America and the
Intellectual Cold Wars in Europe

■■■

America and the
Intellectual Cold Wars in Europe

SHEPARD STONE BETWEEN PHILANTHROPY,

ACADEMY, AND DIPLOMACY

■■■

VOLKER R. BERGHAHN

PRINCETON UNIVERSITY PRESS

PRINCETON AND OXFORD

ISBN 0-691-07479-8 (alk. paper)

This book has been composed in Sabon

Printed on acid-free paper. ∞

www.pup.princeton.edu

Printed in the United States of America

1   3   5   7   9   10   8   6   4   2

TO MY FAMILY

■■■

... *Contents* ...

CONTENTS

... *Abbreviations* ...

AAIB	Archive of the Aspen Institute Berlin
ACCF	American Congress for Cultural Freedom
ADA	Americans for Democratic Action
AFL-CIO	American Federation of Labor/Congress of Industrial Organizations
BDI	Bundesverband der Deutschen Industrie
CBS	Columbia Broadcasting System
CCF	Congress for Cultural Freedom
CDU	Christlich-Demokratische Union
CED	Committee on Economic Development
CFR	Council on Foreign Relations
CGT	Confédération Générale du Travail
CIA	Central Intelligence Agency
CP	Communist Party
DAAD	Deutscher Akademischer Austauschdienst
DCSS	Darmouth College, Stone Papers
DISCC	District Information Services Control Command
ECA	Economic Cooperation Administration
ECSC	European Coal and Steel Community
EDC	European Defense Community
EEC	European Economic Community
FDP	Freie Demokratische Partei
FF	Ford Foundation
FFA	Archive of the Ford Foundation
GARIOA	Government and Relief in Occupied Areas
HICOG	U.S. High Commission for Germany
IA	International Affairs (Ford Foundation)
IACF	International Association for Cultural Freedom
IISS	International Institute for Strategic Studies
INSEAD	European Institute of Business Administration
IPI	Intercultural Publications Inc. / International Press Institute
ITR	International Training and Research (Ford Foundation)
KPD	Kommunistische Partei Deutschlands
MSA	Mutual Security Agency
NATO	North Atlantic Treaty Organization
NSA	National Security Agency
OD	Overseas Development (Ford Foundation)

OMGUS	Office of Military Government for Germany (U.S.)
OPA	Office of Public Affairs (HICOG)
OSS	Office of Strategic Services
OWI	Office of War Information
PCF	French Communist Party
PCI	Italian Communist Party
RIAS	Rundfunk im Amerikanischen Sektor
SA	Sturm-Abteilung (Stormtroopers)
SPD	Sozialdemokratische Partei Deutschlands
SS	Schutz-Staffel
TWI	Training within Industry
USIA	U.S. Information Agency
USIS	U.S. Information Service
USSR	Soviet Union
VVN	Vereinigung der Verfolgten des Naziregimes
WIGO	Wirtschaftliche Genossenschaft der Presse

··· *Introduction* ···

In July 1958 Dr. Shepard Stone, the director of the Ford Foundation's International Affairs program, asked his staff to take stock of "American cultural offerings abroad" and to see if it was possible "to measure" whether the money that Washington as well as the big American foundations were spending on various overseas undertakings, including the sending of orchestras and ballet companies, was yielding good returns.[1] Apparently in the context of this inquiry Waldemar Nielsen was dispatched in 1959 to observe a conference at Lourmarin in France that had been organized by the Congress for Cultural Freedom (CCF), an influential international association of intellectuals and academics funded by both the Central Intelligence Agency (CIA) and the Ford Foundation.

Subsequently, Nielsen submitted a report on this conference in which he expressed his general satisfaction with American cultural efforts in Europe as far as key strategic elites were concerned.[2] Businessmen and politicians, he felt, had by and large given up their constant complaining about America as the leading cultural power of the West; however, the intellectual and academic elites were "lagging well behind" in the "healthy movement going on in other groups." At least Nielsen had been disturbed by the "sickness" of those attending the meeting and "particularly the French." True, a large number of the participants had meanwhile abandoned their former communist or fellow-traveling sympathies. But this did not mean that they had shed their cultural anti-Americanism. Instead the conference participants "spent a lot of time worrying and stewing and griping about the United States, about American domination, about the inferiority of our values and so on."

Stone's suggestion to "measure" America's cultural impact and Nielsen's report on what he found at Lourmarin put in a nutshell the concerns that lie at the heart of this book. In different ways, all subsequent chapters revolve around the nature and quality of American cultural life, around the questions they raise before the backdrop of the superpower struggle against the Soviet bloc in the postwar period, and around the European-American relationship and Europe's anti-Americanism in the twentieth century. But this book attempts to provide more than an analysis of the East-West conflict from the perspective of two opposed ideologies and utopian designs, more than an examination of the long-standing tension between perceptions of culture on both sides of the Atlantic.

Beyond intellectual "discourses" there were also practical policies, the tangible decision making and strategizing by men who had millions of dollars at their disposal and were determined to deploy their resources for winning two culture wars: one against the Soviet bloc as part of a larger world-historical struggle against communism and the other against the deeply rooted negative views of America as a civilization and society among Western Europe's intellectuals and educated bourgeoisie. Nielsen, to his dismay and anger, had once again encountered these views at Lourmarin after Stone had previously asked a perfectly pragmatic, business-like, sensible, and—dare I say it—"American" question about returns on cultural investments that would have horrified European intellectuals, particularly the French.

The overall approach to these themes is integrative. What follows is concerned with some of the major intellectual trends of the twentieth century; but a serious effort is also made to connect them to political and economic developments. Even if, for reasons of space, the latter cannot be given fuller coverage, cross-references will be repeatedly drawn to the tangible shifts that occurred contemporaneously in the realm of politics and economics. After all, the major actors at the time also saw the world in this interconnected way. Consequently what follows is not just an evaluation of journal articles, influential books, and other cultural products and the ways in which they impacted on the course of events; it is also a study in the preparation and execution of concrete decisions that, in turn, shaped (or were at least intended to shape) ideas and sociocultural and political behavior on both sides of the Atlantic in the age of democracy. The methodological challenges of such an enterprise are admittedly great. But I am hoping to overcome the difficulties of integrating different arenas and levels of "structures" by organizing this book around the life and work of an individual, Shepard Stone.

However, this is not a biography. Rather I would like to use Stone's career as a window to the world in which he operated. It is my belief that he embodied and mirrored the larger cultural, political, and socioeconomic trends, shifts, and generational conflicts in Europe and America that are at the core of this book. Stone is therefore the point of departure, but also of frequent return, through which it will be possible to bring together major aspects of both the Cold War and the European-American relationship after 1945.

To begin with, Stone shared a view of the postwar world that was widely held among America's internationalist elites and the East Coast establishment in particular. They were conscious of the fact that, unlike all other participant nations whose positions had been badly weakened by the result of World War II, the United States had emerged greatly strengthened from the conflict. It had become the superpower of the Western world in power-political-military, technological-industrial, and financial-commercial terms, which, they believed, offered opportunities but also imposed responsibilities, particularly in light of the experience after World War I when the United States had refused to assume the obligations of a major power.

Of course, the Soviet Union, in developing its own nuclear capability, was slowly catching up in power-political terms; but the growing East-West competition with a communist dictatorship—perceived as a dangerously aggressive, totalitarian system that was anathema to what the United States stood for—made them only more determined. They wanted to use their superior weight in the world to shape the postwar international order and to make its structures and underlying values as closely compatible as possible with American principles of political, economic, and sociocultural organization.

When Stalin refused to join the One World that would be based on the idea of a liberal-capitalist, multilateral trading system and representative constitutional government, and the "division of the world" became a reality, organizing the West in competition with the Soviet world was enough of a challenge to occupy the best political, military, and economic strategists in Washington.[3] Western Europe was war-torn and exhausted and had to be reconstructed. Defeated Germany, Japan, and Italy, whose brutal wars of exploitation and extermination had lethally threatened the Allies, had to be transformed into viable democratic systems and to be integrated into the emergent anti-Soviet coalition. At the same time, there was always, on the American side and reinforced by the Cold War, the conviction that the creation of an American-led Western alliance would fail—that Marshall Plan economic aid and the security structures of the North Atlantic Treaty Organization (NATO) would evaporate—if Washington's efforts were not accompanied by an equally successful assertion of American cultural hegemony.[4]

On this latter point, though, the United States encountered the greatest trouble. While shattered materially and psychologically by World War II, Europe's educated elites did not shed their old "superiority complex" with regard to what it meant to be a *Kulturnation*. In their estimation, the United States did not really qualify. America's elites, who deeply resented this condescension, wanted to convince European intellectuals and academics that America had become a highly cultured nation, that the

Atlantic was no longer a cultural divide but, on the contrary, a link between regions that not only had common political and economic interests but also a common culture. The life and career of Shepard Stone provide us with a sharply focused lens on a world of people, ideas, policies, and institutions that are central to an understanding of Western history during the Cold War. It is a world of American Ivy League academics and East Coast intellectuals, of "big" American philanthropic organizations and their backers in big business, of U.S. government agencies and their overt and covert operations.

At the most general level this book is about the triangular relationship between the producers of ideas and ideologies, corporate America, and Washington policy makers at a peculiar juncture of U.S. history. But this is only half the picture. The other half deals with Western European intellectuals, politicians, and businessmen who interacted not only among themselves but also with their counterparts across the Atlantic, thus forming a complex web of relationships. What united them and moved them to join forces across the Atlantic was, in the first place, the Cold War against the Soviet Union. They all saw this war as a comprehensive struggle being waged not only on the power-political-military and economic-technological fronts but also in the field of culture and ideas. The men (and a few women) who appear in this book were engaged in cultural production in the widest sense, countering through their writings and other works the ideological efforts of the Soviet bloc to win the hearts and minds of Europe's populations and intelligentsias. This joint European-American cultural front against communism in its different manifestations forms the first theme of this book.

A second theme deals with European history and starts from the observation that, however strong the affinities, the connections that intellectuals and academics established across the Atlantic were never easy and always fraught with tensions. Although these tensions resulted in part from the East-West conflict raging after 1945, they would have existed without it because they were rooted in European perceptions of American society and—no less important—the Americans' determination to change them. Apart from the strong sense of representing the older and "greater" cultural tradition in comparison to the "young" and "unsophisticated" Americans, the feeling of being pushed and shoved, sometimes gently but at other times more roughly, by an extra-European power in turn provided a strong stimulus for the Europeans to resist American plans and policies. This resistance has been shown to exist with respect to political and economic elites,[5] but it was particularly strong in intellectual circles.

However weakened the Western Europeans were power-politically and economically as a result of World War II, they never felt inferior when they compared "their" culture with that of the United States. Because the roots of this cultural anti-Americanism stretch back to the nineteenth century, this book thus examines European attitudes toward American culture in historical perspective.

Partly because of the urgency that the Cold War brought to these matters, we are probably best informed about the political and security aspects of transatlantic relations.[6] More recently economic and business historians have slowly been catching up with the diplomatic historians. Consequently, much is also known today about how the Western industrial nations generated an economic boom and widespread prosperity that proved to be a useful weapon in the competition with the Soviet bloc. In this sense the East-West struggle was about which side was technologically and organizationally more dynamic and better equipped to deliver the enjoyment of consumption and "prosperity for all."[7] Meanwhile, research into the sociocultural aspects of American and Western European history and their connections with the Cold War has only recently been taken up by a new generation of scholars, in both the United States and in Europe.

There is little dialogue, however, between Americanists and Europeanists in the field of cultural history. Especially the former have concentrated on cultural change and have engaged in lively debates among themselves without showing much interest in very similar arguments simultaneously taking place in Western Europe. American scholars have also produced important studies of official U.S. cultural policy abroad,[8] but they have not had much contact with European colleagues who have looked at the impact of these policies on individual European countries. Linguistic barriers have been an obstacle because few American cultural historians read European languages.

Although researchers have studied the "Americanization" of European society in recent years, their focus, due to increased specalization, has been the nation-state, with few going beyond their relatively narrow frame of reference to make intra-European comparisons as a way of assessing the extent and depth of the American cultural impact.[9] On the European side there are some scholars who, like many Americanists wedded to an exceptionalist position, have taken the "inner view." They have played down the transatlantic connection and postulated that the region is in fact on "the path toward a European society."[10] What follows includes an effort to demonstrate the value of transcontinental comparisons and to link American intellectual debates with those in Europe during the Cold War.

Another linkage is only just beginning to be made. Work on philanthropy, at least in the United States, is almost a genre in itself, with its own research centers and professional caucuses. Much of this work focuses on philanthropy inside the United States, whereas the European-American relationship continues to be studied at the level of public and official policy making. Only recently have some scholars connected U.S. foreign policy with the activities of the big private foundations and the millions of dollars they spent on international programs.[11]

Finally, this book hopes to foster work on the American-European relationship during the Cold War that historians have barely begun to explore systematically—the rebuilding of networks across the Atlantic and within Western Europe after the disruptions caused by World War II. Much work remains to be done on what might be called the sociology of international relations.[12] Again, thanks to the work of diplomatic historians, we may be relatively well informed about the creation of networks among politicians, diplomats, and high-ranking administrators who met their counterparts during conferences and long negotiations of what is by now a vast array of transatlantic treaties. Economic historians, with their foible for numbers and hard statistical evidence, have shown much less interest in the many networks that were manifestly reconstituted among industrialists, trading firms, and bankers after 1945.[13] Nor have they been particularly interested in the history of mentalities and traditions. In the field of culture we are still furthest behind in this respect, even though some work is now being done on exchanges and meeting points, such as the Salzburg Seminar. We now also have several solid studies (and one more sensationalist book) on the role of the CCF as an important part of this picture. Yet much of this work has been focused more on the organizational and ideological aspects of the congress's history and its no doubt intriguing links with the CIA.[14]

Against the background of the Cold War era the significance of the Stone Papers, on which this book is partly based, comes into full view. Perhaps because Stone was a trained historian and hence belonged to a human species that habitually collects every piece of written paper, his archive, now deposited at Dartmouth College, his alma mater, is voluminous and rich in materials of all kinds. Hence the more I wormed my way into the stacks of boxes and filing cabinets,[15] the more I came to realize that Stone's public life might enable me to make linkages between the various fields of research that have hitherto been treated separately or, worse, neglected. As the headings of the central chapters indicate, this book would like to stimulate the development of a more transatlantic approach to the sociocultural history of the Cold War and to the ideas and policies that this war produced in both Western Europe and the United States. The history of the European-American relationship is too complex to be compressible into a *Not Like Us*.[16]

Given the very obvious military and economic power differentials between America and a war-torn Europe after 1945, the Europeans were in a poor position to resist American hegemony effectively and persistently in the fields of politics, security, industry, and finance. But the Europeans, led by their intellectuals and artists, thought they had retained their edge over America in cultural production and heritage. They derived this notion from a long-standing perception that there existed, across the Atlantic, no more than a primitive, vulgar, trashy *Massenkultur*, which was in effect an *Unkultur*, whose importation into postwar Europe had to be resisted.

Seen from this perspective, this book deals with European cultural anti-Americanists as well as their allies in the United States, on the one hand, and, on the other, with people and organizations in Europe and America that tried to correct and undermine deep-seated and long-standing Western European attitudes and perceptions. The latter did so not only as part of the Cold War struggle with the Soviets, but also because they believed the critics to be biased and wrong. What made the research for this book so intriguing was that they included, on both sides of the divide and on both sides of the Atlantic, many eminent intellectuals and academics who, through their writings and lectures, promoted very different images of American "mass" culture. Stone occupied a central role in this dramatic story, not only because, as an American who had studied in Europe, he knew about and disagreed with cultural anti-Americanism, but also because he became, during two crucial decades in this other culture war, a key figure with the financial means to help with its prosecution. He was in a position to put ideas into practice.

Initially, while Stone was working as Public Affairs director in the U.S. High Commission in West Germany, this money came from Washington and was spent exclusively on the "reorientation" of the Germans. Later, after he became director of the International Affairs program at the Ford Foundation, the funds were given by the largest private philanthropic organization in the world. This gave him, and his superiors and colleagues who supported him in this effort, a powerful leverage in forging and fostering precisely those networks (and the intellectual force that they could marshal) without which these two cold culture wars could not have been conducted. Finally, we shall have to examine what happened to the European-American conflict in the 1960s and 1970s, as the culture war against the Soviet bloc was gradually being won. Were the efforts of Stone and his allies ultimately ground up between the millstones of the new and even more radical critique of the New Left and the conservative backlash that followed? Or did the arguments produced in the 1950s in defense of American society against European cultural anti-Americanism assert themselves in a different way later, and not merely because of their greater persuasiveness but also because of the material backup they could rely on?

Before coming back to these questions at the end of this book, we must engage in a wide-ranging task of historical reconstruction in which the career of an individual provides the continuous thread. This reconstruction begins, perhaps as the historiographical equivalent of a *Bildungsroman*, with a more narrowly focused account of Stone's background, his early adulthood, and the world of ideas in which he grew up and which later guided his actions and motivations. The experience of Nazism, his participation in the war, and the occupation of Germany were bound to leave a profound impression on him. No less important in this respect, he was not alone and may be said to have embodied the experience of an entire generation that was born before 1914 and came of age in the 1920s and tumultuous 1930s. His time with the U.S. High Commission then enabled him to apply, within the limited context of West German society, some of the "lessons" that he, the historian and keen analyst of contemporary events, believed he had learned before and during World War II.

The analysis of his involvement with the Ford Foundation is preceded by two crucial chapters that try to map out the larger ideological terrain of the two culture wars that Stone became involved in and funded with Ford's millions. There then follow three chapters concerned with the international activities of the foundation, its achievements and programmatic shifts, and its role in the demise of the Congress for Cultural Freedom, which had become a key command post in the conduct of the two culture wars. Although the focus of this book is on the 1950s and 1960s, the final chapter tries to look beyond this period and to put forward some reflections as we search for an answer to the difficult question of whether and how far the entire culture war effort was a success or failure.

It should be clear by now that this effort was much more deliberate and "directive" than some scholars have assumed; they tend to see the

Americanization phenomenon primarily as some inexorable process due to the globalization of markets and of capitalism and the desires of consumers. In a similar vein, resistance to Americanization has been interpreted in terms of a vague yearning of people to define and retain their peculiar ethnic or national identity. Because scholars taking these approaches are reluctant to call this process "Americanization" (and the reaction to it "anti-Americanism"), the tendency is to view everything as an even more anonymous and inescapable process of "modernization."[17] This conception of large-scale sociocultural developments is obviously not completely misguided. There are such *forces profondes* at work. Yet what this interpretation tends to underestimate is the degree of conscious and pragmatic "management" that also goes into the equation and certainly did so in the 1950s and 1960s. Perhaps this American "management" was most tangible in the field of security policy and economics. But it was also very present in the cultural sphere. The experience and memory of fascism and Stalinism were still very strong, and concerned elites believed that they could not just sit back. To do so, they thought, would lead to defeat by a totalitarian enemy who was even more firmly wedded to notions of social engineering and cultural management than the American and Western European intellectuals at the core of this book.

These big "structural" issues occupy the central chapters of the book; however, it seems appropriate to end this introduction with another reference to Shepard Stone, the individual. I never met him and I am not certain if this is an advantage or disadvantage. A few of his acquaintances with whom I talked were not uncritical of him and I wonder how we might have hit it off if we had in fact encountered each other at one of his conferences. After all, he was known to make up his mind very quickly about younger people, about whether they measured up. However, the more I learned about him, I have to confess, the more I came to like the ideas and values he stood for, partly because many of them are my own. I hope that some of my feelings for him do come out in subsequent chapters. Of course, there will have to be an overall assessment of his role and of the institutions he worked for. But the larger questions raised by this study of the European-American relationship will have to wait till the conclusion of this book. Suffice it to say that I found dealing with Shepard Stone's life and work rewarding and illuminating. If I have any regrets, it is that I had to make so many decisions as to what to include in the text, as well as the notes and bibliography. Unfortunately, I had to leave uncited many a good study relevant to the main chapters.

I am grateful to all those who gave me access to the sources on which this book is based. I found the Shepard Stone Foundation, the Ford Foundation's archivists, and various interviewees most helpful, and I wish to thank Margaret MacDonald, James Cooney, Fritz Stern, Horst Niemeyer, Michael Wreszin, Marion Berghahn, Edzard Reuter, Eric Foner, Ulrich Reusch, Sara Bershtel, Alan Bullock, Alan Brinkley, Abby Collins, Oliver Schmidt, Carrie Beckner, Michael Gross, Vicky de Grazia, and Barry Gewen for their advice, comments on the manuscript, and support at other stages of my research. Finally warm thanks are due to Brigitta van Rheinberg of Princeton University Press, Karen Fortgang, and Brian Mac-Donald.

America and the
Intellectual Cold Wars in Europe

■■■

From Nashua and Berlin to Pearl Harbor

ALTHOUGH THIS book is not a biography, its analysis of European-American relations during the Cold War from a cultural-political perspective follows the life and career of one individual, Shepard Stone. Accordingly, his social background and intellectual development are important not only for an understanding of Stone's mind and attitudes toward the world but also for entering the milieu in which he lived and worked.

Nashua (New Hampshire) and Dartmouth College

Shepard Stone was born on 31 March 1908 as Shepard Arthur Cohen into a family of Jewish immigrants who had come to the United States from Lithuania in the 1880s.[1] Like so many other Russian Jews, his grandparents and their children had crossed the Atlantic looking for economic improvement and an escape from the violent anti-Semitism that was rampant in the tsarist empire. His parents had met in Boston, where they got married in 1895 before moving to Nashua, New Hampshire, a small textile- and shoe-manufacturing town northwest of the New England metropolis. Shepard's father, Simon Cohen, for whom this was his second marriage, began to earn his living as a peddler selling haberdasheries. Working very hard, he eventually accumulated enough capital to open a small shop in the poorest part of the town and later moved up to become the owner of a local department store.

In all there were seven children in the family, the two eldest from Simon's earlier marriage. Shepard was the Benjamin in whom his parents, having come into greater prosperity, invested much of their pride and hopes for the future. His father was "Jewish-Orthodox" but—as Shepard stated in his unpublished memoirs—in a "practical" way. Their youngest son, resentful at being sent to Hebrew school, apparently rebelled against an Orthodox upbringing. For a while he seems to have tried to "enlighten" his parents but soon abandoned this effort. Much more appealing was the fact that his father was an admirer of Woodrow Wilson, and the political liberalism and internationalism to which Shepard was exposed as a teenager exerted a crucial influence on his own world view, to which he adhered till the end of his life.

It is more difficult to say how well integrated the Cohens were in Nashua society. They were complete newcomers to a town of some twenty thousand people in the 1920s, a good many of whom traced their roots back to the colonial period; the rest were mainly of French Canadian, Irish, and Polish extraction. There were some sixty Jewish families in town, a few of whom had achieved a measure of affluence. As elsewhere in this part of the world, it was also a solidly Christian community, and the WASPs ran the place politically. Anti-Semitism, while not violent and physical as it had been in Russia, existed in various covert forms; but there was also friendly interfaith contact. Thus his sister Lillian remembered many years later that "on Christmas Eve, Mrs. Duval blest [sic] a candle at the St. Patrick's Church" for young Shepard.[2] Indeed Shepard, having an outgoing personality and being a good mixer, apparently found it easy to overcome whatever social barriers there were. He spent much of his free time with the boys of the Sargent, Whitney, and Marcus families. Phil Sargent, the son of Nashua's mayor (who once also ran for the governorship on a Democratic ticket), was a particularly close friend.

At Nashua High School, Shepard was a popular teenager, though not a model student academically. His membership on the school baseball team was definitely more important than his homework, and he also played the saxophone. However, education was highly valued by his parents. Ten years earlier, his eldest brother had gone to Dartmouth College, the Ivy League institution where the New Hampshire elites traditionally sent their young men. Another brother was accepted by Brown University in Providence, Rhode Island. So, there was an expectation that Shepard would go to an elite college. But as he was to recall in later years somewhat mockingly, "Mr. Nesmith tried to make some of us worthy of Dartmouth, but the material he had to work with was inadequate."[3] There was also Mrs. Mae Sullivan, who for two years attempted "to knock German grammar" into his head but who nevertheless "stimulated an interest in the language" in the youngster. So, even if Shepard was not an outstanding scholar, he turned into a "fanatic reader" and was "most alert on current events," including international affairs.[4]

It was apparently on account of his intellectual liveliness and social skills that he got into Dartmouth at a time when personal contacts and patronage counted for more than certified academic excellence. Still, it must have taken some pushing, and he had to take "a special exam in Math" in order to enter the prestigious college in Hanover.[5] Dartmouth proved to be considerably more challenging than Nashua High. As Stone wrote in one of his memoir fragments, the four years in Hanover were a satisfying though not a particularly exciting experience. He majored in American History and made Phi Beta Kappa in the final semester of his senior year. Beyond these tidbits, he remained rather terse about his life as an undergraduate. There is merely a menu card from SS *America*, dated July 1952 by John J. McCloy, his later mentor and friend, who also came from a humble background and had gone to Amherst College in Massachusetts. It was dedicated, rather ominously, "To the underdog of Dartmouth."[6]

Whatever his experiences, Stone remained a loyal alumnus, conscious not merely of the privileged education he had received but also of the support he was given by one of his professors and the college's president when he began to launch himself into a career in journalism in 1933. As Andrew Hacker put it in his 1997 study of wealth in America, "the years at college and graduate school pay off because they burnish students' personalities. The time spent on a campus imparts cues and clues on how to conduct oneself in corporate cultures and professional settings."[7] Although Hacker probably overstated his case, becoming part of a world of patronage and mutual help was an aspect of Stone's years at Dartmouth that he came to rely upon later. Here he learned about the importance of networking. As he himself put it to the son of a friend some twenty-five years later, who, while studying at Exeter, was thinking about where to get his college education: "I really don't think you would make a mistake if you chose any one of the outstanding private Eastern colleges. As a Dartmouth man I hope you go to Dartmouth where you will find some fine professors, a magnificent library and, of course, a wonderful countryside around Hanover. John Dickey, the President of Dartmouth, is my classmate. Princeton has an excellent faculty, proximity to New York and Washington. Harvard is, of course, one of the greatest institutions in the world, with an exciting faculty and student body. I don't know Duke, though I am sure it is a fine university."[8]

The teacher who took the warmest interest in young Shepard was Ambrose White Vernon, a Princeton-educated minister who had moved to Dartmouth from Carleton College in Minnesota in 1924 and whose official title was "professor of biography." Shepard apparently came to his attention when he submitted a number of good essays to him. It was Vernon who alerted his protége "to the complexities of the human character, to the drives and hopes, the meanness, selfishness and capacity for greatness in men." According to Shepard, "he invigorated an interest in international affairs, stimulated originally by my father who had never had a chance to go to school in the country." No less important, he "encouraged graduate study in Germany" rather than law school in the United States, which Shepard apparently contemplated. The two men stayed in touch until Vernon's death in 1951, at which point Shepard admitted that he had had "the greatest influence on my time as a student and the years thereafter."[9] The professor was not just a good prophet of things to come in Europe; he also had a variety of connections with Germany. He had studied at Halle University and was married to a German woman. Himself fascinated by German high culture and learning, Vernon told his graduating student: "Go to Germany. In a few years European and world politics will be made there."[10]

This advice struck a responsive chord in the young man, who had continued to pursue his high school German and had also taken a number of courses on the culture of Central Europe at Dartmouth. Being a Wilsonian, New England was becoming a bit too provincial for him. He wanted to see the world, not become a lawyer or, like his eldest brother, a businessman. It was apparently also this brother who, in an attempt to make his Jewishness less obvious, changed his name from Cohen to Stone, and other family members, though not his sisters, followed suit. And so Shepard Stone set off for Europe on 13 September 1929 on board SS *Bremen*, the recent winner of a Blue Ribbon. Eight days later, he got off a train at Berlin's Friedrichstrasse railroad station, not far from the glitter of Kurfürstendamm—"inexperienced, ignorant, and hazy about what the next step might bring."[11] While his reading knowledge of the language was probably not bad, his spoken German was "fragile to non-existent."[12] Exhausted and overwhelmed, he spent the first night at a seedy hotel.

STUDENT IN WEIMAR GERMANY

The next day he quickly found a small room with Dr. and Mrs. Julius Lewin in Motzstrasse 63 around the corner from Nollendorf Platz. It was a district in the center of Berlin full of prostitutes and homosexuals, and his parents would no doubt have been shocked if he had told them. On the other hand, the Lewins were a "kindly old" couple who took him in as a paying guest, which included breakfast and a cold German-style supper. Lewin was a medical doctor, "whose patients came up from the streets below." The Lewins "were Jewish, proud of Germany and Berlin and would not believe that in the country of Goethe and Schiller, Hitler could

6

ever come to power."[13] They were a cultured family whose daughter Eva Lewin-Bacher likewise held a doctorate. Writing to him from Jerusalem in 1975, Eva remembered him "as a rather saucy young man—frisch, frech, frei, who learned German with my mother."[14] With the Lewins, he also talked about books, music, and life in general, though he avoided politics for most of the time.

Shepard Stone was lucky in other ways. Keen to begin his studies at Berlin University, he went to the main building where he ran into a German student in front of the bulletin board who initiated him into the complexities of registration and academic life. Also across the hall from the Lewins' apartment lived two American students with whom he quickly became friends. One of them was James Morgan Read, the son of a Methodist minister from New Jersey who was writing his Ph.D. thesis in modern European history. Thenceforth Stone's new life improved very quickly. With the help of his two neighbors, he joined a university society for foreign students where he met Edward Teller, John von Neumann, Leo Szilard, and Raymond Aron. Albert Einstein once came to one of their meetings to give a talk.[15]

He began to enjoy Berlin's rich cultural offerings. On his first Sunday, he went to the reduced-price morning rehearsal of the Berlin Philharmonic Orchestra. As Stone recalled, he "had never before heard a full symphony orchestra in a concert hall or for that matter on radio."[16] He had not heard Brahms's Symphony No. 1 before, and after the concert he went "floating through the nearby Tiergarten near Brandenburg Gate, enchanted by what [he] had heard." And so he became a regular concert and opera goer, seeing the great conductors of the time, among them Bruno Walter, Otto Klemperer, and Erich Kleiber. He heard Wagner's "Walküre" and Brecht's "Dreigroschenoper," and because he had never been to an opera, his first night proved to be "unforgettable."

To him the opera houses of Berlin became "temples of music" and in his view "no city in the world compared with Berlin in the quality of its musical life, on a high level, and, as I was later to know, in the cabarets and bars on a low" one. Indeed, it was "intense [and] vivid." He came to revere "the high culture of the upper middle class, a culture combining the best of the German and Jewish traditions. Here literature and music flourished, the arts flourished with new ideas and creativity. Science, philosophy, and music thrived. In homes, institutes, theaters and concert halls, museums and in the countryside—life was full." Given this fascination with the big city, barely two months had passed when Stone "began to feel like a Berliner." He explored the neighborhood and socialized in

7

cafés where "one could sit forever without being told to move along." There was a serious side to his life when, sitting in the Prussian State Library, he "learned to associate great books and manuscripts . . . with the hardest wooden benches ever designed." Although he later also remembered the images of mass unemployment, poverty, and growing political radicalism and violence, these positive experiences of German society will have to be borne in mind when, in later chapters, we consider Stone's attitudes toward Germany, toward "high" and "low" culture and the European-American culture wars in which he participated.

But there was also the social life for a young American in Berlin. While night clubs at first were as strange to the small-town lad from Nashua as the opera, he also became more savvy about the city's "low cultural" scene after, on one occasion, he and his friends just avoided getting fleeced in one of those establishments. In fact, for a while, before the start of the semester, there was a danger of his becoming more fascinated by "the present, in the streets, cafés, and bars" than by his proposed study of history, of "becoming an Ishmael character." But there was "the family investment" in him to be considered, and he resolved to concentrate on his studies. Not altogether, though.

Jimmy Read had been dating a young woman who was a lodger with a well-to-do family in Meineckestrasse off Kurfürstendamm and who, in turn, had befriended her landlord's daughter, Charlotte Hasenclever-Jaffé.[17] One evening, he arranged a double date and, although Stone and Charlotte did not hit it off immediately, they would meet again and eventually become lovers. By the summer of 1931, they were deeply involved with one another. Indeed, for a girl of good middle-class background it was quite daring to spend some long nights with Shepard in Weimar, registering at the Erbprinz hotel as his wife.[18] Her mother, herself a née Jaffé, had been married to Alfred Hasenclever, scion of a wealthy industrial family hailing from Aachen where they owned a landed estate, Gut Merberich. After the death of Alfred, she had married a distant relative, Joseph Jaffé, who—born in Russian Poland—had opened a successful practice as a dermatologist in Berlin. Another distant relative was the well-known intellectual and writer Walter Hasenclever, not to be confused with Charlotte's brother of identical name.

If the relationship between Shepard and Charlotte had been love at first sight, it is doubtful that he would ever have left Berlin for one semester to study at Heidelberg. Although this town with its *Schloss* ruins overlooking the Neckar River had many romantic connotations, it was also a world-famous center of learning in the social sciences and humanities.

Stone signed up for the lectures of the sociologist Alfred Weber, the jurist Gustav Radbruch, and the philosopher Karl Jaspers. Witnessing the economic crisis and polarization of German society, he had developed an even stronger interest in politics, and this, together with his fascination for Berlin, may explain why he returned to the German capital. In another of his memoir fragments he described this attraction which he retained for the rest of his life: "Berlin in the late 1920s and early thirties was one of the most bubbling, exhilarating cities in the world. New York, Paris, London, like Berlin, exhausted by the world depression, were gloomy and listless. Berlin was mad, a place where anything goes. Brutality in politics, culture and daily life went hand-in-hand with romance, sentiment, adventure and living life to the full. One could live to the limits and limits far beyond anything you imagined before you got there. On the streets, in the subways, on the hiking paths around the town you turned away from the fat, the overweight, the ugly, the thin and hungry, faces too red, too sullen, and there were young women, faces and figures of extreme beauty."[19] It was a view which he cherished throughout his life and which explains, at least in part, his strong attachment to Berlin after 1945.

If Stone had been interested in current affairs since his high school days, Germany politicized him further. In terms of the American political spectrum, he is probably best circumscribed as a left-of-center Democrat and Wilsonian internationalist. In Berlin he regularly read the liberal *Vossische Zeitung*. Having wandered about for a year, he developed into a serious student after his return to Berlin, regularly attending seminars and lectures. It was probably in one of those classes, or perhaps through his friend Jimmy Read, that he caught the eye of Hermann Oncken, a well-known professor of history, who, unlike many of his arch-conservative colleagues, supported the Weimar Republic.[20] He had once held a visiting professorship at the University of Chicago, which may have helped Stone in becoming one of his doctoral students. Stone responded to the challenge and thenceforth buried himself in the sources relating to German-Polish diplomacy during the 1920s.

In November 1932 Stone submitted a 326-page thesis entitled "Deutschland, Danzig und Polen, 1918–1932," the last third of it written in English. It may be that he was under pressure to finish as the dark clouds of a possible Nazi seizure of power hovered over Berlin. Awarding the thesis a *valde laudabile*, Oncken judged it "a valuable attempt" to write the history of German-Polish relations "on the basis of thorough and careful primary research (including [work] with official materials from Berlin, Danzig, and Warsaw)." He felt that it was written "from the

9

objective viewpoint of a neutral person." To be sure, no one would expect this manuscript simply to "represent 'the' German viewpoint, but it shows so much genuine understanding of the German side of the struggle that one can only wish that it will find many readers also with us." Above all, Oncken concluded, "it is to be hoped that Mr. Stone's call for justice will find a lively echo in the neutral part of the world." The second examiner was the much more conservative-nationalist historian Otto Hoetzsch, who read the thesis with "great pleasure." Writing to Stone in his best, though slightly Germanic English, he added that "it is very well built up upon a solid scientific base and is well and objectively written." Hoetzsch hoped that it would be published in English, arguing that it made a contribution to an understanding of a major problem of the present and future and also wondering whether there "can be a durable peace in Eastern Europe with a situation like that between the German and the Polish State?" Writing very contemporary history on a topic of this kind was certainly something highly political. Stone passed his *Promotionsprüfung* on 15 December 1932 and was given a *"cum laude"* for his efforts.[21]

It is possible that the young American doctoral student did not realize until later how his mentors were evidently trying to exploit his work to buttress the German revisionist case against Poland.[22] In early 1933 Dartmouth president Ernest M. Hopkins learned from Vernon that "Stone's work was considered an extraordinarily fine performance and that the [German] Foreign Office stood ready to publish it as a governmental publication if Stone would make a few minor modifications of his argument."[23] But, to his credit, Stone declined to change the text.

If one reviews the first twenty-five years of Stone's life, several points emerge that are important to bear in mind for his future career and intellectual development. First of all, he came from a family that had achieved a high degree of upward mobility. At least as far as their sons were concerned, the Cohens gave them the best education they could get and two of them succeeded professionally. Shepard found it easy to connect with people, and he learned to use networks both for his own career advancement and for the causes close to his heart. At the same time, he never seems to have made much of his Jewish background. The name change of 1929 tended to cover it up, but it is probably significant that his first social contacts in Berlin were with Jewish families. Even if he did not talk much politics with the patriotic Lewins, by 1930 Hitler's struggle against the Weimar Republic and the political and cultural values it stood for could no longer be played down as irrelevant. Stone who had a long-standing interest in current affairs, read the Berlin press, listened to fellow students, saw the posters, and witnessed the escalating civil war in the streets of Germany. He apparently even got involved in fistfights with Nazi students and showed sympathy for the Social Democrats.

He knew and learned to abhor Nazism from firsthand experience and later joined the U.S. Army with the avowed purpose of wanting to help defeat Hitler. After 1945 the eradication of the remnants of Nazism and the creation of a democratic Germany were his top priorities when he was an occupation officer in the U.S. zone, then a journalist at the *New York Times*, and finally Public Affairs director at the U.S. High Commission. But his reaction to the horrific news that emerged in 1945 about the camps and the Holocaust was not one of blanket condemnation and hatred of all Germans—feelings that were quite widespread in the circles in which he moved in New York. One reason for this more subtle response may have been that he had met too many people who did not fit the stereotype and who had opposed Hitler just as much as he had. He learned to differentiate and gained a more sophisticated understanding of what it means to live through a major social crisis and a brutal dictatorship.

Last but not least, he had been exposed to German high culture and had come to love and admire it for the rest of his life. He also encountered, not least from his mother-in-law, European criticism of America as a country that lacked *Kultur*, and he may even have agreed with it. It was only later that he discovered the importance of American art and music.[24] Until the 1960s he also retained a high opinion of the German university system and of German scholarship, although his own exposure to an Ivy League education also convinced him that the best institutions fared well in any comparison with Germany. Later, as will be seen, he also included Oxford and Cambridge in this layer of top universities to be supported by the Ford Foundation, but only after years of extolling the superior virtues of the universities of Berlin and Heidelberg.[25]

Having completed his Ph.D. with Oncken in December 1932 and with the Weimar Republic by then in a state of civil war, Stone decided to go back to the United States. His career plans were still rather nebulous. While still preparing his thesis, Stone had become convinced that he "was not cut out for an academic career."[26] Given his strong interest in international affairs and his knowledge of Germany, he explored, during his last weeks in Berlin, the idea of joining the diplomatic service. On his return home, he apparently prepared himself for the foreign service exams. He also visualized himself as a European correspondent for a major American newspaper.

REPORTING ON EUROPE AND HITLER

Dartmouth had taught him how to go about his job search. He traveled to Hanover and paid a visit to Dartmouth president Ernest M. Hopkins. Hopkins promptly gave the alumnus a letter of introduction to Joe Gannon, "a Dartmouth graduate in charge of advertising censorship on the *New York Times*." Attached to this letter was another one, which Hopkins had "just written to Walter Lippmann in regard to a very promising young Dartmouth boy who has got a high degree of intelligence, a fine background and a definite ambition to get into newspaper work." The president continued that he had told Stone "that you would unquestionably be glad to do anything you could as from one Dartmouth man to another." He left it to Gannon "whether to give him helpful advice for which he is looking or whether this should come from some of the editorial staff."[27]

When Stone met Lippmann in early April, he realized that it was "supremely important that I make a good impression and name now." It is not certain how much help Lippmann, in fact, offered. Gannon was not too useful either, referring Stone to one of the managing editors, who told him that there was a glut of reporters. He also made disparaging remarks about Stone's useless Ph.D. Nevertheless, if an opening arose in Europe, he promised to send for Stone. The budding journalist was not discouraged and began to write for *Current History* and the *New York Times* on a freelance basis. He apparently established a good rapport with Lester Markel, the editor responsible for the paper's Sunday edition, who asked him to submit analytical pieces on such thorny international questions as the Polish Corridor. It was Stone's "first big opportunity," which also enabled him to make "a start in getting my name established." Because payment for his efforts took some time to come through, his family, and his brother Lou in particular, sent him some money, which, as he wrote to his sister Lillian Cohen, helped "a great deal." It was a frugal time, which apparently also led him again to make inquiries about a placement with the State Department; but success in journalism was just around the corner.[28]

Proudly Stone sent his articles to Hopkins, who had meanwhile also received a reply from Gannon, expressing—as he informed Stone—"the pleasure he had had in meeting you and further expressing the hope that he had been of some service to you."[29] That this helpful link continued emerges from the response by Hopkins's secretary to another article Stone had written in *Foreign Policy*. The president, she told Mildred Wertheimer, "is following Dr. Stone's work with keen interest."[30] To keep afloat in difficult times, the young doctor also began to give lectures on the European situation. Thus, as early as February 1933 he had given a luncheon speech at the Nashua Lion's Club, trying to enlighten local notables about Germany. According to the *Nashua Telegraph* he warned that the March elections for the Reichstag "will and must be watched with cool anxiety, for the success of the present cabinet may lead to disquieting developments on the European continent."[31] He gave a similar lecture on the rise of Hitler to the Kiwanis in nearby Lowell. Later there followed speaking engagements at Dartmouth and Princeton. Moreover, he became involved with expert discussion circles on foreign affairs. He traveled up and down the East Coast in pursuit of various projects. *Current History* was interested in getting articles on Europe from him, and anxious not to miss his chance, he wrote to his family to send him his books and newspaper articles together with his collection of documents on Polish-German relations.[32]

Even though he did not join the *New York Times* as a member of staff until May 1934, he continued to garner assignments. In early May, Markel sent him on a trip to Washington where he met the counselor at the Polish embassy, who told him "many interesting facts."[33] The Polish ambassador also gave him half an hour of his time. Later he went to the State Department to speak with Jay P. Moffat, the chief of the Division of Western European Affairs. While he was reporting for the *New York Times*, Stone's trip to Washington apparently also yielded two articles for *Current History* on "The Polish-German Dispute" and "Anglo-American Economic Issues." As the editorial preface for the second piece put it, "Dr. Stone, since his return from Europe where he was engaged in investigating international problems, has been in Washington studying various aspects of American foreign policy."[34]

Finally, during this period he was planning for another important event in his life: his marriage to Charlotte Hasenclever, whom he had left behind in Berlin six months earlier. The wedding was held on 15 August 1933 and the couple spent their honeymoon on a trip to Prague and other Eastern European cities. However, the ten weeks he spent in Europe were also hard work. Having established himself as an expert on Europe, not only the *New York Times* and *Current History* but also the *Boston Herald* and *Vanity Fair* had signed him up. His itinerary included the World Economic Conference in London and visits to Prague, Vienna, and Budapest. Armed with letters of introduction from the *New York Times* and *Current History*, he also tried to gain an interview with Hitler. He failed but was able to talk to Dr. Achim Gercke, an expert in the Reich Interior Ministry, who

Outside the Berlin Registry on their wedding day, 15 August 1933. From left to right: Jimmy Read, Charlotte Stone, Shepard Stone, and Walter Hasenclever. (Courtesy of Margaret Macdonald)

briefed him on Nazi racist policies.[35] He was more successful in Prague where he landed a meeting with President Thomas Masaryk.[36] Three days later in Vienna, he discussed the European situation with Friedrich Stockinger, the Austrian minister of trade.[37]

Back in New York, Stone quickly turned his material into articles, some of which earned him praise and were reprinted in *Reader's Digest*. Clearly, this young journalist who pursued his reporting projects aggressively and whose years in Europe, Berlin doctorate, and social skills helped him to get the information he was looking for, was on the way up. In fact, he was so assiduous that Markel felt obliged to put a damper on his reporting. As he wrote to Stone on 5 September 1933: "As for the pieces you are undertaking for us, you realize, of course, that we are getting huge quantities of material out of Germany, and it might be advisable to have an agreement upon subjects before you proceed," which "might save you a considerable amount of unnecessary work." However, he also felt that a "piece on the racial issue sounds especially interesting."[38]

Eventually the high quality of his articles, his earnest sense of mission, and his tireless activism brought him a permanent position on the *New York Times* news staff. After further solicitations from Markel to write articles for the Sunday edition, Stone moved to the Sunday department, where he held a variety of positions.[39] By the time he joined the army in 1942, he was serving as assistant to Markel, the Sunday editor. However, he did not give up writing articles for magazines such as the *Commentator*.[40] In September 1936 he was in touch with the Columbia Broadcasting System (CBS) network about a job as "current events commentator of the American School of the Air," for which the director of Radio Talks, Edward R. Murrow, sent him some guidelines on CBS's reporting standards.[41] Not all of his projects were accepted. Nor did he cover only foreign affairs. Back home in Nashua, the local newspaper proudly reported in April 1937 that Stone had "interviewed several Congressional leaders directly following the President's message to Congress."[42] He spent much of the rest of 1937 on another extended trip to Europe in the course of which he talked to Masaryk again, garnered an interview with Eduard Beneš, and prepared a CBS talk to be broadcast directly from Paris.[43]

What was the thrust of Stone's reporting on European affairs in the 1930s? It will come as no surprise that overall he was highly critical of the Nazi dictatorship and its domestic policies. But he also subscribed to the reporting ethos of *New York Times* and CBS journalism, which Ed Murrow outlined in 1937 as follows: "We strive, insofar as possible, to present commentaries free from political or religious bias, in a dignified manner, calculated both to inform and entertain the listener. We attempt to avoid advocacy of any point of view by presenting both sides of a controversial subject; thereby giving the listener the opportunity of forming his own conclusions." [44] As to Poland, it may be that, initially at least, Stone remained more sympathetic toward the German position, just as he had been in his doctoral thesis. Thus, the Polish consul general in New York wrote to Raymond L. Buell, the research director of the Foreign Policy Association, in June 1933 that he had read Stone's article on Polish-German relations with the "greatest interest." But he also felt that "Mr. Stone's vast volume of information reflects preponderantly the German point of view." [45]

Closer scrutiny of Stone's piece shows that he tried hard to be even-handed and did not shy away from criticizing Germany quite severely for its nationalist condescension and racism toward the Poles, which, he added, injured Germany's "just claims in the eyes of the neutral world . . . , while Poland's true strength has been misinterpreted. Imperialistic demands in 1919 and repressive measures against the German minority since then have necessarily affected German sentiment toward Poland." [46] He identified "the whole question" of the Corridor as "the fundamental difficulty," adding: "Until this thorn in Germany's flesh has been removed in a manner satisfactory to both countries there will be no peace in Eastern Europe." But he also raised the problem that "if Poland were prepared to discuss the territorial issue with Germany, would not that be the beginning of the end of the Polish State?"

Furthermore, he saw "the danger that a change in the Corridor would release a universal demand from the dissatisfied minorities in all countries" of Eastern Europe. At the same time, "the activities and tendencies of the Hitler government have created a serious barrier to any territorial revision. The experience of many centuries has demonstrated the impermanence of decisions won by force, and a peaceful solution must be reached on the question of the Corridor." Stone ended on a somber note: "Today neither Germany nor Poland wants war, but for over a decade German-Polish relations have been allowed to drift until they have reached an impasse. Present conditions lend force to the belief that an insignificant border incident would suffice to bring about the disaster which the inhabitants near the frontier await with anxious expectation, with fear and, most tragic of all, with resignation."

Stone's pessimism seems to have grown markedly after his visit to Germany in the summer of 1933. In October he published an article that began with the words: "The center of Europe has become an island. A mental ocean separates it from its immediate neighbors and from the rest of the world." Hitler, he continued, had consolidated his power and increased his popularity: "There is no organized and effective opposition" to Nazism.[47] After analyzing the indoctrination of the young and reminding his readers of the roots of the "Hitlerites" in the years of economic crisis, he examined labor relations and the alleged greater independence of German industry. It seems that, like so many other foreigners, Stone was initially misled about Hitler's foreign policy ambitions. Because the "Führer," at the beginning of his regime, posed as a "peace chancellor,"[48] it was easy to assume that no major shift had taken place in 1933 and that Hitler might not last for long. Apparently only after his European tour in the summer of 1933 did Stone become more suspicious of Germany's power-political aims. By the fall his views on Nazi domestic policy and Nazi diplomacy had instilled in him a sense of ominous foreboding.

Accordingly, the piece he published in the *New York Times Magazine* in December 1933 focused almost exclusively on the dangerous power of Nazi propaganda and its impact on the Germans. Titled "Hypnotist of Millions," Stone's article described Nazi techniques of indoctrination through constant marches, rallies, and exhibitions. "With the aid of this propaganda machine a new German myth has been concocted. In the schools the teachers are doing their duty and at universities professors are propounding the party philosophy. Even newspaper columns devoted to the 'German woman' pay due deference, and women are told how to be child-loving and to prepare for their proper place in the home." The results were distressing, in that Germans were now "living in a Nazi dream and not in the reality of the world." Worse, possibly "more Germans are happy now than at any time since the war. They like to play soldier, and under Hitler they play it overtime. . . . And the crowds go home elated in the conviction that the Third Reich is the consummation of a divine development."[49]

On the Sunday before the first anniversary of the Nazi seizure of power, Markel published an article by Stone that examined the situation in Germany just before 30 January 1933 and in the months thereafter. Starting with the setback for the Nazis in the Reichstag elections of November 1932, he argued that at that point Hitler's accession to power appeared to be "remote, if not impossible."[50] He described the intrigues that led to the dismissal of General Kurt von Schleicher, the Reich chancellor, before tracing how Hitler had quickly transformed the country into a one-party dictatorship whose citizens were "now docile." As in earlier pieces, he spent some time discussing the labor situation, though this time he stressed the repressive character of the regime. The only positive thing, Stone wrote, that had been achieved was that "although the living standard had fallen in the country as a whole, work has been divided among larger numbers."

Finally—and significantly, in light of the causes he pursued after 1945—he spoke about the changes that had occurred in the once rich cultural life of Berlin, which he remembered so well from his student days: "Bruno Walter, Klemperer, Adolf Busch, Hubermann and many others have gone to foreign countries, and non-German artists, including Toscanini, Menuhin and Heifetz, have declared their solidarity with the persecuted artists by refusing to appear in Germany." All in all, "German life has been unified and only the pastors of the Protestant Church have risen in revolt against Nazification." Worse, "Jewish families which had looked upon themselves as German for centuries are now degraded inhabitants of their native country. Not only have they been forced out of positions where they made generous contributions to German culture, but they have been definitely relegated to an inferior place and their means of existence has been threatened." Stone concluded: "Hitler is master today and the old President [Hindenburg] only infrequently interferes with the decisions that he makes. Although every German is careful to look behind himself before opening his mouth, Hitler can say truthfully that he has made the German people happier since taking them into the Nazi nursery." Millions believed in a better future and felt "heroic and important in the petty bourgeois atmosphere of the Third Reich." Although the state had humiliated some sections of the population and had imprisoned others because they had "put principle above personal safety," but, "the great majority of the nation" would "join in the fanfares celebrating the first anniversary of the ascension of 'the Leader.' "

A month later, when Stone was interviewed by the *Dartmouthian* about the international implications of these domestic developments, he now saw a "strong possibility of a war." The interview then turned to the position of Austria, which, in light of the weakness of other politicians, including Benito Mussolini, Stone thought might become a powder keg: "I am afraid that no matter which group gains possession of Austria the situation will only become more strained in Europe. The only solution I can see for the European problem is a Pan-Europe," but this looked "obviously impractical" to him. For "most of the German youths believe that there is glory in fighting for the Vaterland" and "since they have experienced sorrow and hardship all their lives in a vanquished and impoverished country, the idea of war holds little alarm for them." To be sure, "there are many who think that imminent war is improbable because of the poverty of these countries." But, he added, "a country is rarely too poor to go to war. They figure that if they are victorious they can easily pay their war debts, and if they lose, the war debts won't matter so much anyway."[51]

The theme of the danger of war and of a desperate move by Hitler continued to preoccupy Stone in subsequent months and years. However, his warnings attained a new sense of urgency after his trip to Germany, Italy, Austria, Switzerland, France, and Britain in 1937. It was mitigated somewhat by Ed Murrow, who welcomed him "to the Continent of Chaos" and commented sarcastically, "if your darling New York Times is any indication, the American press has a war starting in Europe every other day!" Therefore, if Stone agreed with him that "no war is really imminent, it would perhaps be a good idea to say so" in his proposed radio talks from Europe.[52]

It seems that Stone took these cues. Certainly his CBS talk in January 1938 on the occasion of the fifth anniversary of the Nazi seizure of power was relatively subdued, focusing on Hitler's propaganda and general popularity; on his romanticism and on the major changes that had been unleashed. He referred his listeners to Hitler's *Mein Kampf* to gain a better understanding of what the Führer wanted: "Germany, he believes, has a mission; she must expand in Eastern Europe; she must unite all Germans under one flag, she must dominate the Continent. To do so she must arm, militarize her life and fight, if necessary." However, because other nations would resist his ambitions, there would be war if Hitler went ahead with his plans.[53]

Much of Stone's journalistic effort at this time was devoted to persuading an isolationist American public that it was dangerous to hide its collective head in the sand, and eventually this led him to venture into the field of U.S. naval policy. His article in the *Commentator* of April 1938 was evidently designed to justify a strong navy. Taking a firmly internationalist position, he wrote that if the American people saw no danger in developments in Europe and Asia, then the president's request for naval rearmament would be unnecessary. Yet, "if we want to trade with the world, to protect our interests in the world; if we want to make sure that non-democratic powers do not extend their influence to this part of the world; if we believe that eventually our own system of government depends somewhat on the survival of democracy in Britain and France; if we believe that no matter what we do, the United States in the Twentieth Century cannot take an exit from the rest of the world any more than it did in the days of George Washington—then we do need a powerful Navy."[54]

Mindful of how difficult it was for Americans to visualize what was happening across the Atlantic, Stone devoted another piece a few months later to the "two Europes—the one of surface beauty and contentment; the other, a hidden element of brutality and force."[55] Looking back, he wrote: "Not too long ago I was in Rome, Vienna, Prague, Berlin, Paris, and London and from what I *saw* not one of these cities could have been less peaceful than Boston on a summer Sunday." But looks, he continued, are "deceiving," and it is "what you *won't* see in Europe that really counts, that will be responsible for the great changes which coming years will probably bring." This hidden face of Europe included uniformed men forcing "their way into a home to murder a political opponent, only to have the newspapers report the next morning: 'Mr. X committed suicide last night at his home.' " Nor would one see "men being shipped to prison islands because they happen to disagree with the political principles of the dictator who rules over them."

Hidden from view would also be the "executions of alleged 'spies and traitors' in the courtyards of prisons"; or "a boy . . . suddenly ordered to leave the sanatorium where he has been convalescing for six months from a malignant disease, because he is 'racially undesirable' "; or "clergymen of all faiths praying quietly for the rule of God in place of Caesar"; or "officials sitting in government bureaus, plotting and arranging and paying for uprisings in a neighboring country so that the ensuing turmoil will benefit themselves." What, according to Stone, all this amounted to was that Europe was "morally ill." Specifically naming Italy, Germany, and Russia, he gave further examples of dictatorship and repression. Given these realities in the other Europe "of brutality and force," Stone concluded darkly, it "may help to explain events which will be occurring in the days yet to come."

A further illuminating summary of his ideas about Nazi Germany and Europe in the late 1930s is finally to be found in a booklet of just under one hundred pages that he published with Simon and Schuster in 1938. The title gave its basic line away: *Shadow over Europe*. This volume represents, at one level, a rough survey of German history since the Roman period, with an emphasis on the twentieth century. It contains judgments that he picked up during his student days at Dartmouth and in Berlin: "We know today that Germany was not solely responsible for the war. There were many causes: the Slavic-German rivalry; Great Britain's fear of Germany's growing navy; the French desire to avenge the defeat of

1871; Germany's ambition to dominate Europe"; and others.[56] But he also reminded his readers of the treaty that Germany had imposed on Russia in 1918 at Brest-Litovsk and of what Europe would look like if Germany had won the First World War. His assessment of the Nazi dictatorship did not mince words and pointed out that Germans critical of the Nazi regime were thrown into concentration camps that contained not only "Communists and other enemies of the regime" but also, and especially, Jews. Indeed, "owing to Nazi policy, it is rapidly becoming impossible for Jews to live in Germany at all."

This analysis of the domestic situation was followed by an examination of Germany's relationships with its neighbors and of the situation of German minorities in Poland, the Baltic states, and the Soviet Union. He quoted from *Mein Kampf* to highlight Hitler's quest for *Lebensraum* in the East and his willingness to spill blood to obtain more land. At the end of his booklet, Stone raised the inevitable question of where all this might lead. He displayed some optimism but ultimately stressed Hitler's unchanging aims and his continuing persecution of "all people of liberal opinions within the borders of his realm," as well as "his desire to stamp out the Jews of Germany." No less alarmingly, "since he holds Germany in his hands, and there is no organized opposition to him, it seems unlikely that anything but death or war or economic collapse will end his story." Hitler, Stone concluded, had already "harmed the cause of free men everywhere. In an attempt to meet him on his own ground, nations are being forced to regiment themselves as never before. He is forcing men to fight a battle which the western world believed it had won in the American and French revolutions." So, "along with all the good he has done for Germany, he has been responsible for thousands of personal tragedies and for much of the fear of the future which now hangs over Europe and the world."

The booklet found a ready readership. The first edition of 25,000 appeared in October 1938. In December another 5,000 copies had to be printed and a third edition of 10,000 copies was published in July 1939.[57] Sales dropped off thereafter, but by that time Stone's gloomy predictions had come true. Another book of his, *We Saw It Happen*, had come out in the summer of 1938 and sold 7,500 copies from July to December. This volume, compiled with Hanson Baldwin, a colleague at the *New York Times* who was on the rise as a European correspondent, assembled essays by some thirteen *Times* correspondents and critics who discussed contemporary issues and problems in a variety of foreign countries.[58] Judging not just from the sales but also from the reviews and readers' responses that

Stone collected, both books were well received and widely noticed. This success encouraged him to think of writing a further study on Germany for which he began to prepare an outline in June 1938, but it was apparently never completed. A wartime book idea also came to naught and so did a plan to bring out a second volume of *We Saw It Happen*.[59] In the early 1940s, however, he added reviewing books on Europe and Germany to his list of journalistic activities at the *New York Times*.[60]

Several points that are of relevance for later chapters emerge from Stone's career between 1933 and 1942, when he volunteered for the U.S. Army. Firstly, by the beginning of World War II, he had left his mark as a journalist and expert on Germany working in the United States. Looking back on the American press in these years in a speech before the Inter-American Press Association in October 1965, he argued that in general it "left no doubt about what Hitler was doing, where he was going and what the grim implications" would be. "This was reporting in depth, scope and with perspective." Some of "the correspondents covering that story," he continued, "were able to put the complex facts together [and] assess the significance of events. Their reports were brilliant and effective."[61] Although the appeasement-minded papers, such as those belonging to the Hearst press, hardly deserved this kind of favorable evaluation, it did apply to the *New York Times* and also included his own writings.[62] From the summer of 1933 he had no doubt done his best to unmask the Nazi dictatorship and to raise the specter of war. Time and again he analyzed the power of propaganda and the gullibility of the nationalist German "masses." He described the brutality of fascism in its various guises. He juxtaposed these regimes with Western democracy and its principles, warning his fellow Americans to be on their guard, to abandon their isolationism, and to recognize how dependent their country and its economy was on the rest of the world. Following family tradition, he remained a Wilsonian internationalist who was also suspicious of Stalinism. In domestic politics he leaned toward the Democrats, though it seems that Roosevelt's New Deal interventionism made him uneasy.

But given his humble family background and rapid rise into the middle class, not least through his marriage, he also retained his reservations about inherited privilege and an undemocratic elitism. Without this it would be difficult to understand an article he published in the *Commentator* in February 1939 on the British "governing class." At first glance it was directed against London's appeasement policy and the need to get rid of its protagonists. However, the thrust of the argument went beyond this, because to him the appeasers were a small "gang" of upper-class men who controlled Britain politically and economically and who saw Nazi Germany merely as a bulwark against Bolshevism. They lived in a world that was "not the world of the vast majority of Englishmen or Americans." Rather it was "a world of privilege; a world which believes in its own prerogatives; a world convinced of its own wisdom and of its right to rule." With these men at the helm, "the future of Britain does look dark," though not hopeless; for "forces are stirring in Britain; men and women of ability and power know that something is wrong; that some house-cleaning must be done." Indeed, "even among the 'governing class' there are people who oppose 'the gang.' " These people would never want to "sign away the Old World to Adolf Hitler." Stone concluded that "if 'the gang' loses power or changes its policy, then Americans will be able to breathe more freely." The United States would not be able to stand "at the side of a Britain ruled by a 'gang,' " but of those who represented another Britain.[63]

These arguments, too, should be borne in mind later on as we move into Stone's postwar life and try to connect him with the professional and intellectual world in which he operated after 1945. He was not opposed to elitism as such, but it had to be meritocratic and it had to be open to the principles of the parliamentary-democratic systems of the West.

RESCUE FROM THE HOLOCAUST

Finally, his writings of the 1930s invariably mentioned the persecution of Germany's Jews. To be sure, the culture of the *New York Times* was particularly sensitive to this theme. But Stone was now also personally confronted with this question whenever he visited his parents-in-law or learned about the deterioration of their position through the letters they sent to their daughter.[64] Although there are but few indications that the Jaffés considered emigration to the United States before 1939, *Mammchen* and *Pappchen* were repeatedly urged to leave Germany.[65] Charlotte's brother Walter Hasenclever, with Shepard Stone's help, found a teaching position at the Andover Academy in 1936; but, although they knew of Walter's happiness in New England, the elderly couple apparently found it difficult to uproot themselves. Moreover, Joseph Jaffé had problems getting an American visa because of his Polish birth; however, the two elderly people probably also felt that Nazi anti-Semitism had peaked, and they could not imagine that worse was still to come.

23

After the beginning of the war their predicament inevitably became more and more nightmarish. They had already moved from their large apartment on Meineckestrasse to a small sublet on Kurfürstendamm. As the situation for Jews continued to deteriorate, and it also became more difficult to get into the United States, the Jaffés agreed to emigrate to Venezuela. Charlotte had meanwhile become a U.S. citizen and her mother was therefore eligible for an American entry visa. Yet Joseph came under the quota for Polish immigrants and the length of this list so diminished his chances of getting out that the family decided to try the Venezuela route. Unfortunately, in May 1940 the Venezuelan Interior Ministry began to drag its feet despite the financial guarantees that Shepard Stone had given. By December 1940 the Stones were actively exploring the possibility of the Jaffés emigrating to the Philippines.

Fresh guarantees were given that funds for their maintenance would be available. In January 1941 a deposit of $1,000 reserved passage from Spain to the Philippines for the Jaffés in the hope that they would be allowed to travel to the United States from there. The *New York Times* correspondent in Madrid helped to book the first sailing from Bilbao in March 1941. Then disaster struck again. On 10 February Charlotte learned that the U.S. State Department "never cabled Berlin to give Mrs. Stone's parents a visa" and that the whole process was back to square one. Worse, the Philippines had introduced a new immigration law and they had to apply again.

In the meantime the affidavits had expired and had to be renewed in a hurry to be sent to Berlin, this time in the hope that the Jaffés would be allowed to sail directly to New York. The Madrid correspondent of the *New York Times* made another reservation for a ship from Bilbao for early June 1941 and arranged for the issuance of a Spanish transit visa. However, the problem of the American visa for Joseph Jaffé and the Polish quota continued. On 18 April 1941 the *New York Times* correspondent in Berlin telegraphed Stone that the Jaffés had "cancelled [their] passage as [it proved] impossible [to] get [a] visa" for Joseph due to the quota restriction.

It is not difficult to visualize how panicky the Jaffés and Stones must have been by this time. The situation in Europe worsened day by day. The Nazi persecution of the Jews had begun to turn into mass murder. Stone now tried to mobilize the State Department via the *New York Times* in Washington and Joseph Jaffé was put on an emergency list shortly thereafter. On 21 May, Charlotte was informed by the chief of the State Department's visa division in somewhat cumbersome bureaucratic language "that although it was not possible to issue a visa to your father as a Polish quota number was not available, favorable action will be taken in the case in the event that any number allotted to any consular office should be returned unused before the end of the month." Four days later, the Berlin correspondent of the *New York Times* reported that visas had now been promised by 31 May and that the Jaffés were making preparations to catch a boat in June. They arrived in Bilbao by train on 11 June and left on the day before the Nazi invasion of the Soviet Union, arriving safely in New York at the end of the month.

The case provides a good example of how difficult it had become for Jews after 1939 to leave Germany and how easily one could get caught in a bureaucratic maze. Indeed, it is probably not too farfetched to say that the Jaffés would not have gotten out of Nazi Germany had it not been for the network of journalists and contacts that the *New York Times* was able to provide. To this extent the drama found a happy ending. They had escaped certain deportation and murder. However, the Jaffés life in New York offers a distressing example of what it meant to be forcibly uprooted and to be put into an alien environment. After temporary accommodation, the Stones found them an apartment on West 119th Street. It was, as Shepard Stone recorded in December 1941, "a tiny place, and I felt a bit uncomfortable, seeing them in this cupboard after the luxury of Meineckestr. 26. Mammchen cooked and served Sunday dinner—a bit puzzled by the type of work she had never done." Later they moved to Liberty, New York.[66] However, it seems they never felt at home. Now in their early fifties and with Joseph unable to practice, they were virtually at the end of the road. Their unhappiness and stress probably also accounts for their failing physical health. Like so many survivors they were deeply traumatized by what had been done to them. Their lives had been wrecked to a degree that is difficult to fathom some sixty years later.

In the meantime another event had taken place that was to shape Stone's life very profoundly: on 7 December the Japanese had attacked the U.S. naval base at Pearl Harbor and, when Hitler declared war on the United States a few days later, America had entered the world war on the Allied side, more or less guaranteeing, thanks to superior U.S. economic and military resources, that the Axis powers would be defeated. It was an effort that Stone joined with conviction.

Defeating and Rebuilding Germany

WHEN THE Japanese attacked the United States at Pearl Harbor in December 1941, Stone happened to be visiting his parents-in-law, where he heard the news on the radio. After a moment of bewilderment, he quickly realized the implications of the news flash. He rushed to the *New York Times* office on Manhattan's 43rd Street, called his colleagues, and "went to work planning [a] new [Sunday] magazine."[1] After a brief night's sleep, he was back in the office by midmorning on the following day to find "everyone excited [and] anxious to do something." There existed a "great unity of purpose." Most people he met were confident of victory, even if they expected a long war. In this atmosphere Stone immediately thought of joining up as a volunteer. While Hanson Baldwin gave him "a steer," Markel "argued that I could do more for the war effort by staying in 43rd Street."[2] But although at thirty-three he was beyond draft age, he had already made up his mind. As he wrote to Baldwin: "I still think that with my knowledge of Germany and Germans, I might do something with [the] forces who will be trained to go to places where there will be contact with the Germans."[3] With this in mind, he may have thought of joining the intelligence outfit that the Donovan Committee was building up; but Markel enlightened him that men in uniform were considered as being on a leave of absence from their job, whereas "those who take civilian jobs in the government, such as those in the Donovan committee, have no such status."[4]

WAR SERVICE IN EUROPE

And so, on 19 February 1942, Stone wrote to the adjutant general at the Information and Personnel Placement Agency in Washington that he wished "to enter the military service of the United States." He added that he had "a fairly extensive knowledge of Germany, German, and the Nazi mind . . . I gained as a student for many years in Germany." He then gave a summary of his career and listed Arthur H. Sulzberger, the publisher of the *New York Times*, President Hopkins of Dartmouth, Eaton D. Sargent, the former mayor of Nashua, Edward M. Earle at Princeton's Institute for Advanced Study, and Brigadier General Kenneth P. Lord, chief of staff with the First Army, as his references. Shepard and Charlotte Stone had befriended the Lords in New York after discussions on "the European situation, the threat of Hitler to the U.S.A., and . . . years of study and observation in Germany" had brought the two couples together.[5]

Lord was happy to arrange for Stone "to be commissioned [as] a First Lieutenant and posted to G-2 [Intelligence], First Army, at Governor's Island." It was not an easy start for him. First, he barely passed muster because of his flat feet. When introduced to other officers, he had the feeling that they harbored "reservations about a civilian, suddenly commissioned, in their midst." Although there were now more Jewish officers in the army, anti-Semitism may also have been a factor until, "again owing to [his] knowledge of the enemy," Stone became accepted and, indeed, "close friends with many of these dedicated men." No doubt it was a particularly "odd collection in G-2: West Pointers, National Guard[smen], reserve officers from finance, industry, academic life"; and then there was Stone, with his "lonely Ph.D. and *New York Times* background."[6]

For the next nine months there was little change in the daily routine of Stone's army life and training. His wife had meanwhile received security clearance from the Federal Bureau of Investigation (FBI) and began her work in intelligence for the Office of Strategic Services (OSS). For a while Stone appears to have been happy with his work, but soon he felt under-utilized. When making his decision to join up, he had been warned by Baldwin: "Keep your pants on, old man. This war is going to last a long, long time, and we won't be sending any forces anywhere to meet the Germans yet."[7]

But despite this sensible advice, by the end of 1942 frustration had become so bad that—in good old networking fashion—Stone got his close friend Hadley Cantril, a Dartmouth graduate now at the Office of Public Opinion Research in Princeton, to write to Lieutenant Colonel R. E. Looker at Military Intelligence Services in Washington's War Department. Cantril praised Stone as "an extremely personable man with high native intelligence, poise and good judgment," mentioned his Ph.D. and knowledge of German, and highlighted his experience as a reporter and editor. Unfortunately, he explained, Stone was now "afraid that he may have to sit out the war if he remains in the First Army." Looker should consider him for his operations, "if you have any places to fill."[8]

He did get a transfer to the Twelfth Air Force at Gravelly Point in Washington, D.C., as the unit's prospective historian. But the assigment ended quickly because "at Gravelly Point nobody quite knew what to do with me and I could throw no light on the subject." After another spell on Governor's Island he "was ordered to the War Department and met an entirely new breed of officers, including Colonel Benjamin Dickson." He learned "a highly classified military secret," namely, that half of the First Army would move to Bristol in England, "where under the command of General [Omar] Bradley it would become the core of the U.S. forces in the Allied invasion of Europe."[9] Further training followed, in the course of which Stone tried to revive his contact with Eduard Beneš, the exiled president of Czechoslovakia, whom he had interviewed in 1937 and who now lived in Washington, D.C. Writing to Beneš on 13 May 1943, he asked him for another conversation the next time Beneš came to New York.[10] He left for England on 13 September 1943.

With military action still some time away, but doing more interesting intelligence work, Stone seems to have settled into wartime Bristol with ease. Judging from the correspondence in his papers, he was quite a ladies' man. Back in New York and Nashua, his family tried to give emotional support to the young officer, of whom they were very proud. In December 1943 he received presents from his sister Lillian and a "Merry Xmas" greeting from his wife, who, working hard at the OSS offices in New York, did not enjoy life as a grass widow. Money was tight; she missed her husband terribly and was dreaming of having a child by him—"or several, [that] would make my happiness complete."[11] Charlotte was in frequent contact with Markel and saw her Jewish friends. Like her parents, whom she also looked after, many of them were refugees from Germany, among them the Bermann-Fischers of the former Frankfurt publishing house. While his family lived up to its patriotic duty of giving their "man at the front" reassuring news about life back home, Stone, who had been promoted to the rank of captain, became ever more deeply involved in top secret planning work relating to Italy and soon also to the Allied invasion of Normandy in June 1944. In April he was sent on a secret mission to Algiers. After his return, he prepared "an invaluable report on the operations in Italy."[12]

Other information about Stone's work emerged some thirty-seven years later in the draft manuscript for a talk he gave on Berlin's radio station. There he described how General Bradley, the commander of the First Army, received instructions to develop an alternative operations plan should the Hitler regime collapse prior to the projected Allied landing in

28

Normandy. Part of the assigment was to identify factors that might lead to such a collapse. Asked to produce, within forty-eight hours, a number of annexes to the Rankin Plan, as the project was code-named, Stone went into seclusion. Drawing upon his knowledge of German and Prussian history and his memories of Berlin during his student days as well as his subsequent visits, he produced his assessment. According to his recollections years later, he did not believe that there would be "a mass revolution against Hitler"; after all, he knew about the "tremendous power of the Nazi police and [the] fears of the Gestapo, the SA [Storm Troopers], and the SS." He had also seen the "mass enthusiasm for Hitler" as well as heard about the "opposition to Hitler which operated in small circles." Only high-ranking officers in the Führer's entourage, he estimated, would be able to remove the dictator and enter into negotiations with the Allies.[13]

Although the Rankin Plan was never activated, Stone's work was praised and was used in May 1945 in the First Army's recommendation to award him the "Legion of Merit in the grade of officer." According to this document, his annexes proved "to be of remarkable accuracy and an exact barometer of problems later faced in Germany." Next he participated in the Normandy landing on 6 June 1944, during which he "was in direct charge of the General Staff direction of psychological warfare methods and in the application of these methods in combat." With his reputation among his comrades high, Stone now moved with the advancing troops through northern France and Belgium, continuing his G-2 work. He witnessed the liberation of Paris and, as before the invasion, was occasionally sent on special missions to North Africa or London. By early October 1944 the First Army had reached the German-Belgian border near Aachen, and Stone was later commended for his participation "in the final assault on the city."[14]

OCCUPIED GERMANY

It was "through his experiences in Aachen [that] the first measure of the reaction of the German civilian population to Allied occupancy was obtained." His detailed and reliable reports "were of great assistance" to his superiors "in obtaining a clear picture of conditions to be expected as we [the Allies] made further advances into Germany." As we know, there was a good deal of anxiety among the Allied troops about a Nazi underground and "werewolves" sniping at American soldiers. But then it quickly became clear that the native population was too exhausted and

29

Shepard Stone outside his Paris Hotel, 21 September 1944. (Courtesy of Margaret Macdonald)

disillusioned with Nazism to want to resist the Allies. They just wanted peace and "normalcy."[15]

Stone was furthermore concerned to find out what had become of the Hasenclever estate, *Gut Merberich* near Aachen. He obtained a permit and discovered a depressing scene. As war correspondent Harold Denny wrote in the *New York Times*, "the Germans had made Gut Merberich into a formidable strong point guarding the western approaches to Langerwehe. Our forces captured it . . . after a hard fight in which they took ten prisoners, including an officer." As a result, "the grounds were marred and the buildings scarred by shellfire, but the damage was relatively light."[16] On the basis of this report, Charlotte's office arranged a " 'liberation' celebration" in her honor and she received various telephone calls.

It was only later, in March 1945, that her husband sent her a fuller story of the destruction.[17] If the recollections of one of his fellow visitors are to be believed, Stone showed much less emotion at the time than in this letter.[18] This may to some extent be because he had never seen the place in peacetime; but it may also be that more generally he had adopted, at least outwardly, the stance of the sober front-line soldier and matter-of-fact assessor of the military situation. It was his way of coping with the many distressing things he saw.

As Stone's unit moved further east, psychological warfare work expanded. In the Cologne area he apparently came across anti-Nazi youth groups, known as *Edelweisspiraten* and asked Richard H. S. Crossman, the British deputy chief of the Psychological Warfare Division with Supreme Headquarters, Allied Expeditionary Force, for information. Crossman, soon to become a prominent Labour politician with whom he resumed contact in the 1950s, sent him a record of what seemed to him to be "an unusually interesting interrogation, illustrating a segment of the German population which we do not often come across in prisoner of war camps," though such people may be more frequent "in the civilian population as we advance."[19]

The winter months of 1944–45 were another time of long-distance travel for Stone. In January he flew to North Africa; in February he was back in Paris and also paid a brief visit to London. At the end of April he traveled to Weimar, and in a letter to his wife recalled their visit there in 1931, of which Charlotte also still had vivid memories.[20] But it was not really a nostalgic trip. As he wrote to his wife on 20 April: "I stop at Nordhausen, and see quickly, for my stomach isn't used to everything, though I've seen death in many terrible forms since [the Normandy invasion on] June 7, the atrocities of the foreign labor camps." A day later he received a five-page memorandum with "additional information on Labor & Concentration Camps located around NORDHAUSEN im Harz," which must have made his stomach turn. And so we see him "rolling along, forgetting or trying to forget, the horrors, on the Autobahn through Thuringia." He encounters "thousands of foreigners heading God knows where." In the distance he spots "Eisenach with the Wartburg . . . and then suddenly Weimar." He visits the recently liberated Buchenwald concentration camp and on 29 April, the day Hitler committed suicide, returns to Weimar after another trip to Marburg and Kassel.[21]

While in the Harz Mountains region he added another task to his list of duties as an intelligence officer, one for which he was no doubt particularly qualified: he supervised the Documents Team attached to the U.S. First Army, which collected and evaluated captured military documents containing "information on the enemy's capabilities and intentions."[22] No less important, he helped to secure archives that were to be of great importance both at the Nuremberg Trials and for later historical research. He had meanwhile reached the rank of major.

The history of the biggest find can be reconstructed from a correspondence that developed after Marion Dönhoff, of the liberal West German weekly *Die Zeit* and a close friend of Stone, published an article about him in April 1983 when he was director of the Berlin Aspen Institute. Her brief reference to her friend's involvement in the discovery of the massive archives of the German Foreign Office prompted David D. Silberberg, then honorary consul of the Federal Republic in Memphis, Tennessee, to fill in further details, to which Stone added others.[23]

Shortly thereafter, the war in Europe ended. Stone was able to go home for a brief visit in June 1945 when the First Army Headquarters was ordered back. People with his experience and knowledge of Germany were desperately needed in Europe, and so he returned via Scotland, London, and Bristol to take up the position of "Chief of Intelligence and general handy man" with the 6871st District Information Services Control Command (DISCC). Based at Schloss Hohenbuchau near Frankfurt, "the most comfortable and horrible baroque palace in Germany," the duties of this unit included "establishing in the Western Military district a new and democratic press and radio and also book and magazine publishing houses free of Nazi influences and strong enough to carry on in the coming years."[24]

Working for U.S. Military Government

In line with this mandate, Stone, using his experience and standards of good journalism, set to work to help rebuild a democratic press in his territory. A major problem was to find journalists and publishers who were not compromised by their activities in the Third Reich and to put the newly licensed papers and journals on a sound economic footing. After all, they now had to survive against their competitors in the harsher climate of a slowly emerging marketplace. Other Allied policies and complex bureaucratic structures greatly complicated this endeavor. Thus, many of the assets of the once time-honored *Frankfurter Zeitung* had been blocked in 1945. The paper, which the Nazis had taken over, had been put under Allied control with a view to returning it to its pre-1933 owner, Heinrich Simon. At the same time, the printshop had been requisitioned to be used for the production of another paper, the *Frankfurter Rundschau*, the first newspaper licensed in the American zone. While this legal tangle was being sorted out, it became clear that many other papers could not stay afloat economically without subsidies from the Military Government and, from 1949, its successor, the High Commission. In other words, the Americans spent literally millions to prop up a democratic press.[25]

Finding suitable personnel proved to be another thorny problem. As Stone put it in his draft memoirs: "Publishers and editors of newspapers had to be identified; heads of radio stations installed; universities and hospitals staffed; theaters and concert halls opened, all the while making certain that former Nazis were not creeping back with jobs."[26] In the case of the *Frankfurter Rundschau* this did not pose a problem because of the good political credentials of its founders. But questions arose over its left-wing bias and occasional criticism of the occupation authorities. With the Cold War on the horizon, American fears of communist infiltration grew and, from the U.S. viewpoint at least, one of the editors was not above suspicion.[27]

In 1945–46 it was rather more the former Nazi affiliations of prospective publishers and editors of *bürgerliche* papers that gave Stone a headache. Thus, he was very proud to have helped Theodor Heuss to found the *Rhein-Neckar-Zeitung*. He knew Heuss, a former liberal Reichstag deputy, from his student days when Heuss had taught at the Berlin Hochschule für Politik and Stone had attended his lectures. Shortly after

33

the capitulation, while passing through Heidelberg, he had, after smoking "peace pipes" with Heuss, also relied on the German's advice about the rebuilding of a democratic press. Heuss was thought to have an impeccable political record, even though he had voted for the Enabling Act of March 1933. It may have been for this reason that Stone also had to deal with a number of "gentlemen" who "were opposed to Theodor Heuss as co-publisher of the Rhein-Neckar-Zeitung." Supported by John Boxer, Stone did not budge. He "went to Bad Nauheim where I took a strong stand before the Commanding Colonel or General and finally won the case."[28]

After this, Stone was dismayed to discover in the fall of 1945 that Heuss had once written articles in Joseph Goebbels's prestige paper, *Das Reich*. Challenged to explain this, Heuss was deeply embarrassed and, following an interview with one of the DISCC officers, wrote a slightly lame letter of explanation.[29] In not mentioning this aspect of his life under Nazism, he argued, he had not imagined that his contributions to *Das Reich* might become a burden. After all, when the paper was founded, it was supposed to be free of party bias. Its editors were primarily people such as Karl Korn, who, during the Weimar years, had worked for the liberal *Berliner Tageblatt*. Moreover, he had produced no more than six or eight pieces, mostly reviews of art history books and literary analyses about nineteenth-century German novelists. Heuss thought that his last contribution appeared around the end of 1940 and before the time when Goebbels became a regular leader-writer. By that time Korn had also long left the paper.

The Americans once more condoned Heuss's past "sins," and this pardon turned him into an even more loyal ally of Stone in subsequent years when they resumed contact, with Heuss now in his position as president of the Federal Republic and Stone as the High Commission's public affairs director and later as a Ford Foundation official.

In other cases involving media questions, Stone found himself acting as a conciliator. Searching for reliable aides to help him build up a democratic press in the U.S. zone, he had brought Dr. Otto Veit, an economist and banker and a friend from his student days in Berlin, from the former German capital to Wiesbaden to work with DISCC staff and with OSS. When Veit returned to Berlin in early October 1945 to arrange for his move to the West, he traveled in a military vehicle but had not been given proper traveling papers. When he was stopped and searched by an American border patrol at Helmstedt, he was found to carry several letters. One was from Gottfried Bermann-Fischer, whom we have encountered before as heir to the renowned Fischer-Verlag and refugee friend of the Stones in

New York. More incriminating was another letter carried by Veit which contained some eighty thousand marks. Suspected of being a spy and closely interrogated, Veit lost his nerve. He "tore up the letters foolishly and requested that he be shot."[30]

Stone's unit thereupon submitted a two-page explanatory memorandum confirming that Veit had been an anti-Nazi, that he and his wife had suffered because of his Jewish ancestry, and that his house in Berlin had been "a meeting place of OSS personnel and other persons whose work throughout the war was aimed at the destruction of the Hitler regime." The document also explained that "in recognition of his ability, Mr. Allen Dulles and Mr. Gaevernitz of the OSS requested Dr. Veit to submit memoranda on financial and industrial questions, memoranda which have been studied by US Group CC, Colonel Bernstein's office," and that Veit had been "encouraged to gather as much information as possible on industrial and financial matters." His behavior was condoned, but "in order that the future status of Dr. Veit may not be affected," DISCC requested "that a copy of this endorsement be added to all files on Dr. Veit which may exist as a result of the Helmstedt incident." As can be seen, it was not easy to build a strong team to help Stone implement the tasks that he had been assigned. Painful awareness of the Nazi past and suspicions of the Germans in general were ubiquitous among the occupation forces. In these circumstances relying on a network of friends was more vital than ever if blunders and scandals were to be avoided.

Things went more smoothly with a number of journals that emerged next to the dailies. In October 1945 a license was issued for *Die Wandlung*, an intellectual monthly whose title, as Stone wrote to his wife, had been "picked by your old friend of OWI [Office of War Information] days Gene Jolas."[31] It was published by Lambert Schneider and Dolf Sternberger. Sternberger, a journalist who later held a professorship at Heidelberg University and wrote op-ed pieces for *Frankfurter Allgemeine Zeitung*, succeeded in gaining Karl Jaspers and Alfred Weber as contributors. For Stone, who had lent a hand to the creation of the journal, this beginning had been very reassuring. A license was also issued to Eugen Kogon and Walter Dirks for the left-Catholic journal *Frankfurter Hefte*. Similarly, Stone helped with the founding of *Die Gegenwart* after meeting Benno Reifenberg, another former *Frankfurter Zeitung* staffer and soon to become a major influence at the postwar *Frankfurter Allgemeine Zeitung*. As Stone recalled in 1970, "Benno gave many of us the feeling that a new Germany could and would emerge."[32] Although Hamburg was outside his territory, he felt no less encouraged by the journalism that the

35

northern German liberal weekly *Die Zeit* and its editors came to embody. Indeed, Marion Countess Dönhoff later became a close friend and supporter of his work on Atlantic relations, even if during their first encounter in 1949 Stone had been somewhat gruff when her paper sent her to his HICOG (U.S. High Commissioner for Germany) office in Frankfurt to make some request.[33]

The manifold difficulties he was confronted with during his relentless inspection tours up and down the American zone of occupation, and the frustrations this engendered, finally stimulated him to deliver a speech before a meeting of German publishers and editors in Marburg at the end of October 1945. Knowing that the atmosphere in the hall would not be relaxed and trying to take some of the tensions out of the situation, he started by stressing that, whatever the differences of opinion between the American occupiers and the West German press, journalists (and, after all, he was one himself) had one thing in common: "They are critical and mostly very grumpy and awkward people."[34] Having established, in brief references to his career, his own professional credentials and his German expertise, Stone proceeded to tell his audience, also in the name of his American colleagues working in his territory, that the rebirth of the German press would one day be recounted as a story full of drama. He then gave the example of the *Aachener Nachrichten*, a newspaper published under the most difficult circumstances soon after the fall of the city in 1944.

Next Stone cited a proud record of accomplishments: in the U.S. zone there now existed seven weeklies, with another one soon to appear in Fulda. The total number of copies distributed came to 1.75 million, and they all had begun to play a vital role in the country's new public life. However, no editor, he continued, would ever be completely satisfied with his paper and, although the standards of American papers would not necessarily have to serve as a model for West German journalism, there were numerous criticisms he could not avoid making. To begin with, news, whether local, national, or international, had to be truthful, and while papers relied on news agencies for international news, local reporters had to be trained to be absolutely reliable and objective. It was, Stone added, up to the editors to see to it that opinions had no place in local news reports. In fact, Stone made the editors and publishers present directly responsible for training reporters to write about facts, not in providing propaganda. In this respect, the speaker may have been a bit naive, but once again his point has to be seen against the background of the Third Reich and Goebbels's manipulation of news.[35] The same principles of ob-

36

jectivity, he told the assembled newspapermen, also applied to the crafting of headlines.

Moving on to the notion of leader articles, Stone mentioned that the American press strictly separated news pages from opinion pages. Nor, as a rule (and contrary to German tradition), did leader articles appear on the front page. Citing the example of one German paper that had carried not one, but two leader articles on the first page, he criticized such an opinion overload and recommended that no more than one such article be placed in the space regularly reserved for op-ed pieces. He also exhorted his listeners to publish "well-thought-out opinions by men who deserve to be heard." Such articles should be "positive contributions that do justice to all groups and parties." They should not be "petty bourgeois and one-sided." In the same vein, a newspaper should cater to all members of the community, but it should also develop its own style and layout. Yet, whatever the individual features, their overriding duty was to tell the truth, even if that truth was uncomfortable. This applied in particular to the incontrovertible truth that Hitler and Nazism were responsible for the destruction of Germany and the dire postwar predicament of the population. Notwithstanding these realities, journalists must also hold out the hope for a new and better life. Stone concluded his speech by expressing his deep confidence in his audience: "We hope and believe that in your hands the German press will be strong and democratic and that it will be the intellectual bearer of a new democratic Germany."

As can be seen from this account, he tried hard to balance praise with criticism—to make recommendations rather than pose as a bully. But he also found that it was not easy to wrench the German press and its editors away from practices that they had adopted during the Nazi period of strict opinion guidance and news control. This at least was the impression of Dr. Adolf Arndt, the local state prosecutor, who had attended Stone's speech. As emerges from his open letter to the *Marburger Presse* after it printed a report on Stone's speech on 26 October, Arndt accused the editors "of having turned a fanfare into a sweet tune." The gullible reader who had not been at the meeting would have come away with the impression from this report that "Major Stone had been full of wonderful praise for the new German press, when in fact he had subjected it to a sharp and well-founded criticism." Arndt also missed the reporting of news about the East, which was facing mass starvation. He objected to the practice of printing letters to the editor that were in turn criticized by the paper itself. This custom, Arndt believed, violated a sense of fairness that could be expected of a democratic paper. He insisted that letters to the editors be printed without comment, as was common in the United States and in Britain.[36]

As Stone suggested to Markel in September 1945, the Germans needed exposure to a training program, which, he thought, American newspapermen would be able to provide.[37] There was his parallel disenchantment with American occupation policy. The roots of this feeling went deep and resulted from his basic attitudes toward Germany and the Germans in general.

Our analysis of the articles that Stone published throughout the 1930s has already shown that he despised and fought the Nazi regime and believed that millions of Germans had fallen prey to Hitler's propaganda. If resistance were to be expected at all, it would and could only come from small elite groups who saw what was going on behind the Nazi facade of bread and circuses. This belief, as we have seen, had also guided his input into the 1944 Rankin Plan.[38] At the same time, his memories of the Weimar Republic and the wonderful years he had spent in Berlin seem to have counterbalanced what he learned about the Hitler dictatorship after 1933—in particular, the escalating persecution of the Jews and the stories his parents-in-law told him during his visits in the 1930s. Finally, the frantic efforts to get the Jaffés out at the last minute in 1941 left their scars on his image of the country. But even these experiences did not completely blacken it. The industrialized mass murder of millions of women, children, and elderly people was, as Walter Laqueur has argued,[39] still beyond the horizon of human experience and hence unimaginable to most, including Stone, as a possibility in the "cultured" nation that he had gotten to know as a student.

Thus, when in 1940 he received a critical letter from a listener in response to one of his radio talks, he merely reiterated a view that he had heard from his professors at Berlin University, who, as we have seen, had also shaped his views on German foreign policy and World War I: "Most of the German atrocity stories" put out by the British during that war, he asserted, "were untrue."[40] It therefore also took him some time before the full truth about the Holocaust began to sink in. The harder shell that he had acquired as a American officer who had seen many deaths during his advance east from Normandy was probably also responsible for this response. And then there was the rising anti-Germanism that he encountered among his friends.

Ruth Nissen wrote him from New York in October 1944: "I cherish one wish and that is never to set eyes again on any German. The horror, disgust and hate I have for all of them is so deeply rooted in me that I sometimes feel frightened about it myself."[41] It is safe to say that he disagreed. A few weeks later he began a correspondence with Mrs. H. O. "Knaus" Fehling, another friend and refugee living in England, who wrote: "I'm glad about what you said, about your ideas of a real peace and I'm glad that most newspapermen—not all of them!—are much more bloodthirsty than the soldiers who are fighting. Terror and hatred leads to nothing; that the Nazis have proved too well and, as you say, the way for you to act is to be Americans, not Nazis." But then his "soldierly" attitude was put to another severe test when he saw Nordhausen and Buchenwald concentration camps shortly thereafter, as emerges indirectly and rather mildly from a letter Fehling wrote him at the end of December: "Since your feeling towards what used to be Schnuepschen's and my fatherland are about mine, all what you live through right now, must be quite a problem."[42]

No doubt this was an agonizing time for him, made worse in 1945 when he learned that large parts of his family in Lithuania had been murdered. The news came to him not through the papers that had been full of reports on Nazi atrocities and the Holocaust, but through his cousin Jakob Abramavicius who, stranded in Paris, starved and penniless, had asked him for help with clothing and money. He had, he informed Stone, just been released from Dachau concentration camp. His youngest son and father-in-law had been murdered by the Germans. His wife had been sent to Stutthof concentration camp near Danzig and he did not know what had happened to her. Back home in Lithuania everyone had been killed: "Father, brothers and sisters . . . and their children as well." Indeed, "all Jews have been murdered. Of some 300,000 Lithuanian Jews (incl. Vilnius) *perhaps 4,000* (four thousand) are still alive."[43]

However unsettling this news must have been for the old Germanophile Shepard Stone, he refused to move to the other extreme. In February 1945 Jimmy Read referred to a letter he had had from Stone in which he "excoriate[d] the Morgenthau Plan." Read now remarked: "Thank goodness you felt that way, and I hope you still do."[44] If Stone's later testimony is to be believed, he did indeed. When in 1952 Thilo Bode accused him in the *Frankfurter Allgemeine Zeitung* of being a *"Morgenthau-Mann,"* he replied angrily that in 1944–45, when there was great fury over what had been discovered about the camps, opinions were deeply divided over Morgenthau's proposals.[45] But actual American policy, in the implementation of which he was directly involved at DISCC, was guided by a desire to save the Germans from starvation and to help them reconstruct their country. This is why in his view it was quite wrong "even to speak of a Morgenthau policy vis-à-vis Germany." And later still in his draft memoirs, apparently with William Shirer's best seller in mind, we find the following passage: "The Germans like other countries over the pages of history have not always been comfortable neighbors; it is going somewhat far to damn them with original sin. There is no direct line from Martin Luther to Adolf Hitler as some highly successful but problematic journalists-turned-historians would have us believe. The Germans were not alone responsible for World War I, though they share a large part of the blame."[46]

As to World War II, he continued to cling to the view that, notwithstanding the mass support that Hitler had gained, there were many "other Germans," some of whom he knew as friends. At the time of the capitulation he gave renewed evidence for this after seeing Maria Harriet Schleber, née von Alvensleben, about whom he recorded in his diary: "One of the most remarkable women of what must be a remarkable family. Involved in the Anti-Hitler Putsch of July 20, 1944. Uncle hanged, father in concentration camp, sister and sister's husband in Prinz-Albrechtstr. 8 [Berlin Gestapo headquarters, with infamous torture cells in the basement]. . . . A few days before we took Weimar she was there to try to find her father at Buchenwald. In [the town] square she saw SS beating [a] foreign laborer, got up and denounced the SS man as shaming the armband Deutschland he was wearing. A deep quiet woman who is strong and wants to live."[47]

In December 1944 Stone's views on the treatment of defeated Germany also triggered an exchange with Markel, with whom he had made contact again about rejoining his department at the *New York Times* after the war. Stone had commented on American press coverage of Germany in terms that disturbed Markel "a good deal." From Stone's somewhat cryptic remarks, he had gained the impression that "apparently you feel that the stories the correspondents have been writing have been too tough on the Germans." Now Markel wanted to be convinced "that they are, especially the Times men." Moreover, even if they were unfair, he retorted, "what harm does it do?" Stone seemed "to fear that we are going to impose too hard a peace on Germany." His fear, by contrast, was "that the peace will be too soft and that twenty years from now the whole business will start up once again." Markel appreciated that "when you meet a people (I suspect it is true even of the Japs) it is hard to believe the generalized picture that you have had up to that moment." This was a perfectly human reaction. Markel thought that Stone had "run into some very nice Germans, and so, with your big open heart, your viewpoint is slightly altered." For this reason he believed that "we people on this side, seeing the thing in perspective and always keeping in mind the larger issues, are probably safer counselors in the long run." Markel conceded that he might be "cockeyed" and "arrogating . . . too much in the way of judgment" to himself, but at least he had given Stone his honest reaction to his letter.[48]

The reply that Stone sent him on 10 January 1945 did not convince Markel either. Repeating his earlier arguments about no damage having been done even if mistakes occurred in press reports about Germany, he wrote back on 22 March: "As I see it, more lives have been lost by trusting the Germans and assuming they were beaten before they actually were than by depicting the savagery of the beast." Hence all pleas "for a soft peace" should be "condemned at this time." And "as for your 'good Germans' it seems to me you answer yourself when you say 'These were the people who voted or heiled Hitler.' " Markel thought that Stone condoned their behavior and he was not prepared to do this.[49]

Further contemporary evidence of Stone's attitude toward the Germans and his opposition to a harsh treatment is to be found in his exchanges of ideas with Walter Hasenclever when they met in Germany in the spring of 1945. His brother-in-law had originally been reluctant to join the army, apparently because of his background in the pacifist wing of the German Youth Movement. But he changed his mind and by early 1943 worked as a military translator. After the end of the war, he helped to interrogate prisoners of war and former Nazi officials. In this capacity he also interviewed a number of major war criminals, and his notes of these encounters make instructive reading not merely because they reflect the disgust he felt at the cowardice of once very powerful and brutal men,[50] but also because they reveal his many reservations about the Germans. After one of Hasenclever's encounters with his brother-in-law, he wrote to his sister Charlotte back in New York in May 1945 that Shepard had "more understanding for the prevailing situation than the great majority of the people who are going to have the power of decision in this country." In August they had another "long talk," in the course of which Hasenclever was "glad to find the rare sensation of being completely d'accord on all [of the] most pressing problems with an officer of our somewhat uncomprehending Army."[51]

As other studies have confirmed, there was indeed a large gap in comprehension between those Americans who knew pre-Nazi Germany and those who saw the country for the first time in their lives in 1945 or, like

Markel, looked at it from great distance.[52] Stone's anger at the latters' ignorance and misjudgments, which—he was convinced—resulted in many wrong decisions, grew even stronger in the fall of 1945.

Stone's frustration can also be traced in Charlotte's responses to comments in his letters at this time. Thus she wrote on 20 October: "I don't blame you for being disgusted with the way things are going for military government in Germany. I share all your views on the subject and I agree with you that, under the unfortunate circumstances, you should return here, too, and then maybe go back to Germany—with me—as a civilian journalist or lecturer. Or you should try to influence public opinion here in the country and the policies emanating from Washington. At any rate the Times has requested your release, and it may indeed be possible to have you back here by next month. I don't dare to hope it too strongly yet, it would be too good to be true, and I have too little knowledge of the difficulties which may arise. But I look upon my present rather uninteresting life as just a short interim before you come back to me for good, and then I'll be ready to do whatever you want me to do."[53]

Five days later she proved to be an even more loyal wife. The letter was her reply to a letter of 18 October in which he had been very critical of Allied denazification procedures, as well as the lack of courage and the bullying of the occupation authorities: "I'm so proud of you because you have exactly the right attitude, and so much understanding and sympathy where it belongs and also just severity where that belongs. Again, after your long letter telling me so much about your role in Germany and the heartbreaking failure of M[il.]G[ovt.] as a whole, due to Washington's policy of pulling all the high-pointers out much too fast, I feel that I ought to try to come over to you and have you stay to finish your job. It's so important, and you are so wonderful and, apparently, appreciated by all those hard-struggling decent Germans who are getting a chance now and need guidance. And yet, looking at the picture of this globe as a whole, one lone man with a hopelessly inadequate staff to get this enormous task done won't defeat the odds against him which are mounting daily. So maybe we need you more here where a lot of enlightening has to be done and, if you are successful, that will benefit your good Germans more than your local efforts." Charlotte then talked about those "good Germans," her friends in New York who were political refugees who had fought Nazism without losing touch with Germany and their underground connections there: "They never even tried to tear up the bridges behind them because all of them wanted to get back to Germany and put their hands to the wheel" as soon as possible. They were now "being deluged with letters from their former comrades urging them to come back; that there were jobs for them to do and that they were needed badly." And indeed, they were "eager to help although all of them know that it isn't a bed of roses."[54]

Witnessing policy making with which he disagreed, Stone had moved closer to a decision to change jobs. True, he had felt a sense of mission to help effect a redirection of U.S. Military Government policies. As late as the summer of 1945, Charlotte had been trying to obtain a transfer from her OSS office job in New York to one of its operations in Europe, and Stone himself actually talked to Allen Dulles about this possibility.[55] But when this plan fell through, he seriously began to contemplate rejoining the *New York Times*. It would give him the opportunity to be reunited with his wife, who was longing to have her husband in New York and to educate the Americans back home. When he visited Berlin in early September 1945, he was depressed by the apathetic population and the ubiquitous ruins, even if Meineckestr. 26, the old apartment building of the Jaffés, had not been badly damaged. Berlin, he concluded, was "broken," but only for the moment; for "some day this will change."[56] The visit also gave him an opportunity of putting his views to General Lucius D. Clay, the U.S. military governor.[57]

Apparently he did not get very far, and by October disillusionment had conquered his earlier optimism. On 18 October he wrote to Charlotte: "It won't be long now, though I leave this work, if I do, with a terrible feeling. It's like giving up, not finishing the job that I know is more important than anything else you can possibly do."[58] Four weeks later he added: "The situation here goes from bad to worse, and I understand that the recent State Department appointments are impossible so far as this work is concerned. As soon as I get out I want to write an article or talk over the radio on the tragedy of what we are doing when we could do such a magnificent job. If I had charge of this work here—and a few people have recommended to Gen. Clay that I should be put in charge . . . —then I'd order you over here immediately to work with me." This work, he believed, "would make a considerable difference in Germany and in the future. The prospects challenge me and it's a crime that we are throwing away our victory with lack of understanding and foundering personnel. Well, what's the use. I believe you that now more good can probably be done from the outside if one can't really take over the whole organization from the inside. I hate to give up, but it has to be."[59] In December, he voiced his opposition to American requisitioning policies.[60]

CHAPTER 2

BACK WITH THE *NEW YORK TIMES*

What finally facilitated Stone's decision to leave the army in January 1946, after promotion to the rank of lieutenant colonel, was that he had an influential job waiting for him. The *New York Times* Sunday department wanted him back. But there were problems here, too, in the person of Lester Markel. The department head was a somber person and difficult to get on with. In August 1943 in response to Stone's casual inquiry, his friend Hadley Cantril replied: "I have never quite been able to figure Markel out, for he has always been so negativistic in conversation that I never know what conclusion he has drawn from a discussion."[61]

In the fall of 1944, Stone wrote to Markel and also asked Hanson Baldwin for advice about his future career. His own hope was to become the *Times*'s Berlin correspondent. "Are you serious about that one or shall we continue to reserve a desk for you in the Sunday Department?" Markel asked.[62] Meanwhile Baldwin, in talking to Markel about Stone's future, gained the impression that, in Markel's view, Baldwin was the "only one" capable of running a Berlin office. Baldwin, in a fit of modesty, thought that he was given "too much credit" by Markel and assumed that Stone was "scheduled to be Gauleiter of Berlin."[63]

In the following months, Stone and Markel got into the previously mentioned argument over American press coverage of Germany and the treatment of the German population. The exchange did not bode well for Stone's proposed return to the *New York Times*. However, whether or not it was through the good offices of Charlotte who, based in New York and anxious to have her husband back, had been keeping in touch with Markel, in May 1945 she expressed satisfaction to her husband "that you understand each other again."[64] More important, Arthur Sulzberger wanted him back and in June 1945 applied to the Army for his release.[65] Still, by the summer Stone had not quite given up hope that he could achieve more in Germany and that Charlotte might join him there. If he returned to New York, he also wanted greater executive responsibility. Markel got the impression that Stone—as he wrote at the end of August 1945—had "no great desire" to rejoin the Sunday department; but it may well be that Markel was not too keen either.[66] Stone toyed with other jobs even after a concrete and "attractive" offer to become assistant editor of the Sunday edition had come through.[67] But a deal had been struck and the *Times*'s request for Stone's discharge was finally granted.[68]

44

Whatever his feelings of joy at this outcome, he continued to think that he had left "the job for which this war was fought in inadequate hands." Still, his protests had not been completely in vain: "Big changes are coming in information control and some of them, I think, because of talks I've had with General Clay." Apparently there had been some consideration of retaining him with enhanced responsibility. But he was prepared to wait only "if the big job did come through," which would also enable Charlotte to come to Germany "and together we could really do something. I like living here and above [all] doing something creative."[69]

This "big" opportunity was to come along in 1949, when John J. McCloy was chosen as U.S. high commissioner in the newly founded Federal Republic and asked Stone to join him. In the meantime, while working under Markel, Stone did not drop out of the German scene completely. On the contrary, he was keenly interested in developments in Europe and received reports from former colleagues and friends. Thus, in April 1946 he had a letter from Hans Hirschfeld, a returnee soon to work closely with Stone on various projects from the Berlin mayor's office, who was convinced "that Europe is still a very important part of our small world—and 65 million Germans are and will be always an integral part of Europe, materially and spiritually. This fact one may regret but it still remains a fact."[70] If nothing else, for Stone, too, this was axiomatic.

There is also a note from William Stevens, who had helped him to sort out the embarrassment with Heuss in the fall of 1945 and who still remembered "when you told us as we were ready to go home after having fought for the U.S., to stay on and to finish the job because we had the qualifications for it." It now seemed "that we have been expedients: 'Der Mohr hat seine Schuldigkeit getan, er kann jetzt gehen.' " He wondered if there was "any way to fight this injustice" and was dismayed by the current search for scapegoats. Yet, as before, there was not just the concern over American policy, but also over German attitudes.[71] In December 1948 Sternberger gave him a very gloomy view of developments in Germany: "The opportunity of democracy is gone, and overwhelmingly the Germans are to blame."[72]

Not surprisingly, therefore, Stone adhered to the promise he had given himself in 1945 to continue the crusade, this time on the American side of the Atlantic as a journalist and producer of memoranda that he sent to Washington. He also expanded his network of contacts. He started with his immediate colleagues. In a speech in Times Hall in early 1946, he told them about the trials and tribulations of news gathering in occupied

Germany. With Markel sitting in the audience, he was on the whole quite laudatory about American correspondents now working there and also referred to the emergent German press as a source of information. Extolling the virtues of objective reporting, as he had done before the German editors at Marburg in October 1945, Stone tried to give his audience a strong impression of realities in the occupied zones. Providing them with an array of geographic and demographic statistics and with the results of various surveys from the Office of the Military Government (OMGUS) he went on to describe daily living conditions and even "a week's menu in January of a family I know in Stuttgart."[73] It was not a pretty picture. He then talked about German responses to Allied policies of denazification and peacemaking. He mentioned the strength of socialism and the weakness of the unrepentant who, in his estimate, "make up ten percent of the population." The basic point Stone was trying to make was for his colleagues to "see Germany and the Germans as they are. We must put resentment, though not vigilance, aside."

Beyond an assessment of the German situation, his talk finally contained something like a European Recovery Program, as enunciated by George F. Marshall over a year later and presumably reflecting quite well what Stone had been saying to Clay and others in Germany before his departure from DISCC: "If the Germans are not to remain a continuing object of charity, then they are to work themselves out of their ruins, if they are to help rebuild their own and Europe's economy, then Germany must be solvent and self-sustaining. By implication, a solvent, a producing Germany means an industrially healthy Germany." Stone then turned to the political side of his program. Here his ideas were remarkably similar to the reorientation efforts that came to replace the earlier denazification and reeducation practices: "If the Germans are to become a democratically-minded people, democracy must have a chance to grow in Germany."

There is no record of the subsequent discussion; but it is safe to assume that many of his colleagues remained skeptical and continued to advocate a harder line toward the Germans. This was certainly true of Markel; yet, however difficult the head of the Sunday department may have been, somehow the two men respected each other and Markel was happy to send Stone on a two-month assigment to Germany later in 1946, even though he did not like the assessments that Stone produced on his return. When Markel was himself away from the office for two months in 1947, Stone acted as his deputy. In the spring of 1948 he earned laurels when he helped to prevent a strike at the *New York Times*, for which he received a personal letter of thanks and a salary raise from Sulzberger.

More important for its message and its conclusions as well as for its impact was an article by Stone that appeared in the *New York Times Magazine* on 26 January 1947. The "Report on the Mood of Germany" was the fruit of his recent trip to Europe. He started off with a question that frequently preoccupied the American elites in those years, namely, "what is going on in the German mind today. . . . What are the German people thinking, fearing, hoping, hating? Is there any indication of psychological change?" He concluded that "the answer to these questions is a key to the future of Germany and of world peace." For six weeks, Stone wrote, he had listened to people on trains and in public places. It was often bitter, despairing, and resentful talk and weird rumors that he overheard on his travels. He also went to one of Karl Jaspers's lectures and later, at the famous philosopher's house, discussed the mood of the students with his former teacher at Heidelberg University. Overall it was a colorful portrait that Stone gave of the Germans, some of whom, like Eugen Kogon, the editor of the *Frankfurter Hefte* and former concentration camp inmate, tried to give the Americans sensible advice on the economic and political situation.

Stone defended the need for continued censorship and road checks, but criticized "excesses" and "brutality." There had also been, he added, injustices with respect to internment, but "these again have been the exception." Furthermore, "these camps are resorts compared with the hell of the concentration camps with their crematoria and gas chambers." At the end he raised the question of "what can be done to solve the psychological problem in Germany?" He saw only one solution: "A coordinated psychological and economic program," for "unless there is a psychological reorientation in Germany, economic support, improvement and independence would be a dangerous mortgage on the future." At the same time "certain approaches and attitudes" in OMGUS, he believed, also had to change.

Ultimately, Stone put his trust in the ability of small elites to overcome the economic and psychological problems facing the German population: "There are a few Germans, among them newspaper editors, who are trying to show the way, and there are small groups, including youngsters and university students, willing to learn." Hence "the start must be made" here. It was an idea, which not only chimed in well with his own education and the world views of the American elites among which he moved but also anticipated the approach to European reconstruction and German-American relations that he was to take when he returned to the Old Continent in 1949.

47

While trying to create sympathies for Germany's problems among *New York Times* readers and a wider American public, Stone also continued to be active behind the scenes in Washington, warning his former superiors of possible trouble ahead. On 26 February 1946, he wrote to Major General John Hilldring, the chief of the Civil Affairs Division at the War Department responsible for military government matters in Germany. Having presented his credentials, he stated that "in recent months the attention of the American people has been centered on denazification and economic changes," but public interest "and perhaps considerable criticism" might soon focus on "the work being done in reeducation." His letter, he continued, was trying to deal with "some of the strengths and weaknesses in the various echelons" of the Information Control Division that he had observed while serving in Germany until the end of 1945. As before, he minced no words as he offered his critical observations.[74]

On 15 April 1946 Stone reaffirmed his views in a memorandum on "Information Control in Germany," which he sent directly to the secretary of war. Without the usual polite introductory formulas, he came straight to the point: "Unless measures are taken soon to remedy the situation, there is danger that the program to reorient the German mind, the job of the Education Section and of the Information Control Division of OMG [US] in Germany, will disintegrate. This means that of the two main goals we tried to reach in fighting this war, one will be lost." He then became personal, calling Brigadier General Robert McClure and other top people in the information control field "incompetent" and ignorant of German affairs. He attested to their goodwill, but recommended the removal of these "misfits in their jobs." Disillusioned by their superiors, some of the "most capable men in the field have preferred to leave and return home, discouraged by the lack of leadership, foresight, and knowledge." To remedy the situation, Stone suggested that McClure be replaced, the organizational structures be modified, and Lieutenant Colonel John Stanley "be considered for an important position in the new setup." He also wanted the secretary of war to "call on the great newspapers, publishing houses, radio stations, universities for a total of 25 persons who could take the vital media jobs in Berlin, Munich, Stuttgart, and Wiesbaden." Stone would be happy to provide a list of names. Finally, he advised "to send a small group . . . to Germany to report on the present situation."[75]

At this point it is unclear whether any action was taken on this memorandum. Stevens's letter of 30 April 1947, which has been mentioned already, was probably written too shortly after Stone's suggestions reached Washington. However, he kept at it. At his prompting, Sulzberger began a correspondence with Clay in Germany after what appeared to be an unfair dismissal by the American authorities of a left-wing German journalist. What happened next was a nice example of what aggravated Stone: Clay replied by apologizing that Sulzberger's "first memorandum became lost," before confessing that he, too, was "not happy" about the case. He thought "it was handled badly and in a way in which he could become a martyr in the cause of press freedom." Stating that he remembered "Shepard Stone very well indeed" and had "a high respect for his ability and opinion," Clay nevertheless tried to justify the actions taken, causing Stone, who was shown the reply by Sulzberger, to comment to the latter: "This is an evasive answer, and not up to General Clay's usual standard."[76]

Whatever happened to his job in Germany, in 1948 McClure was cheerfully working in the New York Field Office of the Civil Affairs Division, supervising, inter alia, the publication of two magazines, *Neue Auslese* and *Die Amerikanische Rundschau*. Intrigued, Stone called him in early December 1948 to ask for review copies. He was sent some recent issues together with a "statement of purpose" for both publications. In conclusion, McClure asked him several questions: "Do you feel that the function of the magazines, as described briefly above, can contribute to German reorientation and help in supporting U.S. policy? To what degree do you feel that the magazines perform their functions? Do they, in your opinion, meet professional publishing standards?"[77]

Stone composed his reply "based on my observations in Germany and also on fairly close contact with many Germans." While confessing that "these publications meet a big need in Germany" and did "a job which privately-owned and published American magazines seem unable to do," he speculated that larger parts of *Neue Auslese's* contents were probably "above the level of a majority of Germans." As a result, the publication was "probably missing the big target, the important German middle and lower middle class." However, it was this large group "that must know human and democratic values if our work in Germany is to succeed." Throwing in a bit of his own elitism, he cited a statement by Jaspers that had appeared in one of the issues: "I happen to be a former Jaspers student and an admirer of the man's work. I don't think, however, that the average German understands him." At the same time he had nothing but praise for "the political, social and human values" that the magazine was trying to proliferate. The editors, he felt, "without suppressing—and they should not—the more questionable aspects of American life, have a sure touch." Overall, *Neue Auslese*, "redesigned to appeal to a popular audience, would be able to play a big role." Turning to *Die Amerikanische Rundschau*, Stone wrote that it was "on the right track," given that it was "important to reach the leaders of thought in various fields." But he suggested that this magazine be made, "if anything, more detailed and more intellectual." It seemed to him that this publication was "an excellent vehicle for long and detailed articles in the fields of education, economics, public administration, politics etc."[78]

Now, it may well be that deep down in his heart Stone continued to feel the urge to return to Europe and to organize the "psychic" reconstruction of the Germans himself, rather than criticizing or advising people in decision-making positions. As early as May 1946, he had written to Julius Ebbinghaus, the rector of Marburg University, that he had been "very happy in Germany." Somehow, he added, life there had been "at times more satisfying than it is over here." He found it difficult to explain the reasons for his feelings, "because he had an enviable task" in New York. But he sensed that "in Germany it had been a great psychic challenge for me to be able to cooperate in the reconstruction" of the country.[79]

Restless about this matter as he continued to be, he went before the American Press Institute's Council on the Future of Germany in March 1948 to talk about what he saw as the tasks ahead. He urged his audience to work with the generation of the twenty-five- to fifty-year-olds, made proposals for overcoming the faults of the German educational system, and suggested exchanges of students and teachers to break the country's isolation. The "right people" were needed to replace the inadequate ones. Because journalists knew Germany and spoke the language, they could do much to advance these causes. Included among the "right people," it appears, may have been Stone himself.[80]

While exhorting his colleagues and fellow Americans in articles, speeches, or confidential memoranda not to miss the opportunity of constructing a new Germany and through it of solving the "German problem," he also tried to keep in close touch with his friends and acquaintances in Germany. What he heard did not always reassure him. At the same time, with reorientation and the Marshall Plan in place by 1949, some of the developments that Stone had been hoping for had come about.[81] The brief punitive phase of the early postwar years ended. Denazification and dismantling wound down. The start of the Cold War against the Soviet Union helped those policy makers in Washington and occupied Germany who advocated the reintegration of the country into the community of nations. West Germany's industrial potential, in this vision of things, was to be mobilized as the engine for the economic recon-struction of Europe and the West Germans were made part of a more unified Western bloc.

Against the background of these developments and his continuing pre-occupation, as a journalist in New York, with Germany under Allied rule, Stone made a decision in 1949 that gave his career a new turn and offered him a chance to promote policies that he had not been influential enough to effect in 1945.

Public Opinion and High Politics in
Semisovereign West Germany

IN 1949 the strict military rule of the Western zones of occupation came to an end. The West German Basic Law was drawn up, approved by the three Western Allies, and adopted by the Bundestag of the newly founded Federal Republic of Germany. General Clay was replaced by a high commissioner, and John J. McCloy was selected for the job. He had distinguished himself as a lawyer and in war service in Washington where he had risen to the position of assistant secretary in the War Department by the end of the war. Another spell with his old Wall Street law firm and service as president of the World Bank had given him wide-ranging experience and plenty of political wisdom and contacts when he took the job in West Germany. But he did not know that part of Europe well and therefore needed a team of reliable and knowledgeable advisors. A key position to be filled was that of public affairs director, the person who dealt with a myriad of media questions that the high commissioner would have to confront.[1]

JOINING U.S. HIGH COMMISSIONER JOHN J. MCCLOY

It is not clear who drew his attention to Stone. Later it was thought that his name had been tossed into the ring by James "Scotty" Reston, an influential writer on the *Times*; but as we have seen in the previous chapter, Stone was a distinguished journalist whose expertise and strong views on Germany were not unknown in Washington and elsewhere. Stone embodied exactly what the high commissioner was looking for: he knew Germany well and had helped to rebuild the press in the U.S. zone of occupation in 1945; he was a trained historian with a Berlin doctorate, a degree that would be an asset in a country where titles counted. Moreover, the fact that it was a German qualification in a well-regarded discipline and supervised by the highly esteemed Hermann Oncken would give Stone prestige among academics and intellectuals.[2]

There may well have been further reasons why Stone, who had initially merely been hired as a temporary consultant on leave from the *New York Times*, was asked by McCloy to take charge permanently of HICOG's large Public Affairs operation.[3] When they met over lunch in New York for the first time, they probably discovered quickly that they held similar views on Germany and had been on the same side with respect to the earlier debate on how to treat Germany after 1945. Although they were exactly thirteen years apart and, it might be argued, belonged to different generations, another bond, even if never openly articulated, was that both had risen from humble social backgrounds. McCloy's family had immigrated from Scotland and his father had been an upwardly mobile insurance clerk in Philadelphia who died when his son John Jay was only six years old. Without a pension or a larger life insurance payment from her husband, Anna McCloy opened a small hairdressing shop to make ends meet.

Consequently her son had no choice but to start his education at local public schools, but eventually Anna McCloy saved enough to be able to send him to the private Peddie Institute, which John left at age eighteen as "a self-assured young man" with a "simplicity of manners and easy dignity." Considering that he had grown up in a strictly stratified society of wealth and pedigree, it was not surprising that he, "the son of a hairdresser . . . was grateful that Peddie had given him opportunities beyond his origins, beyond Philadelphia's Chinese Wall. He now had one of the prerequisites for membership in the Eastern Establishment: a prep-school credential."[4] The next one was a four-year degree course at Amherst College.

There is little doubt that McCloy and Stone occasionally reminisced about their college years. Speaking at Dartmouth in 1989, he reported how McCloy "often recalled his undergraduate days at Amherst when those 'Green Gorillas' would defeat Amherst."[5] Some thirty-five years earlier he mentioned in a letter to "an Exeter boy" who had sought his advice on the Ivies: "Mr. McCloy often spoke to me about Amherst where he had a few inspiring teachers and where he had learned about the principles and traditions of our civilization."[6] If their social background and education created affinities, there was also the coincidence in the choice of their wives: Charlotte, born in Germany, had come to the United States in 1933; Ellen McCloy, née Zinsser, was the daughter of recent immigrants from Germany who, by the way, were distantly related to the deceased wife of Konrad Adenauer, the first federal chancellor and McCloy's frequent interlocutor during his years as U.S. high commissioner.

For the moment Stone's relationship with McCloy apparently remained informal. But in September 1949 HICOG was looking for a director of educational and cultural relations, and as Ralph Nicholson, the director of the Office of Public Affairs (OPA), informed Stone: "If everything works out as planned, Mr. Sulzberger will be requested by either the Secretary or the President to deliver you to Frankfurt forthwith." He added that "we need you more than the *Times* does, and I am keeping my fingers crossed."[7] One of the tasks was to look after the American "reorientation" effort, about which William Diebold at the Council on Foreign Relations had recently been "very pessimistic."[8] At first Sulzberger proved resistant to granting more than a three months' leave, and as Stone wrote to John Dickey, the president of Dartmouth College, at the end of October 1949, "three months won't make much sense";[9] but eventually this was extended to "more than a year," and ultimately Stone resigned from his position in New York altogether to replace Nicholson.[10] McCloy had been asking Stone since early June, if not before, to assume Nicholson's position and "to get a deputy."[11] In early August *Stars and Stripes* formally announced that he would become the new director of the Office of Public Affairs from 1 September 1950. This was an important position in its own right, but the nature of his relationship to McCloy is tellingly revealed by a comment that his *Times* colleague Dan Schwartz had heard in May 1950 "from a visitor from Germany." This visitor, Schwartz informed Stone, had told him "that you are 'McCloy's Harry Hopkins,' " to which Schwartz added somewhat incredulously, "Is that true?"[12]

Having joined the government camp and facing a critical press corps at the side of the high commissioner or all alone, Stone could not expect to be treated more leniently by American fellow journalists—his *Times* colleagues not excluded—when they tried to obtain information about McCloy's policies. Certainly Schwartz and Markel were not as easy prey to the new director's rhetoric as Drew Middleton, the paper's Bonn correspondent. After Schwartz saw Middleton toward the end of June 1950, "he was full of praise for what" Stone had done "to stiffen McCloy's backbone." He told Stone that "you seem to have sold the occupation to Middleton." But, Schwartz continued defiantly, "I remain your toughest customer. If Markel returns pro-Nazi [from his European trip], too, I'll be all by myself."[13] Others were more obviously delighted than Schwartz with his little pinpricks, particularly the many German journalists, academics, and intellectuals who still remembered Stone from his days with DISCC in 1945. Some of them had meanwhile become important political figures in the new Federal Republic with whom Stone thenceforth worked hard to foster good relations. For a while he had himself been vexed by doubts about whether to abandon the *New York Times*. In February

1950, before accepting an official position with HICOG, he admitted to a colleague that he found his work in Germany "fascinating"; but he asked him to inquire "six months from now if we are going to accomplish anything." Of course, he added, he "wouldn't be here if I didn't think so, but sometimes I am not sure."[14]

When he finally took over as public affairs director, he no doubt had the powers and the organizational apparatus to make an impact on the development of the young Federal Republic. Under Nicholson, the Office of Public Affairs had grown into a sprawling empire with divisions for Education and Cultural Relations, Information Services, Public Relations, and Exchanges. The Educational and Cultural Division was in turn subdivided into sections covering Information Centers, Schools and Vocational Education, Women's Affairs, Religious Affairs, Health and Welfare, Community Activities and Government Institutions. The Information Services Division had a group for Press and Publications, U.S. Feature Service, Publishing Operations, Rundfunk im Amerikanischen Sektor (RIAS, Berlin), Motion Pictures, and Reactions Analysis, the last being devoted to compiling frequent public opinion surveys.

The budget for 1951 overseas expenses and salaries was $4.4 million, with the estimates for 1952 reaching almost $5 million. It declined thereafter, as the High Commission's activities began to wind down and the Federal Republic moved toward sovereignty, achieving it in 1955. The range of activities funded from this budget was considerable. It included the provision of international news "on a factual basis" to the West German press; the publication of pamphlets "with detailed accounts of important world and local subjects, such as NATO, Schuman Plan and Mutual Security achievements"; a German-language American newspaper, *Die Neue Zeitung*; a monthly journal, *Der Monat*, about which we will hear more in later chapters; the RIAS radio station and program assistance to West German stations; newsreels and documentaries "showing American and world-wide events"; Amerikahäuser and, finally, exchange programs.[15] All in all the Public Affairs Office employed about 400 Americans and some 3,500 Germans.

STONE'S GERMAN-AMERICAN NETWORK

Another aspect of Stone's role at HICOG in the early 1950s was instrumental in promoting the aims and activities of his empire. Being a sociable, if somewhat restless man and appreciating the importance of personal contacts and networking, he made it a major plank of his effort to meet people and to bring Germans and Americans together in informal settings. Even if the occasion was more formal, he always tried to create a relaxed atmosphere. He once confided to Fred Praeger, the Austrian-born publisher, the purpose of his "reorientation" efforts: "I have often been struck at international meetings with the decency of many Germans who participate, but also with their stiffness, their lack of ability to communicate, and their remote relation to flexibility and charm. Here, I think, we have a reason for the hostility which affects both personal and international relations." But averse to too much stereotyping, he ended on a more light-hearted qualifying note: "Having said this, I must tell you that one of the most charming people I know in the world is a German."[16]

To provide a congenial meeting space for the German-American encounter Stone was hoping to advance, he and Charlotte ran a house in Falkenstein, north of Frankfurt in the Taunus Mountains, which was staffed by several servants, a butler, a chef, a fireman-gardener, a laundress, and a house cleaner. When he later moved to Mehlem, a few miles south of Bonn, the new federal capital, the building was again chosen to accommodate the tenant's extensive official social life as "a meeting place for Germans and Americans interested in working out, on a cooperative basis, the creation of a democratic, anti-Communist, anti-Nazi Germany which would be a reliable partner of the West." The traffic "at Mr. Stone's house," Boerner continued, "fully justified the six servants." In fact it caused him "considerable personal expense above and beyond the salary he got from U.S. Government."[17] According to Stone's expense accounts, he held a party on average twice a week attended by an average of one hundred Germans and seventy-five Americans.[18]

No less important, he did a lot of traveling, at first in order to renew his contacts from 1945 or to visit people who had been recommended to him. His hectic life, even before he became director of the Public Affairs Office, emerges from two long, diary-like letters he sent to his family in Nashua in May and July 1950. In the first letter he speaks of one hundred telephone calls and thirty-five visitors in three days. More days followed with the "same kind of office madness." Soon thereafter, Drew Middleton organized a large dinner party for some twenty journalists and HICOG officials, who, instead of asking awkward questions, "drank and relaxed."[19] The intention was to reconcile McCloy with the press following a somewhat unfortunate start that the high commissioner had had with the corps.[20] As Stone proudly reported, "newspapermen and McCloy are now friends."[21] Small wonder that Middleton talked to Schwartz in such glowing terms about Stone's activities.

At the beginning of April 1950, he flew to London to meet with British Foreign Office officials and journalists. On the day after his return from Britain, he was off to Stuttgart and back on the same day to have dinner with James Riddleberger, HICOG's political advisor. He worked "all day" on Easter Monday and met with the "owners and editors of *Frankfurter Allgemeine Zeitung*" who came to "ask for financial support." He was off again to Munich the next day "to straighten out the America Institute" at the university there. There followed another dinner party for some twenty people, including the McCloys, this time at Nicholson's house. Earlier that day he had had a "long talk with Ben Shute, our director of intelligence, . . . and with McCloy on [the] future of [the] Ruhr industries."[22] He also had a discussion with Milton Katz, the deputy head of the Economic Cooperation Administration (ECA) under Paul Hoffman, both of whom Stone encountered again in connection with the Ford Foundation.[23] Before the end of April he had been to Berlin and once again to Bavaria. On 25 April, he had twelve Germans for dinner at his house, "among them Inge Scholl, the sister of the two Scholls who defied the Nazis at the University of Munich and were hanged in 1943."[24] For the benefit of his family in Nashua he added: "Inge is the girl who started nowhere in 1945, after the war, and built an adult education school which now has 3,000 students. Marvelous girl. She will get hundreds of thousands from us to develop [the] Scholl school."[25]

There followed another dinner "at our house—guests: Mr. and Mrs. Mac [McCloy], Hamilton Fish Armstrong; Mr. and Mrs. Hilpert, Otto Veit und [*sic*] Frau." On 26 April he took Charlotte on her first visit to Berlin since before the war. She was "shocked by [the] ruins of [the] city, but lifted up by [the] spirit of [the] people in [the] streets." After a meeting with "30 Berlin editors, professors, politicians and labor leaders," he stressed the "cordial relations in Berlin between Americans and Germans." On 5 May the Stones were in Bonn and in the evening joined the McCloys at the residence of Theodor Heuss, his "old friend" of 1945, now president of the Federal Republic. Further travels followed to southern Germany. In Munich he wrestled with Alois Hundhammer, the Bavarian minister of culture, a "bitter anti-Nazi" once imprisoned at Dachau, but also "the most charming and most reactionary fellow I have ever met." Although the fact that Oncken had also been Hundhammer's *Doktorvater* created a common bond, Stone came away feeling that only the future would tell "whether I become as reactionary as Hundhammer or he becomes as leftist as me."[26] This was after another dinner the previous night which included the minister president of Northrhine-Westphalia, Karl Arnold, who was on the left wing of the Christian Democratic Party.

Having told his family about another string of meetings and trips around the country, Stone concluded his account admitting, no doubt from the depth of his heart, "that all this seems mad. But believe it or not, it has to be. It is trite to say that Germany is a crucial place. The big problem is to make Germany a country upon which you can rely to be peaceful and anti-totalitarian. If that can be accomplished [in] the next ten years, it will be a major achievement. Again, I say I must try. And those of us here, using our energies and what ability we have, try to do our best. There is nothing like free and open discussion, social contact, friendliness with the people of good will. I don't know if we are getting very far, but I'm certain we are on the only track that may lead in the right direction." He added that "those of us who speak German try to help McCloy in this policy. We spend our time with every type of German, in every field. I think we are making a little progress." But there was also much to make him pessimistic: "Most German political leaders are not open to new ideas, and we have to push them at every turn. By this I don't mean to say that they are pro-Nazi or anti-Semitic. I really think that certain groups in the USA are hurting the cause by their tactics."

It may well be that when making this point he was thinking of his fellow journalists in America, and Schwartz in particular, who had been wondering if, exposed to Stone's pleas for support of his work, he would become converted. Stone certainly worked hard at it when Markel and his wife came to Frankfurt in early June. Middleton threw "a Times party" in their honor at which Stone found his former boss to be "relaxed" and "in good shape" to face a big garden party that had been arranged for the following day. Among those invited were "the JJ McCloys, the office directors and other big wheels of HICOG, leading German and American newspaper editors and publishers, [and] outstanding Germans from other fields." Stone came away feeling that "the Markels seem[ed] impressed with some of the Germans," even if "up to now Germans haven't impressed him."[27] It looked as if Schwartz would end up as a lonely skeptic.

In mid-June there was another meeting with representatives of the country's newspaper publishers. He also had an interview with Inge Scholl "to discuss her plans for a new type of college," the later Hochschule für Gestaltung in Ulm.[28] Finally, on 14 June, he had dinner with Gerö von Gaevernitz, "sidekick of Allen Dulles in Switzerland during the war." On the other hand, he gave short shrift to men like Ernst von Salomon whose criticism of U.S. occupation policies reflected their more fundamental anti-Americanism.[29]

Stone's encounters with innumerable Germans and Americans formed the basis of his new vastly expanded network of contacts in Germany and back in the United States, a network he cultivated at his subsequent job at the Ford Foundation and during his ultimate return to Berlin in the mid-1970s to direct the new Aspen Institute. All these men and women were carefully categorized with regard to their "fit," often with reference to their Nazi or anti-Nazi past. Thus he informed Sulzberger, half accurately, in March 1952 that Max Horkheimer, the driving force behind the Frankfurt School before and after its move to New York in 1933 who returned to West Germany in the 1950s and had meanwhile become rector of Frankfurt University, "was forced out of Germany by the Nazis because he was both a Jew and a liberal."[30] Former members of the July 1944 resistance movement enjoyed special esteem, whereas the editors and owners of the *Frankfurter Allgemeine Zeitung* were deemed to be rather too conservative and nationalist. He got to know and later nurtured his acquaintances with leading politicians, Adenauer and Reuter among them, and throughout he continued to rely on the *New York Times* to open doors. At OPA he surrounded himself with trusted aides, some of whom followed him to the Ford Foundation or stayed in touch. But even more significant than Stone's style of operation is the light it sheds on the sociology of German-American and, later, European-American relations, the further study of which this book hopes to stimulate.

McCLOY'S "HARRY HOPKINS"

In reviewing Stone's more concrete achievements and the aims he pursued at HICOG, the notes appended to the 1952 and 1953 budget estimates provide a good starting point. According to the "Highlight Statement" appearing in this document, the Office of Public Affairs program was designed "to influence crucial decisions in a geographic area which is vital to the security of the United States; [and] . . . to strengthen the development of German democracy, because a democratic Germany is the only Germany that will be reliable in the struggle with communism or any other form of totalitarianism."[31] These "major objectives," the statement continued, "emerge from the fact that Germany is the front-line battleground between the Soviet Union and the West. Germany is the communist point of impact in the heart of Europe." The document pointed out that "the communists are spending vast sums and are engaging in bold efforts to win over Germany and to drive out United States influence from this key European area." Consequently it is in "the vital interest of the United States to defeat the communist political and psychological attack on Germany and to influence the development of a democratic Germany in association with the nations of the free world."

According to the "Highlight Statement" the following considerations were believed to be "compelling" when it came to "carrying out a hard-hitting public affairs program in Germany":

1. Geographically, the Federal Republic and West Berlin ... are placed in daily contact with hostile elements directing their powerful political and propaganda efforts not only against the Federal Republic but also against the United States.

2. Politically, the Federal Republic is a keystone in the wall being constructed to contain communism; it holds the key to the achievement of European unity and Western defense.

3. Economically, the Federal Republic, with its increasing resources and productive power, is essential to the economic and industrial welfare of the Western world.

4. Culturally, in spite of systematic Nazi destruction, Western Germany is rebuilding from the ground up the institutions upon which democracy rests. The start which Germany has made in this respect has been made with American leadership and financial aid. These cannot be discontinued although, as Germany's efforts increase, the United States contribution is being correspondingly reduced.

The rest of the OPA statement postulated that "seven years after the defeat and moral breakdown caused by Hitler, the people of Germany find themselves in a dangerous position between an aggressive Soviet Union and the free nations of the West, which intend to defend their own freedoms." The Soviets were trying hard to dissuade the Federal Republic from joining the West while at the same time "making large promises to unify Germany and to withdraw all occupation troops."

As the Cold War escalated, Stone's office had also begun to cooperate with other U.S. agencies. Thus "the Mutual Security Agency (MSA) information program has been integrated with the regular public affairs program."[32] No less significantly, the OPA director was "serving both as public affairs and MSA information officer." As a result the "entire public affairs organization, covering RIAS, Berlin, the American radio station which is a strong voice which penetrates behind the Iron Curtain, the Amerikahäuser (information centers) which are used by 14,000,000 Germans yearly, *Die Neue Zeitung*, the American newspaper in the German language which is read by leaders of opinion throughout Germany, and all our other programs" were designed "to carry out the combined public affairs-MSA program."

The explanatory notes to the individual OPA division budgets then offered more detailed statistical evidence of the work already done. The Division of Information Services reported that it had distributed over 13 million pamphlets. *Die Neue Zeitung* and *Der Monat* were said to be reaching a large elite readership, while movies catered to the mass market. Films on life in the United States and American policies were viewed "by 3,150,000 persons monthly." Some "1,650,000 persons see them as part of regular programs in commercial theaters, while 1.5 million people were reached "through non-theatrical showings such as at information centers, community meetings, schools, trade unions, and agricultural organizations." In 1952 the United States produced a weekly newsreel, *Welt im Film*, which was watched by "17,000,000 people each month through commercial theaters."

Much was also made in the statement of expenditures on the rehabilitation of educational institutions "which were destroyed or Nazified during the Hitler regime," and of international youth camps. Moreover, there were the Amerikahäuser, with their average monthly attendance of over 1 million people and a "book circulation of 260,000 volumes during 1951." OPA also funded exchanges that were intended, first, to make "American institutions and culture available to Germans through direct experience of the United States"; second, to assist "the German people with the development of democratic institutions and practices"; and, third, to promote in "cooperation with a European exchanges program . . . policies for [the] integration of Germany with the West." Between 1949 and 1952 the exchange program took close to 10,000 "students and leaders" across the Atlantic until the Fulbright Program came into force in 1953.[33]

Finally, sensitive to the question of their effectiveness, but also knowing that a critical American press and Congress were constantly looking over their shoulders and suspecting them of not being tough enough with the communists as well as the ex-Nazis, Stone and his OPA colleagues developed an elaborate system of surveys. It was their way of monitoring both themselves and the Germans through an unending series of polls that were so typical of this period when empirical social research reigned supreme and belief in "objective science," just as in "objective" journalism, was deeply rooted. While the strikingly strong anticommunism that pervaded the "Highlight Statement" was put in partly for the benefit of the congressional appropriations committees at a time when McCarthyism was powerful and also influenced HICOG policies, the fear of the Soviet threat in divided Germany and isolated Berlin was nevertheless not just window dressing but a defining feature of McCloy's and Stone's experience and cultural politics. Thus, in the winter of 1950–51 Stone was trying to recruit an expert of the Council on Foreign Relations to "sit here and in Berlin and just tell us what is needed in immediate psychological warfare activities."[34]

Beyond the Soviet menace, there were always also the questions of Nazism and of securing democracy in the Federal Republic, casting doubt on John Gimbel's argument that a conservative fear of communism came to replace wartime liberal worries about fascism.[35] In August 1950 Stone explained his brief to his old mentor Vernon, admitting "confidentially" that "one of the new jobs I have here is to run the so-called psychological warfare campaign" against the East. At the same time OPA had "general charge of the so-called orientation program in Germany. . . . What we have tried to do is to assist, advise and persuade." He felt that a start had been made "although advances are slow and a decade will be needed for the Germans to outgrow certain practices." It was, he added, the youth of Germany that gave him hope—a judgment based on "many hours and days spent with individual German youngsters and with hundreds in the schools, universities, and trade unions."[36]

The line Stone pursued at OPA can also be traced in the notes he made for a speech in New York City in 1952. On this occasion he felt that Germany was becoming more democratic, "certainly on [the] surface." "Authoritarian habits," however, continued to be strong and "our work [is] directed towards easing" them. He did not think that the Nazis were a strong force in the Federal Republic. As to whether the Germans were still anti-Semitic: "Undoubtedly many are, but there is no real test [?] in daily life." Stone believed that at the level of government, the German stand on restitution had been "excellent." In general the attitude of the press was also "fine," but overall there was insufficient "recognition of war guilt." On the problem of whether the communists posed a threat, he noted: " 'Not inside, really,' " though it was necessary to remain "alert." With reference to German feelings toward the United States, his response was: "Depends. Overall most favorable. Some jealousy" and wavering between wanting "to be rid of us" and the desire to keep American troops. He concluded his remarks by reiterating his goal "to get at minds and institutions."[37]

Indirectly at least, however, Stone's influence reached beyond these OPA initiatives. He helped McCloy write his speeches[38] or assisted him at press conferences.[39] As the high commissioner's "Harry Hopkins," he was therefore probably also involved in the drafting of a memorandum on Germany that McCloy sent to President Harry Truman on 10 September 1950. "Politically," the document began, "the situation is not as strong as one would wish." Focusing on Adenauer and Kurt Schumacher, the leader of the Social Democrats, the high commissioner was quite critical of the federal chancellor: "While he is clever and intelligent, a thorough 'Westerner' and certainly the strongest man in the government, he is inclined to be querulous and generally uninspiring." Nor did he "work easily with able men and has surrounded himself with rather a weak cabinet." Schumacher was also deemed to be limited, erratic, and negative. Adopting a long-term perspective, McCloy took the view that "our ultimate assurance against future German aggression must lie . . . in the closest integration of Germany into West Europe and not in an imposed system of controls."[40] Hence—and here McCloy probably thought of the Schuman Plan that was being negotiated in Paris at this time—he saw the need to promote European institutions.

Yet, however hard McCloy and Stone tried to maneuver statesmanlike along the East-West divide that ran right through Germany, time and again they found themselves between a rock and a hard place. Back in the United States there were the McCarthyites who suspected HICOG of being too soft on communism; others, like Schwartz, continued to hold that Stone was too lenient toward the Germans. And so he treated Stone to more of his none-too-subtle teasers. To celebrate Stone's installation as OPA director, Schwartz sent him a letter on fake Nazi stationery, headed "*Der Gouverneur*" and adorned with an eagle and a swastika. His words: "How are you doing? Does Maggy [Stone's little daughter] remember any English? Has Musi [nickname for his wife] lost her American accent? Have you joined the [neo-Nazi] Bruderschaft? Heil! Dan." A few weeks later, with the issue of German rearmament having raised new fears about the future of the Federal Republic, he tried the same line: "Are you reforming the Germans or are they reforming you?" He then offered Stone a bet: "Ruth [his wife] showed me the section of your letter to her in which you boasted about how unmilitary the Germans are and how wrong a certain great newspaper was a few months ago. How would you like to bet me a thousand East marks that the German army will be back

Shepard Stone with John J. McCloy, c. 1951. (Courtesy of Margaret Macdonald)

in full power five years from today, whether or not we make them a part of the Western European defense force?"[41] Apparently Stone did not accept, but persisted in his view. As he told his predecessor, now on the *Tampa Daily Times*, on 6 November 1950: "The armament situation is the big overall problem. German aversion to participate in any kind of an Army is much deeper than any of us had thought. In a way, we should be pleased, though obviously there is another side to the picture."[42]

The prospect of West German armed forces inevitably focused German public opinion on the war criminals still held at Landsberg prison. To many it seemed illogical that the Americans were pushing for German soldiers when a number of convicted Wehrmacht generals were still serving jail time. The issue was complicated by the fact that some of the inmates were former high-ranking SS men who had been condemned to death and were awaiting execution by the Allies, just as the Federal Republic, mindful of the Nazi experience, had abolished capital punishment. The details of the ensuing controversy that quickly engulfed McCloy and his "Harry Hopkins" have been well covered elsewhere.[43] The problem was that the Germans accused them of being unbending, whereas in the United States they were attacked, no less unfairly, for undermining the course of justice. What is of interest here is how Stone tried to mount a rescue operation for his boss in the United States. In February 1951 he appealed to Henry A. Byroade at the State Department's Bureau of German Affairs to do his utmost to clarify the situation. McCloy, he wrote, was quite hurt by the reaction in certain quarters back home. Stone hoped that Byroade would intervene to point out that the high commissioner was acting on the advice of a panel of American judges who had carefully considered each case. "One of America's greatest civil servants" should not be allowed to suffer from "unjust attacks."[44]

Because the most serious of these attacks had appeared in the *New York Times*, Stone also wrote to Sulzberger about an editorial titled "Compromise at Frankfurt." McCloy's decision to pardon some war criminals while having others executed, he insisted, was not "dictated by compromise" but was " 'rooted in the firm belief in the basic principle of the rule of law which all must respect and to which all are answerable.' " With this principle, Stone went on quoting his boss, " 'I have striven . . . to temper justice with mercy.' " Stone then explained to Sulzberger the agonizing steps that the high commissioner had had to take, guided by just one idea in the face of thousands of German pleas to commute the death sentences—that is, "to conform to the highest principles of American justice." He had made his decisions, "based upon the recommendations of the Clemency Board, on the basis of new evidence and of his own reading as a lawyer of the evidence." Moreover, the impact on the Federal Republic had been positive: "German leaders and newspapers have been impressed by the documents and by the integrity that led to the decisions. Some of us think that at least a few Germans have learned a good lesson from the action taken." Another benefit had been "that hundreds of thousands of Germans are again reading [about] the blackest pages" of their history. This time, Stone believed, "they will respect the Nuremberg judgments which they previously thought had been trumped up."[45]

However, Stone did not merely fight a war of words against communism and in defense of McCloy's methods of strengthening West German democracy, using his considerable network of contacts in the process. The most intriguing aspect of his work at HICOG, also in light of his subsequent career at the Ford Foundation, was the monies that he distributed in the hope of fostering a democratic political culture. Most of these funds were for overt activities.[46] Thus, it was no secret that the Americans paid for *Die Neue Zeitung*, Amerikahäuser, informational material, newsreels, and RIAS radio to influence the German public and that they frequently polled the population, trying to discover changing attitudes toward political, socioeconomic, and cultural issues of the time.

OPA took particular pride in the success of *Die Neue Zeitung*. As Ernest Cramer, then managing editor, reported, by the end of 1951 the paper came out daily in a Frankfurt and a Berlin edition and reached "a broad cross-section of the German people with authoritative, factual information about American policy objectives on the international scene and in German. Features were "directed to specific reader groups" and overall the paper was therefore deemed to serve "as a model of the best modern journalistic techniques." Reviewing the past six months, Cramer's report focused on one important recent project, the "preparation of the German public for full particpation in the western defense organization." The literary and art sections of *Die Neue Zeitung* "gave prominence to important cultural events in the western world and at the same time exposed the propaganda nature of a number of Soviet-sponsored 'cultural meetings.' " No less important—again also in light of Stone's later work at the Ford Foundation—"by giving proportioned space to American cultural activities, *Die Neue Zeitung* effectively countered the common communist canard that the U.S. is culturally poor." Cramer felt that the effort had been worthwhile. In Berlin the paid daily circulation was 34,700 and 58,100 for the weekend edition; in Frankfurt daily subscriptions were 119,000, rising to 146,700 for the weekend. To these figures, he argued, had to be added the " 'hidden' circulation."[47]

In short, the relatively small direct costs of the paper (without salaries) was thought by HICOG to be money well spent. Much of the credit for this must go to Hans Wallenberg, the first editor of *Die Neue Zeitung*. Stone paid tribute to Wallenberg's achievements after his death in 1977. Writing to his wife Eva, he eulogized that "Hans was a loyal American who had more understanding of the deeper meaning of his adopted country than many native-born Americans. He was proud to be an American soldier and officer and to wear the uniform of the U.S. Army when it became necessary to destroy the Nazi blight. Yet, throughout, he represented and stood up for the enduring in the [*sic*] German spirit and culture."[48] McCloy had found similar words of praise when, in June 1949, he spoke of Wallenberg's "intimate understanding of the German psychology and your splendid record in promoting democratic ideas."[49]

But there were also covert personnel policies and covert funding of activities to promote the aims that Stone had set out for OPA in the previously mentioned "Highlight Statement." In this connection he had also referred to a decision to integrate the information work of the MSA "with the regular public affairs program" and that he therefore had a dual role.[50] Being a journalist who believed in the power of the written word in this pretelevision age, it is not surprising that he looked beyond the American-sponsored daily toward the rest of the West German press. Until the founding of the Federal Republic, Allied controls had been relatively strict. But after 1949 the licensing process came to an end, by which time some 129 newspapers had come into existence. This figure rose to 1,000 by January 1952, if local papers and editions are included.[51]

Given the new constitutional guarantee of press freedom in the Basic Law and Bonn's semisovereign position, it had become more difficult for the Allies to control the press directly. Worse, all papers, of whatever political stripe, were now exposed to the vagaries of the free market that Economics Minister Ludwig Erhard was promoting after the Currency Reform of 1948. Papers that did not attract readers in larger numbers were threatened with bankruptcy, even if their continued existence was desirable from the viewpoint of the stability of the new democratic order. Another worry was that West Germany's voters were still quite volatile. A welter of political parties competed in the 1949 national elections, and Adenauer's first coalition government consisted of several smaller groups. Parliamentary politics therefore remained in a precarious state. Highly emotional issues, such as rearmament and the idea of a reunified Germany, continued to unsettle the electorate. In this situation it was always possible that some papers, by espousing radical views, might succeed by attacking the more sober, middle-of-the-road ones that supported the republic and refused to play on nationalist feelings and smouldering anti-American resentments.

By January 1951 worries over the state of the West German press had become so serious in HICOG that Stone asked his colleagues, through Theodore Kaghan, the deputy chief of the Information Services Division, to "collect some evidence to use in the near future in substantiation of his belief that certain German newspapers have made serious retrogressions from the standards of good journalism by manipulating news to fit their own political concepts and tendencies."[52]

However, OPA did not only monitor German papers and use Information Services reports; the High Commission also distributed money under the table to publications that were deemed to advance the cause of democracy in the Federal Republic and whose financial position was far from secure. The story is as intriguing as it is complicated. We have already seen with reference to the establishment of the *Frankfurter Rundschau*, the first paper to receive a license in the American zone in 1945, that help was essential, if only to obtain the necessary printing facilities.[53] Right after the war, such facilities could be provided by Allied decree but it soon became clear that there were strict limits to OMGUS fiats in an economy that was based on the principle of private property.

SUPPORTING A DEMOCRATIC PRESS

In early 1948 the Information Control Division of OMGUS therefore set up a fund to the tune of 25 million old Reichsmark to make available capital investment loans to licensed publications in the American zone.[54] A committee known as Wirtschaftliche Genossenschaft der Presse (WIGO) was set up to scrutinize applications and to make loans. However, after the Currency Reform, the end of licensing, and the founding of the Federal Republic, a new system had to be developed. From the High Commission's point of view, according to the Kaghan Report, the problem was to ensure "that the ex-licensed press—that is the newspapers licensed by virtue of their political reliability by Allied Military Government in the immediate postwar period (the 'ex-' was added after licensing was abolished)—would be able to survive with no loss of independence or political courage in the new era of fierce competition which had been ushered in during the summer of 1949 by the lifting of newspaper licensing regulations."

The Americans were rightly worried about the survival of their "children," for the "exlicensees were organized on a rather loose, federative basis in the Gesamtverband der deutschen Zeitungsverleger; the post-licensing publishers had their own separate affiliation, the centralized Verein deutscher Zeitungsverleger ('Altverleger' or 'old publishers' because they had been publishing before 1945)." Given their different origins, rivalry between the two associations was not surprisingly "keen" and so was the competition in the marketplace. Worse, there were also political tensions, since the *Altverleger* were generally regarded "as politically tainted" by their Nazi past. The ex-licensee, in turn, was viewed as "an upstart who was enjoying the use of his [the *Altverleger*'s] printing plant at ridiculously low rates established by fiat of Military Government." Of course, the High Commission could and would exhort the newly founded *Altverleger* papers to work untiringly for a strengthening of a democratic press, and this is what Stone did once he returned to West Germany in 1950. He made public statements about the role and ethos of modern journalism, as he had done at Marburg in October 1945, or he organized private dinner parties, which had been much more difficult in the immediate postwar period.

Thus on 20 June 1950 he invited the entire editorial staff of the *Frankfurter Allgemeine Zeitung*, which he thought was "trying to take [the] place of [the] old Frankfurter Zeitung," to dinner. "Professor Stone of [the] New York Times" (!) used the occasion to tear his guests' "paper apart—all in a positive spirit," to be sure.[55] The paper still did not become OPA's lapdog after this session, and in any case Stone had long come to recognize that money can be more persuasive than words. In the spring of 1950 the idea was born to set up a new fund for ailing ex-licensees to strengthen their back against the *Altverleger*. In the middle of April Stone had a four-hour discussion with Gesamtverband representatives about a "50 million D-mark credit to newspapers to permit them to build their own printing plants and to achieve independence" from the *Altverleger*.[56] This was a few days after he had talked to Milton Katz, the "deputy ECA chief for Europe," about the use of Marshall Plan funds for this purpose. Apparently the idea ran into difficulties and in the end it was decided that the Bonn government would ask the ECA Special Mission to make 15 million deutschmarks available out of Government and Relief in Occupied Areas (GARIOA) counterpart funds. By 1951 a formal agreement to this effect had been signed between the Federal Republic and the United States. The WIGO committee, expanded by representatives of the *Altverleger* who could hardly be left out, was to vet and approve applications from individual publishers. After this, the case was forwarded to the Reconstruction Loan Corporation "for a strictly bank examination to determine the creditworthiness of the newspaper" concerned.

Once an application had taken this hurdle as well, the Marshall Plan office would be informed, and in turn would request that HICOG release the funds to the publisher whose application had been approved under this elaborate two-stage procedure. Three months after the WIGO committee had begun its work in November 1950, it had scrutinized some two hundred applications, of which it approved about half. It allocated some 13.5 million deutschmarks and retained the remaining 1.5 million for the support of newspapers in West Berlin. By April 1951 these recommendations had passed through the other prescribed stages, and HICOG was asked to begin allocating the first installments from the fund.

Without going into the various problems that arose over the early versions of the support system, after several changes it seems to have worked more or less satisfactorily. Although set up as a revolving fund with prompt repayment stipulations, the terms were still very favorable. Collateral requirements were more reasonable than at first and interest at around 5.5 percent was much lower than the market rate of about 12 percent. Not surprisingly, according to the Kaghan Report, HICOG soon reported that "the results of the new arrangements have so far been gratifying." Of the newspapers put on the list, 15 were "HICOG top priorities and 19 HICOG secondary priorities." Among these, 25 independent papers received some 6.32 million marks; "9 SPD [Social Democrat] and SPD-inclined papers" were given 2.18 million. There were "7 CDU [Christian Democrat] and CDU-inclined" publications receiving a total of 1.22 million and 3 papers close to the Free Democrats (FDP) benefited to the tune of 510,000 marks.

The other point worth noting is that funds were channeled in such a way that the U.S. government never appeared as the direct funder. It was an arrangement that we shall have to bear in mind when we come to discuss the financial support that Stone and the Ford Foundation, in cooperation with the CIA, gave to the Congress for Cultural Freedom (CCF).[57] To be sure, the grants to the West German press were not as closely kept a secret as was the identity of the CCF's benefactors. Indeed, the communist press was delighted to reveal the existence of the HICOG fund and "to assert that the Americans had bought the West German press for their rearmament plans." Accordingly the East German papers published "numerous violent articles against the 'reptile West German press' and 'American slush-funds.' "[58] In the Federal Republic, however, Allied support for the long list of newspapers did not attract much attention.[59]

For Stone, under whose watch these measures were put in place, it was particularly reassuring that the two favored papers, the *Süddeutsche Zeitung* and the *Frankfurter Rundschau*, got what they needed to secure their viability. The former "contracted with the Bavarian Government to buy a substantial part of the former [Nazi-run] Eher-Verlag printing plant at a cost (including interest charges) of roughly DM 5.5 million." Under the new priority arrangement, the *Süddeutsche Zeitung* received 500,000 marks, the second largest credit given to any paper. The largest, totaling 1.6 million marks, went to the *Frankfurter Rundschau*—rejected (as will be remembered) under the original system, but approved under the new one. It was used "to start building its new editorial and printing premises."

An undated and unsigned memorandum evidently drawn up in OPA provides some interesting further details relating to the *Frankfurter Rundschau* beyond the descriptions of the Kaghan Report cited so far. According to this document, headed "Extension of Credit and Acquisition of Participation (at nominal value of shares) in Frankfurter

Rundschau," the paper's "early appearance on the scene [immediately after the end of the war] and the extraordinary circumstances of the early postwar period, including monetary inflation and a monopoly position of licensed publications, enabled the Rundschau to firmly entrench itself with readers in the important and fast growing city of Frankfurt and beyond." However, the paper's "political importance" far surpassed "the boundaries of its home territory." In the eyes of OPA officials it was deemed to be "the only leading paper in Germany today which has proven its willingness and ability to take up the cudgels for the cause of militant and progressive democracy." The document went on to mention several examples of important political campaigns by the paper. Then came the bad news: "The independence and the editorial policies" were suddenly in danger. The paper required 1 million marks and to find such a large amount "it must succumb to either nationalistic or social democratic influences." It "would have to grow soft vis-à-vis neo-nationalist tendencies in Germany and less reliable with regard to Western cooperation." What this meant in plain language was that, though basically profitable, the *Frankfurter Rundschau* had overreached itself with its new editorial and printing building. There were also "certain shortcomings of management," and, worried that the paper might go under, HICOG contemplated a bail-out. The credit already given was to be expanded by another 1 million marks "from funds blocked in Germany." In return, HICOG was apparently thinking of acquiring a stake in the company by issuing new shares to ensure "a participation equal to that of any of the present two partners in the enterprise."[60]

It is unclear, though doubtful, if a deal of this kind was ever struck. The dating of Henry Kellermann's covering note to Stone and a preceding letter from Karl Gerold of 23 March 1953, following a complaint Stone had made to Gerold a few weeks earlier about the paper's reporting on the United States, suggest that Stone requested the memo about the "Extension of Credit and Acquisition of Participation (at nominal value of shares) in the Frankfurter Rundschau" to refresh his memory of the paper's financial saga and of the help he had given it before responding to Gerold. In his letter Gerold reported that he had already done something about Stone's criticisms. He confessed that he was missing Stone as a sympathetic listener to the problems of the *Frankfurter Rundschau*. He reassured the former OPA chief that he who had lived in a democratic country as a refugee from Nazism would, until the end of his career as a journalist, always adhere to the political course his paper had mapped out in 1945.[61]

71

However, this correspondence should probably be linked to an exchange of views during the spring of 1952 when Gerold, together with his partner Arno Rudert, wrote that "Shepard Stone has a place in the history of our enterprise that cannot be assumed by anyone else: the place of the good American friend." Gratified, Stone replied four days later: "As you know I have only one wish for all German papers: that they become strong, objective, independent, and that they contribute to give firm foundations to the democratic system of Government."[62]

So, irrespective of whether the *Frankfurter Rundschau* got another revolving HICOG loan, the whole affair is highly significant for an understanding of the objectives that Stone and the United States pursued at this time; it is also telling of the political calculations underlying American policies in Germany and, as we shall see in later chapters, in Western Europe at large. If, in the funding of favored West German newspapers, HICOG had gotten close to being the actual benefactor rather than just the conduit, there are two cases in which the subsidies came directly out of the High Commission's coffers. In the first case, concerning the weekly *Echo der Woche*, the funding source was a closely guarded secret until the cover was blown by Hans Habe in 1954.[63]

Such embarrassments notwithstanding, Kaghan, when summing up his more general report on HICOG's newspaper support system, had "little doubt but that the Press Fund will make a sizeable contribution to providing the economic basis for an independent press in Western Germany and, what is probably the same thing, rescuing many of the ex-licensed papers from grave financial difficulties." As to the future, HICOG was determined "to remain in close contact with the papers receiving loans in order to achieve better working relationships with them and in particular to promote the reception and republication of material from American sources, especially AMERIKA-DIENST." Last but not least, HICOG's more active role in the allocation of funds also gave it direct leverage against newspapers and publishing houses that were suspected of accepting print orders from procommunist organizations. Thus, the owner of the *Fuldaer Zeitung* was pressured to pay back a loan after it had been found that he had printed "a special supplement of *Die Tat*," the publication of the communist-influenced Vereinigung der Verfolgten des Naziregimes (VVN). The case was another sign that HICOG's concern over the development of democracy and a democratic press went hand in hand with the perceived need to fight the Cold War against the Soviet Union. But we have also seen that this was not the only consideration. At the back of Stone's mind there was simultaneously always the question of West Germany's "reorientation" toward the West and toward parliamentary democracy, as well as of European cultural anti-Americanism. As we saw in this chapter, the "common communist canard that the U.S. was culturally poor" was very offensive to him, and he used not only the *Neue Zeitung* to counteract this propaganda. In fact, as will be seen in subsequent chapters, it became a major theme also at the Ford Foundation and in the cultural work it supported.[64]

In the spring of 1952 McCloy's time as high commissioner was coming to an end. He had been nominated to head the Chase National Bank in New York and was due to return home. With his mentor leaving, Stone had to think of his own future. As he wrote to a friend soon after McCloy's departure had been confirmed, "we expect to clean up some time in March or April" or even earlier. He added that he wanted "to do something where I can be effective, make some kind of contribution to the general welfare, and earn a little money." He thought he could "go back to The Times," but he preferred "to be more on my own." Maybe Paul Hoffman "might have something" for him. Or maybe "there is a big medium newspaper that needs a publisher" or "a college is looking for a president."Although his future was uncertain, he ended on an upbeat note: "Mr. McCloy is still a marvelous man with whom I have had this great experience in public affairs." However, he considered it essential "that McCloy's successor be more than a diplomat or businessman. He ought to be keenly interested in the development of a free and democratic German society."[65]

In April 1952, as his return to the United States was virtually certain, he wrote to a friend: "My work has taken me into all areas of German life—political, educational, social etc. It has been an interesting and challenging experience, but I am looking forward to returning to private life some time in the next few months."[66] And on 30 June 1952 he informed his former colleague Henry Kellermann at the State Department that he had decided to go. He added: "I want to stay and know that no job I will have in the future will have the importance of this one or its fascination." And yet it seemed to him "that I should go now or decide to enter the career service. I do not wish to do the latter at present. Maybe three years from now I shall be yelling for the chance."[67]

The time had also come for him to thank his colleagues for their support and hard work and to receive praise from others. The Hamburg banker Eric Warburg wrote as early as 1 May: "So many have come back with such glowing reports of all the help they got from your office and particularly from yourself."[68] And on 19 July he received the most important thank-you letter of all from McCloy.[69] To Stone McCloy's warm praise was no doubt a most gratifying confirmation that he had been on the right track when he decided, at the end of World War II, that only the reintegration of a democratic and prosperous Germany into the Western community of nations would avoid a repetition of the past. When he found in 1945 that this view did not predominate in OMGUS, he returned to the *New York Times* to promote his ideas as a journalist and expert voice in various foreign policy organizations. The lunch with McCloy then opened up the opportunity for him to work and fight for the implementation of his ideas about German reconstruction and "reorientation" in a position at HICOG that mattered, one where he could and no doubt did make a difference. Moreover, he had extended his earlier network from the Ivy League and the *Times* to Germany. He had made many contacts that would prove indispensable during the next stage of his career.

At the same time he had also made some enemies, especially among the supporters of McCarthyism. Although we have to come back to this topic in the larger context of American political and intellectual life during the 1950s, this seems an appropriate point to discuss, at least briefly, how Stone and a number of his OPA colleagues found themselves scurrilessly accused of subversive activities. The trouble began when Westbrook Pegler, a right-wing syndicated journalist, began to tour Germany "pursuing my quest of knowledge about our carpetbag administration in Germany." Among other things, he began to look around "Amerika Hause [*sic*], one of the 38 libraries operated by our Department of Public Affairs under Shepard Stone, the 'cultural minister' of the Hicog cabinet at Bonn under High Commissioner John J. McCloy." There he found a biography of Mary McLeod Bethune, "a colored woman who was taken up politically by Eleanor Roosevelt." He listed further titles by other "New Dealers" and in a subsequent attack on Stone added that "something strange and impudent and worthy of public investigation is going on in Germany."[70]

This suggestion was picked up by the McCarthyites, finally resulting in a circular by John Foster Dulles, the new secretary of state, who soon after assuming office instructed missions and posts abroad to inform all U.S. Information Service (USIS) establishments and "specifically libraries" that they "should at once remove all books and other materials by Communists, fellow travelers, etc., from their shelves and withdraw any that may be in circulation."[71] Two weeks later, on 2 March 1953, HICOG confirmed this ukase, announcing that the directors of German Amerikahäuser would be notified by OPA "of those authors whose works are to be removed."[72] On 5 March Stone found his name cited in the *New York Times* as being on the list of Roy Cohn, the chief counsel for the U.S. Senate subcommittee investigating the "Voice of America" radio network, among those "who had applied for transfer to the Voice of America."[73] Stone flatly denied this charge and asked Cohn to retract it.

By May 1953 the suspicions against the allegedly "subversive" activities of former HICOG personnel had become so preposterous that McCloy felt obliged to make an appointment with U.S. president Dwight D. Eisenhower in an attempt to set the record straight. His hope was that Eisenhower would make a "Statement on [the] German Program" vindicating HICOG's activities. The text for this statement that McCloy drafted for the president had an appendix that was supposed to provide further background information. This appendix ended with a quotation by Walter von Cube, "the leading commentator" on the Bavarian radio: " 'Whatever may be said against America—and at present much may be said—without its help, without its initiative, even without its threats, Europe would be lost. McCarthy makes it so easy for the world to become anti-American that for the sake of reason, gratefulness, and a just measure it is time to raise one's voice in America's defense and in the defense of those who trust its leadership.' "[74]

A few weeks later, Eisenhower did issue remarks about "book burners" around McCarthy.[75] But even after McCloy's initiative and with the *New York Times* reporting on the extent of the "book purge" at American libraries abroad, Stone evidently remained so rattled that he suggested to his mentor "to talk with Senator Mundt of the McCarthy Committee." He added: "It is felt that if you told him that the German operation was a big success, that the people working on it were overwhelmingly loyal, and that a continuation of the investigation will damage our excellent position in Germany, he might use his influence with McCarthy to stop."[76] By the spring of 1954, McCarthy's power was definitely on the decline, emboldening Stone to suggest that "everybody should move in now to knock him out of the field."[77]

The McCarthyite campaign, and the fact that he had to defend himself against groundless suspicions,[78] may have left a certain bitterness in him, even affecting the positions he later took up at the Ford Foundation in the American-European culture wars during the mid-1950s. Around the same time, once he had made his decision to leave Germany with McCloy in 1952, he suffered another serious disappointment. As he was exploring various possibilities, he contacted his old newspaper. Sulzberger, to whom he had written as early as September 1951, merely referred him to Markel, his former boss.[79] But Markel could not or would not help him either. It was McCloy who opened up an alternative that would eventually catapult Stone into the most influential position of his career at the Ford Foundation, the largest philanthropic organization of the world. But before analyzing this phase of his career we first have to shift scenes completely and deal with the larger cultural and intellectual context without which his work in the 1950s and 1960s cannot be understood.

Mass Society and the Threat of Totalitarianism

AMERICAN POLICY in West Germany, as represented and crafted by McCloy and Stone, was partly driven by a desire to solve, once and for all, the "German Question" through a recasting of the country's political, cultural, and economic systems as well as its integration into the European and Atlantic community of nations. This policy explains the tireless "re-orientation" work promoted and funded by the High Commission as well as the constant and close monitoring of all nationalist and neo-Nazi tendencies in the Federal Republic.[1] But HICOG was also, to no small extent, motivated by a fear of Soviet expansionism and of a rise of leftist radicalism. Both concerns had larger ramifications, related to the emergence of the United States from World War II as the hegemonic power of the West and to the increasing U.S. competition with the Soviet Union, which proceeded to establish and consolidate its own sphere of influence in the East.

No less important in our context, the resolution of the "German Question" was part and parcel of a larger American quest to promote middle-of-the-road parliamentary-democratic systems and liberal-capitalist economies in Western Europe similar to the ones that existed on the other side of the Atlantic. By the same token, the preoccupation with a perceived communist threat in Germany was inseparable from the growth of communist parties in Western Europe, notably in France and Italy, with their large memberships and support at the polls, and the increasingly global Cold War confrontation between the two postwar superpowers.

Both issues, reintegrating Germany and fighting communism, which had defined much of Stone's work at the High Commission, also consumed much of his time and energy in his new job at the Ford Foundation, though, as we shall see, in a modified form. As the political system of the Federal Republic stabilized and the economy experienced a boom, he now worried less about a possible resurgence of a neo-Nazi or nationalist-conservative right; instead, he promoted projects that were designed further to foster a West German civic culture and orientation toward the West. As regards the Cold War, he joined forces with those people in Europe and the United States who, though staunchly anti-Communist, were anxious to preserve an Open Society[2] at home and to keep the dangerous nuclear arms race from spinning out of control. In other words, they wanted to reduce tensions between Moscow and Washington rather than pursue a hard-line policy toward the Soviets typical of the conservative right, a policy that—as McCarthyism showed—also undermined a pluralistic liberality inside the United States.[3]

ELITES AND MASSES

A third piece in the stage set against the background of which the Ford Foundation and Stone developed their policies in the 1950s and 1960s involved criticism of the United States in general and of American culture in particular. The next two chapters deal with this latter phenomenon, treating it as part of the intellectual and cultural history of the West after World War II; only thereafter do we turn to the role of the Ford Foundation in this transatlantic picture. Stone's career temporarily recedes into the background as we map out the broad European-American milieu in which he operated as a Ford Foundation officer after his return from West Germany.

Fundamental to the debates about American culture to be summarized here was a deep-seated fear among Europe's political, economic, and intellectual elites of the "masses." These fears also had a long history. Worries about how to control and contain the majority of the population surfaced before the eighteenth century, if indeed it had not been a prime concern of all rulers and elite groups throughout human history. During the French Revolution, however, the "masses" had for the first time come to play a decisive role in radicalizing the challenge to the old order. The aristocracies of Europe and soon also the commercial and educated middle classes were terrified by what they heard about or witnessed in Paris in July 1789 and even more so during the subsequent "Terror," when the "mob" and demagogic leaders appeared to be ruling both the streets and the centers of political power. The floodgates to democratic politics, so it seemed, had been pushed wide open. To be sure, eventually the threat to the established order that was symbolized in the Terror and the guillotine was rolled back. Yet it was no more than a temporary relief. Napoleon's military dictatorship, whose power base was the "revolutionary" mass armies that swept across Europe at the beginning of the nineteenth century, soon followed.

In the end this particular threat, too, was contained, and the "masses" even played a major role in the defeat of Napoleon. His *levée en masse* was countered by the popular armies that the monarchs of Europe, though reluctant to let the genie out of the bottle, raised to get rid of him. From the viewpoint of the traditional elites of Europe there was indeed a flipside to the surge of popular patriotism that secured Napoleon's demise in the huge battles of Leipzig and Waterloo: the specter of disciplined universal service armies of young men who had learned to fight not merely against a foreign invader and occupier but potentially also against a post-Napoleonic restoration of the old order back home. This was an even more frightening vision than that of ill-disciplined revolutionary "mobs" roaming the streets of Paris in 1789 and demanding a voice in politics.[4] And so the fear of the "masses" continued to haunt the peacemakers at Vienna in 1814–15 and beyond.

Not long after the end of the Congress of Vienna the nightmare of popular politics seemingly came true. After various smaller insurgencies in the 1830s, were not the "masses" trying to turn the world upside-down during the European-wide revolutions of 1848–49? Were they not trying to seize power or demanding the universal suffrage and other rights of participation in politics? As Frederick William IV of Prussia wrote to his sister Queen Victoria on 27 February 1848 after the revolution had begun in France and subsequently spread to other European countries: "God has permitted events which decisively threaten the peace of Europe. It is the attempt 'to spread the principle of Revolution by every means throughout the whole of Europe.' . . . The consequences [of these developments] for the peace of the world are clear and certain. If the revolutionary party carries out its program: 'The sovereignty of the People,' my minor crown will be broken no less certainly than the mighty crowns of Your Majesty, and a fearful scourge will be laid upon the nations; a century will follow of rebellion, of lawlessness, and of godlessness."[5]

However, the victory in 1849 of the Old Europe and the more conservative middle classes, who abhorred the "masses" and held quite restrictive notions of what they meant by "rule of the people," proved ephemeral. From the 1860s, the tide of demands for popular participation in politics could at most be slowed down, but it could not be halted and even less reversed. Bismarck, in his attempt to undercut the pressure of the Liberals and Progressives to establish a parliamentary monarchy, may have tried to emulate Napoleon III of France. By introducing universal manhood suffrage, the latter had attempted to put up dams against the rising power of the Parisian bourgeoisie by garnering the support of the conservative peasants. Bismarck was motivated by similar calculations when in 1867 he enshrined universal manhood suffrage in the constitution of the North German Confederation and four years later in the constitution of the newly founded German Empire. The first Reich chancellor certainly did not take this step because he was a democrat, and significantly enough he and his successors later bitterly regretted having staged this "revolution from above."[6] Indeed, in the 1890s calls could be heard in Germany and elsewhere to abolish the universal ballot. The demands of the "masses," by now increasingly composed of industrial workers and represented by the socialists, induced some German federal states to curtail their own restricted suffrage systems. Upholding elitist notions of politics, monarchs, conservative aristocrats, and the frightened educated and commercial middle classes combined to stop the further advance of "democracy."[7]

In the countries of Western Europe pressures to block the participatory aspirations of the "masses" were not as strong as in Central Europe. Nevertheless, here, too, many people worried what a future age of mass politics might hold. Most important for the purposes of this chapter, by the late nineteenth century their concerns were also informed by what they had begun to observe more closely in the "New World." Having visited the United States for some eighteen months, Alexis de Tocquèville had published his *Democracy in America* in 1835.[8] It was a study of the society that had emerged across the Atlantic in the age of Jackson, and in his book the Frenchman looked, among many other things, also at majority rule, public opinion, social equality, and democratic leadership.

What he had to say on these issues was no doubt influenced by the deep suspicions of "democracy" that the members of most European elite groups had been harboring ever since the late eighteenth century. For our context, though, the remarks Tocqueville made about the productionist and cultural consequences of the appearance of the "masses" on the stage of history are no less relevant. "In the ages of privilege," he wrote, "the practice of almost all the arts becomes a privilege."[9] The artisan "is not exclusively swayed by his own interest or even by that of his customer, but by that of the body to which he belongs; and the interest of that body is that each artisan should produce the best possible workmanship." If, by contrast, as was the case in America, "every profession is open to all, when a multitude of persons are constantly embracing and abandoning it, . . . [then] the social tie is destroyed and each workman, standing alone, endeavors simply to gain the most money at the least cost. The will of the customer is then his only limit."

In aristocratic societies, he continued, the number of these customers was strictly limited and whatever profit the artisans made therefore depended "principally on the perfection of their workmanship." But "such is no longer the case when, all privileges being abolished, ranks are intermingled and men are forever rising or sinking upon the social scale." On the contrary, "the democratic principle not only tends to direct the human mind to the useful arts, but it induces the artisan to produce with great rapidity many imperfect commodities and the consumer to content himself with these commodities." What was bad in the field of artisanal production was even worse in other fields of artistic creativity. Tocqueville came to believe that "the inhabitants of the United States have . . . at present, properly speaking, no literature." To him there were only superficial American journalists. Of course, he warned, "every aristocracy that keeps itself entirely aloof from the people becomes impotent, a fact which is as true in literature as it is in politics."

Yet again, as he transported himself "into the midst of a democracy [across the Atlantic] unprepared by ancient traditions and present culture to partake in the pleasures of mind," Tocqueville believed he had seen the consequences: "Ranks are there intermingled and confounded; knowledge and power are both infinitely subdivided and, if I may use the expression, scattered on every side." This was "a motley multitude whose intellectual wants are to be supplied." A further consequence of democracy was in his view that by no means all "who cultivate literature have received a literary education." The result was that, "accustomed to the struggle, the crosses, and the monotony of practical life, they require strong and rapid emotions, startling passages, truths or errors brilliant enough to rouse them up and to plunge them at once, as if by violence, into the midst of the subject." Worse, while "democracy . . . infuses a taste for letters among the trading classes," it also injected "a trading spirit into literature." As a consequence, "democratic literature is always infested with a tribe of writers who look upon letters as a mere trade; and for some few great authors who adorn it, you may reckon with thousands of idea-mongers."

For the argument of this chapter, the important point about Tocqueville is the way he connected democratic politics with forms of economic production and cultural consumption and views what happens to a society that discards "privilege." To him they were all parts of the same process. Consequently, the Frenchman "wanted primarily to warn his fellow-Europeans about the perils of the [American] democratic experiment which, he feared, would lead either to anarchy or mass conformity."[10]

Democracy in America did not attract much attention in Europe at the time of its publication; but some sixty years later, around the turn of the century, Tocqueville's views of the United States and of the links he had made between politics, economics, and culture had gained wide currency among the European elites. There were, it is true, many intellectuals on the left who felt that American democracy was at least better than the sociocultural and political order the Europeans and certainly the monarchies of Central Europe were trying to uphold. But plenty of upper-class and middle-class people suffered nightmares at the thought that American practices of democracy, whether in the field of politics, the economy, or culture, might come to their societies. In this respect they replicated the attitudes of their forbears in 1848 when the Liberal majority saw participation in the public sphere as something reserved to men of education and cultural refinement. The difficulty was that in the meantime more and more "uneducated" men had gained the vote, either at the stroke of a pen, as in Prussia-Germany in 1867 and 1871, or piecemeal, as in Britain in 1832, 1867, and 1884–85. And during the Paris Commune they appeared to have demonstrated, once again, their determination to seize power and radically to reorganize society.

In light of all these developments, the cultural pessimists who predicted an impending age of the "masses" and the attendant decline of received "civilized" values had, by 1900, become very vocal in most of Europe.[11] Worse, this age would be one of demagogy and instability, perhaps even of civil war; for the "masses" were deemed to be volatile and unpredictable in their demands and desires. As Hermann Baumgarten warned in 1890, the universal suffrage threatened not only orderly government but "our entire *Kultur*." A good digest of the gloomy, late-nineteenth-century discourses on this subject was Gustave Le Bon's book on the "psychology of the masses," which became a sort of bible to the doomsters.[12] Translated into English as *The Crowd: A Study of the Popular Mind* in 1896, the 240-page volume reached its fifth impression in 1907 and its seventh a mere three years later. By 1939 it reached over forty-one editions in France. Like Tocqueville, Le Bon was an author of the broad sweep who began his study with a fanfare: "The great upheavals which precede changes of civilisation, such as the fall of the Roman Empire and the foundation of the Arabian Empire, seem at first sight determined more especially by political transformations, foreign invasion, or the overthrow of dynasties. But the more attentive study of these events shows that behind their apparent causes the real cause is generally seen to be a profound modification in the ideas of the peoples."[13]

Late-nineteenth-century Europe, he believed, was undergoing such a transformation, caused, first, by "the destruction of those religious, political and social beliefs in which all the elements of our civilisation are rooted"; and, second, by "the creation of entirely new conditions of existence and thought as a result of modern scientific and industrial discoveries." No less important, "the entry of the popular classes into political life—that is to say, in reality, their progressive transformation into governing classes," was to him "one of the most striking characteristics of our epoch of transition." Given these premises, the rest of the volume is devoted to analyzing what Le Bon imagined to be the characteristics, the "sentiments and morality," "the ideas and imagination," "the opinions and beliefs," and the leaders of crowds. He also attempted a "classification and description of different kinds of crowds." He spoke of the mental inferiority of crowds but warned of their power, which they could only deploy for destructive purposes. Accordingly, "their rule is always tantamount to a barbarian phase." He added: "By the mere fact that he becomes part of an organized crowd, man descends several rungs on the ladder of civilization. Isolated he is perhaps a cultivated individual; in a crowd he is a barbarian, that is, a creature of instinct." Le Bon's conclusion was predictably pessimistic: "With the definite loss of its old ideal the genius of race entirely disappears; it is a mere swarm of isolated individuals and returns to its original state—that of a crowd." And so "its civilisation is now without stability, and at the mercy of every chance. The populace is sovereign, and the tide of barbarism mounts."

Ultimately, Le Bon and other collective psychologists of the time tried to generalize their insights to all group phenomena.[14] Even more far-reaching in its consequences—after what has been said about elite attitudes toward the age of the "masses" earlier in this chapter—is that many upper- and middle-class men in pre-1914 Europe were in complete agreement with Le Bon's findings. Some, it is true, continued to hope that it would be possible to avert a civilizational catastrophe by preventive action and reformism. They recommended the adoption of strategies that would deflect the "masses" from their quest for greater equality and participation. Social imperialism as a policy of distracting the lower classes from demanding change in domestic affairs and gearing them toward the acquisition of colonial possessions and great national goals overseas was openly ventilated.[15] Cecil Rhodes warned that the British Empire was ultimately a "bread-and-butter" question: whoever wanted to prevent civil war, he added, must become an imperialist.[16] And the Italian intellectual Enrico Corradini wrote in 1912: "Social imperialism aimed at rallying all classes for the defense of nation and empire and pursued the objective to demonstrate to the least wealthy class that its interests were inseparable from those of the nation."[17] Finally there is the statement by Alfred von Tirpitz, soon to become the kaiser's naval minister, who wrote in December 1895: "In my view Germany will experience a fast decline of her great power position in the coming century if we do not now energetically, systematically, and without delay push ahead with our general maritime interests, to no small degree also because inherent in the new [and] great national task and in the economic gains connected with it is a strong palliative against educated and uneducated Social Democrats."[18]

In this way nationalist imperialism was to be deployed as a counter to the rise of internationalist socialism and its demands for domestic reform or, in its radical forms, for social revolution. Indeed, whenever the term "masses" was used in this period, it tended to be associated with the industrial proletarians in the manufacturing cities of Europe. At the end of the nineteenth century, millions of men and women worked in factories between ten and twelve hours six days of the week. They lived under depressing conditions in large tenement blocks with one- or two-room apartments, accommodating in many cases up to eight or nine people of different ages. Nutritional standards were poor and chronic illnesses were rampant. Fearful of "democracy" and knowing about such conditions in the working-class neighborhoods, the middle and upper classes came to see these millions as a mass seething with resentment and ready to take radical action. As Ernst Heydebrand und der Lasa, one of the leaders of agarian conservatism in Germany, put it: "The masses will assert themselves and take our influence away from us aristocrats."[19]

If the fear of the proletarian "masses" was deep-seated before 1914, it was given an enormous boost by the mass mobilization in World War I, and again it triggered "social imperialist" strategies. As early as the fall of 1914, Alfred Hugenberg, then a director of the Krupp steel trust, predicted that "one will probably have to count on a very increased sense of power on the part of the workers and trade unions which will also find expression in increased demands on the employers and for legislation." It would, he went on, "therefore be well advised, in order to avoid internal difficulties, to distract the attention of the people and to give fantasies concerning the extension of German territory room to play."[20]

In November 1917 the Bolsheviks, who claimed that the world was on the verge of a massive proletarian revolution, seized power in Russia. By early 1919 this revolution appeared to be spreading beyond Russia's borders. Soviet republics emerged in Budapest and Munich, soon to be brutally destroyed by counterrevolutionary volunteer units. Lenin's Red revolution, on the other hand, survived the attempts by the Whites to overthrow it with military assistance from the Western Allies. Thereafter the prospect of the "masses" successfully turning the established order upside down was no longer just a theory and possibility. It had become a reality in one part of the world, which implied it could also happen elsewhere.

Visions of America

Compared to the pessimism that the perceived threat of the "masses" in the shape of socialism and bolshevism generated among the middle and upper classes of Europe, doubts about American democracy, as described by Tocqueville, were initially less well articulated; but exist they certainly did, not least because the United States had meanwhile risen from a distant and seemingly underdeveloped country to the top ranks of the industrialized nations. Until the late nineteenth century, Europeans imagined America as a huge and wild continent where white settlers and trappers fought little wars with "red" Indians and where recent immigrants were seized by intermittent bouts of "gold fever."[21]

These older images, however, were disappearing fast after the turn of the century. In the final decades of the nineteenth century, the United States had undergone a process of very rapid industrialization and economic growth. Suddenly, the Europeans took it seriously as a major power and competitor. In Germany, the other country to experience a similar expansion of its power and influence, politicians, businessmen, and bureaucrats began to speak of the "American danger."[22] The British, although they still held first place among the nations, developed the same consciousness, even to the extent of preferring an accommodation with their former rebel colony to a confrontation. The reason for this shift in European perceptions of America was, of course, also related to the size and richness of the North American continent, its growing population and urbanization. But it had also a lot to do with the astonishing technological advances of American industry.

At the Paris World Exhibition in 1900, U.S. technologies in steel making and steel processing attracted a great deal of attention, and soon European businessmen and engineers could be seen traveling across the Atlantic to study American factories and their methods of management and work organization in which the "masses" figured as producers. The writings of Frederick W. Taylor, one of the fathers of rationalized production, were quickly translated, and some European companies, such as Bosch in Germany and Renault in France, were beginning to experiment with Taylorism.[23] Henry Ford then added the idea that mass production made possible the lowering of prices. He saw it as his mission to supply cheap factory-produced consumer goods to a growing "mass" of people. To American notions of constitutional democracy and mass participation in politics was added the idea of rationalized volume production and mass consumption. The modernity of America consisted in the linkages it had made between all three developments.[24]

Fordism thus defined was welcomed by some Europeans, but watched with skepticism or disgust by others. Car manufacturing presents a good example. While Ford's long assembly lines in Michigan enabled him to reduce the price on the cheapest model before 1914 and thus to unleash the first wave of motorization in the United States, European car manufacturers continued to produce luxury vehicles—custom-made in small quantities in small workshops at correspondingly high prices. Only the very rich could afford a Mercedes-Benz or a Rolls Royce. But the inefficiencies of this system were turned into a virtue and related to the alleged blessings of a sharply stratified society. As Daimler-Benz, the makers of fine motorcars for the wealthy, stated proudly: "Over here we are still a long way from the American situation where every Mr. Jones owns a car. With us the automobile is for the most part a vehicle for the better-off classes." And priding itself on its tradition of solid individual craftsmanship, the company added: "Here [we do things] meticulously and throroughly; over there [in America it is] skimping and rushing."[25]

It is worth pondering these two quotations, also in light of Tocqueville's observations and Europeans' perceptions of the effects of American-style democracy on society. Certainly the Daimler-Benz statements speak volumes about how many conservative businessmen responded to the arrival of mass production and mass consumption on the European side of the Atlantic. It was no different in France or Britain. Taylorism and Fordism made all of them uneasy not just because of cheaper American imports and competition, but also because of the threat the new ideas posed to Europe's much more elitist social and political structures. In the eyes of the European upper and middle classes, the "masses" were not only irrational and volatile at the polls, but also economically "greedy" as producers and consumers. What would this mean for the established hierarchies if popular claims to more equal consumption became linked to mass politics in the age of universal suffrage, a mass circulation press, and more cunning methods of advertising, political as well as commercial, that further stimulated the hopes and expectations of "ordinary" people?

To the growing fears of what this new mix of mass production-consumption with the political mass market might do to existing patterns of privilege and stratification was finally added the concern over mass culture. Before 1914 many Europeans of upper or well-to-do middle-class background defined culture quite narrowly and did not relate it to popular traditions and activities. Culture was seen by them as "high culture," as comprising the great "classical" works of literature, theater, ballet, painting, and music that they enjoyed almost exclusively in the museums and performing arts centers of the cities at prices that were beyond the reach of the "masses." Education and refinement alone enabled a person to appreciate high culture. To go and see or hear these works was beyond the financial means of the "masses" and thus was a privilege of the few who could afford it—those who could go to the theater, opera, or concert, dressed up in expensive evening gowns and tailor-made black suits.

Although the working-class movements of Europe undertook serious efforts to make this kind of "high culture" available to their members through reduced-rate subscriptions, the establishment of "people's stages," and workers' educational associations, sharp divisions between "high" and "low" culture remained, mirroring the structures of class and privilege of European society. "Low" culture, if it was to be called "culture" at all, was thought to be vulgar, primitive, and trashy, something to be disdained and avoided by a self-respecting bourgeois—never mind the heavy dose of hypocrisy that would quickly be revealed if one cared to look behind the facade of respectability and asked after his other leisure pursuits.

Still, with the rise of mass production and mass consumption came the proliferation of mass culture. Technological breakthroughs facilitated this development, and the invention of motion pictures provides the most striking example. Here was a medium that could be made available to millions of people in "movie theaters" and "film palaces." Tickets were inexpensive and "bourgeois" dress codes could be ignored. The new medium provided entertainment, escape from the routine of daily life, and, occasionally, food for thought. After a strong start before 1914, the industry attracted millions of movie goers all over Europe by the mid-1920s. Although the Europeans began to produce their own movies, they quickly found that it was very difficult to compete against the studios in America's Hollywood.[26]

With the cinema came other forms of popular culture and entertainment from across the Atlantic: jazz, the Charleston, the Tilly Sisters, Josephine Baker. It must be remembered that this invasion of "low" culture came at a time after World War I when elitist fears of the "masses" had grown exponentially in the wake of the Bolshevik Revolution, civil war, and the expansion of communist and somewhat less radical socialist movements throughout Europe. The importance of this link and the anxieties it fostered about a new "age of the masses" can hardly be overestimated at a time when virtually all hierarchies, including gender differences, were being called into question. Old relationships, whether between men and women, young and old, or between divergent classes were being challenged.

Worse, with the United States emerging from the war greatly strengthened economically vis-à-vis the industrial nations of Western Europe,[27] worries about American competition and greater productivity had grown even among those businessmen and intellectuals who did not reject, as a matter of principle, the idea of Fordist rationalization and mass consumption and who continued to be willing to learn from the United States. As a result, the debate on the power and psychology of the "masses" that Le Bon and others had unleashed before 1914 intensified. The rise of psychology and sociology as scholarly disciplines added what was taken to be a scientific foundation. Popular demands for the abolition of privilege and for power sharing threatened not only political stability but now, it seemed, also the survival of culture. To the elites of Europe it looked as if sophisticated "high" culture was about to become overwhelmed by trashy and cheap "low" culture and superficial mass entertainment.

The first major wave of anti-Americanism must be analyzed against the background of these economic-technological and sociocultural developments on both sides of the Atlantic after the "Great War" that had devastated Europe's hegemony in the world.[28] Because this anti-Americanism resurfaced in Europe after World War II, its features are broadly familiar to this day: America is depicted as the country without refined and experienced elites in the European sense; the country where the "masses" define values and tastes, having conquered the centers of political power; in essence a nonculture, violent, barbaric; a region that brought out the worst traits in human beings and is devoid of *Bildung* in the classic sense. As educated Germans liked to draw the contrast, America was a cold technological and mass-based *Zivilisation* devoid of *Kultur.* This was the framework within which the debate in Europe operated during the mid-1920s, which implies that there were also many protests against these negative visions of the United States.

After the collapse of the New York stock market in 1929 and Washington's retreat from the world economy into its protectionist continental shell, America no longer looked quite so menacing as it did during the 1920s. Moreover, under the impact of mass unemployment and prolonged economic depression the debate about high culture versus mass culture became overshadowed by the question of mass politics. The polarizing effect of the Great Depression had led to the rise of radical right-wing and fascist movements with charismatic demagogues who, after seizing power on the back of universal suffrage, established ruthless dictatorial regimes, maintained by repression and the mass mobilization of consent and promoted with the help of the latest techiques and technologies of mass propaganda. To most European conservatives, even if they first made their peace with Mussolini and Hitler, these two fascists came to embody the final victory of mass politics. These were the alarming cases where the elites had lost control of the political process, as had been feared might happen ever since the nineteenth century.

The elites were witnessing *The Revolt of the Masses*, in the words of Spanish philosopher José Ortega y Gasset, whose best seller followed the works of Tocqueville and Le Bon. Writing at the height of the crisis in 1932, Ortega proclaimed "the accession of the masses to complete social power," even though they were "by definition" incapable of directing "their own personal existence."[29] The mass had no individuality and felt "itself 'just like everybody.' " He then juxtaposed the masses to "select minorities" and asserted, in typical fashion, that "the mass, without ceasing to be mass, is supplanting" these minorities. In other words, to him "the political innovations of recent times" signified "nothing less than the political domination of the masses." Worse, "the mass crushes beneath it everything that is different, everything that is excellent, individual, qualified and select." Accordingly Ortega believed he was living "under the brutal empire of the masses" in "the epoch of the colossal."

Proclaiming that his book was "an attempt to discover the diagnosis of our time," the Spanish philosopher proceeded with his "dissection of the mass-man." Invoking Hegel's fears of the advancing masses, he looked at the origins of this development in the nineteenth century and inquired into the reasons why the masses had made their intervention into history "solely by violence." He expended a good many words on the primitivism and barbarism of "mass-man," before warning of "state intervention." Because, he asserted, the state had been seized by the masses, its interventionism posed "the gravest danger that threatens civilisation to day." Society, as he saw it, "begins to be enslaved, to be unable to live except *in the service of the State*." All life was becoming bureaucratized, bringing about "its absolute decay" and increasing militarization. That, he concluded, "is what State intervention leads to: the people are converted into fuel to feed a machine which is the State." Ortega's somewhat

incoherent exposition of the ills of the mass age culminated in a nightmarish picture in the painting of which he, as a staunch anticommunist, seems
to have taken Soviet Russia as his model. The only hope he saw in the
end was "the building-up of Europe into a great national State"—"the
one enterprise that could counterbalance a victory of the 'five year plan.' "

Dangers had also been imported to Europe from the United States. If
the "ordinary level of life today is that of the former minorities," this fact,
while new in Europe, had long been "the natural, the 'constitutional' "
situation in America. And when "European life in all orders suddenly
took on a new appearance," people began to say, "Europe is becoming
Americanised." For Ortega this was a false impression. Europe had not
been Americanized and there was merely a parallelism in the development
of the two continents. Both lived in a period of leveling—"a levelling of
fortunes, of culture among various social classes, of the sexes." Yet, even
if his disdain of "mass-man" was generalized, a subtle anti-Americanism
was nevertheless discernible: "The characteristic of the hour is that the
commonplace mind, knowing itself to be commonplace, has the assurance
to proclaim the rights of the commonplace and to impose them wherever
it will. As they say in the United States: 'to be different is to be indecent.' "

Ortega's book clearly articulated the fears that many conservatives harbored of the masses at the peak of the Great Depression. But in the meantime these masses had not only conquered the state, but also found their
charismatic leaders. This alliance between the gifted demagogue and the
enthusiastic crowds, mobilized with modern techniques and technologies
of mass propaganda, had—so it seemed—now in effect begun to turn the
existing structures of power and privilege upside-down. The elites had
definitely lost control and become, in the words of the Italian industrialist
Gino Olivetti, an *ex-classe dirigente*. He meant by this that they had
either capitulated and made their peace with Hitler and Mussolini or they
had gone into "inner immigration."[30]

Unlike Ortega, however, many intellectuals saw anti-fascist communism or socialism as the true antidote against the rise of mass-based rightist dictatorships. Particularly the younger generation of intellectuals in
the West, alerted by such events as the Spanish Civil War, made a commitment to left-wing politics, at this point still ignorant of, or blind to, the
murderous regime that Stalin had meanwhile erected in the Soviet Union.
It is also significant that the rationalism and progressivism of Marxism,
at least in its pre-Bolshevik version, appealed more to writers and avant-
garde artists than did the instrumentalization of irrational popular fears
and ethnonationalist resentments that was typical of fascism. This ten-

dency is particularly true of those who were born in the decade before World War I, cut their intellectual teeth during their ideologically formative experiences of the interwar years, and finally moved into positions of power and influence inside and outside the academy after World War II.

Quite a few of these intellectuals were Jewish, often from more humble backgrounds, who, like Shepard Stone, had achieved rapid upward mobility through intelligence, educational opportunities, and hard work. Some of them, witnessing the turmoil of liberal parliamentarism after the war, had become alienated and were critical of Western capitalism and individualism. But because they also found the racist xenophobia and nationalism in Germany and Italy abhorrent, they believed that the left was the only way for them to go. By 1945 fascism had at last been defeated. World War II had cost over 50 million lives and had produced the industrialized mass murder of Europe's Jews in the Holocaust. With so many of these intellectuals having been under the influence of the communist or socialist world view, searching for the roots of the Jewish catastrophe meant tying fascism to *German* capitalism and, after 1945, broadening this notion to include capitalism per se as an overarching system.

Accordingly many European intellectuals either remained fellow travelers of the anticapitalist Soviet Union (which, after all, had just emerged triumphant from the struggle against Hitler) or they veered toward the socialists who, while fiercely anticommunist, were still searching for a third—European—way between American capitalism and Soviet Stalinism. Inherent in both these positions was a rejection of the United States, not only as a political and economic system, which, with Europe in ruins, now loomed even more powerfully than during the interwar years, but also as a cultural one. The old anti-Americanism of the 1920s had not been significantly dented by the fact that the United States had played a major role in defeating fascism.

For the fellow travelers, the logical move was to join the cold culture war that the Soviet Union began to wage against the United States in an effort to provide lateral support to the military-political and economic struggle that had set in after 1945.[31] With the power-political rivalry between Washington and Moscow and its sequence of dramatic crises— whether over Czechoslovakia, Berlin, Korea, or Cuba—deeply inscribed in the public mind of the West, it is often forgotten that the two sides conducted the Cold War also at the level of culture. As before, congresses and countercongresses of artists and writers as well as youth festivals and counterfestivals became the most visible expressions of this struggle. Experienced in the organization of such events from the interwar years, Sta-

91

linism invariably presented itself as an intellectually and culturally superior system that was destined to remain victorious against exploitative American capitalism and its supposedly trivial, manipulative, soulless, and impoverished "nonculture." Even if the language of Stalin's culture war was more propagandistic and blunt, the basic lines of argument and the words employed were very similar to those that had been common currency in Europe in the 1920s.

Strong reservations about American popular culture were also prevalent among those who were not fellow travelers, but who were nevertheless hoping to create, out of the rubble left by the war, a third alternative between East and West, both as a means of salvaging the achievements of European "high" culture and of preserving their own national or regional identity. They wanted to be neither Americanized nor Sovietized, and to them the two superpowers that had carved up Europe between themselves therefore embodied "the other" against which they tried to define a new European identity. This is why they kept their distance from Soviet cultural overtures. In the 1930s they had been antifascists who had supported the Soviet Union as the only reliable bastion against Hitler. After 1945, with the Axis powers defeated, they turned away from Moscow and its cultural offensives without changing their basic attitude toward the United States as a "culture."

TOTALITARIAN DICTATORSHIPS

Indeed, faced with the distressing news not only of the Holocaust but also with the revelations about Stalin's mass liquidations, they began to connect fascism and Stalinism as two similar forms of modern dictatorship that had betrayed the ideals of a democratic and humanist socialism, a theme that was taken up in fictionalized form in George Orwell's books.[32] The concept that provided the theoretical framework for this interpretation was totalitarianism, most comprehensively formulated by the German-American philosopher Hannah Arendt and later more schematically defined by the Harvard political scientists Carl J. Friedrich and Zbigniew Brzezinski.[33] It was the latter two authors who asserted in their classic study of 1956 that, because they were "basically alike," Stalinism and Nazism could be fruitfully compared through a taxonomy for which they presented six criteria.

However, their social scientific analysis of totalitarianism was not what Europe's anticommunist and antifascist intelligentsia primarily turned to.

To them Arendt's philosophical approach and definition were more appealing than Friedrich and Brzezinski's pragmatic checklist of criteria.[34] She stressed not only the modernity of totalitarian dictatorships but also the role of the individual and the "masses" within them. On the one hand, she discussed the loneliness and helplessness of the individual in the face of anonymous bureaucracies that—backed by the latest technologies— were mercilessly churning out their terroristic and murderous policies; on the other, she examined the relationship of the totalitarian leaders to the "masses." Like many other Europeans or European refugees from fascism living in the United States, Arendt became even more deeply suspicious of the "common man" who, by acclamation and, indeed, delirious ovation in the age of popular politics, provided the dictator with a legitimacy for his inhuman rampage. The familiar theme of the volatility of the "masses" also made its reappeareance in the totalitarianism paradigm. Irrational and driven by instinctual fears and resentments, the "masses" were deemed to be capable of performing radical shifts from one ideological extreme to the other. If they had been taken in by the fascists in the 1930s, they could equally well swing toward the communists after fascism's defeat in the 1940s.[35]

Sociologically speaking, these "masses" continued to be as poorly defined as they had been during previous periods of elitist debates about them; but they now comprised not only the industrial proletarians of the pre-1914 era but also the proletarianized petty bourgeoisie of the 1930s. The persuasiveness of this theory among many Europeans is not difficult to comprehend. For the anticommunists among them it did not require a great leap of faith to turn the former Western ally Russia into a dangerous totalitarian dictatorship after the end of the war, when the enormous human losses of the purges turned from rumor into certainty. They had suspected Stalin all along of horrific crimes and brutalities, not just because his regime fitted Friedrich and Brzesinski's taxonomy but also because the Arendtian analysis matched their long-standing perceptions about the behavior of "mass man" in the age of "mass politics." The fears of the interwar period that Ortega had articulated so clearly did not disappear with the end of World War II, and it is no coincidence that the Spanish philosopher was frequently an invited speaker at conferences and associational functions.[36] At the same time, while the East-West conflict acted as a common bond, older divisions between conservatives, often wedded to a Christian-Occidental vision of Europe, and the so-called Cold War liberals remained.

In this complex web of ideological affinities and divisions, America as the postwar hegemonic power of the West was bound to figure even more prominently than it had in the 1920s. Hannah Arendt, in her 1954 essay on "The Threat of Conformism," put her finger on a key point when she argued that the Europeans dreaded becoming Americanized but that this trend was likely to be accelerated by the unification of Europe. She was less certain whether this unification would be accompanied by a "rise of anti-Americanism" and a "pan-European nationalism, as one may sometimes fear today." But she added that the "unification of economic and demographic conditions is almost sure to create a state of affairs which will be very similar to that existing in the United States."[37] Looking at the overall landscape of intellectual and cultural life in postwar Western Europe, anti-Americanism is not too strong a word. It was prevalent on the socialist and communist left as well as among the Christian-conservative right. And it received a tremendous boost when "trashy" Hollywood films and rock music arrived in Western Europe. While young people, and working-class youths in particular, rioted to hear Elvis Presley and Bill Haley, intellectuals and *Bildungsbürger* were appalled

Notorious public figures like Carl Schmitt, Gottfried Benn, and Ernst von Salomon took their rejection of the United States straight from the 1930s into the postwar era. It was somewhat less explicit in the positions of sociologists like Arnold Gehlen and Hans Freyer or among journalists like Hans Zehrer and Ferdinand Fried. Giselher Wirsing, as editor of *Christ und Welt*, may have abandoned his rabid anti-Americanism of the war years when he railed at the *Masslose Kontinent*.[38] But with him as with many other conservatives, it nevertheless continued to resonate as the basso continuo of their basic outlook on the world. A further dilution of intellectual reservations about the United States occurred, not surprisingly perhaps, among Europe's Cold War Liberals.

French intellectuals, and Raymond Aron in particular, provide a good case in point. As a sociologist with many contacts reaching across the Atlantic, he was a keen observer of the United States. He knew that the postwar reconstruction of Europe required close alignment with America but still felt that the American economic system was "a model neither for humanity nor for the West."[39] With Sartre this was even more marked, politically and especially philosophically. He had no time for John Dewey's pragamatism that so deeply influenced New York's intellectuals. Finally, as the case of Isaiah Berlin demonstrates, ambivalence persisted even among the "Anglo-Saxons" across the English Channel, notwithstanding their many friendships with Americans and their skepticism of many popular British stereotypes about the United States.[40]

What facilitated the intellectual rapprochement between Europe's liberals and their counterparts in the United States was their shared conviction that the totalitarianism paradigm captured the reality of the world they had lived through before 1945 and continued to experience therafter. There was another side to the totalitarian coin, an alternative to the darkness and terror of both fascist and Stalinist dictatorships, which in their eyes was represented by the idea, though perhaps not altogether by the practice, of Western liberal-parliamentary democracy, founded upon basic human rights and civil liberties. Not just some conservative but also some liberal intellectuals in Western Europe, it is true, remained reluctant to see this idea embodied in the "American dream." They persisted in an anti-Soviet as well as anti-American neutralist position. They saw themselves as standing between the two superpower blocs and defiantly upheld the allegedly superior traditions and values of European (high) culture.

Others became more amenable when confronted with the realities of Stalinist rule in Eastern Europe and the escalating Cold War. They were prepared to make a clear and rational choice in favor of "the West." They felt safer, in their precarious positions as intellectuals, under the strategic military umbrella of the United States, even if they continued to harbor doubts about American "mass culture." Above all, it was a constantly shifting picture, and if there was any general drift, it was away from fellow traveling and neutralism. Whether a person completed this ideological journey early or late depended on many biographical and circumstantial factors.

Up to this point we have looked at how, from the late nineteenth century to the Cold War era, Europe's elites in general and its intellectuals in particular tried to explain to themselves and their audiences the advent of the "masses" as voters, producers, and consumers. These "masses" clearly posed a challenge to the established patterns of wealth, privilege, and power; and fears of them therefore persisted and, in view of the experience of the interwar years, indeed intensified. We have also examined how after 1900 the practices of political and economic "democracy" that had been developed in the United States—of participation in popular politics and material consumption—came into this picture. The issue we must now proceed to analyze is how *American* elites and intellectuals grappled with the problems of mass politics and mass culture that arose in the midst of the society in which they lived. As it turns out, reactions to these problems were not dissimilar from those that we have just observed with respect to European discourses about "democracy in America." Given the structures and dynamics of the American political system, tensions had arisen throughout the nineteenth century between the various populist movements that sprang up and the "old," mostly New England, establishment, trained in Ivy League universities and working in the urban and industrial centers of the Northeast.

THE DEBATE ON CULTURE IN AMERICA

In a paper looking at the American experience and produced for a conference on mass culture in Berlin in 1960, Irving Kristol tried to show that the American debate, though rooted in the nineteenth century, began in earnest only in World War I. It was at that point, so he postulated, that discussions of culture came to revolve around the notions of "highbrow" and "lowbrow," "first publicized in Van Wyck Brooks's historic essay 'America's Coming-of-Age' which appeared in 1915." To Brooks "highbrow" "meant the equivalent of the French Academy—the 'genteel tradition' of letters represented by the New England 'Brahmins': Longfellow, Emerson, Lowell, Howells, Aldrich" and others. " 'Highbrow' culture," he continued, "was 'high' culture, that dominating influence on American letters which placed the greatest emphasis, not on creativity itself, but on (1) the continuity of a cultural tradition and (2) the moral role played by art and the artist in the nation's life."[41] Although Brooks conceived of his essay as a criticism of highbrow culture, by this time and with the growth of mass politics, mass consumption, and mass culture before 1914, there were indeed many upper-class Americans who were just as worried about trends in their society as skeptical Europeans were. Still, whatever the rumblings in earlier decades when Americans looked toward Europe for models of high culture, it took until the 1930s for a major discussion to begin in the United States. Until that point the cultural pessimists continued to have a more difficult stand vis-à-vis the optimists who felt that the republican order and the democratic norms and processes laid down in the American Constitution were working and certainly working much better than the aging systems of Europe.

Before 1929 confidence also continued to be strong in Washington and elsewhere that ordinary voters, even populists, were "manageable" and controllable and that elites and "masses" could coexist and even cooperate without one side wanting to obliterate the other. That confidence was shaken by the Wall Street crash and the seemingly intractable mass unemployment of the 1930s. Among the lower classes and a growing number of intellectuals a sense began to proliferate that American capitalism and the political system were failing and that both had to undergo radical reform, if not revolution. Many of the disillusioned turned to Marxism in its different versions and, although Franklin D. Roosevelt's policies prevented a system-destabilizing radicalization of the "masses," writers, scholars, and artists of the generation born in the decade before 1914 moved toward the radical left. If socialist and communist parties had hitherto been insignificant, they now gained new members and sympathizers among the intelligentsia.[42]

In view of the depth of the economic and political crisis, the leftist critique of American capitalism and politics tended to overshadow the criticism of American mass culture that had first set in during the consumer and entertainment boom of the 1920s. In this earlier period, however, cultural critics had come less from intellectuals and cultural producers than from conservative and Christian groups who looked at Hollywood and "Chicago" and felt that the moral foundations of the Republic were being shaken by these two symbols of the modern age. Because some of the new developments in American popular culture, such as jazz, originated with ethnic minorities, racism was—just as among cultural pessimists in Europe—one of the ingredients of the new rightism. No doubt this rightism in American politics displayed tendencies that were fascist or at least protofascist. The difference was that it never grew into a mass movement capable of seizing power, as it had done in Germany and Italy.

Nor were many American intellectuals ever captured by it. Most of the criticism of American mass culture came from the left. The arrival of refugee intellectuals from Europe and especially from Germany, where, as we have seen, the debate on mass culture had been intense in the 1920s, contributed to this process. When Max Horkheimer and Theodor Adorno of the famous Frankfurt Institute arrived in New York as refugees from Nazism and began to influence social scientific analyses of the socioeconomic crisis, their publications may not have been immediately accessible to more than a few American intellectuals who read German; but their ideas began to circulate in New York and elsewhere.[43] Through them and other refugee scholars modern psychology and social psychology came to the United States as serious academic disciplines. Many of the sociologists among them were either Marxists or Weberians. Marxism was taken seriously because of its presumed capacity to explain the prolonged global crisis of the capitalist economies; Max Weber's work helped to foster a sense of cultural pessimism that had by now even begun to affect American liberals. In particular the German sociologist had given early warnings of the desperate predicament of modern man in highly bureaucratized and mobilized "mass" societies. Whatever Weber's own views of America (which he had toured before World War I), his notions of bureaucratic and charismatic *Herrschaft* looked all too plausible in light of developments after 1933.[44] All in all, therefore, an entire generation of young American intellectuals and academics, mostly from the East Coast, was suddenly initiated to Freud, Marx, and Weber or to peculiar combinations of those three men's ruminations upon the urban societies that had now lapsed into a deep crisis.

The intellectual ferment that the Great Crash produced can be traced in the writings of many American intellectuals. John Dos Passos published an important article in the *New Republic* that criticized the limited intellectual and political horizons of business icons like Ford and Edison. He quickly ran into heavy opposition, with his close friend Dinsmore Wheeler accusing him of espousing a "half-baked Greenwich village Communist point of view." Edmund Wilson later remembered "that the writers of his generation had always resented the barbarism of the big-business era" and that "they had been exhilerated at the 'sudden collapse of that stupid, gigantic fraud.' "[45]

Dwight Macdonald, the influential essayist, is of particular interest here because he became a leading analyst and social critic of American mass culture and mass democracy during the Cold War. Thanks to Michael Wreszin's biography of Macdonald, we possess an illuminating analysis of the circles in which he moved and of the intellectual evolution that he and his colleagues underwent. Macdonald's life presents a good example of their journey from the 1930s to the 1950s and 1960s. As Chicago sociologist Edward Shils observed, Macdonald "did more than any other American writer to bring their interpretation of mass culture to the forefront of the attention of the intellectual public."[46] Similarly, Wreszin is no doubt correct when he wrote that Macdonald's "record of observation . . . remains a seminal source for those who would try to grasp our history and what has made us what we are."[47]

Accordingly, we now know how, in the 1930s, Macdonald and his first wife Nancy began to read the *Communist Manifesto*, the work of Leon Trotsky, and Travers Clement's *Rebel America: The Story of Social Revolt in the United States*. Other books on his reading list were Ortega, Friedrich Nietzsche, Konrad Heiden (on national socialism), Hitler's *Mein Kampf*, John Dewey's *Liberalism and Social Action*, and the Lynds's

Middletown: A Study in American Culture.[48] Though he remained critical of Marxism, the crisis of the 1930s badly undermined his faith in liberalism, and in this respect he was no exception. "Liberal Democracy," he wrote, taking up the theme of mass society in now awkwardly sexist terms, "displays an anxious, idealistic respect for the feeling and opinion of the masses similar to the reverence of a romantic young man [for] the woman he loves. But the masses, like the woman, prefer a more brutal, overbearing lover who would tell them what to think and feel. . . . Dictators have discovered this basic fact about the masses. Their love-making, imperious, impetuous, brutal, has easily won the masses away from their tediously high-minded liberal democratic lovers. The nineteenth century was a long honeymoon in which the masses became increasingly bored (and, after the war, skeptical of their powers) with their democratic bridegroom. The dictator is the man of the world who broke up the happy but dull home of the romantic couple."[49]

After this, Macdonald came to believe that "democracy breeds demagogues and demagogues easily become dictators. In the old 18th century aristocratic government, the rulers were a body small enough to know each other, to combine against common enemies, to penetrate frauds. But the 1935 PEOPLE is so vast, so stupid as to be helpless, a dinosaur which drags its tons of flesh wherever the small directing brain tells it to go." And so he remained deeply suspicious of the "masses," insisting that their tastes and capabilities were abominably low. He added: "The growth of popular democratic government is at the root. Up to Rousseau the world was always divided into small bands of rulers and huge unconscious bodies of the ruled. Then Rousseau shattered the walls of class divisions, followed by the French Revolution, the first popular revolt. The 19th century gave more and more power to the people, until by 1914 power was more widely diffused, more people took part in the government than ever before."[50]

Imbued with an elitism that he had been nurturing since his undergraduate days at Yale University, he was at this point in his life drawn to Nietzsche and Ortega because they "confirmed Dwight's own fear of the masses as a threat to culture and civilization."[51] However, he also retained his contempt for dictators. "Do you think," he asked rhetorically, "that in a Nazified Europe Picasso and Léger will continue to paint, James Joyce and Gertrude Stein will continue to write, Stravinsky will continue to compose music, Le Corbusier will continue to build houses?"[52]

Ultimately, the more than two hundred handwritten pages that Macdonald compiled—called "dictator notes" by his biographer—"contained nearly all the themes that were to characterize his political and cultural criticism for the next three decades. The Tocquevillian tone, the traditional stance on high culture, the contempt for the business elite, the fear of the enervating boredom of mass society, and the relationship of such mass organizations to totalitarianism—all can be found in these notebooks."[53] The similarities between the ideas of this influential American intellectual and his European counterparts could not have been more strikingly summarized. When it came to attitudes toward the "masses" and the perceived spirit of the age, the Atlantic—as we shall also see in subsequent chapters—was not a trench, but a two-lane highway along which arguments and conterarguments traveled.

With the experience of World War II behind him and the full horror of the Nazi Holocaust as well as the Stalinist purges emerging, Macdonald's despair grew, but so did his determination to stand up. Disdainful of Bolshevik Marxism, he moved more closely toward the "Lib-Labs" whom he had once likewise despised. He advocated interventionism in Europe to contain communism; he promoted the export of "American goods and ideas abroad."[54] Like other New York intellectuals he proposed to counter the Soviet cultural offensive of the late 1940s not by supporting Russia's rightist opponents in the West, but Stalin's leftist enemies. Typically though, he did not do so in a mood of confidence and optimism. Instead he predicted "dehumanization, bureaucratization, and manipulation" as being the future fate of the West. Worse, he believed that mass culture propelled these depressing trends, which he identified with the "commercialization of culture." Yet it was not an automotive push "from below"; rather, he conceived of mass culture as an elitist invention that was being imposed from above—"as a vehicle used by tyrannical elites to shape a totalitarian society." Hence his insistence on the need for an aristocratic counterelite—not, to be sure, of birth, but of merit—that would uphold the values of "high culture" and its institutions. Given the dangers emanating from mass culture and from the dictatorial ambitions of Soviet communism, the rallying of such a counterelite was in Macdonald's view more vital than ever.[55]

Considering that he spent so many years thinking and worrying about the impact of mass culture on American society, it is easy to see why Macdonald eventually felt compelled to write more systematically about the problem. His first short and critical pieces on popular culture had begun to appear in *Politics*, the magazine he had founded in 1944.[56] To its early issues he attracted many young authors whose names recur in later chapters: Nicola Chiaromonte, Daniel Bell, and C. Wright Mills.

Then, years later, his thoughts on the subject came together in a longer article that appeared in *Diogenes*, the intellectual journal published in Paris. Titled "A Theory of Mass Culture," it asserted that "for about a century, western culture has really been two cultures: the traditional kind—let us call it 'High Culture'—. . . and a 'Mass Culture' manufactured wholesale for the market."[57] The growth of the latter since the nineteenth century, he continued, was due to the fact that "political democracy and popular education broke down the old upper-class monopoly of culture." Moreover, business "found a profitable market in the cultural demands of the newly awakened masses, and the advance of technology made possible the cheap production of books, periodicals, pictures, music, and furniture."

If, according to Macdonald, mass culture began as "a parasitic, a cancerous growth on High Culture," it later drew "on its own past and some of it evolves so far away from High Culture as to appear quite disconnected from it." After a brief excursion to the Soviet Union, which to him was "even more a land of Mass Culture than is the U.S.A.," Macdonald elaborated on its vulgarity, pervasiveness, brutality, and "overwhelming *quantity*" through which it threatened high culture. At the same time "Mass Culture is very, very democratic" in that "it refuses to discriminate against, or between, anything or anybody. All is grist to its mill, and all comes out finely ground indeed."

If his views of mass culture sound familiar and rather "European," his definition of high culture is more interesting, also in light of the ventures that the Ford Foundation later promoted in its European program (discussed in detail in chapters 6 and 7). To him "the High Culture of our times is pretty much identical with Avantgardism," which was now being corrupted by the encroachments of mass culture and producing, next to the cheap *Kitsch* for the masses, a new "tepid, flaccid Middlebrow Culture." Accordingly, the future of high culture looked "dark" to Macdonald, but that of mass culture was even "darker." There was no hope of mass culture ever getting better, because "culture can only be produced by and for human beings." So, once people "are organized (more strictly disorganized) as masses, they lose their human identity and quality." Man to him was "a solitary atom, uniform with and undifferentiated from thousands and millions of other atoms who go to make up 'the lonely crowd,' as David Riesman calls American society."

Macdonald's "Theory of Mass Culture" may not have been a particularly original and profound piece. Nevertheless, it certainly put in a nutshell many of the arguments that were floating around the intellectual worlds of Europe and America after World War II. However, the previously mentioned concept of "Middlebrow Culture" indicated that for Macdonald it was not just the "masses" whose tastes destroyed "high culture" and who were easy prey to the manipulative providers of popular *Kitsch*. He was no less critical of the purveyors of "midcult." This, as he wrote in other essays and in letters to friends and colleagues was the type of "high" culture cherished by the "middle class and at best 'middle-brow' homeowners pridefully hanging [a mass-reproduced] van Gogh" print over their mantel-piece.[58] Midcult in Macdonald's view was a menace in that it proffered an unauthentic version of high culture to the less educated middle classes, yearning for refinement but not endowed "with the intellectual equipment"or "the will to be serious about it."[59] Taking a portrait of Alfred Barr as his starting point, he examined how Barr had been trying "to find a successful way to promote high culture among the Neanderthals."[60]

Whatever one may think of the elitist paternalism that is revealed in Macdonald's "theory of mass culture," his writings on the subject were not merely inspired by aesthetic concerns but also had the immediate political purpose of representing contributions to the winning of the Cold War. As he wrote to his friend Chiaromonte: "If the U.S. doesn't or cannot change its mass culture (movies, radio, sports cult, comics, television, slick magazines) it will lose the war against the USSR. Americans have been made into permanent adolescents by advertising, mass culture—uncritical, herdminded, pleasure-loving, concerned about trivia of materialistic living, scared of death, sex, old age—friendship is sending Xmas cards, sex is the wet dreams of those chromium-plated Hollywood glamor girls, death—is not."[61]

Macdonald's other concern was to preserve the elitist values that guided the efforts of people who were products of the Ivy League and the East Coast metropolitan centers.[62] Not surprisingly, therefore, he regarded Los Angeles, with its film-making citadel of Hollywood, as "a barbarically provincial non-city three thousand miles from our cultural capital and two thousand miles even from Chicago."[63] Conversely he was strongly attracted to Europe and European high culture. He crossed the Atlantic many times and when vacationing on the Cape, he felt that Nantucket was "more like a European village than anything else I have seen."[64] When the European film industry experienced a revival of its fortunes, his rejection of Hollywood as "the preeminent producer of trash" burst forth uninhibitedly, while his movie reviews simultaneously became comments on "the quality of life in America, its culture, its brutality, its

frivolity, the sexual immaturity of the American male, the general obsession with sex combined with official prudishness."[65]

If Macdonald wrestled with the question of "Masscult and Midcult"—
thus the title of his major two-part article which he published in *Partisan
Review* in the spring and fall of 1946—in a pessimistic mode, he of course
did not do so in an intellectual vacuum.[66] On the contrary, he received
plenty of applause, indicating that his "theories" struck a responsive
chord among a good many of his readers. Yet there was also criticism,
early rumblings of which could be heard when in 1952 *Partisan Review*
published articles on the theme of "Our Century—Our Culture." Most
of the contributors displayed not only a newfound self-confidence vis-à-
vis Europe but proudly pointed to the high-cultural achievements of the
United States, as Shepard Stone would do in subsequent years at the Ford
Foundation and then support it with his funds.

One of the most influential responses to Macdonald's writings was
Daniel Bell's *The End of Ideology.*[67] Just like Macdonald's "theories,"
Bell's contributions to the subject of culture were not all that original.
Both men had known each other from the war years, if not before, and
had hence influenced each other's thinking. Bell, a journalist who later
gained a professorship in sociology at Columbia before moving to Harvard, had been one of the early contributors to Macdonald's *Politics.* He
was also familiar with the work of the University of Chicago sociologist
Edward Shils, a man with many links to the New York intellectuals and
another active supporter of the Congress for Cultural Freedom (CCF).
Shils was among the first "prepared to take on the critics of mass culture
as purveying a form of anti-Americanism that did not serve the nation
well during the ideological skirmishes of the cold war."[68] He was seconded
by Sidney Hook, a major voice in this circle who, though not entirely
easy about American popular culture, believed that the Europeans were
"shockingly ignorant" of realities across the Atlantic.[69] They formed, he
complained, their images of the United States from the novels of John
Steinbeck, William Faulkner, or Sinclair Lewis.

Still, Bell's volume of 1960 provides a good summary of how far the
debate had moved by the late 1950s. Overall, it was more than anything
else a strong antidote against the cultural pessimism of analysts of American mass society such as Macdonald, or David Riesman, Nathan Glazer,
and Reuel Denney, whose *The Lonely Crowd* (1950) Macdonald had referred to in his "A Theory of Mass Culture." As we have seen earlier
in this chapter, all these analysts had, much to Hook's annoyance, their
European equivalents.[70] In his introduction Bell emphasized that this was

not a book about Western industrial societies in general but about the complexities and ambiguities of American life. What he wanted to do was to confront "the falsity of simplification and the ideological pitfalls into which such simplifications had led."[71] He believed that many social theories, and Marxist ones about class and the masses in particular, were inadequate for an understanding of the United States. One reason for this was that all serious scholarly efforts had "to begin from the close empirical level before making the grand theoretical generalizations that some of the simplifiers have been prone to make."

Accordingly, Bell's first chapter contained a "critique" of "America as a mass society." Initially he examined here "the sense of a radical dehumanization of life which has accompanied events of the past few decades [and which] has given rise to the theory of mass society." Turning to the much discussed features of this type of society, he identified "five different and sometimes contradictory usages": mass as an undifferentiated number, mass as the judgment by the incompetent, mass as the mechanized society, mass as the bureaucratized society, and mass as the mob. What he found striking about these usages was "how they reflected or related to the complex, richly striated social relations of the real world." In fact, "some of the images of life in a mass society, as presented by the critics," in Bell's view bordered "on caricature." He also criticized the romantic and organicist notions of society that undergirded arguments about the alleged disorganization of mass society. What to him lay at the heart of these arguments was "a defense of an aristocratic cultural tradition . . . and a doubt that the large mass of mankind can ever become truly educated or acquire an appreciation of culture." Instead there was fear of the "masses," which had "its roots in the dominant conservative tradition of Western political thought." Bell pointed out that these conservative notions could be found in Aristotle, in early Christian thought, in the French Counterrevolution "which transplanted the image of the 'mindless masses' into modern consciousness." Although he acknowledged that they were all concerned with the meaning and preservation of liberty in the face of leveling tendencies, collectivism, and democratic demagogy that culminated in Hitler's "nihilistic revolt against traditional culture in Europe," he was dismayed at the "narrow conception of human potentialities" on which those "aristocratic" attitudes rested.

Bell, who hailed from a humble Jewish immigrant background, concluded that, even while the "foundations of privilege go on being challenged in the name of justice, society does not collapse." He approvingly quoted the economist Joseph Schumpeter, who once wrote that capitalism's achievement did "not typically consist in providing more silk stockings for queens, but in bringing them within the reach of factory girls in return for steadily decreasing effort." He praised John K. Galbraith's work on the blessings of a managed, affluence-generating liberal-capitalist economy. But for Bell this did not mean the leveling of wealth differentials. Capitalism, he wrote, "can continue only if it maintains entrepreneurial rewards whose 'short-run inequity' is the price that the masses must pay for the long-run rising living standards that capitalism can achieve."

Having revealed his preference for a Fordist and Keynesian economy of the type that had emerged in the United States after World War II and turning from mass consumption to culture, he was convinced that "the picture of modern culture as debauched by concession to popular taste" was just as exaggerated. He granted "that mass society is compartmentalized, superficial, acquisitive, mobile, and status-hungry"; but the other side of the coin should also be contemplated—that is, "the right to privacy, to free choice of friends and occupation, status on the basis of achievement rather than ascription, a plurality of norms and standards, rather than the exclusive and monopolistic social controls of a single dominant group."

Bell's next step led him to the crucial point: as we have seen, the United States had been the main target of one-sided "aristocratic" criticism of mass society among European and some American intellectuals. Now he wanted to show the reader the bright side of that gloomy picture. If the "mass society hypothesis" argued that the United States might be "exceptionally vulnerable to the politics of disaffection," then how come that neither communism nor fascism "on a European model" ever "gained a real foothold in America?" And, Bell continued, if American society was composed of atomized and isolated individuals, how come that there were "at least 200,000 voluntary organizations, associations, clubs, societies, lodges, and fraternities with an aggregate (but obviously overlapping) membership of close to 80 million men and women?" Even in urban neighborhoods, "where anonymity is presumed to flourish, the extent of local ties is astonishing."

Last but not least, Bell referred to the rising levels of universal education and to "the growth of a vast middlebrow society," which, in the wake of increased productivity and leisure time, would become "an even more active 'consumer' of culture." Time and again Bell therefore tried to put in a positive light what the critics of American mass society regarded as abominable. Thus Frank Sinatra, Sammy Davis Jr., and Dean Martin were

105

turned into rebels against conformity for their refusal to "ape the style and manners of the established status community." He asserted that in Hollywood—a barbaric place to Macdonald—"the old status hierarchies have fragmented, the new sets celebrate their triumph by jeering at the pompous ways of the old." Other groups "at the margins of literary life" like the beatniks similarly fell into this pattern. Bell maintained that rising divorce rates were not merely signs of "widespread social disorganization" and the decline of the family, but also manifestations of a "freer, more individualistic basis of choice and the emergence of the 'companionship' marriage." He even put a different spin on the question of crime and violence, noting "the actual decline of crime in the United States" and debunking the "myth of the Mafia."

In conclusion he asserted that critical theories of mass society were in fact "an ideology of romantic protest against contemporary society" and bore no relation to reality. Bell, by contrast, claimed to have offered an empirical account of mass society, and its American version in particular, at "the end of ideology." Accordingly, other parts of the book contain a reassuring assessment even of McCarthyism. He saw the dangers of an anticommunist witch-hunt, but ultimately arrived at a conclusion that played down its importance and buttressed his earlier positive views of American mass society. If Richard Hofstadter, the Columbia University historian, had dealt with the status anxieties of old aristocracies, Seymour Lipset at Harvard had studied the status fears of the nouveaux riches. As Bell put it in his benign interpretation of McCarthyism: "The central idea of the status politics conception is that groups that are advancing in wealth and social position are often as anxious and politically feverish as groups that have become *declassé*." Consequently, he was convinced that the United States was far too complex a system ever to be overrun by a single obsession and group. For Bell America was "an open society." McCarthy merely articulated status anxieties of certain middle-class groups. They were "part of the price we pay for that openness."

• • • • •

This chapter has been devoted to an examination of debates on the evolution of Western industrial societies and the role of the "masses" in that evolution during the nineteenth and twentieth centuries. The fierceness of some of these debates reflected hopes and anxieties that the upper and middle classes felt when they contemplated the rise of mass production, mass consumption, mass culture, and mass politics and what these developments might do to their positions of privilege and power. When pondering this question, many tended to lapse into a pessimistic mood; but there were also the optimists who saw the age of "democracy" in the widest sense as a blessing and an opportunity, not as a curse. We have also seen how and why America became a focus of debate about these questions among intellectuals on both sides of the Atlantic.[72]

However, it would be misleading to assume that the analysts and theorists of mass society whose positions have been discussed simply voiced their individual views conceived in peaceful contemplative isolation in their studies. For the post-1945 period at least, these individuals must be situated in the groups, networks, and associations within which they met with others and tried to pursue and realize their ideas about the sociocultural future. This means that in the next chapter we must inquire into the organizational frameworks that were built on both sides of the ideological and power-political dividing line—a line that separated not only East and West, and was hence part of the familiar Cold War, but also divided pessimists such as Ortega y Gasset and Adorno at the European end and Macdonald in the United States from optimists such as Shils and Bell and their allies on the other side of the Atlantic. Having dealt with these organizations and the CCF in particular, we will see how Shepard Stone and the Ford Foundation fit into the cultural landscape of a Cold War that was being waged not just against the Soviet Union but also between two groups of Western intellectuals and academics on both sides of the Atlantic.

Western Intellectuals and the Cold Culture Wars of the Congress for Cultural Freedom (CCF)

A T A conference on the "Progress of Freedom," held in Berlin during the third week in June 1960, Edward Shils, one of the leading analysts of American mass culture and critic of cultural anti-Americanism in Europe and the United States, delivered one of the major lectures, "The Quality of Life in Modern Society: Mass Society and Mass Culture."[1]

MASS CULTURE AND THE CONGRESS FOR CULTURAL FREEDOM

The meeting united a group of intellectuals from both sides of the Atlantic, among them Arthur J. Schlesinger Jr., Manès Sperber, Irving Kristol, and Richard Hoggart. Although Bernard Rosenberg is probably correct in asserting that "the conference was rigged in favor of intellectuals who support mass culture,"[2] it was not entirely so. Thus Shils took quite a differentiated view when he discussed mass culture and its relationship to the "masses." Against the background of the three levels of culture— "refined," "mediocre," and "brutal"—that he had presented in a much longer article in *Daedalus*, the journal of the American Academy of Arts and Sciences,[3] his "reassessment of modern societies" rejected the "ideological criticism" that "stressed their atomization, the evaporation of moral bonds, the intensification of class cleavage and antagonism, the decay of those institutions which maintain tradition, such as the family and the church, and the consequent loss of a coherent meaning of life."

This criticism, Shils continued, had failed to acknowledge the durability of traditions and institutions, the "heightened responsiveness to a greater diversity of experience," the "moral equalitarianism," and the individuality that "has come to flourish in modern society." To be sure, there were the problems of bureaucratization, of boredom, loneliness, and youth. But none of them defied resolution. Intellectuals, Shils exhorted his listeners, had the job of improving "the quality of popular culture and to bring it more into line with the standards and content of the greatest cultural achievements," not least because "many of the *genres* of popular culture, such as sports, games, and cowboy films, have their own inherent potentialities of excellence" and because "such excellence possesses an autonomous dignity." If Shils was particularly troubled by any one issue, it was the separation, as he saw it, of the natural sciences from the humanities.

Although Shils's notion of the relationship between high and popular culture was not without a patronizing streak, Schlesinger's intervention at the conference by comparison displayed a much more elitist sentiment with regard to the "masses." He pointed out—with no mention of their notorious inadequacies—that "IQ tests show an unequal distribution of intelligence in the population." He then added the idea of "the existence of an AQ, or aesthetic quotient," arguing that "some few people are naturally responsive to art; the masses are not."[4] Perhaps this was, in a different key, the "aristocratic" view that Bell had been so critical of in his *The End of Ideology.*

The third American at the Berlin conference to discuss culture, under the title "High, Low, and Modern: Some Thoughts on Popular Culture and Popular Government," was Irving Kristol, another old hand of the radical left now halfway on his intellectual journey to the neoconservative right that eventually overran the 1950s Keynesian liberalism of the Galbraiths, Schlesingers, and Bells. Having provided some historical background to the debate on mass culture in the United States since the nineteenth century, this prominent New York intellectual argued that, contrary to the attitude of educated people toward the general population during that century, intellectuals in the twentieth had become "very sensitive to 'popular culture' as representing . . . a threat" to the moral and political order; "or to be exact, we are on the defensive against 'mass culture' which is what 'popular culture' has become."[5] However—and this is where he differentiated himself from the "aristocratic" cultural pessimists such as Macdonald—"whereas 'popular culture' was the culture of a class (the uneducated), 'mass culture' is a culture shared, to a greater or lesser degree, by everyone." After all, "we all watch the same TV shows, read the same advertisements, see the same movies." Kristol saw this as a mixed blessing, though.

To him "the sentimentality, the inanity, the vulgarity of 'mass culture' " became "objectionable when they impose themselves upon society with such vigour as to set the tone, suggest the values, establish the context of life both private *and* public." And this was "undeniably what is happening in modern democracies" at this time. Nevertheless, he wondered if mass culture was really that powerful and the opposition to it that weak. Having illustrated his doubts by reference to the treatment of pornography, into which "mass culture" was in his view degenerating, he postulated that "*someone* has to be able to say, with assurance and a measure of authority, what is culture and what is not; what is decent and what is not." The problem was that, at least for now, there was no such "class of people which can be regarded as both representing and forming 'public opinion' on matters of culture." But according to Kristol there was hope, "for, in the end, democratic government is government by reasonable public opinion"—"the moral fundament of democracy," even if this moral fundament was "under constant assault by much of that 'mass culture' which is now being distributed through the mass media." The crucial question facing modern democracy was therefore whether "leadership will be forthcoming."

Whatever uncertainties Kristol may have felt about how mass culture impacted upon elites and whether a " 'natural aristocracy' of talent and virtue" would be able to retain control, overall there was a marked contrast in tone and content between the American contributions at Berlin and the paper by Manès Sperber, the well-known Jewish writer and intellectual. He had grown up in Vienna, studied there with Alfred Adler, and taught psychology at Berlin until the Nazi seizure of power, when he escaped via Yugoslavia to Paris and then via the south of France to Switzerland.[6] In other words, Sperber had survived the age of totalitarian dictatorship and the Holocaust by a hair's breadth.

In "Repudiated Past—Disinherited Present: Socio-Psychological Reflections on the Theme of Tradition and Mass Culture," Sperber reminded his audience of the older Marxist view "that, in contrast to the hysterical, thoughtless and brutal crowd, the class-conscious proletarian masses were destined to introduce the next stage of history, carrying out a preconceived plan in accordance with a scientific theory."[7] Yet, he continued, "today . . . we know that on a broad level the masses represent nothing more than what in military terms would be called 'une masse de manoeuvre.' " However, there was another concept of the masses "which corresponds to a certain stage of industrial production, namely standardization, which only becomes possible as consumer goods are distributed and used in ever larger quantities during an ever shorter period of time. It is the mass of consumers whose constantly increasing importance has set its stamp on so-called mass culture."

To Sperber, these consumers were "mass men" whose characteristics he then proceeded to describe and with which we are already familiar from our earlier summary of discussions among European intellectuals about this type of person. However, "simultaneously and undisturbed" by the passions of mass men and their "ably organized commercial exploitation," there remained "in the individual's deepest being . . . the uninterrupted self-assertion of the individual who 'lives his life in growing circles that surround things'; the individual in his need to love and to endure with others in a harmony through which he is not only himself but also everybody else with whom he has in common an unnamed, because unrecognized, loneliness." While the basic thrust of Sperber's presentation in Berlin was pessimistic and no doubt marked by his professional training in the Adler school and by personal experiences as a victim of Nazi persecution, he ended on a vaguely upbeat note: "It may be that the term *mass culture* will soon become obsolete. Maybe we are only dealing with a contemporary phenomenon which we have encountered on an apparently endless bridge on which humanity may yet have to lose its way for several decades until it reaches the other bank."[8]

Sperber's philosophical excursion into the present state and future of modern society was characteristic of a Continental European tradition in which he was steeped and which will be examined in greater detail in chapter 9. By contrast, the British sociologist Richard Hoggart struck a less somber and more soberly analytical tone when, under the title "The Quality of Cultural Life in Mass Society," he set out to analyze his country's case with its "loosening of many old 'class' or hierarchical forms" as well as "the emerging in part of a sort of cultural 'classnessless' and in part a compensatory seeking of status."[9] To him the dangers of the future did not so much lie in the fact "that mass culture will be crude and raucous, full of sex and violence. These elements can certainly be seen but they are essentially marginal" and were seen by him as "warning mechanisms or even sometimes as a healthy kicking-back against the main trend." The "real danger" was instead "that a successful mass culture will be too damned nice, a bland, muted, processed, institutionalised decency, a suburban or commuter's limbo in which nothing real ever happens and the gut has gone out of life." Although hopeful that "art—culture—intellectual affairs—education" would "not be neglected by mass society," Hoggart in the final analysis tried to steer a middle course between the "High Bourgeois" who attacked mass culture and the "Populists" who accepted "altogether uncritically the face of prosperous mass democracy and especially its communications."

As he put it frankly and to some extent prophetically in his conclusion, "Behind all I have been saying is the assumption that in our societies class-and-culture have been immensely intertwined, in part disablingly, but also in part fruitfully; that these particular forms of entwinement are now

111

being loosened and that many people are—unconsciously but intensely—trying to find new links, and that the links that are most often promoted in present circumstances are those between culture-and-status-and-commodities." He thought it "idle and wrong to regret the breaking of many of the old links." After all, "none of us can produce a blueprint for a 'decently classless society.'" Nor did he feel able to "accept the present tendencies as the only alternative." Rather, he proclaimed in good old "Anglo-Saxon" fashion, "one can reasonably and pragmatically work in the direction of a society which recognises variety, distinctions, differences and doesn't narrowly relate them to birth-marks, 'prestige-culture' marks or consumption marks."

At the same time Hoggart did not wish to underestimate "the difficulty of speaking to these [general] audiences today." But he was also "struck by the extent to which many of us accept, in our own way, something of those shallow, lowest-common-denominator assumptions about people's tastes and abilities which the popular commercial providers obviously work from." He therefore openly admitted that it was "not easy to find directions in the open society." For the moment this direction "is being decided almost entirely by the commercial providers. . . . The admen are pushing very hard their notion of the good society and the good life . . . , especially with people to whom 'intellectuals' have not been used to speaking." There were hence "most difficult problems of responsibility, perhaps even of 'pastoral care'" that intellectuals needed to confront.

However revealing the various contributions to the Berlin conference may be for our continuing exploration of the European-American dialogue on mass society and mass culture, a further point is of considerable significance for the aims and purposes of this part of our study of America's cold culture wars after 1945: the conference was organized by the Congress of Cultural Freedom. This very influential association has already been referred to at the end of the preceding chapter, when the question of networks and interactions between individual social thinkers and cultural producers was raised. The importance of the CCF in this picture of cultural institutions may be gauged from the fact that it has been the subject of major studies in several languages and many scholarly articles.[10] It is no less relevant for the present volume that the Ford Foundation and Shepard Stone became deeply involved in supporting and funding the increasingly global operations of the CCF. But before dealing with these aspects of our story, it is necessary to consider the larger postwar political and ideological context of which the founding of the CCF in 1950 and its operations during the Cold War are a part.

From the perspective of the twenty-first century and after the end of the Cold War, it is often difficult to grasp what the East-West conflict as well as the world war and the crisis of the 1930s that preceded it did to the intellectual life of the Atlantic region. The question of whether artists and scholars—intellectual producers in the widest sense—can and should engage with the larger political and socioeconomic issues of their time or merely devote themselves to their creative work in the narrow sense had, of course, been raised long before the world crisis of the 1930s. But it was after the Great Crash of 1929 and in the misery and despair that followed that the question of *engagement* assumed a new urgency. With the Western economies in deep depression and reeling under massive unemployment and growing political radicalism, it proved more and more difficult even for the artist, who by disposition was not a very political person, to remain aloof. Some, as was mentioned in the previous chapter, committed themselves to fascism, the new mass movement on the extreme right that had first succeeded in seizing power in Italy in 1922 and was now attracting millions of men and women all over Europe.

COMMUNISTS AND EX-COMMUNISTS

These events and the violent political struggles they unleashed inevitably mobilized countermovements on the left. With fascism also appearing elsewhere in Europe, the stage had been set for major confrontations between the two sides of the political spectrum. While artists and intellectuals rarely joined in the street battles, many of them began to furnish the arguments, slogans, and watchwords that were subsequently deployed in the fight against fascism. Some conservatives, fearful of the right-wing "masses," as well as liberals joined in this effort, but it was most vigorously pursued and organized by the socialists and communists. Viewing fascism as an outgrowth of capitalism and having predicted the major crisis that had now befallen it, the communists could rely on the material and moral support of the Soviet Union and its foreign arm, the Communist International (Komintern). Indeed, as Western governments—often weak, divided and preoccupied with their own domestic problems—were reluctant to join the antifascist camp and looked for ways of appeasing Hitler and Mussolini, the Soviet Union came to be seen as the last dam against the fascist tide that had already swallowed up its leftist opponents inside Italy and Germany in a wave of brutal repression and murder. To confirmed communists in the West, the Soviet Union moreover repre-

113

sented the foundations on which they believed it would be possible to build the classless society.

The phenomenon of "fellow traveling" developed within this larger context of Western official passivity toward Hitler and Mussolini and Soviet efforts to rally all active opponents of fascism.[11] It became the stance of those Western intellectuals who did not openly join the Communist Party of their country but who nevertheless wished to support the Soviet Union in its antifascist struggle. They also saw it as the germ cell of a future egalitarian society, which bourgeois capitalism, in their view, would never be able to create. In 1936 the Spanish Civil War became the focus of the international struggle against fascism, attracting this type of committed intellectual from all over Western Europe and the United States. But next to the rumors about Stalin's purges, this war also became the source of a slowly growing disillusionment among those foreigners who had volunteered to serve on the side of the Spanish Republic. They came to resent the ruthlessness with which the Spanish Communists treated their allies, reinforcing their suspicions that Stalin's policies inside Russia similarly showed no respect for human life. George Orwell and his *Homage to Catalonia* provide the best illustration of this disillusionment that led straight to his novels *Animal Farm* and *1984*.[12] To many others the 1939 Nazi-Soviet Pact proved to be the last straw, although some returned to their more favorable attitudes toward Moscow after the Western Allies had formed the anti-Hitler coalition in 1941.

This time the support of Western intellectuals for the Soviet Union and its population even had the seal of approval from their governments in London and Washington, and those who had a knowledge of German, Italian, or Japanese language and society promptly found themselves recruited into the Allied armed forces or intelligence gathering agencies to collect and evaluate information about the Axis enemies. Yet neither the period of official cooperation with Stalin during the war nor the victory over fascism that ended World War II could stop a slow and piecemeal process of dissociation of a sizable number of intellectuals in Europe and the United States. Some of then peeled off early from the columns of Soviet-organized antifascism; others were unwilling to abandon their rejection of capitalism and their hope for radical change spearheaded by Moscow.

It is not easy to pinpoint where in the West the corrosion set in first. But it is no coincidence that Trotzkyites were among the earliest critics of Stalin's brutal regime. If we start with the American side of the picture, we have already seen that suspicions of Stalin's policies had been widespread before the mid-1930s. The Great Depression had resulted in a leftist shift among intellectual critics of American society and its capitalist system. If anything, Trotsky's revolutionism looked more appealing to many of them than Stalin's faceless bureaucratism. Given also the deep suspicions that existed between the two factions of communism ever since Trotsky's ouster from the Soviet regime, it is hardly surprising that Trotskyite sympathizers such as Melvin Lasky, Lionel Trilling, and Irving Kristol as well as other members of the network of radical American intellectuals centered in New York City began to be vexed by doubts about the future of Marxism more generally.[13]

Above all, there was Sidney Hook who, slightly older than most of the rest and radicalized by his youth in Williamsburg (Brooklyn), had become a communist fellow traveler in the 1920s, interested in integrating Marxism with the philosophy of John Dewey, Hook's mentor and lodestar and a major influence on American thought in the postwar period.[14] Though originally close to Soviet communism and an opponent of Trotsky, Hook became completely disillusioned with the Soviet experiment after the Moscow Trials in 1936–37, in which he saw "the face of radical evil—as ugly and petrifying as anything the Fascists had revealed up to that time—in the visages of those who were convinced that they were men and women of good will."[15] Soon Hook emerged as one of the organizers of a Commission of Inquiry, initiated by Dewey, into the Stalinist purges and crimes. In May 1939 Hook and Dewey founded the Committee for Cultural Freedom, which was supported by Norman Thomas, the chair of the staunchly anticommunist American Socialist Party. The committee's manifesto was signed, next to well-known writers like John Dos Passos, by Sol Levitas and Arthur Schlesinger and appeared in the *Nation*. Other prominent figures who joined after the war were James Burnham, a Princetonian and former Trotzkyite, and Phil Reber, while Macdonald at this point still remained on the other side of the fence.

The important point to be made about the committee's agenda is its criticism of dictatorship in the language of the emergent totalitarianism paradigm. It is quite likely that the interest in this paradigm was stimulated by the work and debates among the refugees from Nazism who had settled in New York since 1933. Horkheimer and Adorno have already been mentioned as the founders of the Frankfurt Institute for Social Research, now in its new home in Manhattan. Among its other associates was Herbert Marcuse, who in 1934 wrote his essay "The Struggle against Liberalism in the Totalitarian View of the State," almost simultaneously with a piece on "The Totalitarian State and the Claims of the

115

Church," which the refugee theologian Paul Tillich published in *Social Research*, the recently established journal of the nearby New School for Social Research.

Whatever the differences in the points of departure and intellectual trajectory of these two refugees, the comparisons they made, implicitly or explicitly, between Nazi Germany and Stalinist Russia provided a conceptual backing for the critiques that America's antifascists had been developing. Even though they were all—Americans as well as European newcomers—motivated by a search for a more egalitarian society at a time when American capitalism seemed incapable of finding a way out of the economic crisis, they also worried about the threat to individualism and freedom of expression that the totalitarian state and its anonymous bureaucracies posed. The seminal book-length analysis of the Nazi system that Franz Neumann, another refugee from Germany, put out under the title *Behemoth* represented the first culmination of a growing preoccupation with totalitarianism.[16] The title encapsulated the dangers that threatened modern societies. Another book was *The Totalitarian Enemy*, published in 1940 by Franz Borkenau, another refugee and former communist.[17] In it the author defined communism as a "red" fascism and Nazism as a "brown" communism. Above all, both systems were out to destroy a world that was struggling to uphold the inviolability of human life and basic rights.[18]

Although the Committee for Cultural Freedom disappeared after the conclusion of the Anglo-American alliance with the Soviet Union, its ideas and notions of totalitarianism continued to be discussed among scholars and intellectuals. Just as the *Nation* had helped the committee onto its feet in 1939, it was now, toward the end of the war, *Partisan Review*, another one of the various East Coast intellectual journals, that opened its pages to the anti-Stalinists on the left, with Hook, Burnham, and Trilling on the editorial board. As early as 1943, Hook was given the opportunity to launch a renewed attack on the myopia of other leftists. What agitated him so much was that it was not just fellow travelers who persisted in hoping that the wartime alliance with the Soviet Union would somehow continue after the war whose end was by then clearly in sight. Similar hopes were held by leading members of the Roosevelt administration, who saw Allied cooperation as a way of resuming and completing the domestic reform program, begun at the height of the economic crisis, but stopped in the 1940s to secure a united front of Democrats and Republicans, of labor and big business in the war against the Axis powers.

The accession of Harry Truman to the U.S. presidency after Roosevelt's death in February 1945 decisively shifted the balance of opinion both against continued cooperation with Stalin abroad and radical reform at home. Instead we see the beginnings of the Cold War struggle against the Soviet Union in other parts of the world and the rise of a neoliberal type of market economy, tempered by moderately Keynesian demand management. In a more general and rapidly spreading climate of anticommunism, fellow traveling quickly became an untenable position in the United States. Nor, with the East-West conflict accelerating, was there a third way. The choice was between a foreign and domestic peace guaranteed by Washington's elected government, which most intellectuals now subscribed to, on the one hand, and a *Pax Sovietica*, whose desirability all but a few 1930s loyalists still propounded, on the other.

In this respect the situation was fundamentally different in Europe. If we start with the French scene, the intellectual climate in Paris, the cultural nerve center of France, had lost little of the complexity that had been its hallmark in the 1930s. During those years the Communist Party (PCF) had been very strong until it was driven underground by the Nazi invasion and occupation in June 1940. The Nazi-Soviet Pact of August 1939, not surprisingly, proved to be a political disaster for French communism, but the PCF recovered ground on account of its resistance effort against German occupation after the defeat of France some nine months later. However, already before 1939, after a good deal of fellow traveling by French intellectuals during the mid-1930s, leading artists and writers had begun to drop out of the networks that had been crafted on behalf of the Komintern by Willi Münzenberg, a refugee from Nazism. Münzenberg had been not only the brains behind the German Communist Party's agitprop apparatus in the Weimar Republic but had also built up a press empire that published a number of successful mass-circulation papers, including the *Berliner Illustrierte Zeitung*. In exile in Paris he had then quickly expanded the work of the Komintern and attracted intellectuals such as Sperber, Arthur Koestler, and Bertrand de Jouvenel, who also became associated with the Institute for the Study of Fascism.[19]

Through their contact with Sperber, two more intellectuals, Raymond Aron and André Malraux—soon to play a prominent role in French cultural life—were also drawn into the force field of the Münzenberg circle. Among the many propaganda activities Münzenberg was involved in were the efforts to undermine Europe's colonial empires and to support anti-war movements, such as the League against War and Fascism and the

1935 "World Congress for the Defense of Culture" held in Paris.[20] German communists in exile were also behind an appeal that was signed in December 1936 by many German intellectuals who had found refuge in the French capital. However, as elsewhere, there were also a number of well-known writers, such as Karl O. Paetel, Alfred Döblin, Arkadi Gurland and Norbert Mühlen, whose Bund freie Presse und Literatur openly opposed Münzenberg's propaganda organization. By 1937, Münzenberg was himself becoming increasingly alienated from the Soviet Union. With Sperber and Koestler who had already abandoned their communist affiliation, he established *Die Zukunft*, a journal that espoused a democratic-humanist socialism.

Fearing for his life, Münzenberg refused to heed a call to return to Moscow and in March 1939 decided openly to turn his back on Stalin. He died under mysterious circumstances in the summer of 1940 when he tried to escape from Hitler's invasion of France. The Nazi occupation of northern France and the installation of the Vichy regime halted all open antifascist activism. The French left was either forced into exile or went underground, where the experience of persecution led to occasional cooperation and discussions between communists and socialists about the shaping of a new postwar French society.[21]

As France emerged from the Nazi occupation, commitment to communism had long ended for intellectuals like Sperber and Koestler. For others fellow traveling continued, as the world kept breaking apart and the victorious Soviet Union appeared to be not merely the only counterweight to American capitalism, but also the guarantor of a future egalitarian society that had remained the dream of many intellectuals in the sharply stratified class societies of Europe. Overall, the intellectual climate in post-Liberation France was tense and inward-looking. Dissociation from the Vichy regime and from collaboration had been swift. A strong desire for self-preservation and national unity had accelerated this process. As one scholar has put it rather bluntly, "this 'exercise in suppression of memory' succeeded in reestablishing the credentials of the nation, but at the cost of building into postwar life an element of bad faith."[22] Close to eleven thousand collaborators had been executed, mostly by summary justice. Where formal trials were held, the defendants, among them such prominent fascist writers as Robert Brasillach, were given short shrift.[23] In this atmosphere, the ideological spectrum shifted sharply to the left. An antifascist government coalition, consisting of the PCF, the Socialists, and the Gaullists, was forged and survived until 1947 when the PCF and Gaullists were replaced by a center-left coalition that mostly failed to tackle the manifold problems of postwar French society but was held together by its opposition to communism and Gaullism.

In the meantime the camp of noncommunist leftist intellectuals had split into those who, in light of the unfolding story of the Stalinist mass murders and Siberian camps, joined the ranks of the enemies of the Soviet Union and those who, while not directly entering the PCF, continued to uphold, in their writings and speeches, its utopia of a new, classless society. This latter position came to be represented most prominently by Jean-Paul Sartre and his entourage. Tony Judt has published a scathing indictment of them in which he spoke, in Bendaesque fashion, of the "treason of the [French] intellectuals."[24] Whether or not this verdict is overdrawn, Judt's analysis also contains an explanation of the peculiar position that the Sartre circle adopted after 1944. It is an explanation that takes account of the fact that the record of wartime resistance of Sartre and other leftist intellectuals was "imperfect" and that, like so many of their compatriots, they, too, felt a need to compensate for their earlier meanderings at a time when the world had gone topsy-turvy.[25]

Several other considerations, which had more to do with hopes for the future than an uneasy conscience about the past, have to be added to this picture. One of them was the conviction that fundamental change was necessary both for France and the rest of the capitalist world. Because to Sartre and his circle the working class appeared to be the only conceivable agent of change, they developed something like a mental block against condemning the Soviet Union and what they thought amounted to a betrayal of the French working class. To them Russia continued to be the state that had put an entire society on the revolutionary road toward the project of genuine equality among humans, a state whose population had, with enormous sacrifices, just defeated fascism, which they saw as an evil outgrowth of capitalism in crisis. Their idea that capitalism was responsible for an unending history of war, exploitation, and inhumanity was thus the flipside of their Russophilia. America, as the hegemonic power of the West, inevitably became the prime target of this anticapitalist critique. As in the interwar period, the deep-seated cultural reservations about the United States became reinforced by the condemnation of its political economy. While for some, such as André Siegfried, the United States equaled the world portrayed in Charlie Chaplin's movie *Modern Times* and existentialists nurtured their abhorrence of technological society, others rejected American capitalism as a system under which they did not wish to live, one that had to be revolutionized before any good could be expected to come of it.

119

The trouble was that Sartre's stance toward communist Russia, on the one hand, and capitalist America, on the other, was barely compatible with his existentialist philosophy that an entire generation of Europeans, faced with the destruction and disillusionment that the war had engendered, found so attractive. But his continued fellow traveling enabled him and his circle to nourish a strong anti-Americanism and to turn a blind eye to the ever more detailed and horrific news about Stalin's terror regime. Sartre went so far as to acknowledge the existence of the *gulagi*, but did not wish to be drawn—as he put it—into a counterrevolutionary posture. He even told Stephen Spender, the British writer and later coeditor of *Encounter*, that it would "be wrong to speak out against injustice in a Communist state" because "to do so would be to provide ammunition for use against a cause which is that of the proletariat and thus, in the long run, of justice itself."[26] For the same reason he also sympathized with blacks and other disenfranchised minorities in the United States. What was to be resisted tooth and nail was the capitalist Americanization of Europe.

Meanwhile, Maurice Merleau-Ponty, "the Sorbonne's most brilliant existentialist,"[27] defended the staging of show trials in Eastern Europe. However, it was precisely over the issue of not wanting to see what could no longer be overlooked that disagreements erupted and carefully nurtured positions began to come apart at the seams. As late as 1947, Sartre still counted Albert Camus among his friends. Camus was probably the most influential writer to come out of the French *résistance*, and—like so many others on the left—he advocated radical change.[28] Yet, as Camus's revulsion against Stalinism grew, so did his distance from Sartre. The friendship between the two men broke down completely in 1952, after Sartre's relationship with David Rousset had come to a similar rupture toward the end of 1949.[29] The latter, a former Nazi concentration camp inmate, had meanwhile emerged as one of the most outspoken critics of the Soviet Union and campaigned for an inquiry into the camp system. It is indicative of the polarization that had occurred in Paris by the early 1950s that even a former hard-liner like Merleau-Ponty now deserted the Soviet camp when he found it impossible to reconcile the invasion of South Korea with his earlier belief that communism, as an essentially peaceful system, would never resort to military aggression.[30]

If we move on to the British case, there had been some early fellow traveling in the 1930s, which soon turned into a growing aversion to, or deep suspicion of, Stalin's policies among intellectuals close to the Labour Party and the influential trade unions. The Nazi-Soviet Pact reduced support for British communism or its sympathizers virtually to nil. At the other end of the ideological spectrum, Oswald Mosley's Union of British Fascists did not succeed in attracting much popular support either. With France defeated in June 1940 and fears of a Nazi invasion of the British Isles rising, it did not take much, in light of the seemingly close cooperation between Hitler and Stalin, for the concept of totalitarianism to take root in England. One of the most indefatigable promoters of this idea was George Orwell, who had returned from the Spanish Civil War as a fierce opponent of Soviet communism. He confessed after World War II that "every line of serious work that I have written since 1936 has been written, directly or indirectly, *against* totalitarianism and *for* democratic Socialism as I understood it."[31] The last part of this statement is important not only for its rejection of Stalinism but also for his views of the United States. Partly under the influence of Burnham's *Managerial Revolution*, Orwell had come to believe that it was not just fascism and communism that were moving in a totalitarian direction, but capitalism as well, a conviction that chimed in well with the latent anti-Americanism that had spread in Britain before 1939 and that never quite subsided even during the period of close wartime cooperation between Washington and London.[32]

Of course, there was also relief and gratitude when the U.S. government first supported the British war effort against the Axis powers with loans and deliveries of military hardware and, after the Japanese attack on Pearl Harbor and Hitler's declaration of war on Washington, joined the Allied camp as a full member fighting on the European front. At the same time it was perhaps unavoidable that tensions arose as American soldiers arrived in Britain in larger numbers in advance of the Normandy invasion, and customs and behavior patterns clashed. Among the elites and many intellectuals there also existed a tendency to treat the "naive" and "culturally unrefined" Yankees with an inimitable condescension that British exposure to American "mass culture" during the interwar years had done nothing to moderate. Meanwhile, British officials and academics in wartime government service became increasingly resentful at the ways in which American negotiators, wedded to the notion that the Open Door and a multilateral global trading system would be reestablished after the war, were throwing their weight about in a thinly veiled effort to weaken the British Empire and the sterling bloc because they were deemed to be protectionist.[33]

So, while anti-Soviet feelings remained strong not just among conservatives but also on the Labour left, and although totalitarianism firmly established itself as a concept for interpreting the events of the 1930s and 1940s and for differentiating dictatorships from the democratic "Anglo-Saxons," many leftist politicians and intellectuals had high hopes that there was, indeed, a third way between American capitalism and Soviet communism. This third way would be one of democratic socialism as espoused by the British Labour movement. When Labour defeated the Conservatives in the 1945 general elections, the noncommunist left certainly had the majorities and political power to put Britain on a track of socialist reform. Only a small minority of intellectuals, among them Eric Hobsbawm and Edward P. Thompson, later to become renowned historians, stayed close to the small British Communist Party in an atmosphere that was far less polarized than that of France or Italy.[34]

When, in this brief survey of intellectual trends, we come to Italy, it is hardly surprising to discover that the ideological spectrum shifted decisively to the left once the more than twenty years of fascist rule and repression had come to an end. For many Italians identifying with communism and socialism, the two major antifascist resistance movements, was, of course, a convenient way of covering up whatever traces their former association with or sympathies for Mussolini had left behind. It was also an effective way of forgetting the past by looking into the future. However, there is also a good deal of evidence that fascism never struck deep roots in Italian society and that attitudes became increasingly unenthusiastic. When the Duce finally fell from power in 1943, his popular base had shriveled up. As to the intellectuals, the picture is similar to that of France in the same period. Those relatively few who firmly and actively committed themselves to fascism were utterly discredited, if they had not been summarily executed in the last years and months of the war in Italy. Others who had not gone into exile but had kept their distance from the Mussolini regime began to join the underground resistance movement. After this it was almost natural not just for many ordinary Italians but also for surviving intellectuals to profess communist or socialist sympathies.[35]

Soon the Italian CP (PCI) had become the largest communist party in Europe, ranking ahead of the French sister party in membership numbers. It was also less Stalinized than its French counterpart. After the early postwar government of the highly esteemed resistance leader Ferrucio Parri, which had advocated very radical reforms, had collapsed, there emerged, as in France, a tripartite power-sharing arrangement between the PCI, the Socialists, and Aristide de Gasperi's Christian Democrats in which the latter party increasingly gained the upper hand. Once the Cold War had begun in earnest and after the split of the Socialists into Pietro

Nenni's radical wing and Guiseppe Saragat's Social Democrats, de Gasperi succeeded in isolating the extreme left. The PCI was ousted from the coalition. In April 1948 national elections, the first under the new constitution, gave voters a choice between an electoral alliance of communists and Nenni socialists, on the one hand, and a Christian Democrat–led bloc under de Gasperi, on the other. The latter swept the board, gaining 60 percent of the seats in the lower chamber.

The shifts in early postwar Italian politics are significant in our context because they provided, as in France, the space for intellectual debate and criticism, both within the PCI and on the left. Some of these debates were concerned with problems of culture. The Italian labor movement—again like its French and other European counterparts—had been involved in the promotion of cultural activity and popular education since the turn of the century.[36] This tradition was revived after the fall of Mussolini and with it the cultural anti-Americanism rooted in the interwar period.[37] The PCI took the lead in trying to create an "authentic" culture opposed to the "trashy" literature of romance and escape or the dream world manufactured in Hollywood. In 1961 it reiterated its belief that the "masses" were claiming access to cultural life and knowledge without the restrictions of class, whereas it accused the dominant classes of trying to contain them. This tradition forms the background to the remarkable rise of Italian film in the postwar period, many of whose prominent directors were either active in the communist movement or remained fellow travelers. The themes they took up were very different from those scripted in California but also from the movies of "socialist realism" made in the Soviet bloc. Thus, films such as Federico Fellini's *8½* could not be shown in the Soviet Union, though it was awarded a first prize by the jury of the Moscow Film Festival. It became a considerable box office success in the West.

Nor did Italy's procommunist writers, such as Vasco Pratolini, conform to the canon of PCI cultural policy. His *Tale of Poor Lovers* belonged to a literature inspired by a humanist impulse and by an optimistic faith in a better future rather than by party doctrine. Occasionally party boss Palmiro Togliatti resorted to what has been called "political harassment"[38] when in 1947 he quarreled with Elio Vittorini, the editor of *Il Politechnico*. But overall the party's relationship with the intellectuals close to it remained quite relaxed and open.

Still, even in Italy there were limits to the intellectual alliances on the left, as the example of Ignazio Silone (pseudonym for Secondino Tranquilli) demonstrates. His career also mirrors well how totally torn European intellectual life had become in this period. A member of the PCI from its early stages, he seems to have worked with a multilevel value system that made it possible for him simultaneously to write reports for Mussolini's political police. He finally broke with communism in 1930 when he went into exile in Switzerland, moving in leftist antifascist circles in Zürich, but during the war also making contact with OSS. His star as a writer rose after the publication of his novel *Bread and Wine*, an account of poverty and exploitation in the Mezzogiorno region.[39] In the book, which belongs to an Italian literature of social criticism, the protagonist pleads for morality in practical life and a sense of social responsibility and solidarity. It was the convictions expressed in this book that furthered Silone's reputation as a prominent "intellectual of liberty."[40] After the war he tried to prevent a much-debated fusion of the PCI with the socialists. Like Carlo Levi in his 1947 novel *Christ Stopped at Eboli*, set in the Italian South, Silone wanted socioeconomic reform but now firmly rejected the recipes proffered by the PCI. Frequently at loggerheads with his former colleagues on the communist left, Silone, like Aron in France, hooked up with the Congress for Cultural Freedom.

The situation in Germany looks at first glance less complicated than that in France and Italy. But there are a number of similarities that deserve exploration. The fierce antagonism that had marked the relationship between the Social Democrats and the Communist Party (KPD) during the Weimar Republic, culminating in the KPD's total underestimation of Hitler and its struggle against the alleged "social fascists" in the Social Democratic Party, had in 1933 been replaced by sporadic underground cooperation against the Hitler regime in a number of industrial centers with strong working-class traditions.[41] After all, it was now clear that, contrary to Stalin's earlier expectations, Hitler had come to stay. Yet by 1935 the Gestapo had become efficient enough to crack most underground resistance cells, either executing their leaders or putting them into camps. We have also seen that there were some fellow travelers among those German refugee intellectuals who had escaped to the West. However, the news about Stalin's purges had turned even a Komintern activist like Willi Münzenberg against the Soviet Union.

Meanwhile those refugee intellectuals who had fled to Moscow either lay low, terrified that the secret police might earmark them for arrest and execution, or, after the Nazi attack on the Soviet Union in June 1941, were eagerly helping to prepare a communist takeover in Germany following the expected victory over Hitler. When this victory came and the Red Army had established its authority in the zone of occupation assigned to it by inter-Allied agreement at the Yalta Conference, several groups of handpicked communists in exile were flown to eastern Germany to re-build the KPD.[42] The hope was that this new party, led by Walter Ulbricht, would quickly gain a popular majority in early elections, defeating the Social Democrats, Christian Democrats, Liberals, and various splinter parties that the Soviets had licensed to operate. Some of Ulbricht's com-rades also had hopes that Stalin would permit them to develop a "German path toward socialism," rather than forcing them to copy the Soviet model of socioeconomic and political organization. Both expectations turned out to be an illusion, ending in a sharp U-turn of communist strat-egy. When the KPD failed to gain anything close to a majority, Ulbricht, in April 1946 and with Soviet help, engineered the forced merger of the KPD and the Social Democrats. And instead of allowing for national vari-ety in the radical changes that the KPD was determined to bring about, Ulbricht initiated the Stalinization of the Soviet zone of occupation.

These developments, which must be seen in the larger context of the incipient Cold War between the Soviet bloc and the Western Allies, accel-erated the division of Germany and Europe along the Iron Curtain and set back the weak communists in the Western zones of occupation. After some early postwar cooperation between KPD and Social Democrats at the grass-roots level in the so-called Antifa committees and some rallying of intellectuals in the Kulturbund zur demokratischen Erneuerung Deutschlands (Cultural League for the Democratic Renewal of Germany), the Western occupation authorities as well as the other licensed political parties began to steer a sharply anticommunist course. The SPD and the trade unions were in the forefront of this drive, and their stance contrib-uted to the fact that there was little fellow traveling among intellectuals in the Western zones of occupation of the kind that occurred on a much larger scale in France and Italy. The Kulturbund membership, which had been impressively large early on, declined. An important turning point in this respect was reached at the time of the league's Annual Meeting in May 1947, when the Social Democratic delegates tried unsuccessfully to steer the league into anti-Soviet waters.[43] These and other differences of opinion exploded six months later at the First All-German Writers' Con-gress in Berlin, and thenceforth the East-West divide became sharper also with regard to relations among German intellectuals.

This did not mean, however, that West German writers and artists were all pro-Western and pro-American. Rather there existed a strong convic-tion, shared by larger sections of the population, that Germany's role was to act as a bridge between the two warring superpowers. To be sure, a widespread hatred of the Soviet Union, exacerbated by the expulsion of millions of Germans from Eastern Europe, prevented popular pro-Soviet sympathies. But, with many Germans convinced that capitalism had failed in the 1930s and had helped to produce Hitler, there was a good deal of support for a "German way" between the Americans and the Russians. Some of these neutralists were outright nationalists who failed to appreciate that the defeat of 1945 had completely destroyed Germany's former power position in Europe; others were more internationalist and talked about creating a larger European federation next to the two superpowers.[44] As we have seen earlier in this chapter, similar conceptions of Europe's future role in the world also existed in Britain, France, Italy, and—though they have not been examined here—in the smaller countries of Europe.

Beyond the many intellectual reservations about America, which had deeper historical roots[45] and were partly cultural and partly power-political and economic, notions about Europe as a third force were also encouraged by fears of a military confrontation between the United States and the Soviet Union on European soil. The development of the nuclear bomb with its horrendous destructive potential greatly deepened these fears. They were also reinforced by a general yearning for peace that was felt, almost inevitably, in the wake of the physical, psychic, and moral devastation that World War II had wreaked

RALLYING THE ANTI-SOVIET LEFT

The communists saw an opportunity. Already in the 1930s they had proved to be skillful "engineers of the human soul"[46] and played on the pacifist sentiments that existed among intellectuals. Accordingly, they had organized major congresses devoted to the theme of peace in the face of fascist aggressiveness. After World War II, Stalin revived this strategy in the hope of supporting neutralist currents and of weakening American efforts to build a U.S.-led Atlantic alliance with Western Europe against the East. In occupied Germany, neutralism received support within an All-German framework to capture those intellectuals opposed to the sealing of the country's division. This was one of the key issues that led to the organization of the previously mentioned First All-German Writers' Congress in October 1947, to which a large number of intellectuals who were not communists were invited.[47]

All in all, it was quite a propaganda event. By the end of the second day some of the anticommunists present had come to believe that the attacks on the West had to be countered in some way and Melvin Lasky, the Berlin correspondent of *Partisan Review*, was asked to prepare a speech for the following day. This speech, which proclaimed the urgent "struggle for cultural freedom," resulted in loud protests and a walkout by the communists. After this there was a new sense among the German and other participants who had applauded Lasky's words that a turning point in the intellectual life of postwar Germany had been reached. The anticommunist left had found a voice and was no longer prepared to leave the intiative on major political issues to the East. The cold culture war against Soviet totalitarianism had begun in earnest, and Berlin became the symbol of the West's determination to resist Soviet power-political as well as cultural offensives.

The next writers' congress, which took place in Frankfurt in August 1948, two months after the beginning of Stalin's blockade of West Berlin, featured no East German authors with the exception of Hans Mayer. Very few speakers upheld the neutralist and anti-Western position of the previous years. After the Czech coup in the spring and the beginning of the Berlin blockade in the early summer, neutralism became increasingly untenable and the dream of a united Germany also faded into the distance. Deterrence and containment, as formulated by George F. Kennan and others, appeared to be a better guarantee of survival against Soviet aggressiveness.[48]

However, there is a context to Lasky's appearance and speech at the 1947 writers' congress that reaches beyond the question of neutralism. To begin with, as an American in Berlin, he was in touch with the U.S. Military Government authorities and the intelligence community that had made West Berlin a center of its information gathering and anti-Soviet activities. Of immediate importance here is the wider European-American context within which Lasky and his speech have to be set because he belonged to a network of leftist anticommunists in the United States. His work for the *Partisan Review* linked him to a circle of intellectuals, some of whom we have encountered earlier on in this chapter: Burnham, Hook, Bell, and Schlesinger. This circle had meanwhile been enlarged by Galbraith, James T. Farrell, and James Wechsler, the editor of the *New York Post*. Apart from *Partisan Review*, other noncommunist journals included the *New Leader* under the editorship of Sol Levitas, while Kristol had taken charge of *Commentary*, which provided yet another forum in which international politics was discussed in terms of the confrontation between totalitarianism and the "free world." The domestic agenda of these people was reformist, and they had links with the American labor movement.

If Burnham and Hook were the anticommunist hard-liners in this circle, their counterparts in Europe were Arthur Koestler and Orwell, whose anti-Stalinist novels had won them a wide and admiring readership.[49] In 1947 Koestler became the British correspondent of *Partisan Review* and subsequently traveled to America. After meeting Hook and Burnham, the fierce anticommunism that they discovered they shared increasingly set them apart from a slightly younger generation of Americans who saw both domestic and international politics through less dogmatic lenses. As confirmed New Dealers they had more in common with up-and-coming centrist Labour politicians, such as Denis Healey, Anthony Crosland, and Richard Crossman, and intellectuals such as Bertrand Russell, Malcolm Muggeridge, and Stephen Spender, many of whom had taken a similar road from a 1930s antifascist leftist radicalism to a postwar "Lib-Lab" reformism. Another influential member in the circle was the Oxford philosopher Isaiah Berlin, a friend of Schlesinger, and the colorful composer Nicolas Nabokov. Berlin was very much a "New Deal liberal"[50] in that he, an émigré from Russia, defended the freedoms of the capitalist West, while always reminding his readers and listeners that liberty and a degree of social equality were inseparable.

Across the English Channel in Paris, Raymond Aron became the main contact. In World War II he had edited the Gaullist journal *La France libre* in his London exile and he continued to maintain his ambivalent and more typically French intellectual feelings toward the American model of culture.[51] He returned to Paris soon after the liberation to help rebuild the country and to renew his friendship with Sartre. The two men had met at the Ecole normale supérieur in the 1930s, and after World War II it seemed natural for Aron to join the editorial board of Sartre's influential *Temps modernes*.[52] But then, as the Cold War sharpened, the friendship fell apart. While Sartre remained a fellow traveler, Aron began to view world politics through the lens of the totalitarianism paradigm.

Meanwhile in Italy, Silone and Chiaromonte, Macdonald's old friend, became the postwar pointmen of an emerging international network of left-wing anti-Stalinists who, despite their reservations about American "masscult," were nevertheless Atlanticists. In the Western zones of occupation, Eugen Kogon, concentration camp survivor and editor of the *Frankfurter Hefte*, acted as a liaison to the left-Catholic wing of the Christian Democrats. Carlo Schmid, Francophile and philosopher-turned-politician, assumed a similar role with respect to the reformists in the SPD. Compared with the French and in light of the moral crisis that Nazism had inflicted on Germany, West German intellectuals were certainly more open toward cultural and ideological imports from the United States, but on closer inspection they, too, were by no means enthusiastic. And when Elvis Presley and Bill Haley arrived on the scene to cause youth riots, they were absolutely dismayed.[53]

While the nuances of European perceptions of America constantly have to be borne in mind, by the spring of 1949 the stage had been set, both in terms of personal contacts and of common ideas, in favor of a plan to copy, in form though not in content, what the Soviet Union had done so well in previous years: holding a major congress of intellectuals with the avowed purpose of openly combatting both communists and fellow travelers. In March of that year the communists had called yet another meeting, which attracted such famous intellectuals as the physicist Albert Einstein, the conductor Leonard Bernstein, the writers Paul Robeson and Lillian Hellman, the composer Aaron Copeland, and the actor Charlie Chaplin. The fact that it was being held in New York had added insult to injury for activists like Hook, but it also gave him and his colleagues the opportunity to stage a show of force. Apart from Hook and Macdonald, the writer Mary McCarthy and Nabokov turned up to ask the Soviet representatives uncomfortable questions about Stalinist repression.

Indefatigable as ever, the Soviets sponsored a second peace conference in Paris a month later, attended by such luminaries as Frédéric Joliot-Curie, Pietro Nenni, and Pablo Picasso. On this occasion, the intellectual opposition went beyond interventions by individuals during the congress's main session. In New York, a group calling itself "Americans for Intellectual Freedom" organized a counterdemonstration at Freedom House with anti-Stalinist speeches by Hook and Nabokov. Judging from the size of the audience, the organizers thought the rally was a considerable success, causing Macdonald to feel that the anticommunist left had finally succeeded in seizing the initiative.

If the New York terrain was favorable for a cultural offensive, the situation was considerably more complex and difficult in Europe—and particularly in France, where fellow traveling and anti-Americanism continued unabated. This is what Rousset found when he organized an "International Day of Resistance to Dictatorship and War" as a counterpoint to the communist-sponsored Paris peace meeting. Although he was able to persuade a galaxy of well-known authors—Hook, Silone, Borkenau, Levi, Farrell—to attend, Sartre, Merleau-Ponty, and Richard Wright refused to come because they believed that the meeting would be too blatantly anticommunist. The irony was that Rousset, in an attempt to steer a middle course, had excluded hard-liners such as Burnham and Koestler for the same reason. Not surprisingly a miffed Hook later criticized the speeches made at the Rousset meeting as so tame as to remind him of "the soap-boxers in Madison Square" in the 1920s.[54]

After this flop, it was clear that a major event had to be planned in Europe. As we shall see later, it was not just the network of American and European intellectuals who were convinced of this necessity; the same was true of the U.S. government.[55] According to Peter Coleman, the plan for a counterconference was hatched in Frankfurt in August 1949 at a meeting between Borkenau, Ruth Fischer, and Lasky.[56] To them, Berlin, with its symbolic significance since the blockade, was the best venue. There was to be the usual format of sessions to debate major issues of the time in smaller circles. The high point was to be a mass rally and the establishment of an "International Committee for Cultural Freedom," with Lasky as the key organizer in Berlin, his elective home. It was apparently also Lasky who subsequently persuaded Ernst Reuter, the mayor of West Berlin, Edwin Redslob, and Otto Suhr to join a preparatory committee—three men who, thanks to their position in Berlin's political and intellectual life and with the encouragement of the American occupation authorities, were able to provide administrative backup. Financial support came not only from the city but also from the American Federation of Labor and HICOG under McCloy's and Stone's stewardship.[57] Some of the ideas that went into the draft program were furnished by Koestler, Burnham, and Hook, thus reinforcing the German-American connection of this particular enterprise.

The meeting took place in the "front-line city" of the Cold War in June 1950. There were five honorary presidents, all of them famous philosophers: Benedetto Croce, John Dewey, Karl Jaspers, Jacques Maritain, and Bertrand Russell. Their basic positions on the great questions of their subject may not have been easy to reconcile, and if they had been put around the same table for a panel discussion, a particularly wide gap would no doubt have emerged between the "Anglo-Saxons" (Dewey, Russell) and the Continental Europeans (Croce, Maritain); but their political credentials certainly fit the larger political context. Papering over these gaps, many stirring speeches were delivered and participants left with a firm feeling that a powerful phalanx not only against Stalinism but also against neutralism and fellow traveling had been created. Overall an estimated ten thousand to fifteen thousand people attended the concluding rally.

The speeches made on themes that were by now typical of the anticommunist left have been recounted by several scholars and therefore need not be repeated here.[58] It is the sociological and organizational conse-

quences of the Berlin congress that are more important here, also in light
of the role of HICOG and later the Ford Foundation in them. As regards
the national background of the participants, the Germans and Americans
constituted the largest contingents. From among them merely those of the
inner circle shall be listed—people whose names that have either already
come up in earlier chapters or who will be playing an important role later
on. The other point to bear in mind about this list is that these are also
the people who would form the core of the CCF. Not all of them became
or remained friends or close colleagues; but they all were part of a clearly
identifiable network of intellectuals that Shepard Stone would rely on
when developing his programs:

1. American: Brown, Burnham, Cohen, Dewey, Emmet, Farrell,
Friedrich, Hook, Levitas, Muehlen, Nabokov, Franz Neumann, Schlesinger.
2. German: Birkenfeld, Borkenau, Buber-Neumann, Kogon, Korn,
Pechel, Plievier, Schmid, Sternberger, Alfred Weber, (Jaspers).[59]
3. French: Altmann, (Aron), Brunschwig, Freynay, Labin, Mauriac,
Philip, Rousset.
4. British: Ayer, Haffner, Koestler, Löwenthal, de Mendelssohn,
Trevor-Roper, Russell.
5. Italian: Silone, Spinelli, (Croce).
6. Swiss: Bondy, Hofer, Lüthy, Röpke, de Rougemont.

If the Berlin congress had been a success and the "Freedom Manifesto,"
drafted by Sperber and Koestler, reflected the ideas that most of the participants stood for, it nevertheless took considerable time for a permanent
organization to emerge from the meeting.[60] It was not just that the various
individuals who were prepared to invest their time and energies in the task
of building an infrastructure tried to push the emergent CCF in different
programmatic directions. There were also the related disagreements over
where the proposed international secretariat should be headquartered.
Nor did it help the early launching of a permanent association that the
question of funding still had to be clarified.

Lasky, who had been the most active coordinator of the Berlin meeting,
decided against taking the job of secretary-general. Still, eventually an
executive committee consisting of Brown (alternate: Haakon Lie), Koestler (alternate: Aron), Kogon (alternate: Schmid), de Rougemont (no alternate), Rousset (alternate: Altman), Silone (alternate: Chiaromonte), and
Spender (alternate: T. R. Fryvel) began its work. Philip, Muggeridge,
Lasky, Hook, and Sperber joined the committee "from time to time with-

out standing on formalities."[61] They were supported by a Paris-based secretariat and a larger international committee as well as a number of national committees, all of which, with the exception of the American Committee for Cultural Freedom (ACCF), sprang up after the summer of 1950.

This American committee was soon rocked by a major internal conflict and, given its role at the Berlin congress and in subsequent organizing efforts throughout Europe, this conflict was then carried into the embryonic European outfit in Paris. The issue in the ACCF was whether to pursue a hard-line anticommunism. A number of its leading members regarded the threat of communism both at home and abroad as so grave that they were even prepared to condone the activities of Senator McCarthy and his supporters inside and outside the U.S. government. Their critics, by contrast, held McCarthyism to be indefensible, both as a matter of the principles enshrined in the American Constitution and because some of them feared they might themselves become targets of the widening anticommunist witch-hunt. Worse, while the hard-liners in the American Committee demanded an expansion of their crusade to Europe, their opponents argued that this was the best way to destroy whatever consensus had been forged with European intellectuals at Berlin; it would not only be grist to the mills of neutralists and fellow travelers in their pursuit of anti-Americanism but would also alienate sympathetic European anticommunists intellectuals who would never wish to be associated with anything smacking of McCarthyism.[62] After all, as we have seen, very few of them were positively enthusiastic about the American "model" even without McCarthy's crusade.

THE GROWTH OF THE CCF EMPIRE

Fortunately, as the struggle over McCarthy's practices continued in Washington, the balance of forces slowly began to tilt in favor of those who wanted to stop the senator and his movement. This broader development also helped the moderates in the ACCF to gain the upper hand. Their gradual victory in turn eased the pressure in Europe, where influential members of the executive committee and the international committee, above all the key people in the Secretariat in Paris, had been working in the same direction. Acutely aware of the general intellectual climate in Europe, they had become convinced that adopting a hard line would only serve to reinforce traditional reservations about the United States and a prevailing cultural anti-Americanism.

This was certainly the view of Michael Josselson, the man who from 1951 until his resignation in 1967 became the most influential permanent official of the Congress for Cultural Freedom.[63] He put the association and its administration on a more solid financial footing and defined the general direction of its programs. Josselson had apparently been suggested as a good choice by Nabokov, who became the first CCF general secretary and then joined him in curbing the influence of the hard-liners. Their first victim was Koestler and he was easy prey.[64] The writer, whose books had meanwhile become best sellers, initially wielded considerable influence in the early CCF, using his home at Fontaine-le-Pont near Paris as his base. Convinced that France would fall into communist hands unless there was vigorous resistance and counterpropaganda, Koestler wanted the CCF to prepare its next major congress for the summer of 1951 in Paris, the stronghold not only of the PCF and the Confédération Générale du Travail (CGT) trade union, but also of the Sartrians. In his conception this was to be a highly political event with fiery anticommunist speeches. Yet Nabokov, though initially ideologically close to Koestler, scuttled the idea, arguing that there was too little time to prepare a major conference.

In view of the CCF's difficulties in the fall and winter of 1950 to get its act together, this excuse was not entirely convenient. The point that a poorly prepared congress that became a flop would be a disaster for the CCF movement as a whole was no doubt a serious one. Koestler disagreed and walked out in disgust. Nabokov breathed a sigh of relief, for in cooperation with Josselson he had begun to develop an approach to the congress idea that was quite different from that of the remaining hard-liners. So, instead of "Koestlerizing" the CCF's activities and turning it into a ideological combat unit, the Secretariat began to "intellectualize" and "culturalize" them. The cultural initiatives of international communism were to be countered not at the level of crude political propaganda of the kind the ACCF had been calling for; instead, Nabokov and Josselson developed a "high-cultural" program that proved very successful.[65]

The underlying idea was to challenge the Soviet bloc at a level on which it was deemed to be most vulnerable—that of the arts, the sciences, and the humanities. It was a program that did not aim directly for the hearts and minds of average Europeans, whom the hard-liners had been hoping to speak to and to win over with their populist McCarthy-style sloganeering. Rather they targeted the intellectual elites, calculating that swaying them would generate multiple effects and their more sophisticated anti-communism and pro-Americanism would complement other efforts and percolate down to the rest of society.

This approach, and the elitist notions of culture that we have already encountered, must be related to the debates on the role of the "masses" that agitated intellectuals on both sides of the Atlantic in the 1950s.[66] The design of the first CCF event after the Berlin meeting, which was finally held in Paris in 1952 and for which the Secretariat took responsibility, fits neatly into this picture. In marked contrast to the Berlin program and to Koestler's 1951 plan, this congress was devoted to the significance of modernism in the arts. Starting from the fact that modern art had been vilified as "degenerate" by Nazi totalitarianism and was now once more under attack from Stalin's cultural theorists who praised the superiority of "socialist realism," the theme of modern art was thought to provide a good platform in the cold culture war against the Soviet bloc. It offered an opportunity not only to present high-quality concerts, operas, and ballets with leading artists and to show masterpieces of the visual arts, but also to organize panel discussions and lectures that commented on these performances and exhibitions and contrasted them, no doubt favorably, with the products and aesthetic concerns of "socialist realism."

Nabokov's career and artistic tastes made him the ideal person to implement this program.[67] But whatever his personal interests in the subject, more important for an understanding of this enterprise is the larger context. This context became all too clear when Nabokov visited New York in the fall of 1951 to explain his plan to the ACCF. Predictably he came under heavy fire from the hard-liners, such as Hook and Levitas, who wanted to know how the proposed themes could possibly be thought to contribute to the fighting of communism. Nabokov stood his ground and, apart from the moderates, convinced at least one influential hard-liner: James Burnham.

As far as Nabokov and Josselson were concerned, however, there was another advantage in putting "high" culture and modern art at the center of the Paris congress. While the influence of the radical anticommunists was waning, the corresponding strengthening of the moderate Americans fostered the rise of Josselson, who, based in Europe, was acutely aware of the anti-Americanism of many European intellectuals. The Paris congress presented an ideal platform for including modern American works and thus countering the widespread prejudice that America was capable only of producing cheap and trashy "mass culture." Indeed, the CCF Secretariat even harbored the hope that the display and performance of modern

American art would persuade European intellectuals to concede that much of American culture had become part of the avant-garde. The Paris congress was therefore not just a challenge to communist art and its aesthetic theories but also to the disdain in which the West Europeans tended to hold American culture. The unspoken claim was one of a common Atlantic tradition and movement in modern art, of which American composers, writers, and painters were an integral and indeed leading part.

Nabokov's festival took place as planned in May 1952, and once more the cultural competition between East and West was very much in evidence: it coincided with an exhibition of Mexican art that, with communist backing, was staged at the Paris Museum of Modern Art. The "Battle of the Festivals" was now truly in full swing.[68] After the CCF executive committee had resolved to encourage the publication of critical reviews of the Mexican venture in order to minimize its significance, the real challenge was to get the press to highlight the accomplishments of European and North American art. Accordingly, "Paris had its first productions of Alban Berg's *Wozzek* (by the Vienna Opera), of Benjamin Britten's *Billy Budd* (by Covent Garden), of Getrude Stein and Vergil Thomson's *Four Saints in Three Acts*, . . . and of Arnold Schoenberg's *Die Erwartung*. Igor Stravinsky conducted *Oedipus Rex*, for which Jean Cocteau designed the set. The New York City Ballet was brought over for the occasion, as were William Faulkner, Katherine Anne Porter, and Allen Tate for literary debates. There was an exhibition of 150 modern paintings and sculptures," which gave due space to French masterpieces but also many American ones. And in case anyone missed the ideological point, Nabokov also had works by Sergei Prokofiev and Dimitri Shostakovich performed (which were banned in the Soviet Union) and arranged "church services for the victims of totalitarian oppression."[69]

If Richard Kuisel is correct, many Parisians "were impressed by the display of the West's artistic brilliance."[70] But significantly enough most of the city's prominent intellectuals kept their distance and André Malraux was the only Frenchman with an international reputation to become an active participant. The press reflected the widespread reservations that the Europans had toward American culture. Conservative papers were happy to write approvingly about the exhibition's main purpose—to establish a positive contrast to "socialist realism." But at the same time they could not resist drawing attention to the fact that the Boston Symphony's performance in Paris was conducted by Charles Munch, a Frenchman.

Worse criticisms appeared in the left-wing press. The communist *L'Humanité* spoke of the CCF's attempt to recruit Europe's intellectuals for a "cultural army," and the leftist *Combat* flatly dubbed the event "Nato's Festival," and then discussed the provincialism of a "nation that lynched blacks and hounded anyone accused of 'un-American' activities." All this led Janet Flanner, writing in the *New Yorker*, to judge the whole affair "an extremely popular fiasco."[71] Europe in general and France in particular were certainly unfriendly territory, and it is not surprising that the big American foundations and the CIA should see the need to support the cultural efforts of the CCF.

Showing a stiff upper lip, Nabokov later wrote to Hook that the event had been "a psychological success in the complex and depressingly morbid intellectual climate of France." But he added somewhat dejectedly: "Of course, in any other country we would have had both more sympathy and more support. We would also have had a finer press reaction." Referring back to Koestler's original plan, he thought that what had been done "was the only kind of action we could have undertaken here in Paris which would have established the Congress [for Cultural Freedom] in the minds of the European intellectuals as a positive, and not only as a political organization." As a result, the CCF was now "not only well-known, but is respected by many intellectuals who don't agree with us." Even more encouraging, "many other intellectuals who were afraid of us before have come to us now as friends and colleagues." Nabokov's defensiveness toward Hook was partly a response to the internal criticism that his conference and festival idea had encountered from the start. Koestler was just waiting to call the event "an effete gathering."[72]

While the influence of the hard-liners was declining, however, European anti-Americanism was, if anything, rising in 1952–53. It was no coincidence that *Combat* in its critique of the Paris festival had pointed to American racism and McCarthyism as sources of this anti-Americanism. Hannah Arendt, who, her basic views on totalitarianism notwithstanding, was too much of a liberal at heart to be a friend of Hook and his followers in the ACCF, wrote to Karl Jaspers in May 1953 that the dangers of the Red Scare were very clear. Although she did not wish to join in Europe's anti-Americanism, she was reminded of the intellectual and academic situation in Germany in the 1930s and saw hope only if McCarthy did not become U.S. president in 1956. Jaspers, himself uneasy about his commitment to the German branch of the CCF as one of its honorary presidents, replied that, because of the hard-liners around Koestler, the Paris CCF was in essence an anti-Soviet organization rather than one that combatted all forms of totalitarianism, and here the German philosopher evidently included the McCarthy movement.[73]

As noted earlier, McCarthy's campaigns impacted disastrously on European opinion, and the CCF Secretariat in Paris found itself right in the middle of these sentiments. Josselson tried hard to distance the international organization, which at this stage was primarily a European operation, from the ACCF in New York and attempted to make it more than a purely cultural association that organized art exhibitions and philharmonic concerts. Nabokov, it is true, convened two more Paris-style events: the first one, significantly, in Rome, the other city with impressive numbers of communists and fellow travelers and in line with a CCF steering committee recommendation that France and Italy be given "first priority"; the second one in Tokyo in 1961,[74] indicating that Josselson's main concerns had begun to move away from Europe. That the International Secretariat was now actively trying to steer the CCF toward an independent political line is reflected in the fact that its managers were prepared to take a stand against McCarthyism and other illiberal developments in the United States. To Josselson this was both a matter of his convictions and of the need to bolster the CCF's standing with European intellectuals.

The CCF repeatedly published statements on political issues. Thus, Denis de Rougemont, on behalf of the CCF's executive committee, sent a telegram to President Eisenhower urging him to pardon Julius and Ethel Rosenberg.[75] Paris also continued its ties with the physicist Robert Oppenheimer after he became the target of an investigation by the House Un-American Activities Committee. Finally, and in contrast to the thrust of Nabokov's 1952 festival, the CCF began to define culture and cultural freedom increasingly broadly. If the Western arts and humanities were to be pitched against the rigidities of Soviet-style "socialist realism" and strict control of artistic creativity, the scientists and social scientists were, in Josselson's view and that of his advisors in the CCF, facing a parallel confrontation with those Soviet researchers who espoused the principles of Lysenkoism as a way of subjecting science to state planning and the alleged needs of society. Most prominent among them was Michael Polanyi, a Hungarian-born nuclear physicist with wide-ranging interests in the social sciences and in philosophy, who, as a refugee from Hitler's Germany, had obtained a professorship at Manchester University. In publications and lectures he made himself a major advocate of a liberal approach to the pursuit of scientific research and vigorously opposed the pronouncements of the Soviet Academy of Sciences.[76]

As to social science research, Polanyi insisted, the choice was between the acceptance of a diversity of methods, on the one hand, and the supposedly iron laws and requirements of "scientific Marxism." The same was true of the natural sciences, which were therefore also brought into the East-West culture wars. However, the sciences also represented a counterweight to the anti-Americanism of Europe's noncommunist intellectuals and scholars. After all, when it came to these disciplines, it was much more difficult for the West Europeans to sit on a high cultural horse. American science research institutes and university science departments were unquestionably among the best.

It is against the background of these developments and a very broad definition of culture that the Paris Secretariat, with funding from the Rockefeller and Fairfield foundations,[77] began to plan the Hamburg Congress under the title of "Science and Freedom." The meeting brought together some 110 scientists, mainly from Western Europe and North America. Though they were treated to Gounod's "Little Symphony for Winds" during the opening ceremony and to some Mozart at the end, for the rest of the time participants debated issues relating to the main theme of the conference, such as "science and the State," "science and its methods," "the organization of science," "science in chains," and "the scholar and the citizen." It was thanks to Polanyi's broad academic interests beyond pure scientific research and attempts to bridge the "two cultures" that scientists mingled with a number of eminent social scientists and philosophers, among them Hook, Shils, Aron, Bruno Snell, Hellmuth Plessner, and Theodor Litt. But again, at Hamburg it was less the hard-liners from the ACCF than the orientation of the people behind the influential *Bulletin of Atomic Scientists*, to which Polanyi was connected, that defined the American input. Lysenkoism appeared badly battered and Josselson was delighted with the overall success of the meeting.[78]

The tensions in the ACCF between the two wings in the American scholarly community became very visible when the *Bulletin of Atomic Scientists* published an article by Aron criticizing new McCarthyite visa restrictions for entry to the United States. Meanwhile the ACCF agitated for keeping all foreign communists and ex-communists out of the country. Because of their former political commitments in the 1930s, quite a few European intellectuals were thus barred from visiting the United States. Tensions also surfaced in Hamburg when James Franck, the renowned German-born physicist, after an attack on Soviet science policy also condemned Washington's assault on the freedom of research and opinion. What seems to have been foremost on his mind when he made these remarks were the political harrassment and discriminations to which his friend Robert Oppenheimer was exposed.

138

After the second art festival that Nabokov organized in Rome in 1954, the CCF supported one further major international meeting, the 1955 Milan congress devoted to "The Future of Freedom." That event, which united some 140 intellectuals, is remarkable for several reasons.[79] In terms of its composition it reflected the final victory of the liberals over the hard-liners in the United States and the addition of a group of prominent members on the European side with a similar world view. Josselson could now rely on the support of a younger generation wedded to reformism at home, welfare state economics, and, in light of the nuclear stalemate that had meanwhile arisen between the superpowers, a softer line toward the Soviet Union. The funding base was also secure.[80] The names of some members of this group have appeared earlier on in this study—Bell and Galbraith, for example. The group had various links with the democratic left and the American labor movement. In Europe many of the new generation were "new" Social Democrats linked to the British Labour Party, to the pro-European left in France and Italy, or to those factions in the West German Deutscher Gewerkschaftsbund and SPD which paved the way for the Godesberg Program of 1959. There was also a stronger representation from India (seven members), Japan (three), the Middle East (five), Latin America (seven), and Africa (two).

Although a good many of the panels dealt with traditional Cold War themes related to the confrontation between the "totalitarian" East and the "free" West, a considerable portion of the proceedings was devoted to a critical discussion of mass society in the age of the mass media, particularly in its American variety. Bell's presentation focused on the ambiguities of mass society, but he also highlighted the complexities of life in America, as he would present them in his *The End of Ideology*, discussed in chapter 4.[81]

Such openness and lack of dogmatism was related to another feature of the Milan congress, namely, the growing sense inside and outside the CCF that communism was losing the struggle for the minds of Europe's intellectuals. There were, to be sure, still dangers, emanating from the Soviet bloc that threatened "the future of freedom." But with the ferment that led to the uprisings in Poland and Hungary in 1956, Western European anti-Americanism loomed larger, excerbated by Washington's stand during the Suez crisis when Britain and France were bluntly told to stop their traditional colonialist policies. As the Cold War along the Iron Curtain became less tense and the French and British were bullied into their full retreat from colonialism, competition increased between East and

West for the hearts and minds of the people in the Third World. Marxism remained attractive to African, Asian, and Latin American intellectuals, and they were supported by noncommunist nationalists who worked for the liberation of the colonial world from Western imperialism. If they were not outright fellow travelers, they often took a neutralist stance, a good expression of which can be found in the 1955 Bandung Declaration.

For Josselson and the Paris Secretariat there was hence yet another job to be done, and the Third World representatives at the Milan meeting, at which a full day was devoted to problems of nationalism and colonialism, subsequently spearheaded the creation of a network similar to the one that had meanwhile been built in the Atlantic region. While for the moment Europe remained the center of the CCF's cultural activities, by the 1960s the balance had begun to shift noticeably in favor of the non-European world.[82]

Finally, there is yet another aspect of the CCF's culture wars in Europe during the 1950s: its sponsorship of a number of intellectual periodicals in France, Italy, Britain, Germany, Austria, and Spain.[83] If the CCF's international congresses represented the annual fanfares of its operations, the Secretariat developed many other activities designed to create meeting grounds for academics and intellectuals, such as exchanges, occasional lectures and workshops, and, above all, printed materials and journals. In 1951 France saw the publication of the first issues of *Preuves*, a review edited by François Bondy.[84] Swiss-born and a native German speaker, Bondy in time turned the journal into a respected monthly that was read not only in France but also in francophone Africa and those parts of Central and Eastern Europe where French cultural influence had traditionally been strong. *Preuves*, as Peter Coleman has written, injected a "measured liberal anti-Communist perspective into French debates, opposing the neutralism of *l'Observateur*, the pacifism of *Esprit* and the 'coexistentialism' " of Sartre's journal.[85]

Its Italian equivalent, *Tempo Presente*, was born in 1954 in response to Alberto Moravia's *Nuovi Argumenti*, which was in turn inspired by Sartre's *Temps modernes*.[86] *Tempo Presente* was edited by Chiaromonte, an antifascist from the start who, born in 1905, had been an anarchopacifist during the Spanish Civil War. He fled to the United States via North Africa after the Nazi invasion of France, and there he became one of Dwight Macdonald's mentors. After 1945 Albert Camus persuaded him to move to Paris, whence he returned to Rome and, with his friend Silone, finally succeeded in launching *Tempo Presente* in 1956. The journal was characterized by its liberalism, but also its openness to other views, be they left-Catholic reformers, renegade Italian communists, Russian dissidents such as Boris Pasternak or Andrei Sinyavsky, or American radicals such as Mary McCarthy or Irving Howe. It quickly earned the respect of a larger readership and became—as the editors put it—"a source of great satisfaction to us."[87]

Although published in Paris since 1953, *Cuadernos* appealed to the Spanish-speaking world on both sides of the Atlantic.[88] Its editor, Julian Gorkin (his birth name was more Spanish: Gomez), had been the founder of the Communist Party in Valencia in 1921, subsequently worked as a Komintern official, and ended up supporting the Trotskyists in the Spanish Civil War. During World War II he fled to Mexico but returned to Europe as a leftist advocate of European unity. In 1953 the CCF encouraged the founding of two other journals, *Forum*, edited in Austria by Friedrich Torberg, a Jewish refugee from Hitler who had fought with the Czech Legion in France in 1940 before reaching the United States via Spain and Portugal after the defeat of France.[89] The journal was supposed to act not merely as a counterweight to Austria's communist *Tagebuch* and the Catholic *Wort und Wahrheit* but also as a bridge to dissident German-speaking intellectuals in Hungary. The second periodical was *Encounter*, which quickly established itself as an influential English-language mouthpiece of Britain's "Lib-Lab" antitotalitiarian and pro-American reformists. The indefatigable Melvin Lasky later became its editor.

The intellectual publications that have been mentioned so far were characterized by an ideological position that rejected all forms of extremism, whether of the right or left. Their anticommunism was not dogmatic, but favored dialogue, also with East European academics and intellectuals, and a de-escalation of the Soviet-American arms race. On the domestic front they promoted pragmatic public management of an active social and economic policy. Each journal had its own national flavor, but also propounded an explicit internationalism or, to be more precise, Atlanticism, which invariably included a critical defense of the United States and its culture. In other words, although many contributors were native speakers and each journal had its own ideological signature, they also drew on foreign authors, many of whom belonged to the CCF network. These foreigners were either commissioned to write on their own specialty or had articles that they had published elsewhere in the CCF "family" translated.[90] It is certainly striking how certain well-known intellectuals recycled their ideas from one journal to another.

Whatever their differences of opinion, the CCF journals were united not only in their vision of an antitotalitarian society, but also in their pro-Americanism. It was this latter stance that repeatedly got them into difficulties. Thus *Cuadernos* found itself in deep trouble in 1953 when anti-Americanism reached a peak in Latin America in the face of the U.S. intervention in Guatemala. *Preuves* and the other periodicals struggled with the traditional cultural anti-Americanism in Europe and with the allegation of being the mouthpiece of Washington.

Der Monat, the oldest of the postwar cultural monthlies, served as a model for the others. *Der Monat* grew directly out of the American experience at the 1947 First All-German Writers' Congress in Berlin. Whether the original idea was Lasky's or Clay's, the crucial point is that the American occupation authorities began to fund the new publication. Directed at intellectuals, it was of course also designed to serve the "reorientation" effort that the Americans had started in order to turn the emergent West German state into a stable parliamentary democracy.[91] It is also significant that instead of the sober and neutral title, Lasky and his German coeditor Hellmuth Jaesrich briefly contemplated "Das amerikanische Jahrhundert," in apparent direct reference to Henry Luce's widely read article in *Life* in 1941.[92] Jaesrich—who had done his Ph.D. with Ernst Robert Curtius, a well-known scholar of French literature, and after 1945 had been on the editorial staff of Alfred Kantorowicz's cultural journal *Sie*—tried to keep German concerns in the foreground, but there were also, in the late 1940s, the larger issues of the Cold War and the American image in Western Europe.

For all these considerations, the U.S. occupation authorities and, after the founding of the Federal Republic in 1949, the High Commission took a close interest in the shaping of *Der Monat*.[93] Funding questions were inevitably a major concern. As HICOG's Public Affairs director, Shepard Stone had dealt with the editors of *Der Monat* and had also funded it. Following his move to the Ford Foundation, Lasky and Jaesrich came to him again when the High Commission decided to divest itself of this journal. Philanthropy, academy, and diplomacy joined forces in the intellectual culture wars of the 1950s and 1960s.

Internationalizing the Ford Foundation

WHEN Stone arrived back in New York from West Germany in 1952 in the wake of McCloy, the Ford Foundation was still coping with the consequences of its recent reorganization and growth

THE BIGGEST PHILANTHROPIC ORGANIZATION IN THE WORLD

Originally set up by Henry Ford in 1936, it was only after his death in April 1947 that the foundation's assets suddenly grew by over three million shares of Class A nonvoting common stock in the Ford Motor Company, valued at $417 million. Thanks to a booming stock market and "with business and earnings in the automobile industry at record levels," these assets reached $492 million by 31 December 1950. After making allowances for grants made prior to that date, "the liquid assets of the Foundation were $68,791,847." Although these figures were subject to the vagaries of the stock market and the state of the world economy, they did make the Ford Foundation the biggest philanthropic organization in the world. As Henry Ford II, the chairman of the board of trustees, put it, the years 1949–50 marked "a turning point in the affairs of The Ford Foundation." If up to 1948 its "modest income" had been spent on "contributions largely focused on the Detroit area and its institutions," it had now become possible to go for national projects and even to appear on the international stage.[1]

In light of these favorable developments, the board of trustees decided in the fall of 1948 to commission "a comprehensive study . . . by competent, independent people to serve as a guide to how and in what areas the larger funds of the Foundation could best be employed in the public interest." This committee, chaired by Rowan Gaither, a lawyer who was then chairman of the Rand Corporation, "agreed at the outset that it should review the needs of mankind in the broadest possible perspective, free from the limitations of special professional interests."[2] The Gaither Report finally before them in early 1950, the trustees, at their September meeting, decided on new foci in the foundation's work and two months later chose Paul G. Hoffman as president.

143

The selection of Hoffman, who took up his position on 1 January 1951, confirmed the larger and more international role that the Gaither Report had envisaged for the foundation. The new man had been president of the Studebaker Corporation before he was sent to Europe to coordinate the implementation of the Marshall Plan, adopted by the U.S. Congress in 1948.[3] In this capacity he had gained a deep insight into the problems and needs of the countries included in this aid program. He had also obtained a firsthand impression of the Cold War confrontation with the Soviet Union and the dangers of a stepped-up East-West arms race that, with Stalin's acquisition of the atomic bomb in 1949, might end in a nuclear war.

The number of foundations in the United States and their assets grew markedly after the war in comparison with the interwar period. There were literally thousands of small foundations in the midst of a few giants.[4] Most charities, including the Ford Foundation, spent most of their budgets on domestic programs. Thus between 1951 and 1960, the Ford Foundation gave $32.6 million for educational programs in the United States at all levels; some $67.5 million was spent on public affairs and urban, regional, and youth programs. Another $74.8 million went to economics and business studies, and $294.7 million to hospitals and medical schools. International grants in this period totaled $256.3 million, to which must be added a portion of the $97.9 million that were allocated to arts, sciences, and—as a major item and pet program within this block—the behavioral sciences. In terms of the geographic distribution of grantees throughout the United States between 1951 and 1959, New England was the greatest beneficiary.[5]

Still, international expenditures also rose throughout the decade, though not as steeply as grants to domestic educational programs. Indeed, it soon turned out that the caution about a possible economic downturn voiced in the foundation's December 1950 statement was unwarranted.[6] With the economy booming, twelve months later total assets had increased by another $15 million to $513 million, from which $10 million had to be deducted in "unpaid grants."[7] These propitious developments encouraged the foundation to initiate two domestic ventures, the Fund for the Advancement of Education, with an interim budget allocation of $7.1 million, and the Fund for Adult Education, with an interim budget allocation of $3 million. The Free Russia Fund, for which George F. Kennan, a former counselor in the State Department and now at Princeton, served as president, had an interim budget of $200,000 and hence looked a bit meager by comparison. But there were other international ventures.

Thus in July 1951 the foundation had given $1.3 million to the Free University in West Berlin, founded in 1948 when Berlin's old university in the Soviet sector of the city became Stalinized.[8] In August 1951 Hoffman visited the Middle East and South Asia, soon to become the beneficiaries of a large overseas development program that was independent of the European initiatives and whose emergence will be traced in this chapter.

A hint to what was coming is contained in Henry Ford's annual report for 1951 in which he mentioned the "creation of conditions for peace." Such a program would "try to reduce tensions arising from ignorance and want and misunderstanding" and "to increase maturity of judgment and stability of purpose in the United States and abroad."[9]

THE CONDITIONS OF PEACE PROJECT

At his headquarters in Pasadena, California, Hoffman had meanwhile put together a team of aides to promote this "conditions of peace" idea, which, after his recent experience in Europe, was particularly dear to his heart. Among his associate directors were, in addition to Rowan Gaither, Milton Katz, his former deputy in the Marshall Plan administration (ECA), and Robert M. Hutchins, a former chancellor of the University of Chicago. As of 1 January 1952, Hoffman had also hired as a consultant another trusted former ECA man, Richard M. Bissell Jr., by then at the Massachusetts Institute of Technology and from 1954 with the CIA.[10] Six months later, on 15 July, appropriations to programs in foreign countries and for the study of international affairs in the United States had risen to $13.8 million, almost half of what had been allocated to domestic programs.

As to the "conditions of peace" initiative, it may well be that Hoffman had temporarily contemplated handing it to the Rand Corporation, the California think tank whose founding in 1948 the Ford Foundation had guaranteed with an interest-free loan. But in July 1952 the trustees had converted this loan into a grant, and the project was to be done in house.[11] Discussions had been going on for some time about the shape and personnel of this work, for which the trustees had already approved $200,000. In March 1952 Bissell had written a sixteen-page paper titled "Creating the Conditions of Peace."[12] This think piece argued that "the object of the Foundation should be to help create an atmosphere in which it will be possible for the West from the new position of military strength that it is achieving to negotiate a just and honorable peace with the East." The

145

convenient method to be employed, the memorandum continued, would be a "discussion of disarmament" in order to obtain a settlement and to generate a "public opinion favorable to it."

While rejecting a strategy of sharp confrontation that might end in a war with the Soviet Union, however, Bissell was skeptical of the chances of disarmament and "real peace." Instead he opted for a third alternative: "That we can live in the same world with the Russians without going to war with them despite profound and continuing differences of philosophy and interest." This, he believed, was what the Conditions of Peace project should prepare and work for at the international level in its dealings with the Soviets. But there was also a domestic problem to be tackled. Bissell thought that "the climate of opinion that now prevails in the United States is too tense and emotional, too close to that of a religious war." A "healthier atmosphere" could be "created only by way of an awareness and understanding of the third alternative and support for it." The trouble with this alternative was that it was psychologically "unsatisfying" and ambiguous because it meant "neither peace nor war." And it would be difficult to sustain, partly because this "less war-like cold war" that he had in mind "would still be burdensome." At the same time, "its cost would be more nearly within the limits of what we can comfortably afford."

With McCarthy's fierce anticommunist campaign clearly in mind, Bissell stressed the need for a "change in temper" and for a "more relaxed attitude toward the East-West struggle and one which promises greater endurance in carrying it on." Because America was in a volatile mood, however, it might be dangerous immediately to organize and to lead the public toward some notion of disarmament. Hence "until there is a pretty well defined objective and until all concerned are satisfied that the means exist or can be found for making significant progress toward that objective, neither the Ford Foundation nor a distinguished citizen would wish to be publicly committed to the creation of a new organization." All Bissell advised to do as a first step was to start "the planning work as promptly and privately as possible." At this stage the task was to talk to leading experts in the broader field of international affairs to obtain their views and to collect relevant materials.

Subsequently Hoffman adopted precisely this cautious approach to the "Conditions of Peace" project. It appears that the "distinguished citizen" was no other than McCloy. If nothing else, the president and Katz certainly consulted the former high commissioner on his return from West Germany and probably Stone's name also came up in this context. The latter was still sad about his departure from West Germany and continued to follow developments there.[13] But he was also looking for a job. Hoffman, though favorably disposed toward him, had no immediate suggestions.[14] But he evidently kept thinking about the former HICOG Public Affairs director, for on 8 July 1952 Stone received a letter from Katz which began by setting out the entire project. The Ford Foundation, he wrote in line with Bissell's advice, had been using the "Conditions of Peace" concept not "in the sense of a set of international arrangements which would constitute a just and stable peace, but in the sense of conditions which should be satisfied if we are to have any reasonable chance of achieving any such set of international arrangements," and so "we have had in mind conditions affecting the range and content of U.S. public opinion, and its relationship to the efforts of our government to achieve peace with justice and freedom." Accordingly, they had made plans "for some preliminary work" to be done "over the next six or eight months." Katz thought of "surveys of current thinking on these problems throughout the United States and of current efforts by various groups to develop an informed public opinion on the subject."[15]

As we have seen at the end of chapter 3, Stone was searching for employment, and on 11 August Katz's secretary sent him a copy of a "Draft of a Proposed Docket Item for Trustees' Meeting, July 15–16" titled "Conditions of Peace: Progress Report and Proposed Action." The preliminary work that the trustees had apparently approved involved: "1. A series of quiet, informal meetings with small groups of carefully selected persons. . . . 2. A comprehensive survey of groups currently engaged in public education or research in foreign policy and foreign affairs. . . . 3. If feasible, a survey of the present state of opinion in the United States concerning the aims of our foreign policy and the available means of achieving them. . . . 4. The organization, in selected communities, of 'test runs', i.e., attempts to help local leadership promote local activities designed to create in these communities an informed and constructive climate of opinion concerning the central issues" of the time. The report added that "our initial idea" had been to explore "possible programs of disarmament" but that they had later opted for a more limited effort organized around questions such as: "What do we want of the Soviet Union? What cost are we prepared to incur to get it? What are the possible means to achieve it?" The "real objective," the report concluded, "would be to help establish a kind and degree of public understanding which would serve as a basis for wise planning and skillful operation by the U.S. government in its continuing effort to move through the current problems toward the goal of peace with freedom and justice."[16]

147

Ultimately, therefore, the initiative was more than developing a counterweight to inward-looking McCarthyite anticommunism or fighting the Cold War with more subtle means. Because the United States had become a world power, but public consciousness was still unprepared for the challenges ahead, the objective was to create the popular underpinning of a democratic foreign policy to be conducted by the East Coast elites and to make certain that these elites did not lose ground through a renewed rise of populist politics and isolationism. In other words, apart from its anti-McCarthyite orientation, the lessons of the interwar period also influenced the design of this internationalist program and the role that a newly confident Ford Foundation was hoping to play in it.

In fact, by the summer of 1952 Hoffman was no longer just thinking of generally aiding the "wise planning and skillful operation by the U.S. government." A supporter of Dwight D. Eisenhower's candidacy for the upcoming presidential elections, he also had "Ike" and perhaps even himself in mind when he began to draft an "address on 'steps to peace.' " At least there seems to be some evidence that he had hopes of becoming secretary of state under Eisenhower. Whatever his motives, by mid-August he had, as he told Eisenhower, reached "a general agreement as to content and outline" with Stone, who was now to undertake "the tough part of the job, which is the preparation of the first rough draft." After further review by McCloy and others, Stone would deliver the finished product during Eisenhower's impending visit to New York in the hope that it would "prove useful" to him.[17]

In early September Stone was still polishing his draft. On 2 September he discussed with Katz the possible addition of "a strong attack on Democratic mistakes in foreign policy" but felt he was too much of a supporter of Adlai Stevenson to be "the man to write that." He also believed that preparing a speech for Eisenhower was not enough: "Either a few excellent 'brain trusters' had to replace the men around Ike and stay with him or Ike was lost."[18] In the end the whole initiative seems to have gone nowhere, and after his election Eisenhower appointed John Foster Dulles as secretary of state. The brother of CIA boss Allen took a much tougher line toward the Soviet Union. Once in power, the new administration began to implement its belief that the policy of containment that Truman had pursued toward Stalin was too passive and needed to be replaced by a more assertive strategy. Accordingly Dulles had already begun to talk about rolling the Soviet Union back out of East Central Europe. At first Eisenhower even seems to have been prepared to bear the additional costs of putting the Soviets on the defensive, but the U.S. Congress was in a thriftier mood and looked for reductions in international spending, especially on culture. Only in 1954 did he succeed in getting approval for an "Emergency Fund for International Affairs" to underwrite a program of cultural exports.[19]

Dulles's position—at least in public—was toughest in matters of nuclear war and peace where he eventually went so far as to proclaim that if the Soviets ever launched an attack, the United States would deploy its entire nuclear arsenal and retaliate "massively." All this inevitably put a damper on Hoffman's plans. On 10 September 1952 and with two months to go to the presidential elections, Stone noted in his occasional diary: "Paul is disappointed in Ike, but still for him."[20] The disappointment was no doubt even greater when the freshly elected "Ike" opted for a more hawkish foreign policy. It was a dialectic of positions that came to be reversed only in the later Eisenhower years and even more explicitly after the election of John F. Kennedy.

As to the role of McCloy and Stone in Hoffman's "Conditions of Peace" initiative and the pattern of U.S. foreign policy more generally, we know that they agreed in September to examine "the Ford Foundation's program for promoting peace with a view to making that program as practical, concrete, and down-to-earth as possible." Having been ignored by Eisenhower, they turned to the Truman administration which at this point was, after all, still in charge. As W. Park Armstrong Jr., a special assistant to the secretary of state, continued in his briefing document for his boss, Dean Acheson, members of McCloy's team had "consulted with numerous officers of the State Department at many stages and on many occasions." He added that "there is of course in the Department a general gratification at the cooperative and helpful spirit which the Ford Foundation has displayed." He reminded Acheson that Hoffman had twice seen him in July 1951 and January 1952 and that there had been "many meetings at lower echelons."[21]

In line with the objectives of the program that had been mapped out at the trustees' meeting in the middle of July, McCloy and Stone began their information gathering among scholars and international affairs experts and to think about the Godkin Lectures that McCloy had been invited to deliver. On 22 September the former high commissioner went to Harvard's Littauer Center to discuss the matter with Robert Bowie and Edward Mason. They also met with Galbraith for lunch and ended the day in Dublin, New Hampshire, at Grenville Clark's house. According to Stone's notes, Clark was "full of disarmament" and wanted McCloy "to stick with Ford and do something on peace."[22]

In his own quest to gain a better understanding of American views on the East-West conflict, Stone had meanwhile kept his ears open. In early September 1952 he had attended a Brookings Institution seminar at Dartmouth concerned with how to deal "with the Soviet threat." The discussions went back and forth and Quincy Wright, the well-known analyst of modern warfare, took the view "that we were threatening Russia as much as Russia was threatening us." For Stone and the rest of the participants it was an ideal meeting to exchange views without fear of being branded "un-American" as well as to network.[23]

Slowly, as he was traveling around the country to gather expert opinions, Stone warmed to his new job. He enjoyed being on the road with McCloy and felt "very happy because working with Paul Hoffman and Milton Katz I am working with the kind of people that made the last few years what they were." What was more, "our problems are similar to those we have been handling" at HICOG.[24] It helped his enthusiasm for his job that after Eisenhower's victory he felt an even stronger sense of mission. Some people, he wrote to Hoffman and Katz on 12 November (with a copy to McCloy), might feel that the Republican victory "means the so-called 'eggheads' will be removed from influence in American life." But, he countered cheerfully, "in the coming years the new President will need the backing of all Americans, including the liberals and intellectuals." After all, "these people . . . developed the atom bomb and they have made and will continue to make major contributions to American life."[25] While the larger cultural context of this statement has already been outlined in the previous two chapters, we shall see in a moment how the Ford Foundation became involved in this effort of America's "liberals and intellectuals" during the Eisenhower years.

McCloy and Stone began their campaign by having "many discussions with people high and low" during the fall and winter of 1952.[26] Pursuing their mandate, they talked "with men and women of ideas" and determined "from these talks what the major tensions are and to try to obtain any wisdom available in respect of (a) the mitigation of tensions, (b) the building up of international understanding, (c) the enlightenment of the American people in international affairs." They found, Stone reported, that some thought it possible to "mitigate tensions" by approaching the Russians directly. But much, they learned, could also be done indirectly by concentrating "on the so-called uncommitted East" and "that the Foundation has large opportunities in developing pilot projects in that part of the world." As to his "survey of organizations," Stone admitted that his work had not yet begun in full. He had been studying the Council on Foreign Relations but wanted to "broaden out to look at other key organizations in New York and the East." He also wanted "to see what the Chamber of Commerce, the [American] Legion and other such organizations are doing in our field." Finally he was hoping to learn more about "men of influence in local communities." His hometown Nashua, he speculated, might yield good material for a case study, and it did. As to influence at the highest levels, he had—since the disappointment with Eisenhower—begun to pin his hopes on McCloy and the impending Godkin Lectures, which, he believed, could make another "contribution to the Conditions of Peace project." Yet it was not easy for him to get a sense of progress. McCloy even wondered whether the "work we are doing is much more difficult . . . than running Germany or trying to establish the European community."[27] Above all, there was so much to do.

To lighten the work load, Howard Johnson, a State Department official, took a leave to join the two men in conducting the dozens of interviews. It is against the background of these realities that McCloy submitted a first interim report to Hoffman and Katz on 18 December 1952. In it McCloy expressed his conviction that the Ford Foundation could "act as a chief stimulant" in rethinking the Soviet-American relationship. This was particularly true with regard to "developing in the United States a mature atmosphere for the discussion of our world problems and for dealing with them; for establishing techniques and institutions to improve the quality of our leadership in world affairs." McCloy's report stressed the preliminary character of its findings, not least because of the impending change of government in Washington. As he insisted, "only after the Eisenhower Administration has been in office for a few months will it be wise to draw up a definite long-range program."[28]

Still, the report contained a number of proposals that indicated the general direction into which McCloy and Stone wanted the Ford Foundation to go, and over time they did succeed in nudging it that way. To begin with, they believed that Western Europe was a key region whose institutional base had to be strengthened and where the Ford Foundation "might usefully sponsor the creation of one institute or a number of institutes for research in the problems of the European Community." Second, McCloy's report voiced a concern over "the problem of anti-Americanism," although this was not just confined to Europe. Finally, it put forward the idea "of a university or institute in the East [i.e., Asia] where young scholars of all Eastern countries, together with students from the West, would study administration, political science, and international affairs."[29]

151

In their response to this report and a subsequent discussion in Pasadena, Hoffman and Katz gave their broad approval to McCloy's suggestion to continue. The ideas it contained, Katz added, would occupy a central position in Ford Foundation activity.[30] More money was made available to enable further work on the Conditions of Peace project; positions became more formalized. As Stone wrote at the end of January 1953: "I am enjoying my work at the Ford Foundation. As you probably know, Jack is keeping up his relationship with the Ford [Foundation]. He will be the chairman of the Board of our so-called Project for Peace and I am the Director of it."[31]

When writing these words, Stone's activities had come to focus on surveys of American and European opinion and on the question of "co-existence" with the Soviet Union. Accordingly, McCloy now submitted to Hoffman an outline of, and a budget for, the two issues. More important, he urged the president to set up a division within the Foundation or a fund for the Conditions of Peace program. An advisory board of eight people would be chaired by McCloy who was to be "in active overall charge of the fund," with Stone at his side as "director." Further advice was to be gained from a group of international consultants, headed by Sir Oliver Franks, a highly regarded member of the Whitehall establishment.[32] The memorandum stressed the importance of making "use of the talents of European statesmen who are no longer in government, but whose experience might permit them to make a valuable contribution." He also advised "that some method must be found to gain support among the Socialists of Europe for international peace." The foundation should therefore "consider the idea of bringing together advanced Socialist thinkers from these countries, men who have prestige within their own parties, to study the problem of coexistence and to propose solutions"—a proposal that must, of course, be seen against the background of our analysis of European-American relations presented in the previous two chapters.[33]

All these points were summarized in a cable by Martin Quigley at the foundation's headquarters to Stone of 21 January 1953 with the request to prepare a docket item for the next trustees' meeting.[34] Working closely with Katz, Stone returned a revised draft to Quigley two days later in which he recommended "that the Trustees approve the use of the $150,000 unexpended balance from the previous appropriation for the Conditions of Peace project plus an additional $220,000 for 'a study of the conditions of coexistence,' 'a comprehensive survey of the groups in this country engaged in research and education in foreign policy and foreign affairs,' and the 'identification and comparative appraisal of what each of several leading nations considers to be its national interest.' "[35]

When these ideas were put before the trustees on 23 February, the docket item "relating to the peace project was considered a report on activities and future planning of the division and not a request for an appropriation of funds."[36] Although the monies were subsequently authorized by the president, the fact that the docket item was judged to be a report of a *division* now dragged the whole Conditions of Peace project into a long power struggle within the Ford Foundation about the overall direction of its future activities. When the conflicts were eventually resolved, the Conditions of Peace project had been handed over to the Council on Foreign Relations (CFR) and Stone had become the key person in a new Division of European and International Affairs within the foundation's bureaucratic structure.

THE STRUGGLE FOR A EUROPEAN PROGRAM

The power struggle was triggered by Hoffman's premature departure as president and his replacement by Gaither, one of the associate directors. The new man had his own priorities. One of these was to move the foundation's headquarters from California to New York City. More important, he immediately ordered a review of "all programs" even if budgets for 1953 were to continue "with such changes from time to time as the President might approve."[37] Considering that the "peace project" had been Hoffman's hobby horse, the whole enterprise that had just been consolidated into a "division" might fall victim to a major reorganization of priorities under Gaither's leadership, and Stone might soon again find himself in search of a job. In a narrow sense this is what subsequently happened.

As chair of the project's advisory group, McCloy had finally had a chance to talk to Eisenhower about his activities. In the course of this conversation it became clear that the U.S. president, while of course not disavowing the staunch anti-Soviet policies of his secretary of state, "welcomed the rather constant survey of this problem by non-governmental as well as governmental interests . . . and felt the two groups should be constantly in touch, particularly if the outside group had the responsibility of the Council [on Foreign Relations] with which he was familiar."[38] His politeness did not cost him anything but suggested closer cooperation with the CFR. McCloy knew that Hamilton Fish Armstrong, the influential editor of *Foreign Affairs*, the council's journal, was "very anxious that this work be undertaken." Quite apart from his political views, it always made sense to prepare alternatives to official thinking. And so,

153

with a grant from the Ford Foundation, the CFR made "a serious attempt to collect the best thinking they can on the subject" of relations with the Soviets. A study group was set up, which held its first "organization meeting" on 6 May.[39] But however high-powered the group may have been, McCloy had begun to have doubts about the entire effort. As he confessed to Kennan, he was "torn between a certain sense of frustration in dealing with the whole Russian problem and a hesitation ever to refuse any requests that are made of me to contribute to the subject."[40]

Throughout the summer, Stone continued to work on the Conditions of Peace project; but he probably realized that its days were numbered.[41] As he listened to the rumors about the new Gaither era, he found that there was "much talk going on about the future organization of Area I"[42] and therefore asked Katz for an appointment to discuss his ideas on this subject, clearly also hoping to get a better insight into the thinking of the Ford Foundation leadership. We have already noted that most of the funding went to domestic projects, and as in previous years the question was what should be the overall balance between different areas of activity. Over the years, five such areas had emerged, among which only Area I was related to international affairs. Areas III, IV, and V were all purely domestic.

Area II supported the so-called Fund of the Republic, intended to strengthen the country's "free institutions" at a cost between 1951 and 1953 of $15 million.[43] This was a cover for a domestic program that tried to counter what the foundation and Henry Ford II personally regarded as the detrimental influence of McCarthyism on American politics and society. Indeed, to some extent the Area II program was a self-defense of leading Ford Foundation people after they had come under attack from the hard-line anticommunists who, quite unjustifiedly, suspected them of being "soft" on bolshevism. With McCloy and his former HICOG subordinates having been subjected to similar attacks, there was a growing determination to hit back. But there was also a genuine concern for the health of public life and for civil liberties that McCarthyism was putting into jeopardy. As noted in chapter 5, in the American Congress for Cultural Freedom at this time many intellectuals became similarly worried about the McCarthyite crusade, not least because they heard from their friends in Europe about its disastrous repercussions for the American image abroad. Finally, as discussed in chapter 7, a connection can also be established between the foundation's opposition to McCarthyism at home and the considerations behind its decision to develop a strong European program.[44]

Up to that point, Area I had been used as an umbrella for the foundation's international activities at large. In this context, the overseas development and poverty programs for Third World countries were initially given by far the largest piece of the international funding pie. The foundation was particularly strongly committed to help increase food production and promote agricultural reform in South Asia. Similar programs of "basic research, vocational education, village development, medical assistance, and leadership training" were started in the Near East.[45] Smaller grants were made to the Far East. Nevertheless, the Third World total for the period 1951 to 1960 amounted to over $80 million, of which close to $10 million went to the Middle East, $67.4 million to South and Southeast Asia, some $2.2 million to Africa, and a little under $1.4 million to Latin America.[46] Compared with the millions that flowed to the Third World, the Ford Foundation did not have much of a European program to speak of in 1953. However, quite early into the Hoffman presidency the question had been raised whether Europe, at the height of the Cold War, might not be the most important region after all. One indication that this argument had begun to gain ground was the reduction of the Third World agricultural program in 1953.

In the meantime a debate had begun within the foundation on whether to expand the European program. The larger context of political and intellectual developments is again important here. For while all of Western Europe was making a satisfactory economic recovery from the ravages of World War II, domestic politics were far from stable. In France and Italy governments had to cope with the continuing strength of communist and socialist trade unions and parties. In Bonn Chancellor Adenauer headed a coalition government that included a number of volatile right-wing splinter parties. The West German communists were unimportant, but there was the constant pressure from a large and quite radical SPD in which the reformists had not yet gained the upper hand. The announcement of German rearmament and the planned creation of the European Defense Community (EDC) had generated heated arguments everywhere about the desirability of having German armed forces just a few years after the end of World War II. To these political difficulties and the suspicions of American economic and military hegemony must be added the cultural anti-Americanism that, as we have seen, was particularly widespread among Western Europe's intellectuals.[47]

The administration in Washington, painfully aware of these problems, had not only provided official aid through the Marshall Plan but also overtly as well as covertly subsidized an array of private cultural activities and organizations. The U.S. High Commission's support, under Stone's stewardship, of the fledgling West German newspaper press provides a case in point.[48] In the meantime, however, the situation had become more difficult in Congress. Partly as a result of the Korean War, public expenditure had rocketed sky-high. The Republicans, since January 1953 with one of their own in the White House, wanted to trim the federal budget. So funds overtly supporting cultural enterprises were bound to be particularly vulnerable to the congressional knife. As to covert monies, the U.S. agencies giving them lived in fear of scandal should their grants ever become public.

Against this background has to be seen a memorandum that Gaither received on 5 May 1951 from Hans Speier at the Rand Corporation. The memo began by stressing that, in light of "the support of organizations making valuable contributions to 'peacefare' in Europe etc.," it had become important for the foundation "to plan for the administrative arrangements which would permit the most effective pursuit of these interests abroad." Speier then gave as an illustration the "organizations in Western Germany and in Berlin engaged in work that appears most valuable in supporting U.S. government policy in the cold war with the Soviet Union." The State Department and HICOG, he continued, had been finding it "embarrassing to support some of these organizations in view of the constraints which the occupation statute places upon the U.S. authorities to lend open, overt support to these organizations." For this reason, the two offices were cooperating with the CIA "to channelize covert funds in such a way as to support worthy institutions and organizations." Speier believed that "for understandable reasons, U.S. Government authorities would, in some of these cases, like to see private initiative play the role which overt government effort can no longer assume."[49]

A major step toward a stronger European focus was taken on 20 March 1952 when Katz circulated a memorandum to the foundation's leadership titled "Notes on Foundation Activities Concerning Free Europe." In it Katz reported on a staff meeting earlier that month at which "a question was raised whether we should seek to develop a program for free Europe, perhaps comparable to the programs in progress or in contemplation for India-Pakistan, the Middle East, Southeast Asia, Indonesia, or Japan."[50] Though not quite certain if such a European program was "advisable," he acknowledged that, however great the "complexity and sophistication of free Europe, the worldwide reach of its culture and trade and politics, its close relations with the United States and the range of governmental programs affecting it" had a special quality.

What, in Katz's view, Europe needed was "release from the fear of war and aggression," increased productivity, "a broad distribution of the increment in production," a better grasp of financial and commercial relationships around the world; "a fresh understanding of the immense human promise of a free society," and finally "a steady growth in the sense of European and Atlantic community and an understanding of the practical steps required to give it effect and to realize its creative potentialities." Indeed, for Katz, the former Marshall Plan man, Europe could not be thought of "constructively . . . except in terms of the Atlantic community." Europe included a Federal Republic of Germany as "a constructive and dependable part of the free West," and the liberation of "the great labor unions of France and Italy from the Communist grip," giving them and workers' organizations elsewhere a sense that they had "a primary stake in the maintenance and invigoration of a free society."

Katz next mentioned a number of Ford Foundation projects that harmonized with these ideas, among them the grant to the Free University, the conception of an International Press Institute, the support for the magazine *Perspectives*,[51] and "the plans for the equivalent of a CED [Committee for Economic Development] for continental Europe."[52] He concluded by raising the question of "the desirability of establishing an advisory panel of Europeans to assist us." He followed this suggestion with a list of potential candidates, which included Jean Monnet, Oliver Franks, Hugh Gaitskell, Geoffrey Crowther, Robert Marjolin, Dirk Stikker, and Dag Hammarskjöld.[53] He added "some American citizens (or residents) of European origin," such as Kurt Riezler, before 1914 Reich chancellor Bethmann Hollweg's private secretary and now teaching at the New School for Social Research, Jacques Maritain, the famous French philosopher, and Carl Joachim Friedrich, the Harvard political scientist, whose brother Otto had been mentioned, next to Walter Hallstein, as a possible choice for a German representative.[54]

Indeed, also his list of European interviewees is of considerable interest for an understanding of the international networks that were being forged here. Moreover, from 1953 onward Stone increasingly found himself approached by prominent Europeans who were either about to visit the United States and asked for his help or counted on his long-distance advice. This was particularly true of West German politicians whom he knew well from his days at HICOG. In February and March 1953 he became involved in the preparations for visits by Ernst Reuter and Konrad Adenauer to the United States. The mayor of West Berlin also used Stone as a go-between when he requested more money from the foundation for the Free University. Stone could not help immediately, but Berlin was so dear to his heart that he held out to Reuter reconsideration of his application for later in 1953, citing the change of leadership from Hoffman to Gaither as the reason for the rejection during the current round.[55]

In June a letter arrived from Max Horkheimer, now rector of Frankfurt University, who reported in almost perfect English "that the forces of yesterday are continuing in the ascendancy." He also summarized "the preliminary results of our large-scale pilot study of German attitudes towards some issues of our time, such as democracy, rearmament, and freedom." Though this study by the reconstituted Frankfurt Institute was not yet ready for publication, its findings, Horkheimer continued, "were not too encouraging." Those familiar with it "realized that much work was still needed in order to somehow immunize the population against totalitarian doctrines and influences."[56] Finally, in October he received a letter from Inge-Aicher Scholl asking him and McCloy to visit Ulm during their impending trip to Europe to see the beginning of the new Hochschule für Gestaltung and to talk to her "about our next development."[57] Later she wrote again raising the question of an English translation of *Die Weisse Rose*, her book on her brother and sister whom the Nazis had executed in 1943 for their resistance activities at Munich University.[58] She wondered if young Americans might find a translation illuminating.[59]

While his continued contacts with his friends in Germany merely confirmed Stone in his view that the foundation should commit itself to a large European program, the new president had made some progress on his plans to have a major review of the foundation's activities and in March 1953 began to circulate a memorandum on "Forward Program Planning." Gaither wanted to increase the organization's efficiency and "develop a statement of the rationale for the Foundation's program in each of the five Areas in relation to the Foundation's objectives."[60]

At their meeting in February 1953, the trustees reaffirmed the foundation's basic philosophy of "assisting in the solution of the major problems of human welfare," and asked for all forward planning to be guided by this philosophy. Gaither, in a memorandum of May 1953, added the principle that they should avoid "doing those things which duplicate or substitute for the proper activities of government or other agencies." After all, "some of the Foundation's greatest opportunities . . . may lie in the direction of complementing the activities of others and especially encouraging and leading others, including government, to improve their activities." Moving on from planning philosophy and structure to the process of planning, the new president outlined six stages of consideration and decision making; an effort that, though admittedly "greatly oversimplified" and failing "to reveal the many difficulties and pitfalls that lie along the route," was nevertheless laudable for attempting to produce a more systematic approach.[61] Its drawback was that it invited rivalry between the disciplines and staff promoting their own favorite agenda.

First of all, there was the competition between the domestic program and Area I internationalism, which had been a rallying force for Area I staffs to get their act together. The result of these efforts was an eleven-page paper that tried "to apply the process of program analysis and planning to Area I as a whole." This memorandum contained an eloquent argument in favor of a stepped-up international engagement of the foundation in Europe and in the "Underdeveloped Areas." As to the latter regions, they were, according to the document, "characterized in varying degrees by a revolutionary ferment, the outcome of which cannot now be foreseen," but which might nevertheless "largely determine whether the world will be plunged into war or will move along a course toward enduring peace." Yet "even in the absence of a Communist threat in the world today," it was "vital to the future of world peace that these underdeveloped nations succeed in meeting the challenge before them." At the same time there were the "weaknesses in Western Europe and Japan" to be borne in mind. There were, of course, numerous government programs, and "the opportunities for a private foundation to contribute significantly" were "not at all self evident." Still, the Area I experts were confident that further investigations would reveal such opportunities, also in light of Soviet behavior. After all, the importance "of Western Europe and Japan to peace over both the short and the long term" was clear: "The nations of the Atlantic community . . . are the bastions of freedom and democracy. Both Western Europe and Japan possess a large industrial capacity and both are on the borders of the Soviet sphere. According to our Secretary of State, if Russia took over Europe, it would so shift the balance of industrial power that the U.S. would be in great peril. The loss of Japan would be equally serious."[62]

Second, if more money were to be spent on international programs, there was the question of balance within the Area I budget and in this respect "Western Europe" was slowly gaining ground. This emerged, inter alia, from another report that Gaither prepared for the trustees' meeting in 30 June 1953. Here the president openly admitted that the Area I program was "unbalanced" because "what we lacked in the past" was "a rationale for the whole of Area One." In trying to overcome this deficiency, the "war-peace problem in all its immensity and complexity" provided the unavoidable starting point. But further exploration and planning might "well result in the conclusion that the Foundation should only seek to undertake activities at a few well-defined but strategic points lying within the broad range of Area I." For this reason, he recommended in the end that "no overseas research and training activities . . . be planned, or commitments undertaken, involving expenditures by the Foundation, after December 31, 1957." He would "evaluate the research and training program in 1956 and recommend whether and to what extent programs of this kind should be undertaken after 1957." While this left basic decisions to the future, there was an increase in funding. If the Area I total had been $6.3 million in the previous two and a half years, the allocation for 1954 was $12 million, "of which $500,000 [went] for the Asia-Near East Development Program." The allocation for 1955 and 1956 was to be 75 percent of the figure for 1954.[63]

It seems clear that Gaither was not a strong advocate of an expansion of Area I programs and wanted to keep his options open. At the same time, among the trustees McCloy was convinced that the relationships with the Soviet Union and Western Europe were the key questions of international affairs to which the foundation should turn its attention. Stone shared McCloy's views and wondered about the future of Hoffman's Conditions of Peace project. On 8 July he met with Gaither to put in a word for a request from the Free University for American-born scholars to be placed on its permanent faculty. He also brought up the idea of establishing an institute in West Berlin "where refugee scholars from the Slav countries can work with Western European scholars to avoid a resurgence of the German-Slav nationalistic forces which have contributed to two wars" and which, incidentally, he had analyzed in his doctoral thesis in Berlin before 1933. Finally, Stone supported the renewal request of the faculty exchange between the Free University, on the one hand, and Stanford and Columbia universities, on the other.[64] Knowing of Stone's personal bias in this regard, Gaither, ever skeptical, subsequently sent a "close friend" of his, the president of Stanford, to Berlin to give him a presumably more objective report on the situation.[65]

In the fall of 1953 he also received an assessment by Ernest C. Hassolt about the state of "American Studies in German Universities—1953." It was grist to Stone's mills since he had been worrying about German anti-Americanism for some time. Hassolt found that "the sudden cessation of grants for special projects [once given by HICOG] was a little chilling, but also challenging to greater resourcefulness [sic]."[66] He had also learned from Eugen Kogon, an old acquaintance of Stone's, editor of the

Frankfurter Hefte and now a professor of political science at Darmstadt Technical University, that he was "interested in fighting the mounting resentment against the Americans." Hassolt thought that exchange programs were the most effective "means of replacing resentment and misunderstanding with understanding and respect." He also felt that "without the Amerika Haeuser [*sic*], American studies in German universities would not have progressed half as far or so fast as they have since the war, since the library facilities of the universities have been supplemented to an extent inconceivable in the U.S."

Whether Gaither liked it or not, Hassolt's conclusion was an indirect confirmation of the argument that Europe was central to American interests during this Cold War era: "When one thinks of Asia, America and Europe seem to fall into perspective. Then the differences between American and European culture are clearly unimportant; the two are one culture." More than that: "European culture has entered into its American phase, which Americans and Europeans must now explore together. How much they have in common will become clear to them when they work together, as they soon will, in Asia, for the advancement of culture, not Western culture, nor Eastern culture, but simply human culture." Hassolt ended with a question and a "new perspective of American Studies which I have learnt this summer among the students of the Free University" in Berlin: "Barring war, or a universal garrison state,[67] is it not likely that the European universities will increasingly become laboratories for the development of experimental models for the use in the advancement of culture in Asia and Africa?"

While the notions of Western culture that Hassolt articulated not only speak volumes about attitudes toward non-European societies but also connect well with the themes of the last two chapters and Stone's later policies, Gaither received a third report about Europe in September from a trustee and U.S. District Court judge, Charles E. Wyzanski Jr. It was even more wide-ranging than Hassolt's but also the most critical. This report devoted a longer section to *Perspectives*, a magazine in which Stone had a personal stake because Walter Hasenclever, his brother-in-law, had become one of the editors of the German-edition. Wyzanski recommended that Gaither "consider whether at some future date the Foundation should terminate or reduce its subsidy to the English edition of *Perspectives*."[68] He added that "if, as I recommend, there is to be a continuation of the edition in German (and in French and Italian which, of course, I did not investigate and on which I express no opinion), then (a) revise and expand the free list to increase the types of persons acquainted with the magazine, (b) make the material more representative of American culture, (c) if *Der Monat* is not continued by the U.S. Government then consider including its type of articles, but in any event do not so rigidly narrow the field of *Perspectives* to art, letters, and music."[69]

With reference to American general libraries in Europe, Wyzanski advised "that if the Congress withdraws or sharply curtails support for . . . [them], the Ford Foundation ought to *assist* in a program for their continuance under local control and partly local financing." Moving on to exchanges, he confirmed that there was in Germany and elsewhere "a real demand for *first-rate* American professors, particularly those who have been educated in Europe, speak German, and are prepared to give generously of their out-of-class time for informal sessions with individuals and student groups." Overall, Wyzanski stressed the advantages of closer cooperation across the Atlantic.

Finally, Gaither's envoy turned to "contacts beyond the Iron Curtain," referring to a 1951–52 Ford Foundation grant of $150,000 to the Berlin-based, more hard-line anticommunist Kampfgruppe gegen Unmenschlichkeit, but then looked beyond this group's mission. Although he knew that East-West contacts posed delicate problems, he nevertheless suggested "that the officers of the Foundation explore the possibilities of further resort to this group to keep us posted on what is going on beyond the Iron Curtain and to initiate contacts on which we may wish to rely when the formal barriers between East and West are let down or are drawn further Eastwards." Accordingly, he came to the conclusion that "private Western organizations can and should develop the material and contacts which can be utilized and built upon by those in governmental authority." In addition to expanding the West European program, Wyzanski's proposal to move eastward was indeed another avenue that the Ford Foundation was soon to take.

By September 1953 Area I was still in a state of flux. The people involved in the Conditions of Peace project continued to "gather the views of representatives of the various branches of the United States Government." In an effort "to implement its work," it had also "made a grant of $100,000 to the Council on Foreign Relations . . . for the establishment of a study group on U.S./U.S.S.R. relations" under McCloy's chairmanship and with Stone at his side.[70] However, the cooperation between the two men had by then moved well beyond looking after this relatively modest venture. On 14 September Stone had sent his mentor a document to brief him on the docket items to be discussed by the trustees at their meeting two days later. He believed that the CFR project would go through. McCloy also received some advice on Area IV matters, including education grants, liberal arts colleges, and educational television. Stone ended with a paragraph on the Free University exchange program. He said he was responsible for this item being included in the board's agenda. He urged McCloy to request further study of American professors going to Berlin for a number of years. This, he wrote, would "be of great significance if in coming years Berlin should be made the capital of a united Germany."[71]

These developments formed the backdrop to a three-week tour of Europe by McCloy and Stone in October 1953. Officially, they went to survey opinions of prominent Europeans about the Conditions of Peace project. Unofficially, it was an opportunity to renew old friendships and contacts from the HICOG days, and evidently the trip was also designed to gather arguments and voices in support of expanding the foundation's European programs. According to Stone's detailed diary-like notes, the two men started off in London, then went to France before traveling to Frankfurt, Bonn, and Berlin. They ended up in Luxembourg to visit Jean Monnet at the High Authority of the European Coal and Steel Community (ECSC). Many people they met, were linked to the CCF network.[72]

The people Stone spoke to repeatedly raised two substantive issues: the value of journals and magazines and European anti-Americanism. Discussions in London revolved around *Encounter*, the recent British counterpart to Lasky's *Der Monat*, and the English-language edition of *Perspectives*, which Wyzanski had recommended for closure or reduction. Stone learned that the latter magazine needed beefing up, not closure. All in all, Richard Crossman, his wartime colleague at the Allied Headquarter's Psychological Warfare Division and now a prominent Labour politician, was more complimentary about *Encounter* than about *Perspectives*. It was apparently also new to Stone that the CCF was said to be behind the journal; to add to the confusion, another interlocutor thought that the Ford Foundation "was, but Crossman said no." The British politician speculated instead that the CCF was supported by the State Department.[73] In short, rumors about covert funding had begun flying about long before the CIA was identified as the major source in the mid-1960s.

Across the Channel in Paris, Josselson was in a self-congratulatory mood. The CCF, Stone recorded, was the "first thing [that was] doing any good among the French." Bondy showed no reluctance to make favorable comparisons between *Preuves* (which he edited) and its leftist competitors; but he complained about the strength of the communists in the market for weeklies: "The Commies . . . publish 5 periodicals, [and have] the best doctors, engineers, lawyers etc. There is no answer to it. There is not a single paper in Paris that can be considered fair and pro-American. No good to tell the French how good things are at home, they want to know how they can do it here."[74]

Bondy added that "there is a great problem of teachers, of newspapermen, of managers in plants who are looked upon as stooges by the workers, as foremen by owners. These men are university people and they will either go all the way to the right, to Fascism or Communism."[75] Apparently Stone also talked to him about *Profils*, a new magazine devoted to "the promotion of knowledge about American culture." Bondy felt (as did other CCF associates in later years) that such a theme was "not quite sufficient to make a magazine in Europe appealing, even if it does so on the highest level." Issues of "European culture and many broader aspects of the continuous European-American debate" on this subject "would be of greater interest." In Frankfurt, the next stop, Walter Hasenclever seemed happy with his work for the German-language edition of *Perspectives*, which was being published by Gottfried Bermann-Fischer, an old friend of the Stones from New York City's wartime refugee community.[76]

Whatever the good or bad news about various journals, Stone also heard about the larger issue of European hostility to American culture. As to England, Nancy Raphael insisted that there was not much of it. When McCloy charged Clement Attlee and the British Labour movement "with seeking to organize hostility to the United States," the latter "demurred" and "said that the newspapers played up the critical and not the positive." Posing as a firm believer in the "Anglo-American alliance," Attlee "was critical of his own left-wingers who were stirring up animosity."

Although it is possible that the British were merely impeccably polite to their American visitor, the French were certainly much more outspoken. Manès Sperber, whom Stone had met at the Calman-Levy publishing house, which published the French edition of *Perspectives*, was not just irritated but quite visibly "depressed about the anti-American attitude and spirit in French intellectual and journalistic circles as well as the right." Stone then paraphrased remarks by Sperber which reveal the full dimension of the cold culture wars that the Americans were fighting in the 1950s and which we have encountered in chapters 4 and 5: "The French right and aristocrats disliked the upstart and what it stood for—mass civilization and culture against the culture of the few. The fact that mass culture was achieving fine things did not matter. Then there were the intellectuals and the Communists who were untiring in their efforts. Wild charges and propaganda were spread and not effectively answered.

He thought our information efforts were particularly bad. For example, a few weeks ago a publication had published a list saying these are the books Hitler had burned and then published a list saying these are the books the State Dept. and American libraries are banning or burning. The list simply wasn't true and the charges were quite false. Nobody answered." McCarthyism was taking its toll in Europe.

As McCloy and Stone crossed from France into West Germany, the intellectual climate became milder. They encountered a strong feeling of regret at McCloy's departure and learned that "our contacts in Germany had diminished, our influence had lessened." As in France, Stone encountered abhorrence and fears of McCarthyism, causing people to wonder "where the United States was going." Stone objected to comparisons between the Third Reich and the silence of Americans in the face of the anticommunist witch-hunts. But this did not keep Eugen Gerstenmaier, once an active member of the anti-Nazi resistance movement and now a prominent Protestant churchman and CDU politician, to assert that the "Americans were going mad at home and ought to do something about . . . [their] own democracy."[77]

Italy was the next stop on their trip. At Castelgandolfo outside Rome they saw de Gasperi who reiterated his old belief that "the European unity idea would help solve many problems." He also felt that "the Germans can be a danger again and will be. The safest thing is to make them a part of Europe." No doubt McCloy and Stone agreed with him but then worried with him about the strength of the PCI. The "Commies," Stone noted, "are spending Lire 2 milliard every month on propaganda, we have no money and must nevertheless prepare." While in Rome, he also met with Nabokov, who was "engaged in working at a conference of composers etc."—that is, he was preparing the CCF's Milan congress. Asked about the American-supported press, the CCF man, who typically was more interested in the highbrow, thought "*Perspectives* [to be] off the mark in content, form etc." At the same time he felt that "more progress is being made in Italy than in France." To him the French situation was illustrated by an exchange of letters "he had had (or somebody in Congress) with Camus. After [the] June 17 [1953] suppression by [the] Commies of [the] Berlin revolt, [the] Congress asked Camus to join a protest meeting. Camus wrote back and said he would like to, but [the] protest [had been] inspired by [the] Americans and if he joined with them, he would be betraying the entire philosophy and meaning of the French left." After this, Nabokov advised Stone that "youth" was a more promising group to go for than intellectuals of Camus's generation. He must have thought of middle-class youths, because this was the time when working-class adolescents throughout Western Europe began to develop a taste for American rock music and other "lowbrow" products whose rising popularity dismayed European liberal intellectuals and academics no less than McCarthyism.

When traveling with McCloy from Germany to Luxembourg on 26 October to visit Monnet on the last leg of their European tour, Stone began to take stock of his experiences. He was fairly optimistic about the future of the Federal Republic. "The Germans," he wrote, "are on the right track and it is to be hoped that they will stick to it." He probably felt similarly reassured about his visit to Britain. It was a different matter with France and Italy. There it was not just the problem of large communist movements that generally toed Moscow's line in the Cold War. Once again he had also come across a good deal of cultural anti-Americanism. As a former *New York Times* man and HICOG's Public Affairs director, one of his immediate reactions was to investigate the successes and failures of pro-American journals and magazines and to find out whether this might be a promising field in which the Ford Foundation might spend more Area I money.

Stone returned to New York in early November with plenty of useful information that went well beyond his fact gathering for the Conditions of Peace project. Nothing he had heard was so reassuring as to convince him that he should stop pushing to make Europe a major field of future Ford Foundation activity. McCloy seems to have been in full agreement with him. On 3 November he saw Katz without delay to provide a full-hour report. By 12 November he had produced an account of his trip. Responding to this activism, Katz sent a memorandum to other Area I officials a few days later, drawing their attention to his own March 1952 "Notes on Foundation Activities Concerning Free Europe." Referring to the problems outlined in section II of this document, he stated: "It will be obvious to you that I have included matters which presumably lie outside the scope of possible foundation contributions." But he had found "Shep Stone's interesting report" significant enough to suggest joint discussions including Don Price, soon to become director of Ford's international programs.[78]

To Stone's dismay, the end of 1953 proved a bad time for a European initiative. Katz was unenthusiastic about expansion, believing that the foundation should not be involved in political crisis points like Berlin.[79] Over lunch with Stone on 3 November, his colleague James Laughlin took a "bleak view of current developments in [the] foundation. He sees hesitancy, fears, smallness." If "anything bold is to happen, J. J. McCloy will have to take [the] lead." He ended by saying that the foundation's "officers all tremble for [their] jobs, even D. Price."[80] One reason for the turmoil at the top was that Katz was on his way out. In the middle of January he went to Harvard to become director of International Legal Studies, funded—as a parting gift—with a grant of $2 million from the Ford Foundation. Several weeks before his departure, Price had been made "temporary" director of international programs. But when Stone met Price on 3 November after his return from Europe, he found, though forming a generally "good impression" of him, that "he was not prepared to take a definite line." Price merely asked Stone "to speak before [the] Program Committee which now apparently runs [the] Foundation on [the] officer level."[81]

In preparation for this meeting and perhaps also because he planned to hand McCloy something in writing, Stone decided to compose a strong statement in favor of an expanded Area I program. Dated 3 December 1953 and addressed to Price, the memorandum began by asserting that "we are facing a long period of cold war. In the years ahead the USSR will use every political, economic and psychological weapon to damage (a) American unity and faith of Americans in their free institutions; (b) the alliance of free nations; and (c) the possible movements of so-called neutral nations in the direction of the free."[82] In this situation, Stone continued, "the United States will need wisdom and maturity to hold the free peoples together. It will need to exercise restraint as well as imagination in dealing with the problems of Asia, Africa and South America." But he also felt that the Ford Foundation "can and should make a larger contribution in the international area." Philanthropy had "an opportunity to take action which our Government is no longer in a position to initiate or carry through."

Next he suggested several international fields where the foundation could be more active, both at home and abroad. At home there was the need for research and training in international problems, and "in special cases, such as the Conditions of Peace project," the findings could be made "available to government agencies." Above all, there was the European area where support was needed for the "training of persons to staff developing European community institutions" and for the establishment of "agencies to study European-Atlantic problems." In the "cultural-political" field Stone wanted to "give aid to some of the activities now being carried on by the Congress for Cultural Freedom in France, Italy, Germany, the U.K. [and in Asia]." He also wanted to "broaden the scope of

167

Perspectives . . . to cover a wider range of cultural activities." Third, he hoped that the foundation would help raise the level of knowledge and understanding about the United States in schools and tertiary education. In a relatively brief reference to "Asia, Africa, etc.," Stone wrote that "in addition to, or perhaps instead of some of our current economic programs, develop programs along the lines of those outlined for Europe."

EXPORTING AMERICAN CULTURE

By early 1954, an Area I program was ready to go to the board of trustees. The supporting memorandum asserted that "the conviction has deepened that the objectives set for Area I . . . have increasing validity." The projects described in the rest of the document therefore formed "part of the plan to invigorate Area I." Since "the struggle with the USSR" was likely to become "more subtle and complex" due to the Kremlin's new "peace-minded and non-aggressive" strategy,[83] there was reason "to believe that under Soviet pressures neutralist sentiment will grow both in the West and in the East." In trying to strengthen the allegiance of other nations to "freedom," the U.S. government clearly had the most important role to play. However, there were "important areas . . . where Government action is unproductive, inappropriate and even harmful"—a belief shared by "leading policy makers in the present Eisenhower administration." And finally, while in the past the focus of international programs had been "the underdeveloped nations of the East," the foundation's activities should now "be extended to all parts of the world, in particular to critical areas in Europe."[84]

There now followed a number of proposals either for action by the trustees at their meeting in February 1954 or for their preliminary approval. Among the projects he had in mind was a grant of $3.5 million to the Council on Foreign Relations as well as further support for the Conditions of Peace project and for the Free University. Four days later, on 14 January, Stone bombarded Price with yet another memorandum with four more projects, two of which were concerned with strengthening the Atlantic connection. The third one was in aid of the American Committee on United Europe, submitted by William J. Donovan, the wartime head of OSS; the fourth to help the World Veterans' Federation.[85]

It is not clear how much progress Stone was making with his European plans in the spring of 1954. Whether out of sheer frustration or a sense of optimism, on 21 April he approached Price with more ideas. His memorandum began with the words: "During the past few months, as a consequence of the so-called Soviet peace offensive and of certain developments inside the United States, the need, particularly in Europe, for vigorous effort has increased." With this in mind, he added, "the International Affairs program of the Foundation is being worked out." There were older issues of support for *Der Monat* and *Perspectives*. However, "in September the officers expect to request approval from the Trustees for a grant to the Congress for Cultural Freedom, whose publications in four languages and whose related activities are among the most effective efforts now being made in Europe and elsewhere (a) to counteract Communist influence on political thought and (b) to develop more vigorous support for democratic developments around the world." Also by the end of the year he expected a request for a grant from the Harvard International Seminar in which Henry Kissinger had begun to take a leading role. Overall, Stone concluded, "the officers [of the Area I program] see the M.I.T. project in the present docket as the beginning of a larger contribution the Foundation can make in the research of American foreign policy problems." Discussions had also begun "with Columbia University with a view to aiding that institution to develop its capacities in the American foreign policy area."[86]

While the struggle over the size of the Area I program, its main focus, and its place within the foundation's spending strategy continued, Stone was making some progress on the organizational front. On 28 June 1954, "International Programs Staff" received a circular from Price that, with Gaither's approval, decreed that Stone, John B. Howard, and Kenneth R. Iverson would "each be designated as Assistant Director of International Programs." Howard was to take charge of "programs of training and research carried on by academic institutions at home and abroad that fall within the scope of the international programs." Iverson was to look after the Overseas Development Program. Stone, finally, would cover the "International Affairs (U.S. and Europe) Program." His group "which takes over the staff of the 'Conditions of Peace' project will have primary responsibility for that part of the international programs carried on in the United States by non-academic institutions, and for such programs as may be developed in Europe."[87] This meant that the Conditions of Peace project officially came to an end.[88] Its remnants were moved to the Council on Foreign Relations, leading to the publication of a book by Henry L. Roberts, and Stone became a permanent official of the Ford Foundation.[89]

Given that the European program had been left somewhat vague, Stone decided that the best way forward was for him to go on another trip to

Europe. This time he went for six weeks and on his return on 28 July produced a twelve-page report. Appreciating that there had been a good deal of resistance inside the organization to a European program, he started off by affirming the need for a major effort. On the one hand, there was still the Soviet Union "trying to advance its objective with a new technique of reasonableness and good manners."[90] On the other, "the prestige of the United States has fallen to what is perhaps a postwar low," even if the Europeans recognized their "basic dependence" upon America's strength. Worse, "American diplomatic representation, itself mixed in quality, is generally frustrated over its inability to act because it is confused over policies and trends in Washington." Although the foundation could not and would not replace official policy, it nevertheless had a role to play and was "in a strategic position to act." Next to Rockefeller and Carnegie, Ford was held in high regard in Europe, "even in the far Left circles of the British Labo[u]r Party, the German SPD, and among many Leftist intellectuals in France."

For these reasons, Stone recommended, that "the Foundation, in the interests of the United States and of carrying out its own program, should begin to make grants in France, England, and other European countries, not excluding Yugoslavia." He was reassuringly modest in his demands on the foundation's budget, stressing that "we should not try to develop a master plan immediately, but rather allow it to emerge over the next two years." He then listed over a dozen Europeans as potential contacts, some of whom we have already encountered in Stone's earlier activities.[91] He also gave examples of projects that the foundation might wish to support. Thus with regard to Britain, the main object was "to overcome both lack of faith in American maturity and fears of what are considered to be 'wild men' in Congress and at the Pentagon." Accordingly, Stone wanted "to bring British leaders in political life, and public opinion leaders in intellectual, newspaper, trade union circles into closer contact with their American counterparts." In France he proposed to undertake no more than a "few careful, limited projects" in order "to aid the process of modernization in French life and to bring about the beginnings of an understanding with the United States." One of these projects was to ask "Raymond Aron, professor of sociology at Paris and the leading political commentator of *Figaro*, if he would be willing to support a project that he would carry out analyzing the French political elite, their attitudes and influence in France."

Turning to West Germany, Stone pleaded for fostering "the pro-democratic elements and to restrain the resurgence of the extreme nationalist

170

elements." This meant that he had identified a "large need to support projects on all levels of German society." He particularly mentioned exchanges and "the establishment of chairs in political science and sociology." In Italy, Stone was similarly told repeatedly "that the most promising effort . . . to develop political and economic institutions designed to strengthen democracy and opposing totalitarianism" was "the [European] Community movement sponsored by Adriano Olivetti, the Italian industrialist." The inclusion of Yugoslavia in his trip indicated that he refused to see the Iron Curtain as an impenetrable barrier and pointed toward programs that he pursued after the Polish and Hungarian revolutions in 1956.

Finally, following Nabokov's advice, Stone saw potentialities in supporting the youth movements of Europe and—not to be forgotten—the Congress for Cultural Freedom. In his view the CCF was "the most effective organization in Europe working among political, intellectual and cultural leaders." He added: "In the past the Congress had concentrated on combatting Communists efforts among the intellectuals of Europe and Asia. It now intends to emphasize the positive aspects of freedom and a free society." It seems therefore that the CCF chiefs, whose activities we began to examine in the previous chapter, were not alone in their reassessment of the postwar world situation. If the threat of totalitarianism and Soviet political, military, and cultural expansion had loomed large in the intellectual debates of the early postwar period, by 1954–55 the Soviets, though still a formidable force in power-political terms, were no longer viewed as serious competitors in the intellectual and cultural field.

Yet this decline in Soviet influence did not mean that the Europeans and intellectuals in the Third World had begun happily to join the American "camp." On the contrary, the old deep-seated reservations about American "mass culture" persisted. The cultural hegemony of the United States was far from secure. While Washington continued to dominate the diplomatic and strategic field, official policy was retreating from the cultural front. The big private organizations now stepped into the breach. Stone knew and loved European high culture; he was also all too familiar with Hollywood "trash" and "vulgar" popular music, which he had heard his European friends criticize ever since his student days in Germany before 1933. But he also knew and loved intellectual America with its Ivy League, its scientific research institutes, museums, plays, novels, painters. *Vordenker* Daniel Bell and others proclaimed a new "can-do" managerial pragmatism for the solution of the relatively few social problems that they said were still vexing the industrialized world and presented mass society

171

and mass culture as something no one needed to fear. Stone, in turn, picked this up and set out to show the Europeans, through the Ford Foundation program, that they were most unfairly biased about American society and its culture.[92]

Accordingly, his report now urged the Ford Foundation to "consider the allocation of funds for sending American plays, art, orchestras to Europe. The main problem . . . is not to convince the Europeans that we have a culture. As a matter of fact, Europeans are becoming bored with our insistence that we are a cultured people. Informed Europeans know it. But they want to see for themselves. They read our books and periodicals, and they now want to see our art, our theatre, and to hear our music.[93] Ambassador Riddleberger in Belgrade has made a strong plea for sending Porgy and Bess. . . . He believes that the political and psychological results of such a visit would be astonishing. Ambassador Dillon in Paris strongly urges us to support the American Art Festival which will take place next spring in theatres, museums and halls being put at the disposal of the American people by the Government of France and by the City of Paris. Cultural efforts of this type can have important effects politically."

The deeper reasons for Stone's preference for the CCF can also be gauged from parallel debates within the Ford Foundation concerning the fate of *Perspectives* with its essays, short stories, book reviews, poetry, and fine arts.[94] Writing to John Howard at the Ford Foundation in August 1954, his colleague Elmer Starch understood the magazine to be "an endeavor that the American phase of western culture deserves a standing equal to that of the European phase. Americans are assumed to have certain freedoms of thought which are essential to advancement towards a higher level of behavioral concepts." Europeans had frequently told him "that the best American culture has the dignity and appreciativeness which they admire as greatly as they do those elements in their own culture, but that Americans also have a dash of candor and liveliness which lead to progress."[95]

As we have seen, however, in the summer and fall of that year the publication had come under scrutiny, first by Wyzanski and later by Stone himself. Although Wyzanski's recommendations were not immediately accepted, his report had pointed to what he thought was a "rigidly narrow" focus on "art, letters, and music." In his note to Laughlin of 19 December 1953, Stone, in summarizing his findings from his recent European trip, had reinforced Wyzanski's points. In Paris, he wrote, criticism of *Perspectives* had been even stronger than in London. The magazine, he had learned, was "not making an impression" and "should be broadened considerably to discuss important issues of the day as well as cultural aspects of American life." Various people had told him that the publication "would have been a success twenty years ago" but that "it was now missing the mark." Today, "the French intellectual is deeply interested in the great political issues of the day and that is what he wants to read about and discuss."[96]

These criticisms induced Laughlin to start his own more comprehensive survey of the magazine's impact, which he extended beyond Europe to Third World countries. At the same time he mounted a defense of its content. Thus, at the end of January 1954, he tried to correct Wyzanski's views by pointing out that "the largest part of the sale of the English-language edition" was "outside England, with splendid circulation in places like Holland, Israel, India, Japan etc." No less important, "one of the great advantages of *Perspectives*" was "that it *selects* the best from our magazines for the reader who has not the time to read a dozen different American publications—and how many do if they are not specialists, ergo, already 'converted' to American culture?"[97]

Writing in a similar vein to Price (with a copy to Stone) a month later, Laughlin referred approvingly to a recent article in *Diogenes*, another subsidized intellectual journal.[98] With the U.S. government withdrawing from funding culture, "if support for the arts is to come only from commercial sources," so he paraphrased Macdonald's attack on American Masscult and Midcult,[99] "their quality in many spheres will continue to fall." This is why "the foundations, with their tax exemptions, are the logical patrons today." Ford was "too big" and "too central" in this picture "to shirk its obligation" to the arts.

A few weeks into March 1954, Laughlin learned that the foundation had "received an application for support for the magazines" of the CCF, which he presumed would be *Encounter, Preuves,* and *Forum.* To him this raised the question: "Should the Foundation in its cultural exchange work participate actively in the war of ideas against Russia, or should such efforts be left to the government or to individuals expressing their personal beliefs?" The position of *Perspectives* had "always been to keep out of the political fight, to think of the field of culture as one where people of opposed ideologies can still meet on friendly ground and learn to respect each other as human beings." He continued: "Little as we may like their ideas or their methods, we are sooner or later going to have to find a way to live in the world with the Communists, or else see the world blow itself apart." Culture to him was "an ideal channel of communication because it so often seems to appeal to the best side of our natures. It is a natural symbol of our aspirations for a better life."[100]

In a further note to Stone a few days later Laughlin worried about "the basic philosophical implications of identifying ourselves [i.e., the Ford Foundation] with so militant an organization" as the CCF. He reminded Stone of the differences of opinion between Milton Katz and Robert Hutchins: "Milt has always felt that we should line up with organizations and programs which are aggressively attacking the Communist position, and Bob has always felt that we should not." He had always sympathized with "Bob's point of view." He then became very blunt: "Frankly, I would hate to see the Foundation make its cultural program a weapon in the cold war. I would rather see them take a much longer view and assume that things are going to get better rather than worse, and that, if we can build up an area of understanding on the cultural level, it may be the basis for communication in many other fields. *Der Monat* is about as far in the direction of militancy as I would really like to go." Consequently, he would reject "a blanket endorsement" of the CCF.[101]

In May Laughlin brought up a new point, querying whether the CCF's journals were suitable for Asia. In Europe, by contrast, the CCF's difficulties were of a different kind. Although the Congress's "Music Festival in Paris was absolutely marvellous; that is, the choice of musical works and groups was impeccable," the event failed, in his view, "to reach the right audience." The theater was small and the ticket prices were high. Consequently, "the audience chiefly reached was the rich snob audience of the Etoile and Neuilly who are already in 'our' camp, rather than the fringe intellectuals and students who need conversion." Still, knowing of his formidable opponents, Laughlin did not want to sound too critical. In the end, he professed to be in favor of the CCF, "but would prefer to see them supported by the State Department."[102]

Laughlin's reference to State Department funding may have been made with an eye to an effort that Eisenhower had meanwhile launched under the auspices of the Emergency Fund for International Affairs. This fund was designed to underwrite a program "geared to the performing arts and sent the José Limon Company—its first dance attraction—to Latin America in 1954."[103] The fund was confirmed by Congress a year later, though without increases. Because the artists who were sent abroad were enthusiastically received, the program was eventually incorporated into the federal budget by law, but the program remained small, and professional selection panels and artists were never quite sure how far, given overt funding by Washington, their no doubt superb avant-garde performances could be separated from politics. This is where the big foundations came in with their reputation of political independence.

Still, the criticism that Stone's friend Fred Burkhardt had made in April pointed to another set of problems. He had been asked by Price to evaluate the first six issues of *Perspectives*. Although he thought the venture to be "on the whole . . . a good one," because "the cultural aspects of diplomacy get very little support from the State Department or Congress," he was nevertheless dissatisfied with the magazine's content. For his taste, it was "too exclusively literary, and *avant-garde* literary at that." Art reproduction was "excellent, but the art might have been better selected." Photography, "which is quite an art in America, and one which has a great following in Europe, has so far been entirely neglected." Music was mostly "confined to talk *about* music." Above all, much of the space taken up by literary material "could have been used to advantage by articles on social issues, philosophy, [and] history." Worse, at least as far as France was concerned, "the critical essays in *Perspectives* strike some French readers as being too journalistic. They are accustomed to much tougher fare intellectually." Although Burkhardt recommended continuation of the magazine and tried to make some constructive suggestions, his arguments were grist to the mill of those in the foundation who did not like Laughlin's purely artistic approach. They had a broader definition of culture and of what the United States should project to the world.[104]

Moreover, they were possibly reminded of experiences that promoters of the visual arts had had with exhibitions abroad in the late 1940s and early 1950s. Thus when Jackson Pollock's paintings were sent abroad as examples of how the United States had taken the lead in the visual arts, European viewers reacted with incomprehension, as they tried to absorb his huge canvases and the ideas underlying abstract expressionism. While Pollock is nowadays granted a position of preeminence in the history of postwar international art and his paintings are much admired for their articulation of space and freedom, an earlier generation of visitors was decidedly unenthusiastic and perplexed, and subsequent exhibitions of American art in Europe tended to assemble a wider range of styles and artists, though the objective of showing the achievements of American high culture remained the same.[105]

By the end of the year and with Stone more firmly in the saddle, the issue had been decided. On 18 November 1954 he sent Gaither the draft of a letter from the president to Laughlin "with a view to terminating the relationship of the Foundation with Intercultural in a friendly manner."[106] Intercultural Publications Inc. (IPI) was to be given a final lump sum of

$500,000 to strike out on its own. On 21 December "at a Special Meeting of the Board of Directors of Intercultural Publications . . . it was unanimously voted to accept the generous offer of the Ford Foundation."[107]

The separation implied that Stone had opted in favor of the CCF. Given his networks, concerns, and overall objectives for the foundation's expanded activities in the international field, it is not surprising that he thought it to be "the most effective organization in Europe working among political, intellectual and cultural leaders."[108] The congress's strategy contained all the elements that harmonized with his own views on what needed to be done at this time: With Josselson at the helm, it was a more dynamic organization. It was more comprehensive in its understanding of culture and had the support of a most powerful group of intellectuals on both sides of the Atlantic. It had undergone a metamorphosis, and the anticommunist hard-liners around Hook and Koestler had been pushed out. The CCF had been turned into an organization that was much more responsive to European intellectuals' preoccupations. Europe and the Atlantic region, but not (yet) the Third World, constituted its primary field of operation. And thanks to the CIA, its financial base was also more secure, an aspect that will be dealt with more fully in chapter 8.[109]

Although Stone would reencounter in the late 1960s the differences of opinion on the nature of the cold culture wars that Laughlin had articulated, within the context of world politics in the 1950s the choice was clear. Like most of the other people we have met so far inside and outside the CCF, Stone, too, belonged to an elite that wanted to unite Europe and the United States in an Atlantic community and culture. In his mind, this region was not just tied together by military-strategic and economic interests in the conflict with the Soviet bloc; it also had the same cultural and intellectual heritage. In terms of its *past* "high cultural" achievements, Europe may have had the edge over America, but the latter had caught up fast with its fine arts and architecture, its music and literature, while it had already overtaken the Old Continent in the sciences and humanities. In Stone's view, America had also surpassed Europe, *vide* Daniel Bell, in the sophistication of its democratic civic culture and was no longer mired in the class politics of Britain, France, Italy, or Germany.

So, there was a major campaign to be launched to let the Europeans see an America that was different from their customary stereotypes.[110] A 1953 opinion poll, designed to discover "What the French Think of the Americans," may not have been as bad as some pessimists believed, but it was not flattering either.[111] From West Germany Hans Wallenberg, writing to Stone at about the same time, confirmed that "there have been and are two groups of Europeans interested in American affairs." The first group thought of "the United States as a stronghold of freedom and democracy"; to the other one "the United States ever since its separation from the British Empire is a dangerous upstart threatening the traditional policies of Europe as well as the entire world."[112] Stone was too political a person not to see that there were two culture wars to be waged: one against the Soviet bloc, although this was already being won, and another one against Western European perceptions of American culture, which posed a more formidable challenge. He knew himself that these perceptions had deep roots, which he enumerated once more on 4 May 1954 in a memorandum for Ellen McCloy.[113]

However, before he obtained the funds to pursue his ideas on both sides of the Iron Curtain in Europe and soon also beyond, there was still the cold war inside the Ford Foundation to be won against those who felt that philanthropy should go elsewhere.

Philanthropy and Diplomacy

IN THE SUMMER OF 1954 Shepard Stone's career took a new direction. He had left the relatively small-scale and uncertain confines of the Conditions of Peace project on which he had begun work as McCloy's assistant in the fall of 1952. In June 1954, after a good deal of pressure on the Ford Foundation leadership to focus its attention on Europe, he had been put in charge of the "International Affairs (U.S. and Europe) Program" as a full-time staff member. His old mentor McCloy sat on the board of trustees. Both men were agreed that Europe was too important a part of the world not to be included in the foundation's philanthropy.

FORD'S INTERNATIONAL PROGRAM

But even now the question remained of how a new program could be fitted into the existing bureaucratic structure. Stone also knew that some of his colleagues were not too pleased with him as a competitor for scarce resources. They wanted to spend the foundation's money on other causes. As Frank Sutton remembered, Stone also caused mild irritation with his name-dropping and elitism, especially after returning from his trips to Europe: "Jean" (Monnet), "Willy" (Brandt) or some British establishment figures, with many of whom he would be on a first-name basis.[1] It is easy to see what he meant when one reads Laughlin's more cautious contemporary account: "Shep Stone has returned full of enthusiasm, arising out of his talks with American diplomats in Europe, for a stepping up of cultural activities in Europe, which might include support for the activities of the Congress for Cultural Freedom, an exchange program for cultural and intellectual leaders and—this one will sound familiar to you—sending American art and theatrical and musical groups to Europe."[2]

While Stone's position within the Ford Foundation was eventually resolved by a ruling from the top, the immediate task was to develop proposals and here, as Laughlin reported to Price on 18 August 1954, some of Stone's strongest interlocking interests lay in (a) "support for the activities in Europe of The Congress for Cultural Freedom, . . . (b) exchange of leaders which would include some cultural leaders, (c) sending American art exhibitions and theatrical or musical groups to key centers in Europe." Unfortunately for Stone, Price continued to procrastinate, even as the conflict over *Perspectives* was being resolved in favor of the CCF. As Laughlin understood it, Price wanted "to ask the Trustees in October to authorize the Program Committee to make a real study of the whole question of activity in the Humanities as such." The inevitable delays that such a study would cause puzzled Laughlin. He felt that "all these [i.e., Stone's] projects can stand on their own feet as valid efforts in Area I as now defined."[3]

Waldemar Nielsen appears to have had similar feelings during a conversation with Gaither, in the course of which he told the president that "we will have substantial new proposals for Trustee action ready by fall."[4] At the top of his list were "Atlantic Community Relations; European integration; [and] East European developments." While the scope of the first two plans had been fairly clear for some time, the "East European Program Possibilities" which Nielsen discussed under a separate heading were striking for their ambitiousness and potential for controversy. The object of this particular program was "to take advantage of [the] present shift in [the] political climate to institute research, exchange and educational efforts important for democratic objectives." In other words, it reflected a growing sense in the United States that the West was gaining the upper hand in the cold culture war against communism. Even in the East criticisms could be heard that the prescriptions of "socialist realism" merely promoted mediocrity in art and literature. A system where recognition and funding depended on orthodoxy and required state approval produced no more than an elite of loyal intellectual hacks whose works were as trivial as they were pure.[5]

Targeted, as Nielsen put it, "primarily [at] the satellite countries, but including also the U.S.S.R.," the project proposed to address academic and intellectual elites, "important technicians, journalists, and university students" through fellowships, the distribution of "Western scholarly and scientific publications to East European university libraries," and joint East-West conferences to discuss present trends in international affairs. None of these and other related activities were merely cultural-philanthropic but also aimed to stimulate "scholarly critiques of Communist declarations and policies and assistance for their publication and wide distribution." Apart from the European aspect of International Affairs (IA) planning, there was also the domestic side of educating Americans about foreign countries.

If Price and Gaither were less than enthusiastic about IA activism, Katz appears to have strengthened their backs from his lair at the Harvard Law School. After his move to Cambridge, he had been retained as "program counsellor" until September 1954. In this capacity he had been sent Stone's "Notes" of his recent European trip. In his response Katz agreed with Stone that there should be no immediate master plan, but that the program be allowed to emerge over the next two years. More than that, "the range and complexity of European society, and the world-wide reach of its political and cultural influence, are such as to make a 'master plan' for our activities affecting Europe almost as difficult as such a plan might be for our activities within the United States." Although he liked the idea of "Lafayette Fellowships" and a "couple of proposals relating to Yugoslavia," Katz was opposed to the foundation "supporting particular projects merely because we feel an acute need to do something about Europe and have been unable to think of any other projects to support."[6]

Although a "European Program" docket was presented to the trustees in October 1954, the meeting apparently opted for the kind of further study that Price had envisaged in August.[7] He got his way. As he was informed—most probably by the chair of the program committee—on 14 December 1954, its members had meanwhile "pulled together our preliminary thoughts regarding the focus which evaluation of the Foundation's international programs appropriately might take and methods for carrying it through." The task, he felt, was "to provide an informed basis for deciding the scope, content and method of future operations in the international field most appropriate to achievement of the overall purposes for which the Foundation was established."[8] It all sounded very sensible, but considering also that the memorandum was written two months after the trustees meeting, Stone was bound to feel rather frustrated. On 17 December he complained to Price that there had been "no developments" since that meeting. He asked bluntly: "Are we to go ahead developing a plan to cover a program, staff and budget, with a view to making the European Program an important part of the Foundation's overall effort?"[9]

It took more than another year before a solution for the integration of IA into the existing administrative structure had been found. On 25 January 1955 Dyke Brown, in a "strictly confidential" memorandum for the program committee about the "European Program," summarized the committee's discussions earlier that day at which it was agreed that "the problems of Western Europe (including Great Britain and Canada) are of sufficient importance, in terms of the Foundation's program interests, to

180

warrant serious consideration from a program standpoint, with the possibility of recommending further and continuing expenditures of significant size." There was also a "general preference" among the officers to extend "the present five programs to parallel opportunities in Western Europe."[10]

In March 1955 Stone began to see some light at the end of the tunnel when he wrote to Hans Kohn, a refugee from Nazism, professor at Smith College, and a well-known scholar of modern nationalism, that "the overall prospects for the development of a Foundation program in Europe are better" now.[11] In the meantime Stone soldiered on with his activities under the U.S.-USSR, Atlantic, and European programs and tried to develop criteria for evaluating individual projects.[12] By the summer the drawbacks of the endless assessment procedures had become very obvious: a growing number of small project applications were piling up. Worse, Stone, who had gone away on another European trip in June and July, came back not only with fresh ammunition in support of a strong European program but also with yet another bundle of funding requests. In an attempt to get a decision and to clear the logjam he recommended to Price, for submission to the September meeting of the trustees, six projects at a total cost of $1.59 million.[13]

By this time, however, the debate on overall strategy had become so convoluted that Nielsen sent a memorandum to Gaither warning that "we may be on the verge of moving from too little to too much talk." There was a danger "that an appearance may be created of uncoordinated schemes cropping up all over." Nielsen therefore advised the president to give the Program Committee a specific amount of money for Europe "in the coming year." Second, Brown and his colleagues should be told "that in setting priority for their program planning for the next year and a half they hold back on European activities." In this connection, Nielsen continued, Gaither might wish "to define the limits of Shep's work under Don [Price] and suggest that Shep confine his work to political and constitutional matters." Nielsen wanted the Ford Foundation to "concentrate, through calendar 1956, on a limited number of substantial projects rather than a larger number of small ones." And finally the president should "state explicitly" that he was "responsible for the continuous coordination of plans, proposals, and activities with respect to Europe."[14]

These recommendations, though perhaps sensible, were hardly cheering to Stone. But the fall brought some relief, particularly to an overworked Price, when F.F. ("Frosty") Hill joined the foundation as vice president in charge of the Overseas Development (OD) part of the international effort. The next major step came in April 1956 when the president directed that Vice-President Price had responsibility for the "continuing development of the Foundation's European program." He was also to be in charge of the assignment of projects to officers within the International Affairs area. After the confusion of the previous eighteen months Gaither also thought it necessary to reiterate that "any application received by the Foundation . . . for assistance to any individual or institution in Europe, or to any individual or institution for work in Europe," be first referred to Price. Finally, Price was told "to consult with other program staff units" in the "development of the European program."[15] Whatever further complications this directive added to the bureaucratic process, at least there now clearly was a European program.

In the end, however, nothing helped more to stabilize and to expand the international area than the appointment on 1 October 1956 of a new president, Henry Heald, a civil engineer by training and a former chancellor (later president) of New York University,[16] the consolidation of the foundation's endowment, and the momentous developments inside the Soviet bloc, triggered by Nikita Khrushchev's speech before the 20th Congress of the Soviet CP and followed by the upheavals in Poland and Hungary. Finally, there was the Suez Crisis in which Washington, by stopping Britain, France, and Israel in their war against Egypt, asserted its power-political hegemony in the West.

After taking over from Gaither, who was kicked upstairs to replace the retiring Henry Ford II as chairman of the board of trustees, Heald moved quickly to resolve remaining uncertainties about the European program. It was now firmly put "under [the] IA Office, [with] Stone [as its] director."[17] Nothing reflected this consolidation more distinctly than the "sharply rising grand totals" of its budget.[18] These rising totals were not only due to Stone's energy but also to the growth in the foundation's overall funding pie.[19]

This development made it easier for Stone to argue his case for more European funding. In the summer of 1956 he was once more on the road. As he wrote to Price on 4 June, the first "superficial, though real feeling" he had on seeing Europe again was one of prosperity. But he added immediately: "If one did not look beneath the surface the conclusion would be that Europe has the resources to take care of itself. Below it all [however] there is an uneasiness" which he was hoping to fathom over the next two weeks.[20]

Condensing his impressions of Europe, Stone produced a memorandum on 13 September 1956 that was billed as reflecting "a new approach to the organization of Foundation activities in Europe and related to

Europe."[21] The document repeated that "the strengthening of Europe and of American-European relations is fundamental to the security and well-being of the United States and to the Foundation's interest in peace, freedom, and human progress." Moreover, "developments during the past three years in Western Europe and in Eastern Europe and the U.S.S.R. have increased the need and opportunity for American action." Stone then gave a brief review of the roughly $24 million already given since 1951 "for projects relating to European problems." But there were plenty of issues left.

As to Western Europe, even though "the Soviet Union has abandoned hope to control" the region, efforts to influence it indirectly continued. For example, the Soviets would "appeal to the youth of Europe by pointing to opportunities for talented young people in the Soviet Union to get to the top." In short, having moderated its once aggressive rhetoric, Moscow "will try to become the economic, ideological and cultural magnet for 200,000,000 Europeans." Conversely, "the Kremlin will continue to try to divide Europe within itself and to split Europe from the United States." And he feared that the communists might well succeed: "The economic and social structure of Europe is brittle. Europe's belief in its own future is fragile." There was no doubt an element of exaggeration in this assessment. He knew that invoking the Soviet threat was still a useful ploy for winning an argument. In fact, when he talked about the brittleness of Europe, Stone also had another point in mind.

This consideration emerged clearly enough when his report turned to Italy, an example of a country where the "social system remains closed and undemocratic. Class differences are relatively inflexible. Education and career opportunities are strictly limited. Social mobility is rare. The measure of human dignity afforded the average man is slight." The picture was not much better elsewhere. Consequently, "a large majority of the young people of Europe, including the United Kingdom, cannot expect to cross the class boundary which now contains them." Europe simply needed a more "democratic economic and social system." But unfortunately, Stone continued, "the drift in Europe may go in the wrong direction unless large efforts are made to counteract it."

Worse, American efforts to support "positive solutions to European problems are complicated by the myopic picture (the Asian view is similar) which millions of Europeans have of the United States." America, he argued, is looked upon by many as the "protector of the status quo" when the people of Europe were really looking for change. At the root of this perception of America lay, in Stone's view, the "lack of understanding of the nature of the American system and the failure of the United States to convey to leaders and peoples abroad the spirit of our society." True, Americans wanted "security and stability, but our secret has been innovation, change, flexibility and progress." Accordingly, "every new development in business and industry, each new achievement in the social and natural sciences, the general restlessness of American life is the antithesis of the status quo." Hence it was "the task of American private endeavor to ignite Europe with the spirit of our institutions, not to try to make Europe copy them." If the Europeans merely emulated the American "example of expanding democracy," then "orderly and rapid evolution will be possible." If, on the other hand, "a new spirit is not infused in European society, revolution, supported by the Communists, may win the sympathies of the people."

Turning toward Eastern Europe, Stone believed that "the shift in Soviet tactics is opening new perspectives for the United States" in those parts. That was why "the West must be alert to study," for example, "the school and university systems which are producing a prodigious number of apparently well-qualified scientists and mathematicians." Soviet satellites, he added, posed a particular "challenge to Western initiative and resourcefulness" in respect of future contacts. All these observations, Stone was convinced, justified an "expanded Foundation activity in Europe" that would include "the stimulation of financial contributions from European sources." Toward the end of his long submission, he finally addressed the question of a possible organizational structure for a European program. In his view, the "minimum requirement would be distinct program status and financing arrangements comparable to those which have been established in connection with the Overseas Development program." However, he also saw "substantial reasons for the view that organizational independence would be the most effective solution."

His conclusion reemphasized that "a Ford Foundation program in Europe would serve vital interests of the United States and the free world." But as a trained historian and advocate of an elitist Atlanticism, tempered, to be sure, by Ivy League notions of American democracy defined in terms of gradualism, meritocratic openness, and high social mobility, Stone identified a further rationale behind his plans: "During the first five hundred years European ideas, talents and inventiveness have made outstanding contributions to the welfare of the world. Government and law, science and industry, culture and philosophy have been enriched by the European mind. In supporting programs in Europe, the Foundation may help to bring about a renaissance of European genius and thought which would benefit peoples everywhere." In this sense the Atlantic represented to him a two-way sea lane on which, with Ford Foundation help, the Americans as well as other nations could not only keep importing the best of a reborn European culture, but the Europeans would also become more appreciative of America's more recent cultural achievements and diverse ways of social organization. Shils, Bell, and the CCF's mission were never far away in this vision.[22]

At the end of September 1956, Price, slowly won over by these arguments, presented the gist of Stone's report to the trustees endorsing its general recommendations. He also concurred with the organizational proposals "in theory," but added "that this problem is so much tied up with broader organizational problems which the Foundation faces that it cannot be considered in isolation."[23] In other words, the administrative question was still up in the air. Katz, now serving as a consultant, put up further hurdles. Although he now agreed that "the Ford Foundation should have a European program," he believed that some of Stone's ideas required "action in the political sphere of a kind inappropriate for the Foundation." Nor did he feel that the European budget should grow immediately to the $5 million that Stone had asked for.[24]

If Katz's points still carried some weight, this time his hesitations were overwhelmed by the dramatic events in East Europe at the end of October 1956. With the Hungarian and Polish revolutions before their eyes, the trustees at their December meeting felt that it had become impossible to draw a line between appropriate philanthropy and inappropriate political foundation activities. They listened to Price and Stone making their case for a total annual appropriation of $5 million, which, as the two officers added, would be "neither more costly than nor basically different from what the Foundation had done in the past with respect to Europe, but that it would be better organized, make the most effective use of Foundation funds, and might stimulate philanthropy in Europe."[25] And this time Stone—firmly supported, it seems, by McCloy—more or less got his way. Of a total budget distribution of $45.8 million for 1957, he received some $5 million and, after a discussion of the Hungarian Revolution, the trustees appropriated an additional "initial $500,000 for 'East European Activity.'"[26] Looking back and remembering the foundation's troubles with McCarthy, Stone called the East European program "the most adventurous and bold decision made by the trustees."[27] But more money was to come. In 1957 $1 million was committed in aid to Hungarian refugee students, while the embryonic Polish exchange program received $500,000.

Still, there was something of an irony in this outcome: after years of internal struggle, his West European program, which was designed to

185

counter not only the Soviet threat but also European anti-Americanism, had been put on a firm basis not because his superiors were particularly convinced of its need but because of the human and intellectual tragedy that was playing out in the East. If, as Hungary and Poland demonstrated, the cold culture war against the Soviet Union had for all practical purposes already been won, waging the other battle of convincing the West Europeans of the value of American culture was also less urgent. At the same time there was a grain of truth in Stone's pessimistic and critical portrait of the state of European societies and the one-sided picture that many European intellectuals had of the dynamics of America. Furthermore, Washington's intervention to stop the French and British in Suez had reinforced resentments among the elites of the two old colonial powers who, until the 1956 debacle, had still seen themselves as major players on the world stage next to the United States. Nor, in his view, did Soviet repression in Eastern Europe create a fresh reason for a renewal of the early-1950s confrontationism designed to "roll back" the Soviets.[28] The events in Hungary and Poland and the intellectual ferment that they had brought into the open rather presented opportunities for dialogue and exchange across the Iron Curtain. These considerations had propelled the Conditions of Peace project at the height of the Cold War and were now paving the way for the official detente that began in the late 1950s.[29]

It also helped that the foundation's funding pie kept growing and that the International Affairs program therefore did not have to make particularly tough decisions. The West European program could still be pursued in the wake of the East European and later the Asian and African one, also by connecting them. In 1958 IA was given $5.7 million; by 1963 Stone's operating budget had grown to $10 million, and in 1966, his last year at the Foundation, he had $19.6 million to spend. This was the high point of Ford generosity. The end of the Heald presidency, during which McCloy had also become chairman of the board of trustees, led to a sharp curtailment of expenditures, the reason for which was a simple one: sitting on a huge endowment which had meanwhile been securely invested and diversified, the trustees began to "invade" their capital. Up to 1962 some $600 million had been spent above net income. The amount had been taken from the endowment. In the "first eleven months" of the 1962 fiscal year the foundation "committed $243 million, almost twice its income," for philanthropic purposes. Although the same document announced that "the Foundation in the next few years expects to continue spending beyond its income by invading capital," there was obviously a limit to this practice and this had been reached in 1966 when McGeorge Bundy became president.[30]

Having traced the genesis and financial base of Stone's little empire, it is time to expand on the substance of his work. Unfortunately the account of his activities after 1956 raises considerable problems of presentation. His uncataloged papers reflect an enormous variety of issues and matters that came across his desk. Recounting them in chronological order simply as they arose would be very confusing. Thus a thematic approach is taken in this chapter to highlight the main areas of IA activity up to 1966–67, when Stone left the Foundation—a story to be taken up in chapters 8 and 9.

LOOKING EAST

The fallout from the revolutionary events in Hungary and Poland at the end of 1956 continued to dominate Stone's life well into the spring of 1957. In fact he spent a good deal of this period in Austria, close to the drama just across the Iron Curtain. The need for funds to help thousands of desperate refugees was overwhelming. Quick action was frequently required. To give just one example: on 17 January 1957 Price got Heald to authorize Stone "to commit the Ford Foundation to making a grant of up to $10,000 for a piece of physical equipment"—in fact, a bulldozer "to clear snow-clogged mountain passes so that more Hungarians could get through them."[31]

The grant of $500,000 that the trustees had voted in December 1956 was soon used up. Price therefore informed Stone in the middle of January that an additional $650,000 had been granted. Originally, the intention had been to use $150,000 of the total of $1.15 million now given "within the United States and the remaining million in Europe."[32] But did all this generosity mean that the program Stone had designed in the fall of 1956 might be thrown back into the melting pot? In a memorandum to Price of 10 January he requested that "we defer a general paper on priorities in the European Program" until his return to New York. He added that "investigations in Europe may suggest a shift" in current priorities. Over the next few months, these priorities would "necessarily be influenced by the critical events" in Eastern Europe. Although he wanted "the objectives of the European Program, as outlined and approved," to remain in force, the immediate focus should be "on programs related to (1) Hungarian student-intellectual refugee problems; (2) the development of East-West

187

contacts on a democratic basis; (3) the strengthening of democratic institutions in Europe, particularly in France and Italy." He also pleaded for flexibility, which had just demonstrated its value.[33]

While Stone worried that "Hungary" might undo a larger strategy that he had just gotten the foundation leadership to agree to, his boss Price, having allocated a lot of money in a hurry, was more concerned that the funds were being properly administered and that no awkward precedents were being created "that would lead us into grants for the contribution of supplies and materials for general welfare or relief purposes with respect to the refugee situation." Nor, he warned, were funds to be expended on particular projects if the Austrian government or other private organizations were already active.[34]

As for Europe, Price had stressed many times how much Hungary was at the top of his list. However, he wanted "to stick with the students and intellectuals." But this time his insistence on tidiness was not meant to restrain Stone. Indeed on 1 February he sent him his "warmest congratulations of [sic] all of us on what you have been able to do in such a short time." President Heald, he added, had also expressed his appreciation. Another concern of Price's was to make certain that responsibility rested with those countries of Europe, large and small, that had agreed to accept refugee students on a Ford foundation scholarship. The foundation was prepared to provide emergency support even where local matching funds were not available but was obviously not equipped to administer them. Nor could it be committed to further contributions "beyond the amount of the grant."[35]

The reasons for Price's administrative worries also emerge from a note that Stone sent him on 21 March after his return from Europe.[36] In the meantime another $280,000 had been added to the original $1.15 million. Of this total, exactly $1,425,505 had been spent, leaving a mere $4,495 in the kitty. Fortunately, though, the whole refugee program that the international community had launched in the fall of 1956 proved to be a great success and the immediate crisis was overcome. The West could now relax a bit and assess what might emerge from the East European upheavals. However, the foundation did not convert the sense of achievement and superiority in its values into a renewal of the Cold War but tried further to open the door to the East Central Europe. This meant that Stone now faced the task of nudging his superiors back to the program that he had crafted just before the outbreak of the crisis.

The only major remnant of the crisis and, as it turned out, headache left was the Philharmonia Hungarica orchestra, whose origins deserve brief consideration. With financial support, totaling around $220,000, initially from many sources, including the Rockefeller Foundation, the city of Zurich, and the Ford Foundation, the former assistant director of the Budapest Symphony Orchestra succeeded in reassembling many of its best instrumentalists.[37] After its first performance in Vienna in May 1957, the Philharmonia Hungarica quickly won acclaim; but money, for which the Congress for Cultural Freedom (CCF) had been used as a conduit, ran out faster than anticipated, and by the summer of 1958 the Ford Foundation was faced with another request for a grant.

Because the mere existence of the orchestra illustrated so well how the West differed from the Soviet bloc, it was thought important to continue philanthropic support for it. Indeed, on 5 August 1958 Heald received mail from no lesser person than Christian Herter, the acting secretary of state, in this matter: "The purpose of this letter is to advise you of the importance the Department attaches to the orchestra, and a strong desire that it continue as a going concern." He urged Heald to review the case.[38]

Heald obliged by recommending to the trustees that Rockefeller and Ford would share the cost on a fifty-fifty basis after deduction of some other financial support that had been promised in Europe. At the end of September a terminal grant of $66,750, to be channeled, as before, through the CCF, was accordingly approved on the understanding that "negotiations are being completed whereby the South German city of Passau will adopt the orchestra on a permanent basis as its own orchestra." The docket document added that "the fundamental reason for Foundation support is that a relatively small grant would assure the continued existence of an orchestra which is a potent political symbol favorable to the free world. . . . Leading government officials, top-ranking musicians and cultural leaders generally in the United States and Europe" had encouraged this action.[39]

With this problem out of the way, Stone's department could concentrate on his more long-term plan for increased academic and cultural contacts with Eastern Europe. Accordingly, in April 1957 the *New York Times* announced the giving of "a $500,000 Ford Foundation grant for the first program to bring Polish and later other East European economists, social scientists, experts etc. to the USA and Western Europe for study and training."[40] The Rockefeller Foundation initiated a similar program for medical and agricultural specialists. It was a risky venture and the foundation expected criticism from hard-line anticommunists who wanted to continue to fight the Cold War by more direct power-political and economic means. But there was also praise, for example, from Senator John F. Kennedy, who congratulated the foundation "for what will be the beginning of important developments between the USA and Eastern Europe."[41]

After working with Stone on the subject over the summer and urged by Allen Dulles to expand the program, Price, on 25 September 1957, sent Heald a memorandum that summarized "the state of our contacts with Eastern Europe under the International Affairs Program."[42] The Polish program was the most advanced, with some "54 Poles . . . already selected for study and travel in the United States and Western Europe," five of whom had started their sojourn the previous week. Beyond the continuing work on the Polish program, IA had also begun to "explore the possibilities of a smaller exchange with Yugoslavia." But "consideration of exchanges with other East European countries" had been deferred "until we are better able to judge current developments."

Price also mentioned that "State Department officials and Allen Dulles, head of CIA, are urging the Foundation to continue and expand the program in Poland and also in Yugoslavia, Czechoslovakia, Roumania, and possibly the Soviet Union." The State Department's advisory committee had looked into the question and the department had "committed itself to ask Congress for money for exchanges with East European countries." According to Price, Stone wanted to "discuss with the Poles future activities which may require an extension of our program there." He had also been invited to go to Yugoslavia. If Stone found conditions there to be favorable, "he may discuss exchange activity with the Yugoslavs," though on a smaller scale than with Poland. Of course, Price reassured the president, these "fall within the limits of the provision made in the 1958 planning budget for these particular activities." He also reiterated that the foundation had decided that it would deal with academic and cultural institutions only if selection of participants were free from communist government controls and if individuals selected would be allowed to travel and study freely in the West. Second, any plans would be discussed "with the State Department and other government agencies to guarantee that our actions are consistent with U.S. policies and objectives." Finally, there would be no "support of covert activities"—a sore, but crucial point to be taken up in greater detail in the next chapter.[43]

If the East European program was from the start guided by political considerations, the launching of the Soviet *Sputnik* space satellite and Khrushchev's triumphant speeches acted as a further boost. As the cold culture war had not just been fought on the social science and humanities front but had always included the competition between East and West in science and technology, *Sputnik* revived a heated debate as to whether the Soviets were winning it, after all. Passing through Vienna in October 1957 during those days of renewed, if ephemeral, American self-doubt, Stone reported that "our European friends are behaving better than I thought they would. No evidence so far of panic and a deep conviction that somehow the USA can outdo everybody in the world if it sets its mind to the problem." He added that "some leading European writers and thinkers are saying we shouldn't lose our faith in ourselves, that we can deliver the goods in a free society." Used to Europe's traditional cultural anti-Americanism, Stone thought that this was "a strange message to the American ear"—though he had no difficulty taking courage from this. As he wrote to Senator Ralph Flanders: "Along with the need to maintain military strength, it seems to me that we should also concentrate on ways to lead in a peaceful competition with the USSR. The fundamental values of our philosophy of government give us a headstart and a reappraisal may show us where greater emphasis must be placed."[44]

Nevertheless, given the anxieties that *Sputnik* unleashed in the United States, it was not too difficult for Stone to obtain the trustees' approval for another $500,000 "for continuation of the program to strengthen Poland's educational, scientific and cultural relations with the United States and other free nations."[45] By early 1958 the Polish initiative was paying its first tangible dividends. On 27 January, Stone wrote to Professor Josef Chalasinski in Warsaw to announce a visit by the distinguished Austrian-born sociologist Paul Lazarsfeld, who would be "available for discussions with individual Polish sociologists, psychologists, journalists and others and perhaps for one or two lectures."[46] At about the same time the IA director brought the "prominent revisionist" Leszek Kolakowski, who was on a research leave in Holland, for a visit to the U.S.[47] In the meantime progress was also being made with regard to Yugoslavia; because it looked as if a program similar to the Polish one might soon be in place, IA asked the trustees in March 1958 to amend the geographic terms of reference for the December 1957 allocation of $500,000 to include "other European countries."[48]

Further investigations authorized by Heald had revealed that "we should soon commence a program in Yugoslavia and be prepared for activities in other East European countries including Soviet Russia."[49] There had also been further encouragement from the State department to go ahead with the expansion.[50] In June the department was itself hoping "to

191

obtain $280,000 in 1958–1959 [and] $1,000,000 in 1959–1960 for Russian, Polish and other satellite exchange[s]."[51]

In July, however, the Yugoslav program was running into trouble, partly, it seems, because of the crisis in Lebanon and Soviet-American tensions over Berlin. Stone found it was the wrong moment to visit Belgrade. Rather than returning empty-handed, he suggested that Waldemar Nielsen go in October to see if the Yugoslavs were minded to give a reply to the foundation's proposals at that point. If progress were still unsatisfactory, "we can always stop the program without any great harm."[52] On 4 September Nielsen was "pleased to report that our negotiations with the Yugoslavs have now had some concrete results," after he had made it clear to the Yugoslav ambassador to the United Nations in New York that "either the Yugoslav government was prepared to get on with a trial project as we had proposed or it was not," in which latter case "we were disposed to put the whole matter aside indefinitely."[53] This ultimatum—and perhaps also William Deakin's visit to Belgrade, where the warden of St. Antony's College in Oxford saw Tito—did the trick. In any case, further contacts revealed that Belgrade was now "prepared to have us proceed" and that the Yugoslav government would cooperate and discuss details of the selection process.[54]

If toward the end of 1958 the Yugoslav project looked brighter, the Polish program had suddenly been developing various snags. In November Dr. Ludvik Leszczynski, the director of universities at the Ministry of Higher Education, had visited the United States after Stone had dealt with him in Warsaw and come to view him as "a cynical man who has been of great use to us."[55] While in New York, Leszczynski "repeated what we have heard from ministers and other high authorities in Poland"—that is, "that the Poles are happy with the program and want it to be continued and expanded." However, he had also indicated that his government wanted greater influence over the selection of Polish academics for the exchange program. Stone promptly replied that if the Polish authorities interfered with the foundation's free choice of candidates, the program would be stopped. After this, Leszczynki hastened to confirm "that he would not make an issue" of his proposal. Stone should "drop all consideration of it and assume the question had not arisen." Clearly the Ford Foundation was not without power.[56]

The complicating factor on the Polish front was that Leszczynski was on his way out and resigned shortly after his return from New York to Warsaw. According to the official version, he left for reasons of poor health; but it was no secret that he was not a dyed-in-the-wool communist. Stone caught a glimpse of his innermost feelings when he drove Leszczynski to Idlewild Airport on his way back to Poland. During the ride Leszczynski became "rather emotional as he looked at the lights of New York from Triborough Bridge." Evidently thinking of Khrushchev's recent propaganda offensive, he did not understand, he remarked spontaneously, why the Americans were so fearful of Russia. If only they were more confident of their own strength and vitality, "within a few years," it would be the Soviet leader who would "be answering you people and not always the other way around."[57]

When Stone visited Warsaw at the end of January 1959 "to determine the effects of the resignation of Mr. Leszczynski," the latter was quite open about "the old, more rigid Communist wing of the Party" which had "become increasingly perturbed by developments at Polish universities." Revisionism, he believed, had grown "too strong in the universities," and "the young people" as well as professors were "wandering too far away from Marxism."[58] There was also the conflict over the continuation of compulsory lectures on Marxism. At the same time Stone came to feel that Leszczynski's resignation had also been triggered by more personal factors. He found the latter rather gruff and discovered that the academics for whom he was responsible disliked him. He allegedly treated them rudely and did not get on with Eugenia Krassowska, the vice minister for higher education and other superiors.[59] Nevertheless, although he had lost his staunchest supporter in the Polish bureaucracy, Stone left with a strong sense that the program should be continued.

Unfortunately for him the administrative hurdles that had complicated the exchange at the start reappeared soon after Leszczynski's departure. Time and again academics selected by the Ford Foundation under the agreed procedure had difficulties obtaining a passport and exit visas. In May 1959 the foundation gave the U.S. embassy in Warsaw a list of people whose passports had been denied. This happened less than two weeks after Stone and Heald, on an extended European tour that also took them to Warsaw, had had discussions with the top leadership of the Ministry of Higher Education and the Polish Academy of Sciences. In the course of one of these meetings, Stefan Zoelkievski, the minister, had personally reassured the two American visitors "that there was no change in the Polish attitude toward the Ford Foundation program" since his last meeting with Stone. He then thanked Heald for what the foundation "had done and is doing" and in fact asked for an expansion of the program.[60]

These words provided further encouragement to Stone to remain firm on the question of unfettered selection. He merely agreed to interview not just those scholars who appeared on the foundation's lists but also those put forward by the ministry. The concession did not stop the trouble over exit visas,[61] and in December 1959 IA gave the Polish ambassador to the United Nations yet another list with the names of Poles "who, according to our information, had not yet received passports."[62] Stone told the diplomat that positive action was "vital for the program"; in response the latter pleaded with him not to abandon the program. Doing so, he said, would "be a heavy psychological blow to leading thinkers in Poland and have a political significance comparable to an important governmental action." It would also, as Stone phrased it, "defeat Western interests in maintaining an important opening into the 'socialist' orbit."[63]

These problems and difficulties with other East European countries notwithstanding,[64] contacts with the Soviet bloc were now being maintained on a very different scale than a mere few years earlier. The trustees felt encouraged and in December 1959 approved a grant of $300,000 "to support exchanges and other activities involving the Soviet Union, the U.S. and Europe."[65] Taking a global view, in the fall of 1958 the foundation had even begun to look toward the other communist great power, China, and, as before, after consultations with the CIA's Allen Dulles and the State Department. As Frank Ninkovich put it in his retrospective analysis: "In a real sense it was believed that the struggle for Europe's future was being waged in the rice paddies of Asia."[66]

Midwife to European Philanthropy

The consultations with Washington revealed two further aspects of IA's proliferating activities. First, by the early 1960s its operations expanded increasingly into Third World countries, ultimately necessitating an agreement with Stone's colleagues in Overseas Development (OD). This expansion has to be seen in connection with the fact that the upheavals in Poland and Hungary had been one half of a double crisis, the other half being the Franco-British-Israeli attack on Egypt. The forced retreat of France and Britain at the insistence of the United States and the sharp blow to European prestige and power in Asia and Africa that this defeat brought with it had two consequences. On the one hand, it led the Soviet Union, weakened in Eastern Europe, to woo the "bloc-free" countries in the hope of moving them into the Soviet orbit; on the other, it drew Washington into the Third World to fill the gap left by the former colonial powers. And since the United States had to move cautiously to control the damage to the pride of its NATO allies while raising suspicions of a new American imperialism in Asia, Africa, and Latin America, the foundations were willy-nilly sucked into this power-political whirlpool. As had become more general practice, they responded by providing humanitarian-philanthropic aid with indirect support from American diplomacy.

It might therefore be argued that there was a certain inexorability to IA's expansion. Nor was it surprising that Japan should be among the countries to appear in Stone's telescope. After all, Japan offered many similarities with the American experience in Europe and Germany. Defeated by the Allies in World War II, the Japanese, like the Germans, had undergone reconstruction and "reorientation" under an Allied occupation that was almost exclusively dominated by the United States.[67] With the escalation of the Cold War, it came to be seen as an important counterweight to communist China. But it was also no secret that parts of its population, particularly its elites, still harbored many reservations and resentments about the United States.

All this seemed to Stone to provide plenty of opportunity for IA activity. Accordingly, the foundation became involved in developing Japanese studies in the United States; other programs offered exchange fellowships. In yet another IA initiative, the foundation made grants to Japanese institutions. Between 1954 and 1960 over $1.3 million were allocated to promote these projects.[68] Further pledges were made in the early 1960s. Thus the larger items in the proposed 1962 budget included support for urban planning in Japan ($500,000), English-language promotion ($500,000), "professional and intellectual contact" ($2 million), American studies ($700,000), contacts between Japan and Europe ($3 million), "training in Japan for Asians" ($500,000), and Asian area studies ($750,000). The grand total came to $8.1 million.[69] Even if not all these projects were approved, they reflect clearly enough both Stone's relentless activism and the new directions in which IA was moving by the early 1960s.

Thenceforth IA routinely operated beyond its original European scope, sometimes on the immediate periphery, as in the case of the "Algerian situation" in 1962. On 30 January David Heaps reminded Stone of earlier discussions with the State Department on this point during which the diplomats "had indicated a certain degree of official interest in the Ford Foundation looking at this particular region." Heaps had also been told that the department had talked with French officials and "cleared the way for the possibility of private program activities in Algeria."[70] Secretary of State Dean Rusk personally favored a foundation commitment since "even if Algeria were to be granted its independence in the near future, it was unlikely that any official U.S. activity could be undertaken other than grain shipments or similar general aid projects." On other occasions, IA ventured further afield as, for example, in its support of the International Press Institute, a Swiss-based organization devoted to bringing journalists from countries all over the Third World together for conferences and information sessions.[71]

Whether it was in connection with the developing "Algerian situation" or with problems further south on the African continent, as early as February 1960 IA felt the time had come to form a closer liaison with OD and Frank Sutton, who had a special interest in Africa. On 3 Feburary Stone met Sutton in Paris to introduce him to some of the pointmen with whom IA had been working. He also arranged a meeting for Sutton with Josselson and John Hunt of the CCF, whose activities had similarly begun to reach well beyond their original home territory in Eastern and Western Europe. Having been briefed on IA's programs, Sutton was also told by Stone that they "would have to take up the organizational question of the European aspects of the African program" after their return to New York. Officially, Stone aimed at closer cooperation with OD. In this endeavor, he did not see, as he put it, "any jurisdictional problems"; nor did he anticipate "personal or other problems." Sutton, after all, was "a fine fellow."[72]

Similarly he wrote Josselson on 9 March 1960 "that there will be the friendliest and best cooperation between Frank and our office." But on closer inspection the relationship seems to have been more complicated than this, given that the foundation was by then a very large organization and that, like all bureaucracies, it too—as we have seen more than once— was plagued by interdepartmental rivalries and competition for scarce resources. Remembering this from his own bitter experience in 1954–55, Stone therefore insisted that his memorandum about Sutton was "only for IA eyes." His colleagues back in New York were advised that the matter would be discussed "thoroughly upon my return." There was the additional problem of the CCF's operations in Africa. So, here, too, it was important to prevent wires from getting crossed. Consequently, "the normal line of communication" of the CCF with the foundation was to run through IA, "and we shall see to it that the other parts of the Foundation are always informed wherever appropriate." Clearly, Stone had learned how to operate within a large-scale organization and how important it was to be able to rule when the passing-on of information was appropriate.[73]

Six months later, on 3 August, Nielsen sent Stone a letter in which he reported on a "long and fruitful talk with Frosty [Hill] about our plan to open a European office and set up a European representative."[74] This was an old idea of Stone.[75] Nielsen also felt that the training and research facilities of Europe could be used to support the Asian and African programs.

Finally, there was a development that was implicit in Nielsen's remarks and that was leading Stone to seek closer cooperation and an understanding with OD. He was convinced that the Europeans should make private contributions to the development of the Third World. By the late 1950s, as Europe had been experiencing almost continuous growth and prosperity for the entire decade, Stone began to launch a campaign telling the Europeans and soon also the Japanese that the time had come for action to help not only themselves but also the poorest nations. One of his first steps was to raise the matter privately with the influential and the mighty, especially in Germany, where he had the best contacts going back to his HICOG days and where he also had the greatest moral leverage among the guilt-ridden elites who were trying to rebuild the positive international image that the Nazis had destroyed.

Thus, on 8 March 1960 he received a letter from Max Kohnstamm, a Dutchman and former close aide of Jean Monnet, who had learned from a German lawyer "that Krupp was seriously considering turning his property into a foundation of the Ford Foundation type." Kohnstamm added: "The thing seems to be treated as a great secret and . . . only a few people, working on the legal aspects for Krupp, were in the know." He then discussed some good advice which he had given his contact and concluded that in light of "the immense prestige which Mr. McCloy has in Germany it might not be entirely out of the question for him to exert a certain influence on these developments."[76] With McCloy (who as U.S. high commissioner had once signed Krupp's early release from his imprisonment as a war criminal) in the background, it was Stone who, over the next two years, personally pursued this matter, raising it with Berthold Beitz, Alfried Krupp's trusted *major domus*.[77] Finally, on 19 February 1962, McCloy and he heard the gratifying news at a luncheon with Beitz that a Krupp Foundation would definitely be established.[78]

Beitz informed the two Americans in "strictest confidence" of a settlement that had been arranged for Krupp's son Arndt and that Alfried had recently changed his will so "that the Krupp Company—or fortune— would be turned into a Foundation." A few of Krupp's confidants, he added, "were studying Ford and other American foundations as guides to Krupp." They had also had before them the "FF charter etc." that Stone had sent to Beitz, Krupp's designated executor. Although Beitz "spoke critically of the Thyssen Foundation as a tax dodge," he listened attentively when Stone told him "that European lawyers were working with us to loosen up the laws for purposes of supporting foundations." Obviously, McCloy and his protégé were delighted with the news and stressed "that it would be good for human welfare and for Germany's and Krupp's name if the objectives of the Krupp Foundation were worldwide and similar to Ford's." It would be particularly helpful "if the Krupp Foundation made grants, for example, to Harvard, Oxford, Delhi, etc., and other non-German institutions"—an idea with which Beitz agreed and that was later partially realized. Apart from a genuine philanthropic interest, there may well have been another one that McCloy pointed out at the meeting: "When old John D. Rockefeller had first established the Rockefeller Foundation his name was anathema to Americans. Today the Rockefeller name is held in great honor and esteem."[79]

While the Krupp Foundation soon began its philanthropic work, there is a larger context to the Beitz-McCloy-Stone connection. In the meantime Stone was no longer just privately advising and prodding the wealthy in Europe; nor was he just working with legal experts in Europe "to loosen up" tax laws. Rather he had also begun to make public speeches on the need for the Europeans to become philanthropists and to organize seminars offering practical advice on technicalities and tax rules. The big difference was, of course, that in the United States setting up a charitable trust was tax deductible. European tax laws by contrast were much less favorable to private donors. Consequently Stone also began a campaign for a simplification of Europe's laws and their adaptation to the American system.

He can have had few illusions that it would be easy to effect these changes in mentality and legislation. In the long run, however, changes were made. Prosperity continued and by the 1990s enough wealth had been accumulated for parents and grandparents not merely to pass it on to their heirs,[80] but also to set up charitable trusts. As the annual reports of the *Stifterverband*, which acts as an umbrella organization for many smaller trusts in Germany, show, their number has grown remarkably.[81] Although the United States remains the classic country of large private foundations, they have also mushroomed in Western Europe. Stone's lectures stood at the beginning of this development.

Now, if European private foundations were still relatively few in 1960 and big semipublic philanthropic organizations like the Volkswagen Foundation had only just been established,[82] were there perhaps other ways in which the Europeans could be made to share the burdens, especially in the Third World? Believing that they were wealthy enough to give privately, Stone raised the Indian "food problem" when, in early March 1960, he met with Fritz Berg, the president of the powerful West German Bundesverband der Deutschen Industrie (BDI) and some of his colleagues at the house of the Cologne banker Baron von Oppenheim.

Considering that experts viewed starvation as one of the fundamental questions in South Asia, the West, Stone wrote to Berg afterward in almost perfect German, "should try to help India to become self-sufficient in food production within the next ten years." To make clear how much American philanthropy was already doing, he added for good measure that the Ford Foundation trustees would probably approve next week, in addition to the current program, $11 million for programs to increase India's food production. This is why he was asking Berg, "if Germany would support the program in the seven other states" that were in need of help. Stone hoped that Berg and his colleagues as well as Economics Minister Ludwig Erhard and Hermann Abs, the chairman of Deutsche Bank, would study the Ford Foundation project and send experts to India to gain a firsthand impression of the problem. He and his American friends would "consider it a big positive step [forward] if Germany would support this food program outside the [official] German credit and investment program." In other words, the time had come for West German private interests no longer merely to point to efforts by the German state, but to complement, in the style of American foundations, public development aid with private efforts.[83]

Although Berg's response is not known at this point,[84] Abs certainly took the cue and got busy. As Stone learned on 24 May 1960, the influential banker had "nothing but praise for the Ford Agricultural project in India" and felt that "it should serve as a model, especially to the Germans."[85] He had also seen Heinrich Lübke, the president of the Federal Republic, about the matter and had furnished him with translations of Stone's memoranda, urging him "to back some specific project in India along the lines you suggested." At the same time Abs had been trying to prevent Lübke from proceeding with his own scheme "for collecting money on a private (charity-type) basis for a general purpose." In Abs's view, the president was "going about the problem of Germany and the less-developed nations in a fuzzy way and in a manner which is very disturbing to the German Executive Branch which is trying to stop" him. Abs, Stone was informed, was "very anxious to work with you and is hopeful." The trouble was that, according to Abs, there was "no focal point now in Germany to work out these problems."

Although it was difficult "to get good people to be willing to go abroad and work in the less-developed countries," the Germans, Abs was convinced, "must greatly increase their assistance" to them. Chancellor Konrad Adenauer had "told him recently that this is difficult from a political point of view before the [upcoming national] elections"; nevertheless the banker believed—perhaps still not quite getting Stone's main point—"that the German people would be willing to pay higher taxes, if they understood the purposes and were convinced Germany had a good plan." As to German foundations, Abs remarked that the Volkswagen Foundation would "concentrate on German education (particularly at the secondary level) and would not work on problems of the less-developed nations." However, a large special fund would shortly be set up "out of old ECA counterpart [monies] for loans and projects" in the Third World. Otherwise Abs liked "U.S. tax incentive and insurance schemes to stimulate private foreign investment;" but this point demonstrated once again how far removed the well-to-do in West Germany still were from Ford-style philanthropy.

Stone did not give up. Thus, when he talked to the trustees on 24 June 1960, he argued once more that Europe's economic recovery "makes it possible for a number of European countries to finance many of their own institutions and puts Europe in a position to increase [its] support for underdeveloped countries." It therefore remained "important for [the] Foundation to stimulate a small number of Euro[pean] institutions, including institutions in some of the less developed parts of Europe, where the benefits go beyond local tendencies and help to extend positive dev[el]opments] in free countries." The "new and significant function of [the] IA program [was] to stimulate European contributions of funds and talents" to the Third World.[86] This was also the message that he had left with the Japanese, but only to find that local traditional structures and mentalities were no less difficult to change overnight than in Europe.[87]

However, it would be giving a misleading impression of the Ford Foundation's international activities in the late 1950s and early 1960s to imply that everything now revolved around relations with OD and the Third World. Appearing before the trustees on 24 June 1960 also gave Stone an opportunity to discuss the East European program as well as those activities that were really dearest to his heart, namely, the "strengthening of the European-Atlantic Community." For "in the long struggle or competition [with the East], it is the community which has the resources, talents, skills which, put together, can give the Free World a chance to come out on top." Especially "when the chips are down—this and no other area is the crucial area for [the] USA and for [the] developing countries." Accordingly he stressed once again that the "Foundation can make [an] important contribution here to strengthen [the] intellectual, scientific, institutional and even political community."[88]

We have thus reached the final and core element of the international program that Stone began to build in 1955 after the conflicts over strategy and organization within the foundation had been resolved and his plans had been accepted by the new president and the board of trustees, on which McCloy was now a major voice. In recounting Stone's work in this field, a return to the previously mentioned East European program presents a good starting point. As has been noted, not all funds spent within this program went into exchanges and direct support of academic institutions in Poland and elsewhere in the Soviet bloc. Instead some of the foundation's grants were channeled into West European institutes for studying the Soviet world and communist China and to train experts in the problems posed to the West by those parts of the world.

CULTURAL AND POLITICAL INVESTMENTS

A good illustration of this type of Ford Foundation philanthropy is the support given to St. Antony's College, Oxford. Founded in May 1950 with an endowment from the French millionaire Antonin Besse of Aden and headed by William Deakin, St. Antony's was conceived as an international center for graduate training and specialized research in the humanities. Running one of the poorest Oxford colleges in terms of its endowment, Deakin was constantly on the road in search of external funding. He was well connected and polished, highly decorated in wartime as Churchill's liaison to Tito's partisans in Yugoslavia, and author of *The Brutal Friendship*, a major study of German-Italian relations under Hitler and Mussolini.[89] It is not difficult to see why Stone took to the warden of St. Antony's and was spontaneously disposed to support Deakin's project proposals. There was also the aura of Oxford, with its elitism and the sense of a "special" Anglo-American relationship fostered by World War II, that attracted the American ex-officer to the British one. Above all, however, St.Antony's had hired a number of fellows working on those Eastern parts of the world about which Stone felt more knowledge was needed in the interests of both deescalating the East-West conflict and buttressing the Atlantic community.

201

This was the background to a grant proposal for $300,000 put before the executive committee on 19 March 1959 for the "development of a program in East European and East Asian studies at St. Antony's College over a five-year period." The submission added that the foundation had a "sustained interest in the deepening of knowledge in the Western world of Communist ideology and practice." The college had already attracted an illustrious group of experts, among them "David Footman, a former member of the British Foreign Office; Max Hayward, who translated [']Doctor Zhivago['] into English; Carew Hunt, author of a dictionary of Communism which has been translated into many languages; and George Katkov and Wolfgang Leonhard, who have written important books on Russia."[90] Professors Hugh Seton-Watson, Max Beloff, and Isaiah Berlin, the expert journalists Victor Zorza and Richard Löwenthal, were also mentioned as "frequent participants in the work of St. Antony's."[91]

Thanks to a 1955 grant of $125,000 from the Rockefeller Foundation, the college had been able to establish "close relations with European scholars at the Free University of Berlin, at the Sorbonne, and at other European institutions."[92] Its Middle Eastern Centre had been funded by grants from Shell, British Petroleum, and the Gulbenkian Foundation. Finally, the Leverhulme Trust and Australian organizations had put money into an embryonic Far Eastern studies development. For all these reasons St. Antony's looked like a good match when Stone, with the CIA's encouragement, began to work on a Ford Foundation program relating to China.[93] The fellows working in the Far Eastern field were not quite as well known as their colleagues attached to the East European center; but the idea now had the blessing of the key authorities in Washington.

If support for research on Eastern Europe and China in Western European institutions was one way for Stone to build bridges across the Atlantic, he and his like-minded colleagues were always also motivated by considerations that went beyond fighting the Cold War in the East with intellectual and cultural weapons and keeping the power-political competition between the Soviet Union and the United States from ending up in a hot war. From 1955 onward if not before (and occasional bouts of self-doubt notwithstanding), the protagonists of this "coexistential" kind of East-West relationship had become convinced that their ideological weapons were superior to those of the Soviets, communists in Western Europe, and fellow-traveling intellectuals. In this respect, the challenge of *Sputnik* was no more than a temporary crisis of confidence that moreover confirmed Stone's belief in the value of his decision to include the hard sciences in Europe in his program. Accordingly, the foundation had given, from 1956 onward, grants to the tune of $1.8 million to CERN, the European nuclear energy research outfit in Geneva, and to the institute of the famous Danish nuclear physicist Niels Bohr.

Thanks to John Krige's work we are well informed about this intriguing aspect of the foundation's activities. Richard Courant of New York University had first drawn Gaither's attention to Bohr in August 1951. His letter not only highlighted the latter's achievements as a scientist, but also portrayed him as a man who was deeply concerned about "the problems of international relations and the maintenance of peace."[94] Given Gaither's own academic background and Hoffman's recent Conditions of Peace project, it is not surprising that the Ford team in California should be very interested. As Krige has put it: "What was important to Gaither and to the Ford Foundation was not Bohr the physicist but Bohr the man of international stature, Bohr the sure friend of democracy and the United States. Here was an extremely efficient way to spread an appreciation of America and its values to a wide and influential audience, including that in Western Europe where both France and Italy had strong Communist parties."[95] A connection with Bohr had the additional advantage of possibly facilitating contacts with scientists in the Soviet bloc. Clearly, if the dialogue between East and West could also be kept alive at this level, the hope was that these contacts, like the exchanges with social scientists, would contribute to easing tensions and building confidence between the two superpowers at a time when the nuclear arms race was gathering speed and Cold War tensions were rising. Nor would the Soviets immediately suspect the Danes of being in the pocket of the CIA.

For reasons that are not quite clear, an application to give support to Bohr's institute foundered at this stage. It may have been that the disagreement over Ford's international strategy played a role and perhaps also fear of McCarthy. However, once the decision in favor of a European program had been made, Stone as the driving force behind it helped to revive the idea. When he saw Bohr on his European trip in Copenhagen in August 1955, they talked about grants to CERN and to Bohr's institute.[96] Nine months later, a first grant for Bohr was approved. It is telling that Stone, in his letter of 30 April 1956 informing Bohr of the trustees' positive decision, still asked that the funds not be used "to support persons from Soviet Russia, Communist China, and the so-called Satellite countries."[97]

After the events in Poland and Hungary Stone dropped the foundation's objection to Bohr inviting scientists from Poland, and soon Soviet colleagues were also no longer excluded. The last obstacles to Ford-funded visits to Copenhagen and to CERN by Chinese scientists were finally removed in 1958. And always careful to coordinate policies with Washington, Stone saw to it that the CIA was fully informed when Bohr put forward a proposal to establish a scientific dialogue with China. As Stone told Nielsen in February 1958: "I spent two days in Washington with Niels Bohr and we had some fine talks with Allen Dulles and his boys."[98] Once again the Danish physicist used the occasion to argue that such open exchanges presented golden opportunities for the "free world." But there was always also the sense during those tense years that as long as the creators of the nuclear bomb kept talking in East and West, missiles would not be fired. Similar motives were also behind the foundation's temporary support of the *Bulletin of Atomic Scientists*, which discussed in its pages the dangers of a nuclear holocaust at a time when top leaders in Washington were speaking about "massive retaliation" as an allegedly viable strategic option in the age of multimegaton hydrogen bombs and long-range delivery capabilities on both sides.[99]

While the projects with St. Antony's, CERN, and other research institutes were progressing, the trustees were presented with proposals whose connection with the Cold War in the East was very tenuous at best. West European colleges and universities were given grants that were not designed to generate research of the kind undertaken by the Russian and Far Eastern centers in Western Europe. The first Ford Foundation monies to Berlin's Free University were still inspired by a strong sense that the front-line city in the Cold War against Stalin deserved a show of solidarity. Although this consideration never disappeared completely in the case of the Berlin, subsequent appropriations of funds were made to strengthen the social sciences and American studies there.

When in February 1958 a docket item on the Free University had to be postponed in light of the fact that "had we put everything at this meeting ..., we would have had about forty-three cents left in the bank until Oct. 1," as Stone confessed, it broke his "heart to hold up on the Free University." He did not know, he added half-seriously, how he was "going to face my former constituents" in Berlin.[100] But only a few months later the trustees were presented with another recommendation to approve "a five-year grant of $1 million to the Free University of Berlin to strengthen and expand its academic program through international exchange of professors, instructors, and students; development of its institutes; and establishment of a tutorial system."[101] And less than a year later Stone got his president to sign a memorandum for transmission to the executive committee of the board of trustees that recommended an allocation of $1 million to a "Special Berlin Project." This grant, of double the amount that had originally been requested, was earmarked for the city's Technical University.[102]

Echoes of the Cold War may also be detected in the plans to strengthen "the cultural and intellectual situation in Vienna" after the CCF had first established a base in the city. As Stone justified the initiative to Price and Nielsen: "The city has a strategic location between East and West; a positive and important factor is that Vienna and the Austrian tradition is [sic] all Western and the sentiments of the country are solid[ly] with the West. Vienna had always a great attraction for the people in the Balkans and also in Poland." At the same time, Vienna University was run by "mediocrity."[103] Consequently he was unwilling to do more at this stage than to consider supporting a few small research projects there and getting Paul Lazarsfeld to investigate further. By the spring of 1959 IA had received several proposals relating to Vienna. On 30 March Stone, anxious to exploit it as "a free, Western city of great magnetism for leading thinkers and students in Eastern Europe," invited Professors Hayek (Chicago), Lazarsfeld (Columbia), Sturmthal (Roosevelt College), von Klemperer (Smith College), and Hulla (New School) "to discuss the possibility of reviving Vienna as an intellectual center."[104] Lazarsfeld had some pretty depressing words about the situation in Vienna, but his remarks may only have acted as a stimulus to do something.[105] Stone agreed to make soundings at the foundation, and eventually Ford money also flowed to the Austrian capital.[106]

Other grants were made, however, that could not even remotely be considered to have had a link with the East-West conflict. In 1958 Oxford University received $1 million for the restoration of some of its time-honored buildings. After this endeavor had encountered criticism within the foundation, Alan Bullock, the biographer of Hitler and founder of St. Catherine's College in Oxford, approached Stone with a request for help at an unpropitious moment. He was told that the trustees were "unwilling to make any commitments to this new institution."[107] Another submission on behalf of the newly founded Churchill College in Cambridge for $1 million over five years was also put on ice, but later approved by the trustees. This College was to have a strong science and technology orientation, stemming "from [the] recognition that Britain's survival as a modern industrial nation is based on scientific development." Its exports and "role as a partner in the Atlantic Community" were portrayed as being dependent on this base.[108] What needed improvement and what Churchill College was expected to help remedy were both the inadequate numbers and the poor quality of trained scientists.

There was also a proposal from Oxford's Nuffield College, a graduate college like St. Antony's with a strong social science orientation. This proposal was justified to the trustees by reference to the notion that "the relations of the United Kingdom to the continent of Europe are of vital importance to the Western nations." The idea was to achieve "greater unity of thought and action" between Britain and its West European neighbors at a time when Britain had applied for membership in the European Economic Community (EEC).[109] Although some hard-nosed American experts opposed the application, believing "that the more analytical social sciences were stifled by historians on the other side of the Atlantic" who were to be involved in the project, Stone "cared more about scholarly traffic across the Channel than disciplinary mistrusts."[110] He was also himself a trained historian.

Finally, Isaiah Berlin, the eminent Oxford philosopher and fellow of All Souls, came to Stone in 1965 after the University's vice-chancellor had asked him to become principal of Iffley College. Berlin was tempted but knew that he had to raise a lot of money. After an intriguing journey through the thickets of Oxbridge academic politics, he got £1.5 million from the British philanthropist Isaac Wolfson (after whom Iffley College was then renamed) and, again with Stone's help, $4.5 million from McGeorge Bundy, just after he had become president of the Ford Foundation in 1966. Never had Ford made a larger single grant to a European academic venture. The reasons for such favoritism emerge at least in part from a scanning of Berlin's biography and basic ideological stance. Michael Ignatieff has called him a "New Deal liberal,"[111] a man who, born in Russia but finding a haven as a boy with his family in England in 1921, thought of himself as a firm anticommunist and as "liberal defender of the capitalist world and its freedoms." But he was not a laissez-faire marketeer; rather he was convinced "that individuals could not be free if they were poor, miserable, and under-educated." A believer in the Enlightenment traditions, he warned of the "counter-enlightenment" that kept threatening the modern world.

His old friends similarly tell a lot about him; in Britain they included the democratic-socialist philosopher Stuart Hampshire, Stephen Spender, and Noel Annan. On the other side of the Atlantic, he was close to Arthur Schlesinger Jr., and in Paris to Nabokov, impresario and CCF man. He was strongly committed to the Anglo-American connection, and when one reads his essays and books and relates his positions to the intellectual debates of his time, it is not surprising that he should be found in the pro-American camp of Europe's eminent academicians.[112] But he remained European in his attitudes and thinking about the dilemmas and contradictions of modern society and the darker sides of the human psyche. Indeed, however well integrated he may have been into British intellectual life, there was a "Continental" streak in his basic outlook on the world and he certainly believed that a technocratic style of politics "displaced moral disagreement," while creating the illusion of resolving it. He despised the "positivistic pedantry of American social science" and did not succumb to the rationalist dream "that, with sufficient social engineering, human evils could be abolished and individuals happily assimilated into a seamless social consensus."

This short excursion into the Berlinean world of ideas helps us to recall the larger ideological context in which the foundation's activities have to be seen in this period. It explains why American East Coast intellectuals should be attracted to his writings.[113] But these writings were also sufficiently different in style and message from those of the technocratic optimists on the other side of the Atlantic. They point, once again, to a gap that existed between Western Europe and the United States and may also explain why he did not assume a prominent public role in the CCF empire. It was to the bridging of this gap that Bundy and Stone, as confirmed anticommunist Atlanticists and believers in the high cultural achievements of their country, thought they were contributing when they enabled Berlin to realize, in the shape of Wolfson College, his idea of a liberal academic elite institution.

Next to Britain, where the foundation also supported the founding of the International Institute for Strategic Studies (IISS) in London and promoted the hard sciences at London University's Imperial College,[114] France became a major beneficiary of American beneficence. Perhaps the most important among a variety of ventures was a $1 million grant in 1959 in connection with the establishment of the Maison des sciences de l'homme.[115] Spearheaded by Gaston Berger, the director of higher education in the French Ministry of Education, the plan of a research and graduate training center for the social sciences and humanities came to be promoted by prominent academics, including the rector of the Sorbonne and the distinguished historian Fernand Braudel as head of the Sixth section of the Ecole pratique des hautes études.[116] Similarly the Ford Foundation helped Raymond Aron to launch his Institute of European Sociology in Paris.[117]

Like Berlin, Aron was another of those major European intellectuals whom the foundation supported because he embodied the transatlantic cultural connection that it hoped to promote both against the Soviet bloc and against the Sartrians in France. Unlike Berlin, Aron operated as a public intellectual throughout his life. We have already encountered him in chapters 4 and 5 as a pro-American who had "no patience for those who condemned 'consumer society' while poverty still stalked much of the globe," as well as for those who fetishized growth rates and prosperity levels. He was a typical antitotalitarian, and yet for him modern society insofar as it was democratically organized, was a "society to be observed without transports of enthusiasm or indignation." Putting him into the Parisian context, Tony Judt was probably right to call him a "peripheral insider"—a man rejected by his French fellow intellectuals but also despising them because they sought "neither to understand the world nor to change it, but to *denounce* it." But he was also a mandarin, and this drew him toward the academic elites of the United States.[118]

Given his peculiar position in France, he felt more at home with the Atlanticists in the rest of Western Europe. He was an active contributor to the CCF's cold culture wars, and we will meet him again in the next chapter when, for a brief period and with the encouragement of the Ford Foundation, he became chairman of the CCF board.[119] At the same time he was a difficult person, not easily integrated into the world of congress intellectuals. The fact that he did not shed his Gaullist sympathies indicates that he, too, remained rooted in a Continental tradition of thought and never warmed to "*les Anglo-Saxons*," and their discourses and styles of thinking.

Indeed, since his time in Berlin Aron had been familiar with the writings of Heinrich Rickert, Edmund Husserl, Max Weber, and Martin Heidegger and believed that they had been more sensitive to the extent of the European crisis than some of their French contemporaries and certainly much more so than the pragmatists and utilitarians of the English-speaking world. Still, for those Americans who were reaching out across the Atlantic there were not many Frenchmen like him, and it is no surprise that the Ford Foundation should be generous toward him. As Nielsen wrote to Stone in March 1961: "This is after all an investment in a man and his ideas, and I think it is very important at this stage to build it [i.e., the Institute of European Sociology] clearly around him and to leave his full authority unimpaired."[120]

When, as mentioned at the beginning of this chapter, Stone outlined his plans for a Eurocentric program in 1956, he also highlighted, next to projects for individual countries, the need to support transnational institution building in the Western European community and to foster ties with the United States. He closely observed the emergence of the EEC and kept in touch with his and McCloy's friend Jean Monnet, who was constantly pushing for the implementation and acceleration of the Rome Treaty of 1957. While it would have been inappropriate for the foundation to try to influence the economic integration process directly, Stone persuaded the trustees to provide collateral support that would benefit both the West Europeans and the United States. Since the late 1940s, all of Europe had been engaged in a vigorous program to modernize its industries and industrial infrastructures. Much of this modernization was purely physical. The replacement of war-damaged or obsolete machinery by the latest equipment and production arrangements on the shop floor was clearly an urgent task. However, there was also the immaterial side of productionism and Fordist efficiency drives that reached Europe from America: the need to replace the all-too-often patriarchal methods of industrial leadership and administration by modern management practices.[121]

Since the interwar period, if not before, American entrepreneurs had turned their attention to precisely these aspects of industrial organization and a number of universities had built up business schools to train people for white-collar careers in industry and commerce.[122] The case-based curriculum developed by the Harvard Business School had become particularly influential and in the late 1940s the first younger European managers had come to Cambridge, Massachusetts, to receive advanced training in business administration. One of them was Ludwig Vaubel, a rising star at Vereinigte Glanzstoff, a Rhenish chemicals trust with Dutch connections. He returned to Europe convinced that German industry must adopt the Harvard model of management training or a Germanized variant of it.[123] Accordingly he founded the Wuppertal Circle and was behind the establishment of a West German management training system.

In France, which after the war had begun a comprehensive and ambitious program of industrial modernization and reequipment under Monnet's leadership,[124] the training effort was spearheaded, among others, by a French-born professor of manufacturing at Harvard, George Doriot.[125] Similar initiatives were launched in the rest of noncommunist Europe, even as far away as Greece and Turkey. An official American stimulus for these developments was also provided by the productivity councils. Funded by Marshall Plan monies and promoted by Paul Hoffman, then still the Marshall Plan administrator in Europe, the councils sponsored informational trips by European businessmen to the major manufacturing centers in Pennsylvania, Michigan, and Ohio. There the visitors studied firsthand not only assembly line work but also management methods and industrial relations practices. European trade unionists were likewise invited to the United States to see the high living standards of American workers and to inform themselves about a system of labor relations that was not wedded to a Marxist class conflict model, then still widely upheld in Western Europe.[126] Those who could not go learned about the American system through lectures given by returning visitors or through the sessions of the Training within Industry (TWI) program.[127]

The impact of all these exchanges of information and experience and the resultant networking among people interested in American methods was no doubt considerable. So much is nowadays being written about the myth or reality of "Americanization" as a subtly creeping influence of cultural transfer through the media and Vance Packard's "hidden persuaders" of mass consumption that the other side of the coin—that of mass production, management, and marketing—is often underestimated. Even more underestimated are the very tangible efforts that the United States made actively to change European habits and traditions. We have seen in chapter 3 how Stone was involved in a well-funded official effort to change West Germany's political culture.[128] Similar efforts of recasting deeply rooted structures and mentalities were undertaken by OMGUS and HICOG on the business front.[129]

To be sure, in West Germany the Americans had greater leverage as an occupying power than they had in France or Britain. Among their wartime Allies they had to rely more on persuasion and on like-minded native activists such as Monnet. They could not intervene directly in their economies and hence took a more indirect route. But take it they did, and the process, at least in the sphere of business and production, was therefore driven much more by the intervention of individuals and organizations than meets the eye, blinded as we tend to be by assumptions about "dynamic anonymous forces" of the market as well as about self-generated and uncontrollable desires of the mass consumers and their individual choices.

In the field of labor relations American interventionism certainly accelerated already changing attitudes among employers as well as trade unionists. A growing number of them adopted an approach to collective bargaining that abandoned the class-conflict model still espoused by the communists. Gradually the protagonists of this approach began to replace the confrontationist traditions of the past, reflected in political or politicized strikes to advance the cause of socialism, on the one side, and inflammatory lockouts to destroy the dreaded "revolution," on the other. It must be said that this particular cultural change was slow. As far as trade unions were concerned, even the American AFL-CIO whose representatives, with Washington's backing, spread the message in Europe, found the job of nudging their European comrades toward a more reformist and procapitalist position difficult. But over time notions of class struggle on both sides of industry gave way to a "tripartism" that was also promoted by the predominance of the Keynesianism and "liberal corporatism" that Galbraith was popularizing in the 1950s.[130] This take on the development of modern industrial societies must, of course, in turn be linked to the cultural optimism purveyed by Daniel Bell and others, which has been analyzed in chapters 4 and 5. If one accepted the intellectual framework of the "Cold War liberals," it all fitted quite neatly together. American mass production, mass consumption, and mass culture were something to be adopted joyfully, not something to be rejected in a fit of old European cultural pessimism and traditional anti-Americanism.

The Ford Foundation was only indirectly involved in the labor relations effort—through the CCF and through the contacts that Stone and others had established over the years with Social Democrats all over Western Europe. It was a different matter on the management training side. Here the foundation became very active in the promotion of business education, helping European management schools to get off the ground, arranging for visits and consultancies by American experts, and funding summer courses on American campuses.[131] By 1960 there existed a European Association of Management Training Centers in Brussels whose president was Pierre Tabatoni, a confirmed "pro-American" and a major force in the whole movement. In the previous year, the European Institute of Business Administration (INSEAD) had been founded at Fontainebleau "to help meet the new requirements for top-quality management of European and international business organizations."[132] The Ford Foundation supported this venture in December 1960 with a grant of $120,000, which was renewed and increased to $150,000 in 1965.

All these IA activities had little to do with the East but all the more with Stone's Atlantic community. More precisely, they were designed to undermine the cultural anti-Americanism of Europe's economic and intellectual elites. In this respect the foundation's management education program, together with the many other efforts that were being made, must be considered a success. The programs not only helped the proliferation of American business practices, but also created a better appreciation and understanding among industrial and commercial elite groups for the strengths and complexities of American society. They may not all have read Bell's *End of Ideology*; but the title was no doubt appealing to pragmatists in industry who also found much that was plausible to them in the idea of a new age of industrial democracies in which all basic problems had allegedly been solved and the future merely required some reformist management and tinkering.[133]

This, at least, was what Waldemar Nielsen emphasized when he reported on a conference he had attended at Lourmarin in 1959, as discussed at the very beginning of this book.[134] Responding to an earlier memo by Stone to study "American cultural offerings abroad—orchestras, ballet etc.—and try to measure if we are getting the most out of our (including government's) money,"[135] he confirmed that the businessmen and government officials he had met on his trip to Europe had been brought around. And if the griping of the intellectuals at Lourmarin "about the inferiority of American values" was depressing, other events were a success. For example, a performance of "Shakespeare with Jazz" in Vienna, using Duke Ellington tunes, gained plenty of applause and a rave review in Berlin's *Tagesspiegel*.[136]

As we have seen in previous chapters and as Stone had complained again in his memorandum of 13 September 1956,[137] the United States did have image problems that had been worrying the East Coast establishment for many years. With the Cold War against the Soviet Union seemingly being won at the intellectual level from the mid-1950s onward, the struggle began all the more determinedly against Western Europe's cultural anti-Americanism. The argumentative arsenal against the Europeans' cultural superiority complex and their fear of "mass" society, politics, and culture had meanwhile been developed by American intellectuals and academics, and their feuds with Dwight Macdonald and other indigenous critics helped them to strengthen it. The notion of totalitarianism was applicable to communism and fascism but not to American society. Against the background of a changing Cold War in the East, the task was to strengthen the idea of an Atlantic community and to convince Europe's educated elites of the vitality of America's high culture and of the innocuousness and diversity of its "mass" culture.

Stone, who had often experienced Europe's disdain for the United States, joined this effort and deployed Ford Foundation funds in pursuit of his goal of reconciling the two continents in terms of their ideas and ideologies.[138] The effort occurred at the level of individual West European countries, where he supported, as we have seen, a large variety of academic and cultural projects. He also promoted the idea at an international level, as the grants to the Dutch-inspired Bilderberg Group demonstrate.[139] In addition, he funded a variety of initiatives to strengthen a new Atlanticism that were born around the indefatigable Jean Monnet.[140] Finally, Stone also used the Congress for Cultural Freedom as a major transnational conduit and mediator, and it is to this connection and the CCF's ultimate collapse that we must turn in the next chapter.

The CIA, the Ford Foundation, and the
Demise of the CCF Empire

THE FINANCIAL HISTORY of the Congress for Cultural Freedom reveals a peculiar relationship with both American philanthropy and the CIA, continuing until its demise and conversion into the International Association for Cultural Freedom (IACF) in 1967. Before analyzing the CCF's links with U.S. government agencies and with the Ford Foundation, however, a number of background factors must be introduced so as to make the subsequent account of CCF finances more comprehensible. The previous chapter has shown that the world of big private philanthropic foundations, especially when it came to international affairs, was not sealed off from official American diplomacy and its objectives.[1] Indeed, in the early postwar period, U.S. government agencies had been more deeply involved than ever before in supporting an array of associations in Europe and in other parts of the world that were either openly fighting the Cold War against the Soviet Union or encouraging an economic and political reconstruction for which American institutions and practices were offered as a model.

The Marshall Plan is just one example of support for the economic modernization of Western Europe. It not only provided deliveries in food and raw materials and paved the way for the importation of American technologies and investments but also paid for visits of European businessmen and trade unionists to study large-scale production and Fordism in Ohio or Michigan. We also saw in the preceding chapter how, after the gradual withdrawal of American government agencies, private foundations continued these efforts—how they helped Western Europe's industries to reorganize and adapt their factories and management styles to the peculiarities of an emergent mass-production and mass-consumption society along American lines. To be sure, these Americanizing trends caused many agonies and a good deal of cultural resistance among European businessmen; this, in turn, must be related to the previously mentioned intellectual debates on both sides of the Atlantic about the blessings and dangers of American "mass culture."

THE U.S. GOVERNMENT AND THE FUNDING OF CULTURE

In the funding of simultaneous American efforts to strengthen demo-cratic-parliamentary institutions in early postwar Europe, West Germany probably presents an extreme but nevertheless telling case of "encourage-ment," not only through words but also through financial incentives. As we examined in chapter 3, funds from Washington flowed, overtly and covertly, into West Germany and West Berlin, first during the OMGUS period and after 1949 via the U.S. High Commission under McCloy. Stone, as McCloy's director of the Office of Public Affairs (OPA), spent literally millions of dollars to foster democratic traditions in the newly founded Federal Republic. Targets included major regional newspapers whose economic position was still precarious in the early 1950s as they struggled to gain a loyal and larger readership. "America Houses" as cul-tural centers with libraries and programs of lectures and English-language instruction were part of the same "reorientation" policy.[2]

But West Germany was not the only target. Worried about the strength of communist parties and unions in France and Italy, Washington also invested in other West European countries in an attempt to contain the spread of leftist radicalism and to foster the idea of an "Atlantic commu-nity of nations" in its fight against "totalitarianism" in both its Stalinist and fascist guises. On yet another level, the United States also became deeply involved in Western Europe militarily in the effort to contain "So-viet expansionism" through NATO.

Not least under the pressure of the cost of the Korean War and the escalating expenditures for NATO, where the Allies tried to fill their man-power deficiencies vis-à-vis the Red Army with the deployment of nuclear weapons, the U.S. Congress began to look for reductions in its overseas financial commitments. Washington's cultural operations were, not sur-prisingly perhaps, the first to become earmarked for cuts. McCarthyism also played a role in this when hard-line anticommunist politicians and journalists, such as Westbrook Pegler, accused Stone and other members of HICOG of being "soft" on communism and of spending money for liberal and leftist causes.[3]

Early casualties in this development were the subsidies to a number of publications that had been established by OMGUS and were continued by HICOG. The most influential among these was *Die Neue Zeitung.* Another one, which has also already been mentioned and which was

215

threatened with closure after Stone's departure from OPA, was *Der Monat*. Founded by Melvin Lasky soon after his celebrated intervention at the 1947 Writers' Congress in Berlin, the monthly's first issue had appeared in October 1948. Eventually it became an "American-sponsored, but internationally edited review" with a circulation of some 20,000 copies.[4] Although HICOG initially continued its sponsorship of the journal, by early 1953 Lasky saw the writing on the wall and began to look for alternative sources of funding, because *Der Monat* could not survive economically without a subsidy.

By August 1953 he had produced a revised and fuller version of a memorandum that presented a "Proposal for 'Transition Planning.'" "Against the background of larger reductions in the State Department's budget, Lasky discussed the specific situation in the Federal Republic, where it was, as he put it, "altogether likely that within the next months the last vestiges of the Occupation . . . will be eliminated." This meant that "the financial support of a publication like *Der Monat*, hitherto part and parcel of a large '[re]orientation' or 'public affairs' program becomes a matter which will inevitably be reconsidered." However, because it appreciated the value of the journal, the State Department had also been "seriously concerned to guarantee its continued publication under one sponsorship or another." If a release were therefore to be granted, *Der Monat* needed—Lasky continued—"a financial guarantee of support which would enable the journal to 'convert' to a private bi-national or multi-national basis" for a period of "at least three years." More specifically, "a grant of about" $350,000 would have to be sought and "a U.S. grant-in-aid and a Ford Foundation subsidy have been among several suggested approaches." He concluded by expressing his belief, in light of the cooperation going on within NATO and "with the Marshall and Schuman Plans," that "a new independent *Monat* would be a kind of pioneer effort in the field of international cultural understanding."

Not surprisingly, Lasky was hence looking toward McCloy and Stone for help but with both of them working, as they were, on the Conditions of Peace project, they were not yet firmly enough established at the Ford Foundation to push the plan through. The crisis point came sooner than Lasky had expected. In March 1954 Alfred Boerner at OPA informed him that HICOG would end its sponsorship of the journal in December of that year.[5] Ted Streibert, the director of the U.S. Information Agency (USIA) in Washington, subsequently confirmed this date, causing Lasky to exclaim: "It is a bit shocking, to put it frankly, to think of the July number as the last in the 'Hicog series' without being quite sure how it will continue from there!" But Streibert had also assured him that he would "be glad to promote and facilitate the takeover [into private hands] in any way possible."[6] Laughlin at the Ford Foundation, when mobilized by Lasky, "was upset to hear that Washington is forcing your hand." He wrote back that Stone, barely installed in the foundation's embryonic international affairs program, "will ask for money at the May meeting [of the trustees]." Laughlin had therefore written a memo with arguments and figures that he had "rushed to Shep, hoping that it will be of some help to him in the effort." For good measure he had "upped the figure for [the] circulation drive to a total of DM 300,000" on the assumption that "this figure will be just about enough to do the trick."[7] On 21 April, Stone wrote to Price praising *Der Monat* as "an outstanding publication which has deep influence on political and intellectual leaders in Europe."[8]

And so the trustees at their May meeting had a recommendation to ponder that they approve "a grant of $175,000 to the Ernst Reuter Stiftung in Berlin (or a similar tax exempt Berlin institution) for the publication over a three-year period of the monthly international review, Der Monat." In justifying the submission, it was pointed out that the State Department had subsidized the journal with $100,000 per year; but with increased advertising and circulation, the editors hoped to succeed "over a three-year period in putting Der Monat on a commercial basis." Several "reliable German publishers" had expressed an interest in taking the periodical, but were "not in a position to do so without a subsidy." Accordingly, "since the Foundation cannot make a grant to a commercial organization," it had been "requested by Government officials responsible for Der Monat to make a three-year grant to a tax exempt institution." The details would be worked out between the U.S. government and the Ernst Reuter Foundation. At the end of that period a German publishing house would step in.[9] Anticipating some opposition from within the Foundation, Stone also provided the trustees with supplementary material and a set of questions about the causes of the crisis and its resolution, to which he circumspectly also provided the answers in writing.[10] He also briefed McCloy in advance.[11] In the end, the grant was approved.

Unfortunately for the foundation, no private entrepreneur could be found. In August 1954 Lasky and his coeditor Hellmuth Jaesrich therefore founded the Gesellschaft fur Internationale Publizistik, in which each of them held a 50 percent share. They also obtained a license from the High Commission, and from that fall on the journal operated under this new legal framework. Although monthly sales increased by one-third, the economic position remained so precarious that in September 1956 the trustees were asked to make another appropriation of $75,000 "for assistance in publishing the monthly international review, Der Monat, over a period of approximately two years."[12]

But toward the end of November 1958, *Der Monat* was financially still not on an even keel. Stone had to tell Lasky that no further grant would be forthcoming, even though he added the hope that this decision might be reversed in the future.[13] When this proved illusory, he contacted Cord Meyer, his liaison at the CIA in Washington, expressing the hope that "it will be possible to maintain *Der Monat* on the same level."[14] He asked Meyer to let him know at the beginning of the new year. Meanwhile he asked Lasky to be patient. The latter was by this time commuting to London to devote himself to the running of *Encounter*, the English-language review founded in 1953 and modeled after *Der Monat*. From the start, the Congress for Cultural Freedom had taken this particular journal under its wing, subsidizing it partly from its various foundation grants and partly with covert money from the CIA. However, Lasky was never happy about Allen Dulles's benevolence and continued to look for a private publisher to foot the entire bill. As regards *Encounter*, which he told Stone in June 1961 had some 24,000 subscribers,[15] he finally succeeded in 1964 when Cecil King's Mirror Group in London offered a seven-year contract that guaranteed the journal's independence and covered its deficit. Thereafter its position once more became precarious and, as will be seen in the next chapter, Stone was once again drawn into the crisis to prevent *Encounter* from being shut down.[16]

Der Monat similarly found itself shunted around. In the early 1960s, when the Swiss journalist Fritz René Allemann came in as its editor,[17] the CCF continued to help out in hopes that a private publisher could be found. In early 1966, Josselson was in touch with Klaus Happrecht of the time-honored S. Fischer Verlag in Frankfurt.[18] It is safe to assume that Stone had a hand in the establishment of this contact via his old friend Gottfried Bermann-Fischer. As Harpprecht informed Josselson on 27 April, Bermann-Fischer's partner, Georg von Holtzbrinck, had involved himself in the resolution of the legal complexities of a proposed takeover of *Der Monat*. A few weeks later, with the arrangement still in the balance, partly because of a leak by "our old friend Allemann,"[19] Harpprecht suggested a meeting between Holtzbrinck, Stone, and Josselson.[20] The marriage did not last, and other publishers were brought in to sustain the journal as their loss leader until it ceased publication like its sibling, *Encounter*.[21]

The appearance of the CIA in the European journals business must be viewed in a broader context.[22] In the early 1950s, when the State Department decided to withdraw from many of its international cultural programs, Allen Dulles found himself in a more advantageous position vis-à-vis a miserly U.S. Congress because the agency did not have to reveal and account for all of its operation, on which it spent millions of dollars. Accordingly, it not only continued its intelligence and subversive operations against the Soviet bloc but also began to support organizations that fought communism on the intellectual and cultural front and counteracted anti-Americanism in Western Europe. Thus in early December 1952 Stone told Milton Katz that "the other day a friend of mine in that famous agency asked me if the Foundation had given any support to 'The Twentieth Century' published in London." Because Stone replied that he did not think so, his contact had added "that a serious situation was developing in England, particularly among intellectuals, in regard to attitudes toward the United States and that it was important for us to give certain important pro-American Englishmen opportunities to speak out."[23] Evidently the CIA man was hoping that the foundation might agree to help.

How the issue was resolved is not clear, although Katz probably kept his distance. A further conversation developed in July 1956, this time between Stone and Dulles in connection with another journal. As the CIA chief reported, he had been able to step in "from time to time" but could not "support the publication regularly" for reasons that were related "to domestic politics." He confessed that he regretted the public expenditure cuts in Washington no less than his colleagues dealing with cultural affairs in the State Department, and finally came up with the idea of complementing the CIA's covert support, by urging the big foundations to fill the gap left by the U.S. government.[24]

The fact that Stone allowed himself to be drawn into this arrangement is best explained in generational terms. Like many other men with an Ivy League background who had witnessed the rise of fascism and Stalinism and who participated in World War II, often in intelligence positions, Stone accepted, as a matter of course, the principle of cooperation between government and private organizations. After all, the country was involved in a life-and-death struggle, and winning the war was a national task overriding all other considerations. He and others of his generation similarly viewed the Cold War against the Soviet Union that followed in 1945 as a comprehensive conflict that justified the continued application of the principles of close cooperation that had guided the hot war against

Hitler. Stone's wartime and early postwar experience in the intelligence and information branch of the U.S. Army had reinforced his convictions when he served with HICOG in West Germany and was in frequent official contact with the local American intelligence community. He took these convictions with him when, after his return from Europe, he appeared, so to speak, on the other side of the fence, as an officer of the Ford Foundation.

THE FORD FOUNDATION'S WASHINGTON CONNECTIONS

For Stone Europe was the major intellectual and cultural battleground in the Cold War against the Soviet Union and, while attempting to build up an international program in New York, he repeatedly traveled to Washington to exchange information with his contacts at the State Department and the CIA. On 3 and 4 June 1953 he was in the U.S. capital for "consultation and attendance at [a] State Department conference on U.S. foreign policy at [the] request of Mr. Katz to represent [the] Ford Foundation." On his return he charged, inter alia, a "luncheon for 7 officials of [the] State Dept. and CIA" to his expense account.[25] However, as his marching orders from Katz also indicate, Stone was not the first to establish this link. Even before he arrived at the Ford Foundation to help with the Conditions of Peace project, discussions had taken place between the foundation and top CIA officials. Thus in early April 1951, Ford Foundation officer John Howard took notes on a "conference with Beadle [sic] Smith, Allen Dulles and others," at which the CIA gave Paul Hoffman and his team information about its defectors' program. They also talked about the Free University, which the foundation was considering for a grant and which Smith thought to be a "worthwhile project." As to the Congress for Cultural Freedom, the CIA's Frank Wisner believed it offered "great possibilities." The CCF "must have private support," because government subsidies would be the "kiss of death." According to Johnson's notes, Wisner apparently also raised the question: "Could Ford receive government funds for disbursement[?]"[26]

Two weeks later, on 18 April, Gaither came back to this request "that we might on occasion serve as intermediary for some projects" in which the CIA had an interest, when he wrote from Hoffman's headquarters in Pasadena to Bernard Gladieux in the foundation's New York office. Gladieux replied that "nothing concrete in the way of a CIA request" had developed in the meantime. But should the agency ask the foundation "to handle such a project for them and it should seem [appropriate]," he would have to clear it with Tex Moore and Hoffman.[27] As Howard reported to Gaither on 25 April, he had had a follow-up meeting with Dulles, in the course of which the CIA man confirmed that he was cautious in raising the conduit question again because he was concerned "to safeguard the interests of the Ford Foundation."[28] Howard did his best to explain the risks for the foundation, adding that Hoffman and the trustees would have to make a basic policy decision on the matter. Dulles indicated that the CIA might have another channel for the particular case that he apparently had in mind.

Two days later Gaither wrote to Gladieux that, as he may already have heard, "the staff is opposed [to the CIA proposal] as a matter of policy." Hence, there was no need to obtain "a legal opinion." He offered to "recite the reasons if you need them for guidance in any future discussions with the CIA."[29] Subsequently Gaither also informed Johnson that his latest letter to Gladieux obviated "the need to consider further whether the Foundation should act as a channel for CIA funds."[30] As far as is known, this remained the foundation's position in the years to come. But there was an alternative whose risks may have dawned on Gaither when, on 5 May 1951, he received a memorandum from Hans Speier, who confirmed that "there are a number of organizations in Western Germany and in Berlin engaged in work that appears most valuable in supporting U.S. government policy in the cold war with the Soviet Union." However, "the State Department and the Office of the U.S. High Commissioner in Germany find it embarrassing to support some of these organizations in view of the constraints which the occupation statute places upon the U.S. authorities to lend open, overt support to these organizations." State and HICOG had therefore begun to cooperate with the "CIA to channelize covert funds in such a way as to support worthy institutions and organizations." In other words, "U.S. government support is concealed."[31]

If the foundation found it easy to reject Dulles's idea to act as a conduit for covert CIA funds to "worthy" organizations, the more difficult question was whether Ford should give money to organizations that also received covert CIA support. Much has been written on what happened in 1966–67 when CIA funding for the Congress for Cultural Freedom was revealed.[32] To be sure, the full story will not be known until the CIA finally opens its files to researchers; but as long as they remain closed, some new insights can be gained on the basis of Shepard Stone's papers.

A good starting point would seem to be the internal "report on the financial history of the Congress for Cultural Freedom," which Josselson produced, with various handwritten corrections, when the scandal blew up in 1967. In accounting for his activities he went back to the founding of the CCF in 1950 when he was still a U.S. occupation officer in Berlin and also met Lasky and Nabokov for the first time.[33] When his tour of duty ended in October 1950, he had "returned to Paris where, prior to the war and until the German occupation, I had been the Director of the European buying offices of a number of American department store chains."[34] But instead of resuming his former career, his "close association with writers, publishing, and other intellectual pursuits during the five years after the end of the war" led him to accept the task "of creating a permanent organization fathered by the [1950] Berlin Congress."

At first, Josselson hoped the CCF would be financed out of Marshall Plan counterpart funds. When this failed, "Irving Brown jumped into the breach." But since the AFL-CIO could hardly be expected to become a permanent benefactor, the CIA, which Josselson knew well from his OMGUS days in Berlin, "came directly into the picture." It is likely that he knew of the covert "channeling" practices that Speier told Gaither about in May 1951. Josselson was assured by the CIA "that they would provide all the funds needed." It was merely their interest to help "set up an autonomous group of intellectuals who were opposed to Stalinism and to Communism in general." He therefore received reassurances that there would be no interference by the agency "with any activity" and that "no attempt [would] ever be made to use the new organization for any intelligence or penetration purposes."

As we have seen in earlier chapters, however, the CCF became a rapidly expanding empire. A growing number of sponsored intellectual journals in the major foreign languages had to be subsidized. There were also the ambitious and expensive congresses at which the intellectual heavyweights who were invited expected to be treated well. Realizing that the covert financial link had placed the CCF on a powder keg, Josselson constantly tried "to secure other funding for the Congress which would free it from any need for CIA support." He added that he also tried hard "to protect all those associated with the Congress from any damage to their reputations which might result from a discovery of the CIA connection."[35]

The big foundations were the obvious source for alternative funding. The Rockefeller Foundation was one of the first to be approached and in 1953 Warren Weaver, who was a close friend of Michael Polanyi, agreed to fund the CCF's Hamburg Congress on Science and Freedom.[36] Not surprisingly, the Ford Foundation became the CCF's next target. Josselson knew Stone from his days in postwar Berlin, and it so happened that its secretary-general Nabokov acted as McCloy's guide in Rome when his tour of Europe in connection with the Conditions of Peace project took him and Stone to the Italian capital. When Stone wrote Nabokov after his return to thank him for his help, the latter in his reply seized the opportunity to praise the work of the CCF, asserting that "our Congress is one of the most positive forces on the cultural horizon of Europe, and of all the organizations around it should be helped first."[37] Agreeing with this statement, Stone subsequently arranged for Nabokov to take his salesmanship to New York where, accompanied by Denis de Rougemont, then head of the Swiss-based European Cultural Center, he met McCloy on 26 February 1953.

In preparation for this meeting, Stone sent his mentor a brief note, which he urged him to read before the meeting on the following day. As Stone put it, the "Congress and the European Cultural Center, through these gentlemen, are submitting projects to the Ford and Rockefeller Foundations to cover some of their activities in the coming years." The CCF, Stone added, was "made up of statesmen, writers, scientists and artists and everywhere fights totalitarianism, either Communist or Fascist." He also mentioned that "its main efforts are centered on publications, such as monthly magazines in England and France," which were "largely patterned after the successful example of Der Monat." It was Stone's "impression from the experience in Germany, from our observations on our recent trip in Europe and from many talks I have had with leading Europeans . . . that the Congress is really doing one of the worthwhile jobs in the political and psychological struggle." The two visitors would have further discussions with Price and himself during the following week. Stone concluded his note by expressing the hope "that the Foundation will see its way to supporting parts of this enterprise." His stress on partial support apparently related to a most intriguing sentence that Stone had written earlier on in his note for McCloy.[38] "You know," he reminded his mentor since their HICOG days in a veiled reference to the CIA, "the sources of funds that have hitherto been supplied to the Congress, but in our conversation with these gentlemen we should not reveal what we know."[39]

By the middle of April, Nabokov's and de Rougemont's discussions with Price had made some encouraging progress in the sense that the latter agreed to consider putting to the trustees a proposal for "strengthening cultural and intellectual ties in the Free World." More specifically, the trustees were to be asked to appropriate "$500,000, to be expended over a three-year period, to the Congress for Cultural Freedom in Paris for

[the] publication of magazines in English, French and Spanish and for other related activities of the Congress."[40] While the strategy behind this request was clearly to wrench the CCF journals free from CIA support, the sum involved was quite large. With monies requested in the same breath for *Der Monat* ($200,000) and for de Rougemont's European Cultural Center ($200,000), the trustees turned against awarding another large sum to the CCF. Only in 1956, when Stone, who continued to be a vociferous advocate of the CCF, was more firmly established at the foundation, was a first grant of $40,000 made—"for partial support of an international seminar on 'Economic Growth in Underdeveloped Countries' to be held in Tokyo in May 1957."[41]

Thenceforth relations with the CCF became increasingly closer. In 1957, against the backdrop of the events in Hungary, grants jumped to $290,000. After another good year in 1958 ($210,000), Ford Foundation support for the CCF reached $550,000 in 1960 and $200,000 in 1961.[42] The reasons for Stone's favoritism are not difficult to discern if we compare his own aims and concerns about the European-American relationship (as examined in chapter 7) with the CCF's objectives (as outlined in chapter 5).[43] Clearly there were many ideological affinities not only as regards the Cold War against the Soviet bloc but also with reference to the kind of liberal-capitalist, "managed," and reformist mass-production and mass-consumption society that the Ford Foundation's IA boss and the CCF intellectuals had in mind. This is why the congress became a conduit for foundation funds to facilitate the exchange of ideas and academic visitors across the Iron Curtain; and also why the two organizations joined forces in combatting Europe's anti-Americanism and cultural superiority complex.

Success, especially on the latter front, may at times have been elusive, as Nielsen discovered when he attended the CCF's Lourmarin conference in 1959.[44] Although both sides, in highlighting the value of their activities, occasionally fell victim to their own skillful hype, the fact remains that there were two cold culture wars going on and that many intellectuals who thought it important to fight them both were relieved to have found an organizational focus and voice.

Still, however close the relationship between the CCF executive and its patron Shepard Stone may have grown, the dark cloud of covert CIA funding continued to hover over both organizations. The dangers Josselson saw in this link for the future of his creation led him to pursue, ever more urgently, the idea of financial independence from the agency. For the Ford Foundation the covert CIA connection constantly put its worldwide prestige in jeopardy. This prestige was based on its high reputation as an independent philanthropic organization. Stone's office never tired of stressing that it was not an arm of the Washington administration. Anxious not to damage this image, Hoffman and Gaither had politely refused to use the foundation as a conduit for covert CIA monies, as Allen Dulles had gingerly suggested in April 1951. But there was also the other question and danger: would the foundation's reputation be damaged if it gave money to organizations that it *knew* also received covert government support? Stone and McCloy, as Stone's note of 25 February 1954 testified,[45] recognized how government agencies were related to the CCF. Whatever their other sources of information, at HICOG they had, after all, been party to the arrangements that Speier told Gaither about in his report of 5 May 1951.[46] And if they did not get the full story then, they certainly learned it later when IA personnel began to travel to Washington at regular intervals to exchange information with the agency about their programs.

Thus, on 5 September 1956 Stone had another meeting with Meyer, after which he wrote to him: "Your ideas last night were stimulating and we are grateful to you for coming up to New York." Nielsen would see him in Washington next week, and Stone hoped that "you can go into specific proposals with him." He looked forward to meeting Meyer "a week or two thereafter" and in the meantime he would keep him "informed about developments here."[47] When Nielsen met Meyer on 12 September, he did have some "specific proposals."[48] They discussed "the possibilities of [an] exchange of top flight professors between Eastern [Western?] Europe and satellite universities." They also "talked at some length about CP subsidization of intellectual publications and recent [Communist] moves being made to reestablish contacts with emigré writers," wondering what the West might do to counteract these efforts. A third problem raised at the meeting was the future of various projects in the area of management training, productivity, and "Labor Union leadership programs in France and Italy." Most significantly, Meyer started his meeting with Nielsen by referring "to a recent letter from CCF to us proposing our support for another meeting in Europe of satellite and Western intellectuals" and expressing the hope "that we [i.e., the Ford Foundation] could give the idea favorable consideration."

In the end it seemed to Nielsen "that we should not undertake to salvage the wreckage of some of these worthwhile governmental efforts in Europe that are now being finished off." He did recommend, however, "that in particular cases we might find some special opportunities in supporting projects that have now been well started with other funds." In this context it occurred to Nielsen "that a very appropriate general program objective for Henry and Edsel Ford's Foundation would be the invigoration or the modernization of European capitalism. Under such a rubric might be included our interests in such things as social stratification, productivity, development of responsible and progressive leadership in non-academic fields . . . and so on." As we have seen, IA under Stone did move into these areas and with exactly the objectives that Nielsen had outlined, namely of changing European class structures and industrial traditions in the direction of what was thought to be the superior "American way" of organizing a capitalist manufacturing society.[49] And, of course, the contours of Bell's and Galbraith's technocratically managed economy and society can be discerned in these efforts.

As he left the meeting with Meyer, Nielsen apparently "emphasized that we would remain strictly within the boundaries of appropriate scientific and educational work in anything we might do, but at the same time we wanted to act responsible [sic] and responsively in this hazardous area—that is, we certainly wanted to maintain effective communication with the Government on the needs as they saw them and on our own plans." And responsive he and his colleagues did indeed remain, especially when requests and suggestions came from the very top, for example, from Christian Herter or Allen Dulles.[50] Although IA was always conscious of the fact that this was a "hazardous area," there was no sense that these contacts were in any way wrong. To Stone's generation this was the kind of cooperation that was justified by the pressures of the Cold War, and this is also how he defended the frequent trips to Washington and the initiatives that followed. It probably also helped that Stone got along well with Josselson and Nabokov and that, when enjoying a good meal at a meeting in Paris or New York, they never stopped convincing each other of the importance of their work.[51]

If moving foundation monies into fields that the U.S. government had abandoned was "hazardous," supporting organizations that Stone knew also received covert CIA funds was even riskier. In fact, as rumors about the sources of CCF finances had become more widespread by the early 1960s, the stock-in-trade justifications of this dual support were increasingly challenged within the organization. A growing number of people in the foundation's executive offices and among the trustees believed it was wrong for an organization that received covert CIA funding to be a simultaneous beneficiary of private philanthropy. This opposition gained strength when the trustees confronted large but unspecific CCF requests.

Thus the $500,000 grant of 1957 was for a vague "two-year program in international activities."[52] Two months later, and probably at the request of the foundation leadership, a budget was submitted that itemized the dozen or so projects on which the $500,000 was to be spent.[53]

Stone and Josselson did their best to draw attention to the CCF's accomplishments. In July 1959 Theodor Heuss, Stone's old friend from the early occupation days, now retired from the presidency of the Federal Republic, agreed to become one of the association's honorary chairs, and Stone expressed his delight to Josselson, writing that "he is really a remarkable man."[54] The IA chief's papers also contain undated notes from the fall of 1959 in which he detailed the CCF's mission once again. The Congress, he recorded (possibly during or after a conversation with Josselson), was steering a "middle course in politics and promotes intellectual contacts." It gave "Asians and Africans contacts [and] friends," and provided them with a "chance to expand intellectually with the rest of the world." Freedom continued to be the "objective," while the "methods" consisted of conferences, seminars, periodicals, and activities by national committees. The overall theme outlined in the notes was reminiscent of the familiar antitotalitarianism: psychologically and intellectually a tendency was seen to exist toward "atomization and loneliness." The CCF pulled people together and gave them a "sense of unity against communism."[55]

Yet, over time such arguments cut less and less ice. Criticism of foundation support for the CCF apparently reached a high point in December 1959 when the trustees were presented with a recommendation for a blanket "grant of $750,000 to the Congress for Cultural Freedom for a three-year program of international activities." There was no itemized budget, but a list of "four general topics," namely, "effective government and individual freedom," "nationalism and federalism," "the civilization of the cities," and "economic growth and human rights."[56] Although these topics were important, the foundation ultimately lopped some $200,000 off the original recommendation.

Worse for Stone and Josselson, in early 1961 IA received an "excerpt from [the] Minutes of [the] Executive Committee meeting of February 10, 1961," which read: "The President then introduced for discussion the question of the Foundation's relationship with tax-exempt organizations the source of whose financing is not totally clear from their published records. After discussion it was agreed that grants should be made only to those organizations which were prepared to provide full reports as to the sources of their funds."[57] To complicate matters further, later during that year the trustees set up a special committee under McCloy's chairmanship to review the foundation's activities and to make recommendations for the future. However, with his old mentor in the chair, this review also presented fresh opportunities for Stone.

The first paper that IA prepared for the special committee, titled "Evaluation (1951–1961) and Statement of Current Objectives and Policies," summarized the wide-ranging activities that had been funded over the past decade. It highlighted the efforts to strengthen "the Free Developed Countries," to build up the Atlantic community and the ties between Europe and the developing world; it mentioned the "contacts with Eastern Europe" and the work to increase an "Understanding of World Affairs in the U.S." There was, at the end of the paper, a brief discussion of "Successes, Failures and Missed Opportunities" which, it was promised, Stone's oral report would elaborate upon.[58] The opportunity for doing this came when, in the middle of December 1961, he was asked to lead off the presentations before the special committee. As he later wrote to Josselson, he spontaneously found himself "making some very positive statements about the work of the Congress for Cultural Freedom." He anticipated "more intensive discussions" later on, but for the moment "many of our Trustees know about the Congress and hold it in high regard."[59]

Encouraged by the response to his exposition of past IA activities, Stone sat down to compose, for the benefit of the McCloy committee, a "Program Submission Concerning Future [IA] Program Activities." The document began with generalities about the period of rapid change that the contemporary world was going through, in which the Ford Foundation had the opportunity of being "in the vanguard." It talked about the Atlantic community, relations with the communist East, science and technology, "intellectual-creative activity," the role of the mass media and "efforts to further economic and social progress." With reference to the "Major Objectives of the IA Program," it was clear that its ambitions were no longer confined to Europe, but had become global. Only on page 13 did the paper become specific and begin to argue for a project that sounds familiar: the development of an "Atlantic partnership." The "task of putting together the resources, talents, and skills of the Atlantic area," the argument continued, amounted to "a major challenge and opportunity" that the foundation should seize. This is why IA was now proposing "to establish an Atlantic Foundation with an international board of trustees and an international staff to support the development of the Atlantic Community in the next decade."[60]

The fact that the trustees evidently liked the ideas contained in the IA paper of the spring of 1962 was of course very cheering not only to Stone but, as we shall see in a moment, also to Josselson.[61] In June the trustees approved "Directives and Terms of Reference for the 1960s," one of which requested the president "to submit to the Board recommendations for substantial program efforts to strengthen the comprehensive development of the Atlantic partnership." More specifically, the "Terms of Reference for International Affairs" stipulated that IA should "help accelerate the development of the Atlantic partnership by support of private and public efforts" in a variety of fields. It also encouraged assistance to strengthen "European educational, scientific, and cultural institutions"; to improve the Atlantic nations' "joint capacity to deal with the Sino-Soviet challenge"; to "stimulate the growth of European philanthropy"; to support European aid to less developed countries; and to "develop closer relations between the Atlantic Community and Japan"—all activities for which Stone had been laying the groundwork since the late 1950s.[62]

The trustees' brief encouraged Stone to produce a thirty-one-page paper titled "Strengthening the Comprehensive Development of the Atlantic Partnership," which was completed in March 1963. The document contained, in its substantive parts, recommendations on the foundation's role in the scheme and the activities that IA envisaged supporting. But no less significant in our context were the proposals for the organizational and financial framework within which the program was supposed to operate. As to finances, it was recommended "that the Ford Foundation Trustees approve an authorization of $100 million over ten years for the purposes outlined in the paper."[63] The administration would either be in the hands of a (no doubt considerably expanded) IA staff or, preferably, rest with the "new Atlantic Foundation" and its proposed international board of trustees.[64]

It should be obvious that the broader context of relations within the Western alliance formed the backdrop to Stone's ambitious plan. The new Kennedy administration was itself talking of the need for a new Atlantic partnership that would organize relations between Europe and the U.S. on a new basis. Washington also felt that the rise of Gaullism in France, and its attractiveness to some European politicians and intellectuals needed to be counterbalanced, not least because of its anti-Americanism. There were also fears of economic and technological stagnation. With regard to technology, it was certainly helpful that, on assuming office, Secretary of Defense Robert McNamara promptly spotted a "missile gap" vis-à-vis the Soviet Union that led to expenditure on high-tech weapons developments and was only much later discovered to have been nonexistent. As to economic growth, the hope was that an improvement of East-West trade might further stimulate it. All this should, of course, be seen in the larger context of a vision of managed and reformist industrial societies, espoused—as we have seen—by Galbraith and Bell, and worries that the postwar boom that had facilitated this "Keynesian" vision might come to an end, suggesting the need for anticipatory planning and action. At the same time and focusing on McCloy and Stone, it is also true that the ideas in the March 1963 paper represented something like a summary of everything that they had been working for since 1945, first in Germany and later at the Ford Foundation.[65] The initiative was another example of what has emerged several times before—that all issues were closely interconnected and, no less important, were seen as such by the major actors in different fields.

Now, with McCloy chairing both the board of trustees and the special committee, the opportunity had arrived for McCloy and Stone to realize their vision of a massive philanthropic program that would propel the creation of an Atlantic *cultural* community. This was something more than military and economic cooperation: it was the roof overarching institutions like NATO that had been created at the height of the Cold War. Although the power of personal dreams should not be underestimated, another aspect seems to have come into play at this point: Stone's connections with the CCF and, in turn, the latter organization's financial dependence on the CIA.

Rescuing the CCF

If, as he had written to Josselson on 19 December 1961, Stone had found particularly warm words for the CCF in his first oral presentation to the McCloy committee, it was not just because he genuinely thought the congress's work to be especially valuable. Barred from offering Josselson further support by the trustees' decision not to give any more money to associations whose financial basis had not been made fully public, Stone hoped that he might be able to get one exemption from the new rule: approval of a terminal grant for the CCF of $1 million—in itself no small request. Accordingly IA prepared a draft recommendation that started with a paragraph showing how close Stone's world views had moved to those of the intellectual gurus of the CCF: "Perceptive men have pointed to signs in Europe and in many countries of Asia, Africa, and Latin

America that we are entering a period which may see the 'end of ideology'. Around the world, intellectuals are decreasingly concerned with the infallibility of old-line Marxist theology. There is growing interest in ideas for practical and realistic approaches to political and social problems."[66]

The draft then recounted the achievements of the CCF since its founding in 1950. It also enumerated other grants, "including [some from] a few European governments . . . , the Catherwood Foundation and the Merrill Trust." Because the Ford Foundation grant was not intended to be used "for general expenses of the Congress or for . . . its monthly and quarterly publications," but to support specific seminars, lectures, and international conferences as well as individual scholars and artists, the document reassuringly added the names of the Rockefeller and Cini foundations and of the German Künstlerbund as examples of other groups that had given money for specialized purposes. The draft ended with a "discussion" section that put the problem of the "hazards" as follows: "The Ford Foundation Trustees have discussed the work of the Congress on several occasions and have assessed its assets and liabilities. In view of all the factors involved, this proposal for a terminal grant is presented as the most reasonable action."

Being a practical and realistic person, Stone must have had a hunch that this request might well fail to get past the trustees. After all, the money applied for was no pittance and more than once the trustees had seen a recommendation for a terminal grant, only to be confronted with a further request a few years later. The story of the funding for *Der Monat* was one such case in point.[67] But the most serious threat to the CCF proposal came from the recent trustees' decision "that it will not support institutions which also receive funds from undisclosed United States Government sources."[68] On 6 February 1962 Stone therefore drew up a confidential memorandum that recommended reconsideration of this policy. Over four pages he looked at the pros and cons of the issue and, not surprisingly, tried to play down the question of the damage that a possible revelation of covert government funding to an organization that also received support from Ford might do to the foundation's good name.

Soon thereafter, it appears to have dawned on Stone that a complete reversal of the anti-CIA resolution was not obtainable, however tirelessly Josselson might collect praise for the CCF from prominent Europeans and Americans.[69] He now tried the alternative route of urging that a "terminal" grant be made. He knew that, in order to succeed, he had to pull out all the stops. At the same time he still had a proposal up his sleeve for full funding by the foundation, which would make it possible for the CCF to cut all its ties with the CIA. As the showdown was approaching and the shape of the CCF proposal kept changing, he informed Josselson on 18 April 1962 that "we have succeeded in forcing a full discussion before the entire Board at the June 22 meeting on the problem of the Congress." It was a decision, he added, that had been "made after a serious internal debate which involved our top people." He would therefore find it "extremely helpful . . . if you could write me a memorandum for 'my eyes only' answering . . . questions to which I must address myself in talking to the Board." These questions were concerned with the consequences of Ford's complete retreat from the CCF, the advantages of full Ford Foundation funding, and the possible damage to the foundation's reputation "if certain things became public." Then he added another reason why this was a decisive battle: "We have some good friends in this situation who would want to approve the proposal I am making—the full financing (partial financing is now out)."[70]

Unable to take his "mind off this whole business," Josselson provided additional material, hoping "that when it comes to the final judgment of the merits of our cause, you will find it possible to give us a longer lease."[71] Stone also received a longer paper that Shils had written in March 1962 on the subject of "Further Thoughts on the Congress in the 1960s." It was a perceptive piece that pinpointed the conceptual strengths and weaknesses of the CCF. Two of his points indicate that Shils was trying hard to think ahead. He urged that "we must make a very powerful effort to build up a list of younger people between 25 and 35"—a major problem indeed, on which the congress and its successor would eventually founder.[72] Second, he pointed out that "our female component is much too low," adding that "there is an unnecessary prejudice against women, just as there is a blind spot regarding younger people in general." These were telling observations on the behavior of aging gentlemen who would soon find themselves embroiled in a generational conflict whose causes left many of them confused and bitter. Finally, Shils suggested a rejuvenation of the membership.[73]

This was all very well but would remain useless if Stone's plan came to grief before the board of trustees. In anticipation of the crucial meeting on 22 June, he began to draft a memorandum for McCloy as the chair. His papers contain several versions, which were revised on 8 and 11 June, with the clean copy for McCloy finally emerging on 12 June. As well as reviewing the CCF's work since 1950, the document contained legal and financial recommendations. Stone proposed that, notwithstanding the earlier decision to deny foundation support to organizations that "receive funds from covert governmental sources," in "carefully-selected situations which are considered to be of unusual significance, the Foundation may make substantial grants to institutions which are prepared to give up all financing from, and all connections with, covert agencies." But what would it cost the foundation if the CFF volunteered to give up all CIA support? Out of a current annual budget of $1.8 million, $1.4 million "came from government sources, approximately $250,000 from The Ford Foundation, and the remainder from European and other American foundations." What, according to him, was therefore required "for a complete and total separation from Government financing" was a Ford Foundation guarantee of some $2 million per year "for the next five years"—up to $10 million in all. Stone added his belief that during this period "it will be possible to work out arrangements with other American and European foundations to assume part of the support for the Congress." Although Stone urged the trustees to take risks, his submission and presumably his presentation on 22 June made abundantly clear that these risks were considerable, and his request was ultimately turned down.[74]

After this defeat, Josselson discussed alternative solutions with the CIA and the State Department. But there was no immediate resolution because the CIA apparently wanted more certainty about the future of what in its eyes was, after all, a successful venture. According to Josselson, Heald had been impressed by the plans; but Rockefeller and other foundations were no more enthusiastic than the Ford Trustees had been.[75] There was another flicker of hope in the fall of 1962 when Stone thought he had "managed to get a favorable change" in the foundation. As he put it to a somewhat bemused Josselson: "Months ago, as a matter of deep principle, the man who has been the major opponent [i.e., Heald] said he was 100% opposed. In the intervening period, owing to the position of the other Trustees and particularly of my great and good friend [McCloy], he has become convinced that perhaps some type of favorable action is unavoidable and therefore he has been willing to talk about alternatives." As a result, "the 'terminal' grant idea" had once again "come to the fore."[76] Speculating about the reasons behind this shift, Stone felt that "to our top two it seems somewhat less expensive, though my great and good friend says 'at the end of the terminal period' we probably would be willing to make another grant as we have done in other cases." Second, "our top two have honestly had the impression that our [CIA] friends really don't want to get out entirely," and clearly this was another impediment to changing Heald's heart.

233

While Stone's tidbits throw further light on some of the assumptions behind the 22 June decision of the trustees, the rest of his letter to Josselson showed that his sense of realism had slightly weakened. He wrote assertively that he would "continue to do everything possible for the full takeover." But he was sober enough to add: "If it doesn't work out, the fault will not be fully on our side." When hopes of a second attempt at a "full takeover" faded, Stone began to cast around for other solutions, and in this context the wider significance of the Atlantic Foundation plan becomes clearer. At least it seems likely that this idea was fully elaborated by IA in the second half of 1962 because it might have been the kind of well-funded umbrella organization under which all the CCF enterprises could have found a new home. However, the trustees did not want to commit themselves to a venture that would have cost them not some $10 million over five years (as with the "terminal grant" solution for the CCF) but a clean $100 million over ten.

Other solutions appeared on the horizon, one of which brought at least partial relief. In January 1962, when the idea of an Atlantic Foundation was still topical, Stone's IA colleague Joseph Slater, whom we shall meet again in connection with Stone's Aspen Institute project in the 1970s, had two conversations with Nabokov at which the general secretary of the CCF posed as an ardent protagonist of the Atlantic Foundation idea, this most ambitious of all solutions.[77] But as these and other plans to secure a CCF future independent of CIA monies faltered, Nabokov began to think of his own favorites, the performing and visual arts, and of how they might find a safe haven *outside* the congress framework. The project envisaged creating a cultural center in West Berlin and putting Nabokov in charge of a program that would bring international artists and intellectuals to the divided city for performances or longer sabbatical visits. This idea appealed to Mayor Willy Brandt, who had his own plans for "a significant development" of West Berlin's "cultural and artistic life." He therefore approached Josselson with the request to dispatch "our joint friend Nicholas Nabokov as a consultant" to this particular enterprise.[78] His duties in Berlin would make it necessary for him to spend most of his time in the city over the next two years. Brandt hoped that the CCF would release Nabokov for this time from his position as CCF general secretary.

Knowing of Stone's strong feelings of allegiance to the city, it did not take Brandt, Nabokov, and Josselson long to bring him into the picture. The request for funding that they were hoping to make to the Ford Foundation was, after all, not for an established organization with compromising links to the CIA, but to a brand new one. As Nabokov wrote to Stone on 11 December 1962 with reference to the "Berliner Kulturprojekt," budgetary estimates were still in the works, among them those for an "Artists in Residence" program and a "New York City Ballet [Berlin] Branch" project. The CCF executive director thought that Ford would have to chip in some $2 million to get the various schemes going, but that "the Berlin authorities should be induced to include this amount in their next year's budget and to reimburse either the Foundation or the Federal Government" at that stage.[79]

This time Stone succeeded in persuading the trustees that $2 million was a worthwhile investment, and on 9 January 1963 press notices appeared announcing the establishment of a *Stiftung* that would provide fellowships for foreign artists, support for an expansion of the Amerika-Institut at the Free University, and the creation of studio stages for opera and drama.[80] Former Harvard president James Conant, McCloy's successor as U.S. high commissioner in 1952 and later the first U.S. ambassador to Bonn, was to act as a resident consultant to the educational elements of the project, with Nabokov as the impresario for the arts program. Thenceforth Nabokov was busy selecting candidates for the "Artists in Residence" enterprise[81] and organizing events in Berlin such as "Black Encounters," illustrating—as the *New York Times* put it—"the impact of Negro creative gifts on the arts and music of the twentieth century."[82] The whole project was yet another variant of the CCF's and Stone's quest to counteract European prejudice against American culture but, in the particular case of "Black Encounters," implicitly also racism.[83]

Meanwhile, Josselson and Stone, worrying about the future of the remaining parts of the CCF empire, pursued other avenues in their quest to rid the Congress of its funding by the CIA. One of these avenues was "to set up a consortium of several foundations" centered around the Rockefellers.[84] On 10 June 1964 Stone met "Laurance Rockefeller, the head of the Rockefeller Brothers Fund and other funds, . . . to discuss the financing of the Congress." Because Laurance Rockefeller "was very positive," it was agreed to "have meetings with the Rockefeller Foundation head, the Rockefeller Brothers Fund, the Sloan Foundation, and one or two others." Stone felt that "we may have started something here that can be potentially of great significance to the kind of development you [i.e., Josselson] and I want to see."[85]

Hoping that Stone's optimism was justified, Josselson continued to work on various papers, singing the praises of the CCF for the benefit of the Rockefellers. At the end of April 1965 he drew up "a new angle for the presentation of the new plan which, I think, will make it very much

A luncheon honoring Mayor Brandt at the American Hotel, Berlin, 15 May 1964. From left to right: Shepard Stone, General Lucius D. Clay, and Willy Brandt, Mayor of West Berlin. (Courtesy of Margaret Macdonald)

more appealing to the [foundation] Consortium." The "new angle" was a proposal to transform the CCF "into an International Council for Cultural Cooperation." Ideally, he added, "such a transformation should coincide with a complete transformation of the financial backing. The new Council would have to count on solid backing from private sources and it would publish an audited financial statement annually." It would also take over *Preuves, Minerva, Survey*, the *China Quarterly*, and *Censorship*, after *Encounter* and *Der Monat* had found private publishers.[86] Perhaps the most significant sentence in the document, though, appeared at the very end: "Those two or three officers who have hindering connections [i.e., who were in the pay of the CIA] would sever these connections once and for all before the transformation into the Council was made."[87]

According to Josselson's later report, he had a meeting with David Rockefeller "to sound him out about the consortium idea and about a

Rockefeller participation" in it. Rockefeller was said to have been "sympathetic, but saw no possibility of raising the amounts needed by the Congress without heavy Ford participation." Yet, as long as the foundation's president stuck to the anti-CIA resolution of 1961, its help was out of the question. Josselson continued: "The break came when McGeorge Bundy replaced Henry Heald. . . . Contrary to Mr. Heald, Mr. Bundy was for culture and did not mind the CIA background. Thus, with the tireless support of Shepard Stone, after renewed protracted negotiations which lasted through the spring and summer of 1966, a new submission to the Trustees of the Ford Foundation was worked out" and was finally approved. The CCF was to be given "a total of $7 million for a period of six years . . . on condition that all ties with the CIA were broken which had in fact already been done in the early summer of that year."[88]

This summary is broadly accurate.[89] Heald had indeed been the man who had been opposed to the attempts to turn the CCF into a fully Ford-financed venture. It was not malicious obstructionism. This, as will be remembered, was the period when the foundation, flush with money, decided to go for very big grants and even to dip into its growing endowment to cover them.[90] But it seems that Heald was doubtful about giving large sums to Atlantic and European projects. As a man devoted to the improvement of American secondary and higher education, he continued to believe that more important jobs were to be done, even after Stone had dragged him around Europe on several trips to convince him that the Ford-sponsored programs there were worthwhile. Moreover, if large grants were to be made at home, Heald favored giving them "to non-ivy league universities."[91] A cautious and basically conservative man, the president, as the foundation's chief executive, probably also wondered about how the 1960s spending spree might end. It is also safe to assume that some of the other officers were likewise opposed to Stone's schemes because they, too, had different spending priorities. These appear to have been the circumstances in which an unsigned and undated comment on the IA paper critical of the whole idea, "Strengthening the Comprehensive Development of the Atlantic Partnership," was produced.[92] Nor did it make Stone popular that he continued to put forward requests for smaller projects that all added up.

For example, the trustees were presented with a long list of recommendations at their meeting on 12–13 December 1963. On this occasion, the total to be approved came to just under $63 million, of which $25 million was to go to Overseas Development. Various domestic educational programs were to receive about $19.5 million; but there were also no less than sixteen projects submitted by IA, all of them in the hundreds of thousands rather than millions, that came to some $5.2 million.[93] The minutes of the trustees' meeting of 24–25 September 1964 record a presentation by Stone at the end of which he had obtained approval for grants to strengthen relations between the Massachusetts Institute of Technology and Berlin's Technical University ($500,000); to enable the International Press Institute (IPI) to organize the training of African journalists in Africa ($300,000, to be shared between IA and OD as part of their recent collaboration); to enable the Carnegie Endowment for International Peace to establish "a series of conferences among Western Hemisphere leaders ($300,000); and finally to help with the "construction and equipment of the new United Nations International School in New York" ($7.5 million).[94]

At the end of October 1965 Joseph M. McDaniel called a meeting of "officers and directors" to discuss eight docket items to be presented to the trustees by IA, totaling almost $2.2 million.[95] And on 16 April 1962, Stone had sent Heald a memorandum commenting, of course positively, on a letter that General Clay had written in support of "two specific proposals: (1) A Center for Advanced Studies in the Arts and Sciences; (2) A Center of Urban Development" in Berlin.[96] Heald cannot but have wondered how Clay, the U.S. military governor in occupied Germany until 1949, learned of the proposal and was now throwing his weight as an "elder statesman" about. Nor will the president have failed to notice that Nabokov's plans for building an ambitious Berlin program in the arts were also in the making.

Given the president's basic skepticism, relations between him and Stone began to deteriorate. It also seems that some of the more spend-happy trustees grew dissatisfied with Heald and even began to think of replacing him. Although McCloy later claimed not to have taken a firm stand on the question of full funding for the CCF, he wielded considerable influence as chairman of the board of trustees, and it was widely known that Stone was his protégé. He also seems to have favored large grants with few strings attached. Interviewed in 1984, he remembered "very distinctly having a fight myself with Heald" about juvenile crime and funding for the Boys Club of America. The president wanted to do a study first, while McCloy was prepared to allocate some $10 million for the project. Relations got particularly bad between Heald and Donald K. David, a trustee who "rather regarded himself as Henry Ford's personal representative on the board." Over time the trustees, as McCloy put it somewhat mildly, became "a little too doctrinaire in terms of their interference and their desire to control and influence the staff to a degree that was resented by Heald." And so, one day the name of McGeorge Bundy, who had been working in the White House, came up. Trustees "went and importuned him to say that he would be ready to take over." In the end, even though he felt more warmth for Heald than did his colleagues, McCloy went to Washington "and recruited Bundy."[97]

Although Bundy, soon after assuming the presidency, had to look for cutbacks in the foundation's budget if Ford did not want to spend itself out of existence,[98] he was—as Josselson had indicated in his 1967 report—favorably disposed toward full funding for the CCF. In June 1966, IA produced a "Planning Budget Request for Fiscal 1966–1967–1968," which listed a number of old and new projects and postulated the need "to strengthen a limited number of institutions within the developed countries which are of significance to Western civilization or which could become a national or international resource in scientific, intellectual, or cultural areas related to the program."[99] At the subsequent June meeting of the trustees, the new president received "general authorization for a study" on a large grant to the CCF.[100] While these preparations were moved forward, Stone had been corresponding with Josselson, who was clearly taking the cue. On 28 May the CCF executive director reported that at Stone's suggestion he "had arranged to have all funds which the CCF requires for the calendar year 1966 deposited with our accounting division in London." He added that among the factors that had "contributed to morale recovery" among congress personnel had been "the hope that Ford will come through."[101]

Over the summer Bundy, Stone, and James Perkins, the president of Cornell University, whom Bundy had asked to undertake an independent study of the CCF, had separately visited Paris to vet the CCF and had talked to experts in other places. By September 1966 negotiations by Bundy and Stone with the CCF had progressed to a point at which Bundy was "prepared to make a strong recommendation that the Foundation provide basic underwriting for the Congress" to the tune of $7 million over "the next six years." The document confirmed that "the Congress has completely cut all ties of every description with its principal previous financial sponsors." There was also "definite assurance of first-class leadership both in the continuing service of the excellent staff under Michael Josselson."[102]

A deciding factor was also that Raymond Aron, after some hesitation, had accepted "the Presidency of a reorganized Board of Directors." In

239

light of all these developments, Bundy was "convinced that this appropriation is unusually strong in its quality and in its timeliness." The new president realized that the recommendation "may raise a few eyebrows among those who know or think they know the previous financial history of the Congress, but it is the right thing to do at the right time." He ended by confirming that "additional supporting argument will be available in the [trustees'] meeting in a confidential memorandum prepared by Mr. Stone."[103]

With these endorsements the trustees at their next meeting approved the $7 million requested, with the first slice of $1.5 million to be paid in "October or November."[104] The appropriation for November 1967 was to be $1.3 million, to be followed by $1.1 million per year in November 1968 and 1969. For November 1970 and 1971 $1 million each had been earmarked in the expectation that other foundations would by then have joined the deal. The allocation for 1966 was a little over a quarter less than envisaged by the current CCF budget;[105] but after the organizational changes that had already been made and with Nabokov more or less happily settled in Berlin, Josselson believed that Ford's contribution would secure the survival of the CCF without CIA funding.

Stone was no less elated than Josselson. He was particularly pleased about Aron's assuming of the presidency. As he later wrote to Manès Sperber: "I know what Raymond and you meant to each other, and what you and Raymond mean to me. One could not always be at ease with Raymond, but his mind and voice were European culture at its highest."[106] Stone was no doubt right about Aron on both scores, and his last point once again put the European-American problem, which he and the CCF had been working so hard to resolve, neatly into a nutshell. The French sociologist embodied the tension between the cultural and philosophical traditions of the "Anglo-Saxons," on the one hand, and the Continental Europeans, on the other.[107] And he had also worked hard to overcome them. When the CCF collapsed, he felt let down.

Twelve months after this outcome, which Josselson and Stone had been working for since the early 1960s, Aron had resigned from the presidency of the CCF board, Josselson had stepped down as executive director, and the CCF had been formally shut down. Its successor, the IACF, continued for another decade until it, too, folded. No less significant, within the IACF the old European-American tensions resurfaced, while it simultaneously faced a new culture war with a younger generation of leftist critics on both sides of the Atlantic.

SCANDAL AND COLLAPSE

In explaining this dramatic turn of events in which the CCF's former links with the CIA played the key role, an analysis of the larger picture provides, just as in earlier parts of this book, the best starting point. We have seen how the Cold War with the Soviet Union had lost much of the sharp ideological edge it had had in the early 1950s—a shift that was tangibly reflected in the changing focus of IA's activities. As the sense grew that the intellectual battle against the Soviet bloc had essentially been won, Stone concentrated on combatting Western Europe's cultural anti-Americanism, promoted exchanges with Eastern Europe, and, partly in cooperation with OD, funded projects all over the world. Meanwhile the CCF's operations had undergone an almost identical evolution.[108]

The policies of the Kennedy and Johnson administrations seemed to confirm the general direction of socioeconomic and political trends that Galbraith, Shils, Bell, and other intellectuals associated with both the CCF and Stone had been writing about in previous years. After early doubts and fears, optimism that the problems of modern industrial societies were masterable after all had returned. In the economic sphere Keynesian management and liberal corporatism had swept the board. Social reformism began on a broad front, culminating in Lyndon Johnson's idea of the Great Society. Men like Robert McNamara and Jerome Wiesner embodied the confident belief not only in the power of modern technology but also in technocratic solutions to human problems. The "end of ideology" was finally at hand—or so it seemed.[109]

Rumblings, however, were soon to unsettle the era of pragmatic macroeconomic and macropolitical management. European intellectuals, with their more somber view of modernity, had never quite shared American optimism about a bright future for the industrial West, and Isaiah Berlin had been one of those who, though always pro-American, had given expression to this skepticism.[110] In West Germany, too, technocracy suddenly became a public issue, and in France Pierre Emmanuel similarly returned to a difference in the way the "Anglo-Saxons" and Parisian intellectuals defined the essence of culture.[111]

One of the most ominous signs of the period of instability that lay ahead was the botched American invasion of Cuba and the growing suspicion of a misuse of governmental power and trust. Given the role it was suspected of having played in the attempt to topple Fidel Castro, the CIA became the focus of criticism in ways unknown during the Cold War

241

1950s. Mistrust of government, especially among a younger generation, was exacerbated by the escalating Vietnam War and the incipient wider questioning of the aims and motives of American foreign policy around the globe and in the Third World in particular. Meanwhile, in Europe Gaullism was feeding on growing doubts about America's role in the world.

Consequently, the activities of the CIA came under increasingly intense scrutiny, and not just, as might be surmised, by the leftist and liberal press in the United States. This period saw the ascendancy of an academic criticism that went beyond the question of technocracy. It was spearheaded in the field of history by scholars such as William A. Williams and his students writing about the "imperial" tradition of American foreign policy since the nineteenth century.[112] C. Wright Mills's analysis of the American *Power Elite* and his scathing essays on the CCF "ideologues" and Bell in particular similarly were no longer unheard cries in the desert.[113] With the examination of elitist power structures and the questioning of the "end of ideology" came the renewed dissection of the role of capitalism in domestic politics and what it was doing to popular culture. The incipient civil rights movement focused on the glaring inequalities to which minorities continued to be subjected. Michael Harrington's *The Other America* demonstrated that poverty in wealthy America had not at all been solved.[114] Herbert Marcuse's essays were read with approval by that segment of the postwar generation that was trying to assert itself against the graying generation of the 1930s and 1940s and that wanted to wrench politics and public morality away from the totalitarianism paradigm that had informed Cold War discourses.[115]

At the same time there was always also the opposition to government policies that arose in the U.S. Congress and was frequently driven by party-political rivalry. Indeed, as we narrow our focus on the immediate circumstances that triggered the 1967 crisis of the CCF, congressional criticism crucially came into play. On 31 August 1964, Representative Wright Patman, a Texas Democrat, revealed that the CIA had used the J. M. Kaplan Fund of New York since 1959 as a "conduit" for its monies. He quoted an unidentified CIA source who had given him the information about this arrangement, which was now being investigated by the Internal Revenue Service.[116] Three days later the *New York Times* gave further details on what the paper's editorial writer called the "misusing [of] CIA money,"[117] but thereafter the matter, which was also taken up by other papers, appears quietly to have dropped from sight. Two weeks later the *Nation* carried a column on Patman's disclosures, which raised the question of "foundations as 'fronts.' " It mentioned how CIA money, channeled through the Kaplan Fund, had been donated to various causes and how eight other foundations had been used in this way.[118] In a letter to the *New York Times* Rutgers University professor F. K. Berrin had the last word on 19 September when he urged investigation of CIA activities.[119]

The Kaplan Fund affair and similar rumors about the Fairfield Foundation did not go unnoticed in the Ford Foundation and the CCF. It seems to have pushed Josselson and Stone, always sensitive to the "hazards" of covert CIA support, to redouble their effort to find full private funding for the Congress. It also seems to have reinforced President Heald in his doubts about a multimillion dollar bailout. In May 1965 he issued a memorandum to foundation staff on "Relations with Government Programs." The document, while not discouraging contacts with officials in Washington, laid down clearer operational rules and stressed in its conclusion that the new procedures "do not indicate any slackening in the efforts of the Ford Foundation to maintain its own independence and autonomy as a private philanthropic organization which is regulated by the Federal government only through provisions of the Internal Revenue Code." Heald further insisted that "none of the procedures should be carried out in such a way that would invite Washington officials to make proposals for Ford Foundation grants or to use the Ford Foundation as a means of developing particular government interests."[120] Overall, the memorandum thus tried to put a stop to the kind of relationship that had existed with the State Department and the CIA when, as we have seen, Herter and Dulles openly encouraged the foundation to move forward with certain East European and Chinese programs.[121]

After the September 1964 debate in the press, the matter rested until 26 April 1966 when the *New York Times* reported on "How [the] CIA Put Instant Air Force into Congo to Carry Out U.S. Policy." The article, in which the CIA was called a "child of Pearl Harbor and [the] Cold War," briefly summarized the agency's history as well as its various "official" duties.[122] The next day the paper expanded on this latter theme, giving details on the CIA's spying methods. But the really explosive news appeared toward the end of the article, when the CIA was stated to have funded "anti-Communist, but liberal organizations of intellectuals such as the Congress for Cultural Freedom, and some of their newspapers and magazines." *Encounter* was said to have been "for a long time—though it is not now—one of the indirect beneficiaries of CIA funds."[123] The *Times*'s series on the CIA was widely noticed and led to concern in academic circles about future Ford Foundation funding.[124] Above all, it triggered several letters to the paper. The first one appeared on 9 May and was signed by Galbraith, Kennan, Oppenheimer, and Schlesinger. It did not confirm or deny CIA funding but instead extolled the independence of the CCF. The organization's record showed that it "has had no loyalty except an unswerving commitment to cultural freedom."[125]

Signed by Spender, Lasky, and Kristol, a stronger statement regarding *Encounter* was printed on the following day.[126] By 16 May the *Times* had also published the letter from Denis de Rougemont and Nabokov. Again it did not directly deny the receipt of CIA funds, but insisted that at no point in the "history of the Congress has any donor sought to interfere with or shape its actions, policies or programs."[127] On 17 May, Lasky protested to Clifton Daniel, the managing editor of the *New York Times*; clearly concerned to put oil on the water, Daniel was "sure that some satisfactory solution can be arrived at."[128]

Similarly, the *Nation* received a letter from Nabokov and de Rougemont and from the editors of *Encounter* in response to its account of the CIA's involvement in the CCF and the journal. While the replies essentially reiterated the points made to the *Times*, a sentence in the *Nation's* critical essay deserves quotation: "The undisclosed acceptance, over a long period, of CIA funds by two organizations avowedly dedicated to 'cultural freedom' provides an ironic notation to the cultural history of the cold war."[129]

As in 1964, the press debate had no serious consequences for the CCF. On the contrary, the plans to obtain full Ford Foundation funding proceeded at a quick pace after Bundy had taken over from Heald. It is therefore an even more "ironic notation to the cultural history of the cold war" that after several earlier discussions in the press that barely left a ripple, a third wave of debate that began *after* the CIA's withdrawal became so acerbic that it destroyed the CCF. This third wave seems to have started with an article in the *Christian Science Monitor* on 16 February, which plainly reported that the State Department had acknowledged CIA funding for the National Student Association (NSA) for more than ten years.[130] A further report in the paper published on the following day and titled "Loss of CIA Funds Called Blow to Youth Movements" did not contain a whiff of scandal either.[131]

Four days later, Walter Lippmann stoked the fire with three articles sharply critical of the CIA's totalitarian methods. Americans, the influential commentator added, no longer felt as if they were at the height of the Cold War.[132] On 23 February Lippmann widened his attack on the CIA's practice of engaging in more than genuine intelligence work.[133] Finally, on 28 February he went so far as to call the agency's actions outside its intelligence mission "self-defeating," because they represented "the methods of a totalitarian state, and without a totalitarian environment of secrecy and terror they are unworkable. This most unpleasant and embarrassing affair is the proof that an open society cannot act successfully like a totalitarian society."[134] This charge was perhaps the most ironic notation of all, and one that caused the greatest bewilderment in the CCF, which had always defined itself as being the antitotalitarian association par excellence.

While Lippmann pursued his traditional liberal agenda rather typically within the framework of the totalitarianism paradigm, other journals escalated the scandal into a more fundamental attack on an "immoral" and "bankrupt" political system as a whole. This, it must be remembered, was the period of a growing opposition, especially among students and leftist intellectuals, to the Vietnam War and to the handling of major domestic problems that had resurfaced by the mid-1960s. Above all, they presented more and more extensively researched details on the various covert operations that had been going on. Thus in early March the relatively unknown *Ramparts* published a longish story of the NSA-CIA link.[135] This was followed in April by a look back on the long history of "The CIA and the Intellectuals," which appeared in the *New York Review of Books*.[136] Finally in May 1967 Thomas W. Braden poured more oil into the flames. Identifying himself as the now retired head of the CIA section responsible for "subsidizing student, labor, and cultural groups abroad," he confirmed the press stories and defended the program as "essential."[137]

By this time the CCF was, not surprisingly, also fully in the firing line. As late as the end of February, a Ford Foundation official reported Josselson as saying that "they still have not completely lived down the New York Times charges" of the previous year.[138] After the fresh revelations and suspicions, it proved impossible to hold the dams. Press reports also appeared in Europe, Asia, and Latin America, where the attacks quickly undermined the CCF's credibility. Josselson received letters from all over the world demanding an honest explanation.[139] Depressed and exhausted, he tendered his resignation and called a meeting of the CCF's General Assembly.

As he recounted the story to the assembly members, "the CIA, knowing of our approximate budgetary requirements, would indicate to me, or at a much later date to [his deputy] John Hunt, the name of a foundation which was likely to respond favorably to a request for a grant to the

245

Congress." He or Hunt "would then write to the foundation, explain the Congress's work and needs, and apply for a certain amount of funds which in 99 cases out of a 100 was subsequently granted." However, "before approaching a foundation . . . we would check out its bona fides in the official Foundation Directory," a precaution that, "as has now become known," did not prevent the CIA "in a couple of instances" and "in their only violation of the promises made to me, from resorting to a dummy foundation in order to get the funds to the bona-fide foundation." Josselson concluded his report by outlining the arrangement that had finally been made with the Ford Foundation at the end of 1966 to enable him to sever all links with the CIA.[140]

This good news did not stop the uproar within the organization. Josselson saw no alternative to leaving his position, though he agreed to stay on until September to initiate the transformation of the congress and was hired as a consultant thereafter. Stephen Spender resigned, along with Frank Kermode, from the editorial board of *Encounter*, now that the rumors he had heard in earlier years but had allegedly not been able to verify were formally confirmed.[141] The reproaches from abroad and particularly from India were no less bitter, and when Hunt, the only other person in the congress leadership to share Josselson's secret, saw himself accused of "moral weakness" by Jayaprakash Narayan, a member of the board of directors and former honorary president of the CCF, he too stepped down.[142] Another crunch point came in September when Aron decided that "he would have nothing more to do with the Congress."[143]

While Josselson wrote long letters trying to explain the situation to prominent members all over the world and to keep them from leaving the congress, the Ford Foundation posed a no less serious threat to the CCF's future. The revelations were obviously deeply embarrassing to all philanthropic organizations, now that the public wondered how many of them had been involved in the CIA's conduit mechanism or in the covert system of mixing private and official support. On 2 March 1967, shortly after the first press reports had appeared, representatives of five big foundations met with a special committee that President Johnson had established on 15 February under the chairmanship of Attorney General Nicholas deB. Katzenbach to deal with the CIA scandal. At this meeting there was general agreement that the CIA's policies had been "not only stupid, but wrong" and that "the damage has been immense to the reputation and actual programs of legitimate groups, to their believability as truly private agencies, independent of governmental influence."[144]

David Bell also told Bundy that the CIA's schemes had "(unnecessarily) damaged the reputation and effectiveness of institutions and individuals in the United States, especially vis-à-vis the less developed and more apprehensive nations." Closer to home, he added, "the activities adversely affect the reputation and effectiveness of the Ford Foundation."[145] In light of such strong feelings, the Katzenbach committee, in its final report, sent Johnson two recommendations to overturn National Security Council policies that—in place since October 1951—had been reaffirmed as recently as December 1960 by the Presidential Committee on Information Policies Abroad.[146]

Stone shared the embarrassment felt at the foundation but remained assertive, as a memorandum he wrote to Bundy on 17 April 1967 reveals. While he felt that "notwithstanding The New York Review of Books, Ramparts, Commentary and certain intellectuals spread among the universities, it is likely that the Republic will survive," he thought "the situation . . . somewhat depressing." There was, he continued, "a nihilism, a contempt for self and country, a boredom which reminds me of European intellectuals at the end of the Weimar Republic." But he was in no mood to give up and suggested to the president that "you and a few of us might talk this over with a few open-minded intellectuals, Americans and Europeans, of the Left and other persuasions." He mentioned an unsurprising group of people, which included Bell, Berlin, Lasky, and Aron.[147] Bundy's response: "Shep, this is a great problem, but I'd rather *not* start activities on it through your office at present."[148]

The president also proceeded cautiously on the question of what to do with the large grant that had just been approved fully to fund the CCF over the next six years at a time when the congress was in turmoil. As we have seen, the CIA's practices were, of course, not just rumored at the Ford Foundation. Stone, McCloy, and Heald had known about them for years. At least one trustee, Charles Wyzanski, was also in the picture. When in 1960 he attended a CCF conference that featured Kennan, Silone, Spender, and others, he asked Galbraith if he realized who was paying for this expensive event. When the latter guessed that it must be "some foundation," Wyzanski corrected him: "You should know it's the CIA."[149] Bundy, too, is likely to have been in the know before he arrived at the foundation. According to the *Wall Street Journal* of 24 February 1967, the CIA, in subsidizing various groups, had not acted "on its own but in accordance with national policies established by the National Security Council."[150] It is therefore not too farfetched to assume that Bundy learned about these policies during his spell as special assistant under Kennedy.

If he approved of the CIA's subsidies while serving in the White House, as president of the Ford Foundation and having listened to the critical remarks of his colleagues during the meeting with Katzenbach on 2 March 1967, he was bound to wonder if the millions that he had approved for the CCF in the fall of 1966 were still monies wisely spent.[151] Consequently he traveled to Paris to see for himself. He also sent Sutton out to talk to people associated with the CCF and others to test precisely this question. The Ford emissary found that Josselson, in anticipation of his withdrawal in September, had been busy trying to find a successor and to reduce the membership to build a more effective and more diverse board of directors.[152]

Sutton furthermore discovered that some favored a straightforward continuation of the congress if the Ford Foundation stood by it. Others seem to have spoken for a new name along the lines of Josselson's idea of 1965 when, in connection with the consortium plan,[153] he had proposed transforming the CCF into an "International Council for Cultural Cooperation." It seems that Sutton was inclined to recommend to Bundy adherence to the Ford funding plan until he met Aron shortly before the latter's resignation from the chairmanship of the board, a position he had held since 1966. According to a handwritten note, "Sutton had come back from the talk with Aron shaken." If the Ford emissary had been "very positive" until then, he was now "talking of alternative plans."[154]

Fortunately, though, Sutton's basic attitude remained unchanged. His final report to Bundy and David Bell began with a reassuring statement: "In the wake of the disclosures and the withdrawal of Raymond Aron and Arthur Lewis, there had been fears that other defections were occurring or would occur. These fears seem to be groundless." Indeed, "practically everyone I talked to who has been associated with the Congress believes it should continue and proclaims his loyalty to it." Thus Minoo Masani, the chair of the Indian CCF, and his colleagues did not even want to change the name.[155] Although Sutton recognized "that there are reasons why the leaders of the Congress may want it to continue which do not follow from a cool appraisal of its value," it nevertheless seemed "hardly likely that they would have come loyally through the late unpleasantries if the Congress had not served important functions with distinction."[156]

Much of the rest of Sutton's memorandum represented a summary of what the congress had been in the past and of its future potential. But even if he did not make any explicit recommendation, he evidently hoped that Bundy and Bell would not abandon the CCF. What apparently they had meanwhile been contemplating was a reduction of the proposed grant instalments for 1970, 1971, and 1972 by over $500,000.[157] Commenting on this idea to Sutton on 21 September, Stone signaled that these cuts would be acceptable in principle but should not go below $500,000.[158] Meanwhile Josselson, writing to Sutton on 20 September, had raised the question of continuity once more. He had "given a great deal of thought to the idea that one might conceivably give the Congress a decent burial and replace it after a brief interval with a new organization," though one that continued to rely on the old networks.[159] This, in the end, was the solution that was adopted. The congress was not buried for good but saw its resurrection under a different name: International Association for Cultural Freedom. Its new president was—Shepard Stone.

Coping with the New Culture Wars of the
1960s and Beyond

W HEN IN the fall of 1967 Stone became president of the International Association for Cultural Freedom (IACF), the CCF's successor after the turmoil of the spring and summer of that year, he knew that the new post would not be a bed of roses. True, he was able to move from New York to a beautiful apartment in the heart of Paris with views of Notre Dame. But there is even some question about how much of a lure this was. Culturally he had always been more attracted by Berlin. His French was by no means as fluent as his German, and Parisian social life was certainly very different from the informality of relationships in an American urban or academic setting. When Paul Hoffman congratulated him on his move, he wrote, in a teasing little reference to the American-European culture war that we have traced in previous chapters: "So you have gone cultured. I was always afraid this would happen."[1] Stone replied, slightly more seriously: "I have always been cultured. So have you, but you haven't wanted to admit it."[2]

THE ESTABLISHMENT OF THE IACF

Whatever his private reservations, he liked the challenge that the IACF posed. There was an urgent need to put it, with its many affiliates and journals around the globe, on a sound organizational and financial basis. As he wrote to John Dickey, the president of Dartmouth College: "The risk, the world-wide ramifications, the belief that leading intellectuals (for better or worse) are likely to play an increasing political role—all this appealed to me."[3] Six months later in a letter to Ludvik Lesczcynski, his former interlocutor in Warsaw, he remarked that, having been in the comfortable position of distributing money at the Ford Foundation, he was "now on the other side of the table."[4] But however strong the loyalties he felt to the ideas that the CCF had stood for, there was also the fact that his days at Ford had been numbered. He knew since the end of 1966 that he had to find something else and, although he had a lot of administrative and political experience, this was not easy for a man in his late fifties.

This chapter examines how Stone handled the dual challenge of providing the IACF with financial and intellectual direction and why he ultimately failed. As throughout this book, however, there is not just the biographical element but also the larger context of the times to be considered. This is why this chapter is divided into a first section dealing with the financial and organizational woes of the IACF, and into a second one concerned with the intellectual challenges that ultimately overwhelmed it. In fact, this second section will be linked back to the CCF and its failure, whose deeper causes we have yet to analyze. Among these causes the old and unresolved tension will have to be considered between two definitions of what kind of "culture" should be promoted. For after Josselson had prevented the "Koestlerization" of the CCF and had successfully "culturalized" it, there was, beyond the preference for "high" and the rejection of "low" (pop) culture, the question of how comprehensively culture was to be defined. In this respect—as we have already seen—by including the sciences, the American notion was wider, more pragmatic, and also more political than that of some Continental-European and especially French intellectuals.[5] A third and final section will deal with what Stone did after leaving the association and how he came to be the director of the Berlin Aspen Institute, which enabled him to resume, free from financial worries, the work of intellectual bridge building both across the Iron Curtain and the Atlantic.

The fact that Bundy, on assuming the Ford Foundation presidency, approved a multimillion dollar rescue package for the CCF could be taken to mean that Stone, who had lobbied hard for this large grant for several years, was at the height of his influence. But this is a very deceptive impression; he was really on his way out. Among the reasons for this were the familiar ones: the arrival of a new president who had his own program priorities and who knew that a sure way to implement them was reorganization with the tacit intention of replacing an older group of officers with his own trusted people. Stone clearly belonged to the former. He had been very successful at building up his IA program, but as the focus of foundation activities had begun to shift even before Bundy's arrival, his reputation remained that of a "pro-European." Nor did it help that he was—as Bundy himself phrased it—a " 'McCloy Action' man,"[6] now that his mentor had stepped down from the board of trustees. Because they belonged to different generations, Stone and Bundy also had divergent conceptions of where the big foundations should be going. In short, even if Josselson

251

had written in his May 1967 report that, unlike Heald, the new president was "for culture" and did not worry too much about the CCF's connections with the CIA,[7] Stone quickly sensed the gulf that existed between him and Bundy.

It is against this background that, on 14 October 1966, Vice-President Bell sent Bundy a memorandum with suggestions that had emerged from "several discussions" he had had with Stone "about his future work." The plan was to make the IA director "an adviser to the President in the international field to undertake special assignments from the President, the Vice President (International), and on his own initiative." Bell then listed a number of immediate jobs to be done.[8] Realizing that this meant a lot of traveling without much influence at headquarters in New York, Stone and his colleague Joe Slater subsequently tried to insert a clause that would have given Stone a more active role.[9] But it is doubtful that that would have made much difference in view of the new power realities under Bundy.

Beyond the movement of personnel there were the institutional changes. The new president wanted to revamp the foundation bureaucracy into four entities: the International Division, the Educational Division, the Humanities and Arts Division, and a Division X. In preparation of this reorganization, Bell held a number of meetings with IA and International Training and Research (ITR) staffs "at which we have reviewed the current and prospective activities of those programs with a view to allocating them to one or another of the new divisions."[10] Two days later Bell sent Bundy another memorandum titled "The 'International Division'—General Shape and Content," which confirmed the dissolution of the little empire that Stone had built since 1955.[11]

Stone took all these developments to mean that he should really be looking for another job, and in the following months he explored various possibilities. By the spring of 1967 one of these had resulted in serious negotiations to assume the presidency of Hunter College in the Bronx.[12] But a few weeks later, on 3 May, when the scandal of the CIA's covert funding schemes reached its peak, he received a telephone call from Josselson "about the crisis of the Congress" for Cultural Freedom. The CCF executive director told his patron and friend that "his health was giving out" and that "the Congress needed urgently a new head." Various names had previously been mentioned, but now Josselson insisted that if Stone "would take over, the Congress would be saved" and he could write his "own ticket." Stone replied that he was really looking elsewhere but that, "without giving a final answer, I would be interested." Josselson was overjoyed and agreed to talk to Aron. Galbraith, who had just been advising Stone to take the Hunter College job, was also brought into the discussion. The Harvard economist now reversed his earlier position and promised to call Bundy after Stone had heard a rumor that the $5.6 million that Ford had approved in the fall of 1966 was again in doubt.[13]

For reasons that are not too difficult to comprehend, Bundy turned out to be "favorably disposed" toward a deal that would keep in place the rescue package and put Stone in charge of the CCF. Stone would leave the foundation, yet still be close enough for it to be able to keep a check on the use of the multimillion dollar grant.[14] However, there was a flip side that worked in Stone's favor: he knew the foundation and its peculiar ways well; some colleagues sympathized with him and were prepared to provide inside information that helped him to assess the terrain. Nor, for the same reason, did officers find it easy to turn down his requests when he showed up on their doorstep.[15]

The upshot of all the negotiating was that Stone agreed to become president of the CCF successor. In the summer of 1967 there was still some question as to how well he would be able to cooperate with Pierre Emmanuel, the prospective director general of the new IACF. Emmanuel was an old CCF hand and a well-known French writer who had his own ideas about European-American cultural politics.[16] Stone was an optimist, and on 31 August reassured Emmanuel "that you and I would work together admirably, without rivalry, as you say, and with loyalty, respect and affection." He was also convinced that "the intellectuals in our fragmented world need the Congress." Of course, there were "heavy burdens from the past." But to Stone the achievements of the CCF were "examples of what can and should be done in the future."[17]

The fact that it took Emmanuel until 26 September just to tell Stone that he had not yet accepted the job offer extended to him by the general assembly of the IACF, is likely to have dampened Stone's optimism. It was no less disconcerting that Emmanuel went on to specify his position on key issues of future IACF policy and constitutional questions. Thus he wanted Josselson in his proposed advisory role to be no more than an "elder statesman" who was retired and merely acted as "a consultant from *outside* our organisation."[18] Second, and even more tellingly, Emmanuel insisted that the board of directors be the IACF's "sovereign body" and warned that he "would be unwilling to accept the post of Director," if this "international and 'sovereign' character" were weakened; "if, for instance, certain conditions should be laid down as to our programs or fields of activity." The IACF, Emmanuel continued, "must not appear as part and parcel of the Ford Foundation or of the American Establishment at large." If in a document he had submitted to the general assembly he had argued for making this sovereignty explicit, it was in order to take account of "the uncertainty of most of our friends who do not want to appear as the instruments of any American cultural policy."

This larger point and polite reference to the CIA scandal finally led Emmanuel to state "some of my intellectual convictions which you [i.e., Stone] ought to know because they are not necessarily those of the majority of our friends." These convictions are worth quoting at some length because they reveal the persistence of a European-American divide that Stone and the Americans in the CCF had been trying to overcome during the preceding fifteen years. Emmanuel's words also illuminate some of the causes of the IACF's impending failure: "First of all, I am a 'Gaullist.' This does not mean that I approve all the methods used by General de Gaulle in his Government. But I think that in [sic] the whole his foreign policy is sound and corresponds to the changes of the time. . . . Secondly, I am very much against war in Vietnam and I think that it would bring the United States to a state of external and internal crisis where all the values of freedom we believe in would be endangered if not crushed. A complete change in the American psychology of power must happen and the American intellectuals must help it take shape. Moreover the image of America throughout the world must be made clear and discussed both by Americans and non-Americans."

Having found some quite critical words about the United States and its global role and having articulated his worries about the "period of revolutionary change" that was happening all over, Emmanuel, knowing that he had to be cooperative, proved in the end to be the polished French intellectual that he was: "After reading this letter you will judge, my dear Shep, whether it is possible for us to work intimately together." If Stone had any doubts, he, Emmamuel, would not stand in the way.

In the end Stone and Emmanuel accepted their respective IACF posts. They divided their work of reconstruction between them, appreciating that they came from quite different cultural backgrounds. Stone concentrated on fund raising and on the world of Anglo-Saxon academics; Emmanuel tried to restore confidence in the IACF's worldwide operations among his fellow intellectuals, particularly in the Romance-language regions of Europe and Latin America, where he enjoyed a high reputation as a writer. Meanwhile staff at the Paris headquarters drew up organizational charts reflecting the CCF's legacy: an array of national committees and affiliated institutes, affiliated journals, and seminar program groups.[19] Papers were drafted explaining the past and future of the IACF.[20]

FINANCIAL STRAITS

For Stone the most pressing task was to persuade the Ford Foundation to release the second installment of the five-year grant. On 13 October 1967 he wrote to Howard Dressner, the foundation's secretary, to inform him that the $1.5 million tranche paid out at the end of 1966 was running out and to request payment of "the new 1967/1968 grant of $1.3 million."[21] To reassure Dressner that all was well, he enclosed a copy of the new statutes and the membership of the board of directors.[22] When, soon thereafter, Stone received the most recent budget projection for 1968, expenditures added up to $1.2 million, with $100,000 to be kept in reserve. Estimates for four seminar programs for the year came to $107,000. Institutes and affiliates required close to $500,000. Subsidies to journals amounted to some $250,000. The estimated costs to run the Paris headquarters, including travel and a "Termination Fund" for Josselson and Hunt, added up to almost $380,000.[23]

Stone was also well aware that the yearly Ford transfers would soon decline. Worse, he had already been told of an additional $500,000 plus that Bell wanted to lop off from the last three instalments.[24] Virtually from his first day in office, the new president had to look for ways to effect a gradual reduction of recurrent commitments. In the journals area, efforts had been made by Josselson for years to find publishers, though his experiences had not been encouraging in this respect. But Stone had no choice but to continue the search. Publishers were reluctant to take the bait once they learned about the debt burdens, or else they dropped out again after a few years when the deficits could not be reduced. Thus, *Encounter* had received over £193,000 from the CCF until 1964, and Cecil King's publishing company lost further undisclosed sums—until December 1970, when it threw in the towel. A period of uncertainty then began that ended in the journal being closed down completely.[25] Stone fared no better in his efforts to save *Der Monat* after the Fischer-Verlag was no longer prepared to foot the bill.[26]

In January 1968 Stone told Rajat Neogy, the editor of *Transitions* (published in Kampala since 1961), that, his respect for the African journal notwithstanding, "our budgetary problem is real." All he could promise was that the IACF would clear the journal's 1967 deficit "within the first six months of 1968." As to the anticipated 1968 deficit, Stone wrote that he would make "as substantial a contribution as we can" in the second half of the year.[27] On 16 May then, he stated unambiguously that it was impossible for the association to continue giving "large subsidies for publications with poor circulations." Hence "all the journals and magazines, including *Preuves*, are on notice that unless there is an improvement in quality and circulation we may have to discontinue support."[28] Stone tried his best to secure the survival of *Preuves* and *Tempo Presente*, of *Quest* and *Aportes*, but without lasting success.[29]

The CCF's scholarly journals also became a headache for Stone. Trying to save *China Quarterly*, he corresponded with Professor C. H. Philips of the School of Oriental and African Studies at London University, and with Roderick MacFarquhar, to see if the university's China Institute might take the journal under its wing.[30] With respect to the well-regarded Soviet studies journal *Survey*, attempts to obtain a long-term arrangement with the Hoover Institution and Stanford University proved particularly agonizing, not least because of the need to secure the livelihood of the editor, Leo Labedz.[31] Overall it was probably easier to find a way out for the scholarly periodicals than for the intellectual reviews. The tastes and expectations of potential readers were shifting in this period of rapid political and socioeconomic change. The next generation of intellectuals turned to publications that served up ideas and information in a different format or pursued a different and more appealing ideological line. Daniel Bell was out; Herbert Marcuse and C. Wright Mills were in. Ultimately, the demise of the former CCF journals is therefore bound up with the failure of the parent movement and the new culture wars that developed in the 1970s.

At the same time as Stone was imposing budget cuts on the various parts of his new empire, including the national groups,[32] and turning down requests for support of research projects,[33] he tried to raise money. He offered the CCF archive to Harvard University,[34] and visited the big European foundations with requests for help. But they were all reluctant to contribute larger sums.[35]

By the middle of August 1968, Stone had become so concerned about the IACF's future that he went to see Bundy and vice-president Bell with a rescheduling proposal. As Bell subsequently summarized the meeting to Sutton, the IACF president "would like to have $200,000 of the grant we have scheduled for 1972 brought forward and made available in 1969, bringing the 1969 total from $1.1 million to $1.3 million."[36] Stone admitted to "having much greater difficulty in raising money than he had anticipated"; the German foundations in particular had "not come through as he [had] hoped they would." Stone realized that if his proposal were accepted, Ford funding "would taper off [even] more quickly at the end of the support period than had been previously assumed." However, he felt "that he needed next year to maintain his going rate of operations and that if he could not get substantial additional money during the next year it would be a sign that he would have to make major changes in his plans in any event." Stone assured the two top Ford officials that he had "made all the economies he could possibly make," but in the end Bell was still uncertain whether the IACF president should be pushed to face the grim realities. For the moment, Bundy and Bell remained "noncommittal on this rather startling proposal" and suggested that he have further discussions with Sutton.[37]

The IACF directors were more fully informed about the association's plight at the board meeting on 5–6 December 1968. With Bullock in the chair, Stone once again "stressed the need for strict economies until our situation was eased by new grants, hopefully from German, Italian, and American foundations." He also raised the idea of transferring the Secretariat from Paris to London at an annual saving of $100,000. Yet, although Bullock liked the plan, there was immediate opposition from Shils and Sperber. Most tellingly, Emmanuel added his observation "that a move to London might 'Anglosaxonize' the Association and limit its effectiveness in Latin America, East Europe, Spain, Portugal, and in the French-speaking world."[38] It was a theme to which he returned during the crisis of 1973 and that raised the question of how far Stone's work to overcome the cultural divide between "Anglo-Saxon" and Continental European intellectuals ever succeeded.[39]

The severity of the reductions that Stone was forced to contemplate emerges from a summary of estimated expenditures for 1969 and 1970, which he produced in October 1969.[40] Another statement of receipts and disbursements from early 1970 demonstrates how little progress Stone had made with European foundations, even though he approached many of them.[41] In 1968 only the Agnelli Foundation had come through with a grant of $25,000, the first half of which was paid in December. For the following year, three German foundations are listed: Thyssen ($27,300), Krupp ($26,250), and Volkswagen ($38,996). There was also one unnamed "French donation" of $193! Apparently, the German grants were annual amounts over a period of three and four years and therefore seem to tally with the total of "approximately $400,000" that Stone proudly informed Howard Swearer at the Ford Foundation had been garnered from European foundations.[42]

Unfortunately, though, over the next twelve months, none of the major European foundations signaled that they were prepared to support the IACF on a scale that would have allowed Ford slowly to retreat from its commitment. American foundations were no more forthcoming.[43] Meanwhile in New York, the transfer of funds to Paris hit bureaucratic snags because Dressner's office claimed to be confused about "what the Association does."[44] Dressner was told by Sheila McLean, "a newcomer who knows from [sic] nothing about grants,"[45] that the monies would be spent on publications, seminars ("the contents of which for 1970 are as yet undefined"), as well as "staff support and staff travel." It was clear that the foundation's accountants had regained a stronger voice and were asking some sharp questions about spending habits.

While this was being sorted out, Bundy and Sutton on 23 March politely welcomed Bullock, Shils, and Paul Doty who had come to New York "to present the case for continued support to the IACF" for another five years. This was precisely the situation that the Ford leadership had been dreading. It was difficult enough to tell Stone, who had been their colleague, the hard truth. As was to be expected, the visitors were "strongly persuaded of the need for the IACF and its importance." At the same time, if the association could not expect help beyond 1972, they did "not now want to begin efforts which would have to be cut short." Instead in this case they wished "to make ample provision in good time for an orderly close-down." Stone, the three academics continued, had done his best to attract European foundations, but not more than $500,000 could be expected from that source. Although it was clear that the association could not survive without Ford, Bundy merely listened patiently and made no promises. Sutton spoke of "a review of the IACF's functions, particularly with regard to the developing countries," noting that David Heaps would shortly be seconded to undertake this job.[46]

There was, as happens often in "awkward" situations like this one, a certain degree of deception and self-deception in the meeting. Bundy was too much of a gentleman to tell Bullock, Shils, and Doty that the Ford Foundation wanted to get out, and the latter did not really want to hear this truth. Consequently, they left with the impression that the negotiations had gone well. But Stone was told a different story by Moselle Kimbler, his former trusted assistant and now "spy" at the Ford Foundation. She described to him a recent staff meeting at which Bundy announced that "for the first time he had been able to impress the trustees with the fact that we are nearing bankruptcy. . . . now this was a Bundy joke but with some serious tone, too. He then went on how hard choices would need to be made over the next period." Kimbler concluded: "Well, dear S[hepard] S[tone], we can put two and two together. I think it is going to be hard sledding. That's my assessment, and I'm sorry."[47]

Stone, taking these warnings seriously, redoubled his effort to tap other foundations. He applied to American foundations, among them Mellon and Rockefeller. The Japanese gave him some $30,000. But when all this income was added up, the bill for the Ford Foundation still came to $1 million per annum. This at least was the figure at which Heaps arrived before the meeting of the Trustees in December 1970. Having scoured all IACF accounts for potential savings, he had finally reached a "budgetary point below which meaningful survival is not possible." This point, he thought, was "somewhere in the $500–$600,000 range."[48]

Faced with difficult choices, however, the Ford leadership was unable to come to a decision, partly, it seems, because it was internally divided. Some officers wanted to move the IACF money elsewhere; others supported Stone. Heaps, who in principle favored an extension of a reduced grant beyond 1972, suddenly found himself charged with presenting the IACF's case to the international committee of the board of trustees at its December meeting in the presence of no lesser persons than Robert McNamara "(who is evidently a bear, but this MUST BE CONFIDENTIAL with you), Loudon, Bechtel,"[49] and this only shortly after Bell and Sutton had told him to expect tough questions. Still, they did not press Heaps for an immediate decision. As a result the decision on an extension beyond 1972 but also of the transfer of monies already approved was further delayed. Nor were these delays merely due to doubts about the value of the IACF's work but also to macroeconomic developments and the bear market on Wall Street, which, in the wake of the war in Vietnam and rising inflation, had badly affected the foundation's assets and hence its disposable income.[50] The years of largesse of the early 1960s were clearly over.

On top of all this came an administrative muddle: in the middle of December a letter resurfaced that Bullock had written to Bundy six weeks earlier, requesting more money for 1971 and 1972. The president had passed it on to Sutton who had never answered it. Finally, on 6 January 1971, Bell sent a reply to the chairman of the IACF board of directors. Referring back to Bullock's visit to New York in March 1970, he confirmed that Heaps had prepared a report on the IACF. Notwithstanding the high regard that the foundation had for the work of the Association, Bell noted, "our review has also confirmed the severity of our budgetary situation." For this reason there could be no increases in the current five-year grant of the kind Bullock had been hoping for. The amounts would remain as previously planned, $750,000 for the current year. Bell also expected "to hold to our earlier intention of providing $600,000 for

1972." As to the future, "a careful review of our forward budgets" had shown "that the limit of our possible support for the IACF for the five years beyond 1972 would be in the order of $400,000 annually." He recognized "that funding from the Ford Foundation in these reduced dimensions would entail a difficult reconsideration of the IACF's program." But he hoped that Stone might find other resources.[51]

It is not difficult to imagine how the IACF president reacted to all this, the more so since, through Moselle Kimbler, he had his own sources of information, which gave him further details of the conflicts within the foundation. According to Dressner's estimate, the IACF president was now spending around 70 percent of his time on fund raising and 30 percent "trying to think."[52] Later that year Stone remarked half jokingly to Jack Hubbard (Dartmouth '29): "After years at the Ford Foundation on the grant-making side, I have become a beggar with all that implies for one's character."[53] It was of little comfort that Sutton was prepared "to worry with you on the finance of future years," after he had told Stone once more that he had come "to a discouraging estimate of prospects for help in the budget problems you face this year."[54]

Stone still did not give up. On 11 February 1971 he wrote to Rémy Schlumberger, a Parisian banker, to ask for an extension of the support he had given in 1970.[55] In June he raised the question of whether other French businessmen might be brought together to make contributions via the Fondation de France.[56] He also renewed his efforts with American foundations and started another round of cuts in subsidies for the association's journals. Shils's *Minerva* now became one of his targets.[57] IACF regional groups suddenly had their funding stopped or were told to tighten their belts further.[58]

Meanwhile the uncertainty about the foundation's verdict continued. In July 1971 McCloy was told that "the Ford Foundation is likely to give us another five-year grant, but the level is such that our entire worldwide effort will be in jeopardy."[59] In view of the upcoming meeting of the IACF board of directors, Stone warned Bullock on 22 September that "the most difficult item will be F[ord]. We must discuss it in such a way as to maintain belief and enthusiasm for the organization while at the same time being realistic." The information he had "from New York is that the $400,000 is reasonably certain annually over a five-year period."[60] On the day after this assessment of the situation had been mailed, Sutton dictated a letter to Stone with more specific news about Ford's intentions. After the usual compliments on the IACF's work, he came to the main problem "that we cannot foresee a level of funding as high as we have been providing, and I don't think the gap can be filled, however manfully you keep up your impressive efforts to stir up other donors." Nor had a further review "turned up any new promise of support." All he would be able to supply would be $350,000 to 400,000 per annum after 1972.[61]

As in the previous year, there were again delays in the final approval of the grant extension.[62] Still, courtesy of the Ford Foundation, the IACF had been given another lease on life until 1977 on a much reduced budget. For this reason alone 1973 was the year in which truly major changes would have to be effected, and the Ford leadership was sure to keep the heat up. Ironically, the foundation had already intervened in the affairs of the IACF and would continue to do so at levels the CIA had never even contemplated during the years of its largest covert support for the CCF.

This interventionism became very evident as Heaps completed yet another review of the association, this time for Michael Goodwin on 7 February 1973. Although Stone and the board had made significant changes, he "detected a certain institutional tension which seems to arise in good part from an implicit conflict between the 'global' viewpoint of the Board and the President, on the one side, and the continuing preoccupation, on the other, of senior secretarial staff (Emmanuel, Jelenski) whose primary concerns lie with 'western' values conceptually and with Europe geographically." In equal parts, Heaps added, this conflict had arisen "because of differences in conceptual approach between the same groups, as the IACF becomes more entrepreneurial and less 'intellectual' in its substantive functions." Besides these conceptual differences, other issues also required immediate clarification. First was the retirement of Stone, who would reach the age of sixty-five in March, and the need for a successor.[63] Second, "future policy and program direction" had to be worked out, including the "actual utility of an IACF presence in the developing areas," the ability to support the eleven journals "still published under its auspices," and the viability of the Eastern European program and the "Fund for Intellectuals," which had been established "to provide *ad hoc* assistance to intellectuals constrained to leave their native countries to escape physical or intellectual repression." Finally, and given that "the IACF is now in large part the Ford Foundation baby," Heaps admitted that his further active involvement would be required.[64]

Heaps must have felt confirmed in this interventionist posture when it became clear that a successor for Stone could not easily be found. As a precautionary measure the board therefore persuaded the president to stay on until July 1974. Stone also had gloomy news "on the financial front" following the recent devaluation of the dollar, which "over night" had shaved 10 percent off the association's budget.[65] As to the high cost of another sensitive budget item, the Parisian Secretariat, Bullock had meanwhile pursued the cost-saving idea of moving the headquarters either to London or to Germany.[66]

The Oxford historian and chairman of the IACF board was the next to feel the heat. On 6 April he received a letter from Bell expressing his dismay "that the Board has not found a suitable successor to Mr. Stone." He also wondered whether the association had succeeded in developing "a fresh set of purposes and a program framework to enlist the active involvement of a wide range of leaders, including younger men and women, in the international intellectual communities," adding sternly, "there would seem to be grounds to doubt whether this goal has been achieved, or is in the process of being achieved." In light of these problems, the foundation leadership felt "it necessary to ask whether it might be timely to consider alternative arrangements to the planned continuation of Foundation support to the IACF." Anxious not to sound too bullying, Bell suggested at the end of his letter to hold discussions "in a constructive and cooperative spirit" and mentioned his next visit to Europe at the end of May as a possible date.[67]

Bullock was so alarmed by this missive that he did not want to leave things hanging for that long. A meeting was arranged with Sutton and Heaps four weeks earlier. When they came to see him in Oxford on 23 April, the board chairman, with President Stone at his side, immediately launched "into a vigorous defense of the IACF." Bullock then discussed the various plans for a move from Paris and for attracting a younger generation of intellectuals and scholars. All in all, Heaps came away with the sense that this "lengthy and impressive *tour de force*" was designed "to take the initiative away from us." On closer inspection, this initiative consisted primarily in tossing the ball back into the foundation's court by stressing that the association could not move forward with any of the proposed changes "until they know whether the Foundation intends to continue to provide general support funds at the maximum envisaged level of $400,000 annually."[68]

And so the *pas de deux* continued. A few weeks later, Bell met Stone in Paris, where the latter once more outlined "our ideas" and also discussed a serious candidate to succeed him. The IACF president apparently thought that the meeting went well, and in his subsequent report to Bullock thanked his board chairman for his forceful words four weeks ago. During his conversation with Bell, Stone continued, "it became obvious again that your statement at Oxford had been the turning point for the FF."[69]

Unfortunately, the turning point, in whichever direction, was still some distance away. But the IACF leadership had at least succeeded in making the Ford Foundation staff feel mightily guilty about its indecision. As Sutton confessed to Bell on 8 June 1973, he felt "chagrined that we have not been able to come to a clear position to state to Bullock and Stone."[70] Of course, the dilemmas were serious. Referring to Bullock's cost-saving idea of moving the association's headquarters away from Paris, he expressed doubts about "the IACF's viability from a German headquarters," even if this would considerably reduce administrative costs. He was particularly worried about student radicalism in the Federal Republic and feared "that the identification of the old IACF crowd, in particular Rix Lowenthal [sic],[71] with a rather conservative opposition to the youthful left wing of the SPD and the university radicals might push them into rather narrow German disputes that would affect the IACF's general work and image around the world."

Second, Sutton became aware of an issue that Heaps had raised previously in a different key: Paul Doty, he wrote, had "raised into prominence the issues between Emmanuel and Stone and Bullock in a way that I had not previously heard them." The famous Harvard scientist had revealed "that there was a division in the Board on the emphasis to be given to public affairs versus more purely intellectual matters." Doty felt that "the German representation on the Board provided by Marion Dönhoff and Richard von Weizsäcker,[72] excellent as they are, represents a thrust towards the public affairs side." Although Doty leaned more toward the "intellectual side," he was hesitant about Emmanuel, who had made a bid to become Stone's successor. He believed that the French writer and IACF director general was "a valuable man in his own right," but that there were "important arrays of intellectuals who would be negative or indifferent toward any identification with him" if he became association president.

The deeper reasons for moving the Secretariat to London now become somewhat clearer: from the viewpoint of the "Anglo-Saxons" the idea of a move was more than a cost-saving device. It would also have solved the "Emmanuel problem" and the conceptual rifts that ran through the association. Moving to the Federal Republic would not only have added further fissures and complications of the kind Sutton and Doty had spoken about, but would also have been difficult for psychological reasons: a Germanophile like Stone might have liked to see the IACF headquartered in Berlin under a German president, but for many other members this was no welcome prospect. The Nazi past still loomed large in the

263

memory of this generation. Meanwhile the Ford Foundation had no desire to get caught up in these larger disputes. If leaving the IACF headquarters in Paris meant that Bell would have to "meet Bullock's concern for more resources,"[73] it also made it easier to say that enough had already been done.

While Bell continued to ponder a solution to these "IACF puzzles," the board had to grapple with the "Emmanuel problem," when it met in Colorado on 1–3 July 1973.[74] The Aspen Institute, of which Joe Slater was now the president, offered a congenial setting. Eloquently and with plenty of gravitas, the director general presented his claim to the IACF presidency. There followed a longer general discussion about the future program, at the end of which the board offered Emmanuel Stone's position and decided to search for a new director general to take charge of the day-to-day business. After another and almost comical hiccup, which might be labeled the Duffey affair, the director's position was finally filled by Adam Watson, a retired British foreign service officer.[75]

Functionally, Watson stepped into Stone's shoes and thenceforth spent his time trying to attract money from other foundations and to find new homes for the remaining journals. Because success eluded him just as it had Stone, however, he in effect became the IACF's liquidator. Emmanuel had never seen himself as a panhandler and abandoned ship in June 1975, invoking "the great pressure of work involved in his new government job" with the French State Radio and Television Network, "and his various other activities like his column in the Figaro and the operations at Hautvillers."[76] With the last installment of Ford Foundation support due in 1977, Watson, in the summer of 1976, entered into fresh negotiations with Heaps and was told that his grant for that year would be reduced to $240,000.[77] Because his estimates came to $557,000, it was obvious that the IACF's position was even more serious than it had been during the Stone era. No doubt the foundation people found it easier to be blunt to a rather formal former British diplomat than with the outgoing Stone, who, moreover, had once been one of their own.

Consequently, worse was to come. At the board meeting in October 1976 it was agreed that the association could only "continue in what Paul Doty called a project mode, with a devolution of authority onto the 'third generation' of operations which would become autonomous."[78] Further discussions in New York in the spring of 1977 revealed that the Ford Foundation definitely did "not want to pay any more administrative expenses for [the] IACF after the end of this year." Watson was urged to "close the Paris office by then, and to 'wind the Association down.' "[79]

However, the foundation was "prepared to support directly the 'next generation' activities, like the Fondation Entraide, Survey etc."[80] Other foundations that had been persuaded by Watson to support various projects were also prepared to have them seen through to completion and some of them even favored the survival of the IACF. Yet the director knew that "we cannot keep the Paris office going without Ford Foundation support, and must therefore close it." After this, Watson loyally offered to manage, "with much reduced emoluments and a minimum of expenses," the association's affairs "from London for a year or so," because it would "take time to get the 'third generation' to the point where they can manage their own affairs and receive funds direct[ly]."[81]

The funeral came at the board meeting in West Berlin in October 1977, at which, on the advice of a Swiss lawyer, the legal arrangements were also made to effect the transition to the "third generation" in terms of various national tax laws.[82]

THE CULTURAL ROOTS OF FAILURE

If the successive reduction and ultimate refusal of Ford Foundation funding and the IACF's inability to persuade other foundations to step into the breach represent the most obvious reasons for the death of the association, this in itself is hardly the full story. Although after the cornucopia of the early 1960s, grants were more difficult to come by everywhere, not just philanthropic parsimony explains Bundy's, Bell's, and Sutton's growing reluctance to continue their support for the IACF. On the one hand, as we have seen repeatedly, the Foundation under Bundy was rethinking its overall strategy of international giving by looking even more toward the Third World; on the other, there were the nagging doubts about whether subsidizing conferences of intellectuals, journals, and exchanges run by an expensive Secretariat in Paris was still worthwhile at a time of rapid political, socioeconomic, and cultural change in Europe and global economic crisis. In other words, we must now begin to search for the deeper causes of Stone's and Watson's failure.

One of these causes was the legacy of the CCF and its peculiar financial history. The IACF was referred to within the Ford Foundation as one of the "CIA orphans,"[83] and the origins of the CCF scandal, as we have examined them, certainly explain to some degree why Bundy and his colleagues felt obliged to honor their promise of full funding after the CIA link had been cut. At the same time, the IACF was a constant and awkward reminder of the foundation's involvement in America's covert culture wars of the 1950s. The public, and the younger generation in particular, refused to forget about the CIA connection, which in turn raised suspicions about Ford's philanthropic motives. Nor did it help that Bundy had worked on national security issues in the White House, CIA matters included.

Inevitably there has been a good deal of speculation about who blew Josselson's cover and why.[84] Although, as we have seen, the agency had shown a certain reluctance to hand the CCF over to a private organization, it is unlikely that the CIA, in a fit of envy or for whatever other reason, had leaked the story. While it is difficult to imagine that Braden spilled the beans without a prior nod from his former masters, he merely confirmed the story of covert funding to defend the agency against mounting criticism from all sides. Nor has any evidence come to light so far that locates the leak inside the Ford Foundation. To be sure, some of Stone's colleagues opposed the costly CCF rescue package, but it is not very plausible that one of these officers hoped to scuttle the plan by leaking it and thus embarrassing the entire organization. In fact, the uproar may have made Bundy all the more determined not to renege because of public criticism.

In the end, the most convincing explanation would seem to be that for years so many rumors had been swirling around about covert CIA funding that, in the volatile political climate of the mid-1960s, the day would come when a news item could no longer be brushed off as misinformed. Conflicts in American domestic politics and over the handling of the Vietnam War had changed attitudes toward the U.S. government. The collaboration of private foundations with Washington in the fighting of the Cold War was no longer as acceptable as it had been to Stone's generation.[85] The young at home and abroad, with some of their academic teachers providing seemingly powerful evidence, began to rail against American "imperialism"—cultural, military, or economic. They promptly targeted the CCF as one of its organizational manifestations. After two attempts in 1964 and 1966, which could still be contained,[86] the investigative journalism of the spring of 1967 finally triggered a huge public outcry.

So, while there appears to be little reason to look strenuously for a conspiracy to unmask the CCF's "liberal conspiracy,"[87] the scandal led to a good deal of heart-searching and debate both within the Ford Foundation and the CCF/IACF about its tainted past and about a fresh start. As Marion Bieber wrote in August 1971 in a Ford interoffice memorandum, it had become "difficult to reconstruct the truth about the circumstances, the moral and intellectual intent and, most of all, the quality of what it [the CCF/IACF] did since 1950;"[88] it was even more difficult to explain all this to the student movement. It was a painful realization, as these students represented the future elites of Europe and America who, it was once thought, would carry the Atlantic banner into the future.

Accordingly, the IACF, shouldering the burdens of its predecessor, struggled hard to operate in an intellectual climate in which the former unquestioning trust in government and its representatives was fast evaporating. "The sixties were years of distrust, both of the leading institutions in society and of those who were their spokesmen," according to Peter Novick "Not all official lying was delegated to those with impeccable scholarly credentials like Professors Schlesinger, Bundy, Rostow, or Kissinger, but enough of it was to destroy the presumption that in judging veracity the pronoucements of highly regarded academics should be automatically accepted, or even get the benefit of the doubt."[89]

Confronted with these problems that now deeply impinged on the viability of its operations, the IACF first tried to undertake a diagnosis of the new intellectual climate in which it sought to find its place. According to this diagnosis, the 1950s had been "dominated by the cold war on the international plane and by related problems of industrial society and of the end-of-ideology in the developed countries of the temperate zones."[90] This period had also been marked by "the disillusionment of intellectuals with Marxist utopias, the apparent pragmatism of the post-war decade in the United States and in Western Europe, and the growing erosion of ideology in Eastern Europe." Accordingly, "the basic attitude of the Congress for Cultural Freedom—an attitude historically derived from the Enlightenment—was a clearly stated opposition to the totalitarianism of the left and right."

However, "few foresaw that ideological passions of a new kind would soon reappear among a large section of Western intellectuals, or that the young generation would favor them." Accordingly, the IACF wondered if "some of the ideological confusion of the 'New Left' " was "due to the fact that the last great ideological battle of the right has been fought—and lost—in terms of Fascism." But there were other historical roots and the statement promptly began to "draw a parallel between the present Western 'malaise' and the *fin-de-siècle* sense of discontent, decadence and pessimism"—that is, the pre-1914 "*Kulturpessimismus,* cult of violence, youth movement, Art Nouveau, dissatisfaction with modern civilization in its various manifestations."[91]

One of the intellectual sources of the "new 'schism' which divides Western intellectuals and tends to cut across generations," but which—as we have seen in chapters 4 and 5[92]—was really very old, was said to be traceable to "the central concept of 'alienation' in the works of such masters of the New Left as Herbert Marcuse. Anti-Americanism and anti-capitalism in their latest versions are directed in the first place against the 'affluent society,' against the 'civilization of consumers.' " The quest "for a 'third revolution,' looking to Mao, to Fidel Castro, to the 'Maquis International,' to 'Black Power,' can be understood better if we keep in mind that Herbert Marcuse's 'One-Dimensional Man' contains lyric passages extolling the world of the *ancien régime* (the village, the court etc.) at the expense of the 'horrors' of the modern world."

Furthermore, the IACF discerned a "growing restlessness in advanced industrial countries (including communist ones) against increasing technocratic and bureaucratic decision-making," raising "the cry for 'participatory democracy,' 'student power,' for 'the right of the people to control the decisions that affect their lives.' " The association believed this impulse to be "a valid one"; yet since the analysis rarely got "carried beyond rhetoric, the emotional current becomes focused on an attack against all authority and leads to a new passionate destructiveness." In view of all these trends, the IACF proposed to center its program around a "clarification of these problems" to be treated from the perspective of "one major theme: *the crisis of rationality*." It was a theme that bore Daniel Bell's signature,[93] just as many of the other arguments presented in the document mirrored an old debate in a new key, except that the end-of-ideology intelligentsia now found itself swimming against the tide. For "the new ideological revival" was seen "in terms of one syndrome of which the New Left, the shift from solidarity with the working-class to solidarity with the people of under-developed and former colonial countries, the cult of youth, the cult of violence, the revolt against advanced industrial society, neo-populism are but various aspects."

With the United States constituting the center of these new movements, the association wanted to provide a forum to debate the "implications of the war in Vietnam, the growing opposition of American intellectuals, the radicalization of the racial issue, [as] the student revolt (the 'New Left' and the new version of 'anti-Americanism' can both be traced to the United States: the Berkeley campus has been a model for students in Berlin and elsewhere)." There was also the related theme of "the 'Americanization' of the world, the *défi américain*," as raised in the early 1960s by Jean-Jacques Servan-Schreiber's book with this title and leading to the question "to what extent America is the model for advanced industrial societies."[94]

Looking back in 1973 on what he thought were the IACF's achievements, Konstantin Jelenski, another former CCF *Vordenker*, was moderately satisfied. He felt that "the negative effects of the disclosures concerning CIA funding" had been overcome, "owing to the joint efforts of Shepard Stone and Pierre Emmanuel."[95] Stone, he argued, had made the association " 'respectable' again in U.S.A. liberal circles, which were far more shaken by the CIA involvement than Western European intellectuals." Meanwhile, Emmanuel had been "instrumental in preserving the Spanish and Portuguese committees, as well as the Latin American program." Moreover, he enjoyed "the trust of our friends in Eastern Europe who were (from a Western unsophisticated standpoint paradoxically) less troubled by the CIA revelations."

At the same time, Jelenski was dismayed that the growth of radical movements in the 1960s had sharpened the division in the IACF "between those who saw in these new movements a healthy reaction to the deficiencies of Western contemporary societies and those who dismissed them as irrational and irresponsible epiphenomena." And he complained that the association had little appeal among the younger generation: "Nearly all our most active associates and friends are over 50 years old."

Still, overall Jelenski had remained an optimist. In his view, the "cultural 'schism' which recently seemed to divide Western societies is on the wane." The IACF now had a fresh opportunity to influence the agenda of intellectual debate more decisively than in the late 1960s. In making this point, he was no doubt conscious of the hard questions that the Ford Foundation was asking the IACF leadership at this time.[96] After all, "many of the ideas and concepts which throw new and creative light on contemporary societies (and some of those which have specific appeal to the young)" had emerged from the "intellectual 'milieu' " of the CCF and its successor. More specifically he listed Michael Polanyi's "criticism of 'scientific objectivity' and of shallow rationalism"; Shils's "opposition to behaviourism and to 'quantitative' sociology"; Bell's and Aron's "concept of 'Post-Industrial Society' "; Emmanuel's "conception of culture as a non-elitarian integrating relation of the individual to society" and his "revival of the 'sacred.' " In line with these ideas, many of which we have encountered in earlier chapters, Jelenski proposed to hold high-profile seminars focusing on notions of culture.

The trouble with the agenda that Jelenski mapped out in his 1973 memorandum was that it was hardly capable of healing the rift that so puzzled Sutton at this time and that Doty had circumscribed so well.[97] In 1968, the association had tried, "on the suggestion of Daniel Bell," to build its program "around a 'Defence of Rationality.'" We have quoted extensively from the paper that tried to outline precisely such a program. But in 1973 Jelenski had come to the conclusion that this approach had failed, partly because "the Congress itself was founded on what I would term a rational belief in the need for respecting irrational levels of human experience." With the retirement of Stone, who had always veered more toward a pragmatic "public affairs" position of "Anglo-Saxon" intellectuals and academics, others saw an opportunity of nudging the IACF into a more cultural-"philosophical" direction, of which Emmanuel, the contender for the IACF presidency and "Continental" European intellectual par excellence, was a representative.

What was Emmanuel's position? When the IACF was trying to develop its new identity in 1968, the director general wrote down his views on this matter. His "Personal Remarks" of 9 May began with a discussion of the challenge that the younger generation had issued since the mid-1960s to received notions of the primacy of technological progress and the evolution of the "great societies of consumption." Against the background of his own critical assessment of this position, of which Bell and other American social scientists had been the prime protagonists, Emmanuel launched into a criticism of the association and its precursor. In particular he was unhappy about the "sociological perspectives" that had determined the IACF's orientation. Meanwhile the term "culture," he argued, "has been suffering from its misused and generalized deployment in a world where the value that gives meaning to words was . . . lost sight of."[98]

The Frenchman did not elaborate this point in his "Personal Remarks"; but the IACF position paper of the same year quoted a pertinent observation that Emmanuel had made before the CCF executive committee as early as 1963. On that occasion, when another struggle for the "soul" of the Congress and for full funding by American private philanthropy was in full swing, he had warned: "To limit our action to the formulation of a new political philosophy would be to underestimate the needs of the spirit in our time. Culture is the field of the spirit, and not merely of an organizing intelligence. The conception of a better society and of more equitable political and economic relations cannot be efficient in the long run, if philosophical and moral questions are left aside. They should, on the contrary, be given a primary importance. It seems that we have reached a point of saturation in terms of sociology, economics and of what may be called *Kulturpolitik*. It is time that we *also* speak about other problems and give to the artists of language, *philosophers and poets in the first place*, the feeling that they are not exiles in a world in which the only apparent changes are those taking place on the sociological and economic plane. Unless we help these men of language to express themselves, we shall remain one more instrument of universal planification."[99]

The attack on the Deweyian positions that the Americans had carved out for the CCF and about which Bell, the sociologist author of *The End of Ideology*, and Galbraith, the economist author of *The Affluent Society*, had written, could hardly have been more explicit. As long as Josselson was around and American foundations and Washington provided the money, Emmanuel's critique did not carry much weight. But in 1968 the French intellectual, who called himself a "Gaullist," saw fresh opportunities, as director general of the IACF, to put his intellectual stamp upon the association's activities. He left it to Stone to go out fund raising and to concern himself with issues of contemporary practical politics. Meanwhile Emmanuel spent his time reaching out to intellectuals in the Romance-languages regions of Southern Europe and of Latin America to promote his own particular Continental-European notion of culture and of the role of writers in modern society. The tension between the two visions was not resolved.

The conflict erupted when in 1973 the ultimate future of the IACF was to be determined, and he laid claim to becoming Stone's successor. His hope was to steer the association away from the American social sciences into a "French" culturalist direction, which also explains why he was opposed to Bullock's idea of moving the headquarters from Paris to Germany or to London. In other words, Doty had hit the nail on the head when he enlightened the slightly bewildered Sutton about the intellectual dynamics inside the board of directors chaired by the very "Anglo-Saxon" Alan Bullock. In a handwritten statement, Emmanuel reminded his colleagues of what he had "many times underlined in the past"—that "our so-called 'cultural action' stems more from moral liberalism than from the need to define a specific cultural aspiration in today's changing society."[100] He complained that "we seem to be brewing the same stew as twenty years ago, without the real and direct cultural ingredient; we rarely look at the various *shapes* of our society, cultural, educational or in the mass media." Consequently, there were "intellectual and even spiritual factors that we rarely, if ever, take into consideration." He appreciated that it was "very difficult . . . to make all our members sensitive to that aspect of *culture* (which is *properly* culture), but I cannot help feeling a growing frustration and dissatisfaction when I see that practically all we do is to foster average middle-of-the-way middle-class liberal values, and we come back always to the same worn-out topics."

271

He then urged the IACF to *"invent* alternatives,"* among which he listed, just as Jelenski had done, a discussion of the mass media: "Are they a cultural instrument and, if yes, in what respect?"[101] He wanted to examine "how can the mass media escape the process of massification" and remain, "up to a certain extent, under the control of the users; what will be the effect on the media of the cable system, when every community will have its own network?" Emmanuel also worried about problems of the environment and new threats to the concept of freedom at a time of "complacency towards totalitarian regimes." In his view then, much had to be reexamined, including "freedom of thought, power, authority, value, the idea of man versus technology and nature, the limits of science etc."[102]

It seems that Emmanuel's programmatic ideas, many of which were conceived in a "Continental-European" mood of cultural pessimism and which he, so as to emphasize his point, presented in the French language, did not go down too well with his English-speaking colleagues. Already at the board meeting of 9–10 January 1970, chairman Alan Bullock had stated "in reply to those who believed that [the] IACF was putting too little emphasis on matters of the spirit (Philosophy, religion, esthetics) that they were perhaps losing sight of the fact that the 'agenda at the end of the 'Sixties is a social science agenda,' and that the social sciences lend themselves more naturally to collective discussion."[103]

Adding up what the two sides had been debating since the founding of the IACF, it appears that more was at stake than the primacy of the social sciences over philosophy and the arts. It was also the old disagreement about high culture and American "low" culture and the dangers posed by the latter—about whether cultural trends in the industrial countries of the West gave reason for pessimism and alarm or, as Bell had asserted in *The End of Ideology*, for optimism and self-confidence.

This in turn has to be put into the wider context of the 1960s rebellion of the younger generation with its escalating criticism of America. Stone, being a long-standing observer and opponent of European anti-Americanism, immediately responded to this upsurge as soon as he had established himself as IACF president in Paris. In March 1968 he suggested a joint Franco-American declaration, and Jelenski also had an insight to offer. "French anti-Americanism," he wrote to Stone on 8 March, "has two sides. It is represented by the government (de Gaulle) and—for different reasons—by the left-wing opposition. Thus, curiously, government and opposition are at one on this point. This leads to such curious phenomena as the declaration of the French left-wing writers, published in *Le Monde* (from Sartre to Natalie Sarraute) who, protesting against American 'imperialism,' appeal for the denunciation of the Atlantic Alliance."[104]

Consequently Stone saw himself embroiled not merely in a debate about Emmanuel's "cultural" conception of the IACF but also in the old culture war with European intellectuals and politicians and their anti-Americanism that he had tried so hard to counter during his years at the Ford Foundation. It is intriguing to follow the various reflections of this in his correspondence with friends and prominent personalities. His exchanges may not have been as intellectualized and theoretical as Emmanuel's, but they certainly reflected the mixture of consternation, annoyance, confusion, assertiveness, partial understanding, and pride in past achievements that was more widespread in the circles in which he moved. Among his correspondents were many West Germans, with some of whom he was on a familiar *Du* basis.[105] More than once did he invoke the situation of the late Weimar Republic and his memories of it, as, for example, in a letter to Aron of December 1970.[106] Writing to his brother-in-law, he thought that it was "perhaps one of my mistakes" that he had helped to rebuild the Frankfurt School: "Horkheimer, Adorno, Marcuse—would not have been there if the U.S. High Commission, under my stimulation, had not given Maxie [Horkheimer] very substantial funds to make his Institute possible."[107]

On the one hand, as he wrote in July 1969, "the entire student problem was [to him] part of a complex cultural development of our time," which Shils had recently analyzed in *Encounter*;[108] on the other, he saw a new totalitarianism emerging, in the face of which it seemed "a pity" that "at a time when there are so many threats to intellectual and cultural freedom . . . the few people and groups trying to do something about it should not have friendly relations."[109] This applied to those like-minded outside the IACF, such as Spender who, still bitter about Lasky's "betrayal," was reported in 1967 to be planning, with the support of Hampshire, Berlin, and Auden, a rival to *Encounter*.[110] It applied even more so to the situation inside the IACF whose aims, Stone thought, were becoming more fragile.[111] Of course, he continued to believe that the association represented the "junction for the exchange and stimulation of ideas" and "that many of the political, social, and academic problems involved can be approached most effectively if the best international thinking is made available."[112]

There were moments when Stone put his finger very precisely on what was at stake. For example, when Silone resigned from the IACF in May 1969, Stone recapitulated that with the end of Stalinism had grown the belief in the end of ideologies, making possible pragmatic solutions to social conflicts. However, the revolt of the younger generation and the renaissance of the New Left had swept away these calculations. He did not think, he added, that a technotronic society could be governed by an elite without genuine involvement of the "masses." This led him to raise the question as to whether a society that respected spontaneity, community, and democractic participation might not be capable of exploiting as well as controlling the technological progress that was indispensable for its survival.[113]

There were other moments, however, when Stone inclined toward the more straightforward views of his *Duz-Freund* Axel Springer who, in February 1973, highlighted the "latent anti-Americanism" in Germany, which after the defeat of George McGovern in the U.S. presidential elections and the recent national elections in the Federal Republic had assumed "alarming aspects" (*bestürzende Formen*)."[114] Meanwhile, Lasky bemoaned that "the forces of unreason and indifference have been gaining too much ground in our societies for any voice of reasoned intellectual concern to be stilled."[115]

At the same time, Stone never shared the criticism that Springer (and also many prominent Americans) voiced of Willy Brandt's *Ostpolitik*. This was partly because he continued to feel a deep friendship for the chancellor and former mayor of West Berlin in which there was no room for distrust of the kind that the critics of his foreign policy toward the Soviet bloc displayed. To be sure, ultimately, these were lesser problems than the challenge posed by the radical left. Because the wave of leftist criticism of Western capitalist-industrial society continued unabated on both sides of the Atlantic, he began to discuss with the American office of the IACF, based in Cambridge, Massachusetts, and headed by Diana Michaelis, a fresh mobilization of Ivy League social scientists to analyze this development. In May 1970 Stone proposed to constitute "a group of thoughtful Americans trying to define a platform and relay [?] wider thought for constructive purposes at this time of chaos and violence."[116] But, with even the Harvard campus in turmoil, Michaelis had to tell him that "we do not have any strong leadership within the American group to devote time to exploring ways that the IACF *uniquely* can make a contribution." Everybody, she added, "is trying to do this anyway—through Harvard faculty meeting[s and] professional associations." In the face of the present challenge "very little academic or other work is being accomplished right now." How, she asked, "can the IACF add a further schedule of meetings to this overloaded academic community?"

However, the association suffered from another handicap: "It is not and can't be an activist organization." If Michaelis sensed "the mood correctly, most middle ground people, while revolted by the violence, feel that the next important step is for strong political action—for such things as the vote for 18-year-olds, peace candidates in the Congressional elections etc." In an indirect reference to the conflicts between the hard-liners around Hook and the "moderates" in the ACCF during the early 1950s, Michaelis thought there was some consolation in the fact that the American IACF lacked people ready to devote their time to its affairs: "If there had been a strong American group for the past five years, it would probably—as was the case with the earlier U.S. group during the McCarthy period—have been torn to shreds by the crises of the last two or three years." Men like David "Riesman and others are terribly bitter and the general air of depression is pervasive and frightening. The best hope surely lies with the young and this is the avenue that I want to further explore with you in June."[117]

Four weeks earlier Michaelis had urged her boss in Paris that "it is essential that we move the IACF away from an elitist approach where it can be accused of bringing together a small group of like-minded people who already have adequate forums for knowing each other's point of view." It was, she reiterated, young people who needed to be attracted.[118] Yet, several years later, at the October 1974 board meeting, the IACF was still struggling "to bring younger people into the organization," and Shils remarked on this occasion that the "Association was in danger of becoming a shrinking band or brotherhood which never added any new adherents."[119]

While Stone was wrestling with politics, Emmanuel kept moving in a culturalist direction that, as we have seen, was deeply suspicious of American society and culture. And because the association was being pulled in different directions by its "Anglo-Saxon" and its "French" wings there remained in the end but one common denominator: the IACF's traditional liberal opposition to all restrictions on intellectual freedom. Accordingly the association, like its predecessor, continued to send protests against the repression of intellectuals not only in the communist world but also in countries with right-wing dictatorships such as Spain, Portugal, and Greece. Whatever their differences regarding the substance of culture and cultural politics, a telegram to some petty dictator was a measure that "Anglo-Saxons" and "Continental" Europeans could always agree upon.[120] As Sperber, an intellectual very much in the "Continental" mode, put it after siding with Emmanuel's plea "for greater participation by *creative* intellectuals" in the work of the IACF: "Even though in some parts of the world the danger to cultural freedom was less acute than it had been 20 years ago, [the] IACF must continue to stand against authoritarianism from whatever direction."[121] Or to quote Jelenski once more: "I have stated often that in many ways the IACF's main *raison d'être*— that of solidarity with non-conformist intellectuals in oppressive regimes—is more necessary than ever."[122]

THE BERLIN ASPEN INSTITUTE

In trying to run an IACF facing a grim financial future and still torn by an old European-American culture war, now reignited by Emmanuel's sharp criticism and plan for action, Stone became increasingly disenchanted.[123] As he was traveling to the United States to meet his former Ford Foundation deputy Joe Slater or to Germany to socialize with friends and politicians there, he probably more than once grumbled about his present job in Paris and his difficulties. In these two milieus, back home and in Germany, a new idea was conceived that enabled him to leave the IACF and to take up a position that truly suited him at this late stage in his career: the directorship of the Aspen Institute in his beloved second *Heimat*, Berlin. There, in the city that since the 1948 Soviet blockade had been cherishing the Americans, free from constant financial worries and without having to listen to the perennial cultural anti-Americanism of French intellectuals, he could complete his long career as "impresario"[124] of the Atlantic community and promote its dialogue with the East.

The Aspen Institute in Colorado had originally been founded by Walter and Elizabeth Paepcke. He came from a wealthy Chicago business family of German origin; she was the daughter of William A. Nitze, a Romance languages professor at the University of Chicago, and sister of Paul A. Nitze, international security expert and well-known arms negotiator. As philanthropists with a ranch in Colorado, the Paepckes decided to use some of their money to build, as Walter once said, a place "for man's complete life . . . where he can profit by healthy physical recreation, with facilities at hand for his enjoyment of art, music, and education."[125] By the 1960s, the Aspen Institute for Humanistic Studies, as it came to be named, had grown into precisely such a retreat where the best and the brightest would meet for conferences, seminars, or simply to escape from the stresses of urban life.

It was apparently in the spring of 1966 that Stone was invited to the institute for the first time. He was to be a resource person at a one-week program for executives.[126] A few years later, the relationship grew closer when Joseph Slater, his former deputy at Ford who had subsequently moved to California to head the Salk Institute, became Aspen's president in March 1970.[127] It seems that the institute leadership had been thinking for some time about establishing branches in other parts of the world, including Europe, and in this connection had begun to consult Robert Schaetzel, the U.S. representative to the European communities in Brussels. Writing to Slater on 5 August 1969, the diplomat tried to set out "the broad context within which . . . the Aspen Institute and the Anderson Foundation might wish to move with respect to American-European relations." His question was: "What kinds of relations do we wish to see between a united Europe and the United States in the year 2000?" One of Schaetzel's suggestions was "to encourage the development of a 'European Brookings' " Institute.[128]

What became of these projects is not clear, but Schaetzel and Slater apparently discussed the founding of a "European Aspen" when they met in March 1970. On this occasion Schaetzel "promised to prepare a paper on the general subject of the Aspen Institute and Europe." Returning to the subject four months later, Schaetzel wrote to the Aspen president that he was "more than ever persuaded that something along these lines is not only desirable but urgent," because "we are rapidly approaching a crossroads in Atlantic affairs." To him the crisis in American-European relations, which had been fueled by recent political and economic troubles, had led to a situation in which "either we shall be able to exploit impressive new opportunities or we shall drift back into some 19th century form of uneasy mutual suspicion." He had "real doubts that in the short term governments will be capable alone of preserving what has been so laboriously constructed during this fruitful post-war period or certainly [be] able to lay down the lines of new realtionships." By contrast, "the 'new businessman' with his greater involvement in national and internnational affairs, allied with his deep corporate self-interest, has the potentiality of making a crucial contribution." Schaetzel also thought it necessary to see to it "that the European businessman, in his social and political awareness, does not lag too far behind the American counterpart." After all, "the Europeans have much to learn from us in this area." The paper that Schaetzel appended to his letter contained a number of proposals and ended with a discussion of the vexing question of funding. He thought that "after a trial period" it should be possible to "obtain contributions . . . from major European foundations such as Agnelli, Volkswagen, [and] Thyssen." He suggested that "Europeans close to these foundations should be drawn into the planning process of this program from the beginning."[129]

In subsequent months, however, Slater evidently did not make much progress on the concept that Schaetzel had developed. One reason for this may have been that the Aspen Institute's backer, Robert Anderson of the Atlantic Ritchfield Oil Corporation, the man behind the Anderson Foundation and Walter Paepcke's successor, was reluctant to fork out the money at a time of considerable upheaval in the world economy.

A new stage on the road to an "Aspen Berlin" was reached on 28 December 1971 when Slater cabled Stone that he had been elected as a trustee of "Aspen Colorado." The Aspen president said he hoped for close cooperative relations with the IACF.[130] But with the association's affairs not going well, the new link also gave Stone an opportunity to tell his old colleague of his woes. And when he talked to his German friends, including Willy Brandt, the erstwhile mayor of West Berlin who had meanwhile become federal chancellor, he probably also indicated that he was not particularly happy in Paris. Brandt and his former colleagues in West Berlin pricked their ears. These were the controversial years of *Ostpolitik*. Brandt faced strong opposition from the Christian Democrats back home, and abroad men such as Secretary of State Henry Kissinger had become suspicious of the strategy and tactics behind the Social Democrat government's negotiations with the Soviets and other East European communist regimes. Was an "Aspen Berlin," conceived along the lines of the parent institute in Colorado, supported by the city's government and headed by the old Berlinophile Stone, perhaps one way of keeping German-American relations on an even keel and overcoming Washington's skepticism as regards Brandt's *Ostpolitik*?

It is important to bear these calculations on the German side in mind when reading Stone's side of the story. According to his memoirs, the trustees of the Aspen Institute formally decided in 1973 to establish overseas branches. It must have been soon thereafter, when taking a stroll "down Fifth Ave. near Central Park," that Stone and Slater agreed "that Berlin would be the ideal place" for one of those offshoots. Another key moment—again if we follow Stone's draft memoirs—came in early July 1973 when the IACF board met at the Colorado Aspen Institute and when Stone, after a hard day's work, was sitting with Marion Dönhoff and Richard von Weizsäcker "next to the sunny pool, looking up at the mountains: 'We became more excited and more convinced that an Aspen Institute in Berlin would be a creative step, of benefit to Berlin, to Aspen, and to the world. There was no stopping us.' " Stone reports further that on returning to Europe he began to talk to his "friends in the Mayor's office."[131]

Charlotte and Shepard Stone with Henry Kissinger at an Aspen Institute dinner, Berlin, 2 December 1978. (Courtesy of Margaret Macdonald)

There can be little doubt that Stone had become the driving force behind the idea, but not all its roots were in the United States. On 18 July 1973 he wrote directly to Klaus Schuetz, the city's mayor, who was vacationing in Switzerland, reminding him of a visit that he, in his capacity as IACF president, had paid him in the spring accompanied by Marion Dönhoff. Officially, they had come to discuss a possible move of the IACF Secretariat from the French capital to Berlin. While this plan had to be dropped, "Countess Dönhoff and I were nevertheless agreed that Berlin has to offer to international institutions [much] that is excellent." It was, he added, "from these considerations that my idea stems to found [an] Aspen/Berlin."[132]

Stone appended to his letter to Schuetz a "Vorschlag/Proposal" that was "based on Mr. [Robert] Anderson's ideas" and started from the following assumptions: "*Berlin* is seeking to attract institutions which will help to make the city a vital international center and East-West crossroads. The Aspen Institute is a unique institution for this purpose. *Aspen* is investigating the possibility of widening its international impact and dimension and Berlin, given its substantial cultural resources, appears to

279

offer remarkable opportunities for this purpose." The proposal also discussed a possible administrative structure, listing Slater as president, Stone as vice-president "(to be replaced eventually by a European)," and as director "a German to be appointed—Professor Arnulf Baring of Berlin?" With Anderson as chair of the board of trustees, Bullock and Dönhoff appeared as vice-chairs, and Brandt, Schuetz, and Richard von Weizsäcker as honorary trustees. As regards the budget, the proposal suggested that "the cost of the central office, meeting place, residence for visitors, staff and overhead . . . be financed by the City of Berlin, German private and foundation sources and grants from the Marshall Plan Fund and possibly other foundations."[133]

Thenceforth things moved forward at great speed. On 23 August Slater sent Schuetz "the Aspen/Berlin Planning Memorandum and Budget which Mr. Stone, Mr. Anderson and I have worked out after Mr. Stone's discussions in Zuerich on August 2 and in the light of other exchanges with you and your office." The draft agreement mapped out a program of "executive seminars," workshops, conferences, and a scholars-in-residence scheme, an adminstrative structure similar to the one contained in the July proposal, and personnel as well as space requirements. The estimated budget total came to 550,000 marks per annum, with the American Aspen Institute agreeing to cover Slater's periodic visits to Berlin and the costs of Stone, who as vice-president "will spend substantial periods in Berlin."[134]

In his reply to Slater, a draft of which he evidently cleared with Stone in advance, the Mayor signaled his full agreement with the memorandum, pending more detailed discussions with Stone in Berlin in early September. He added that he was "pleased to inform you [Slater] that I have talked with Chancellor Brandt and he is prepared to announce and greet the establishment of Aspen/Berlin on September 28, at the time he is awarded the Aspen Prize" in Colorado.[135] When Stone arrived in Berlin on 7 September, he talked not only with Schuetz and Hanns-Peter Herz, his chief of staff, but also with old friends such as Günter Grass, Richard Löwenthal, Hans Wallenberg, Ernst Cramer, and Hellmuth Becker,[136] all of whom were enthusiastic about the plan. Indeed, in some ways Stone must have felt as if he was back in the memorable HICOG days.[137] He suggested raising the budget to 2.5 million marks over four years, just to be on the safe side, and, as if money was no problem, Herz subsequently called Stone to confirm that this amount had been firmly put into the city's *Haushalt*.[138]

Brandt duly made his announcement on 28 September 1973, and during his visit to Aspen he apparently said to Stone: "*Du musst die Sache in Berlin leiten.*"[139] Subsequently it was over this question and the question of control that Slater and Anderson expressed some unease. Writing to Stone on 5 November, the Aspen president felt that Berlin's peculiar political climate might magnify "the sometimes not-so-subtle internecine warfare that goes on between institutes and individuals anywhere" and that the planned institute "must steer clear of these political intrigues." This is why Anderson had "concluded that it is not wise for a senior person to be resident in" Aspen/Berlin. Slater had also "become increasingly convinced of the wisdom of making our program decisions and basic policies about Aspen Berlin centrally." Because the city was raising so much of the money, however, he was apparently afraid that this centralized control might be challenged. He was therefore at great pains to tot up, in the second half of his letter, all the direct and indirect contributions the American parent would be making to demonstrate that "the Institute is at least matching the resources being put in by the Germans."[140]

In his reply of 22 November Stone went along with the control question but was clearly unhappy "that you and Mr. Anderson feel that I might get involved in internal German and Berlin controversies or personal intrigues." This notion he refuted vigorously. He insisted that the project needed a senior person and that he would undertake the job "with enthusiasm." But if Slater and Anderson had "another concept of what it will take to do the Aspen Berlin job and what kind of man you want for it," he, Stone, would simply bow out.[141]

Slater knew, of course, that he could not do without Stone, who in the winter months continued to work hard to navigate the proposal through the Berlin bureaucracy. Now listed as "acting director" of Aspen/Berlin, he told Slater on 26 March 1974: "Putting the budget through is a weary matter, though . . . they are taking action on this with a speed unknown previously in Berlin."[142] He also traveled to Munich to see Alfons Goppel, the Bavarian minister president, whom Brandt, in a shrewd political move, had suggested as another honorary trustee. And, indeed, the Germans had meanwhile made a considerable financial commitment. The city of Berlin under Schuetz's leadership provided not only the previously mentioned 2.5 million marks over four years for personnel and administrative costs but also a plot of land and a building in Schwanenwerder, a high-class residential area on a small, idyllic island in Wannsee. On 27 May he wrote to Slater that the first 677,000 marks payable to the new institute for the rest of 1974 had been confirmed.[143] Two months later, Stone was happy to report to Anderson that the conversion into a fully equipped conference facility was on course.[144]

If Slater still had doubts about Stone's crucial role in the establishment of the Berlin Aspen Institute, Alan Bullock explained it to him in a letter he wrote after a trip to the city in June. He talked "of the unique position which Shep enjoys in Berlin . . . and the many proofs of this" he had seen. Stone's name was "an 'Open Sesame' " in the city and his heart was "very much in the job."[145] But the director of the new Aspen Institute was also richly rewarded. The Schwanenwerder center was officially opened in early October 1974 and for the next fourteen years until his retirement he was virtually his own impresario and master.

From 1975 onward, between fifteen and twenty conferences and seminars were held per year, lasting on average three or four days. The themes covered topical subjects of acute contemporary significance and broad issues of philosophy and education.[146] Some took a global, others a regional perspective, but each time Stone tried to get an international mix of people around the table that would stimulate lively discussion. If one looks for the main foci in the rich menu, it is probably fair to say that they were those that had been dear to his heart since his earlier return to Germany in 1949 and later at the Ford Foundation: the European-American relationship and the dialogue between East and West. The scale was not perhaps as grand as that of the CCF and the choice of themes more eclectic and spontaneous than those of the congress. Nor was his influence as great as it would have been if the Ford Foundation had called him back to a top position, as he apparently hoped in 1983. But the basic assumptions were not all that different from those that had inspired the postwar reconstruction of international networks of intellectuals, scholars, businessmen, and politicians under American aegis. The same applies to the role he played in the founding of the Berlin *Wissenschaftskolleg*, an oasis for scholars from all over the world to work and discuss together.

Ultimately, however, what most attracted him to direct the Aspen Institute until age eighty was not just the constant contact with ideas and important issues of the time or the extended vacations he was able to spend on his farm in Vermont during July and August when there were no conferences at the institute; it was above all the affinity he felt and had been feeling since 1929 with Berlin and with Germany, that "other Germany" that Hitler had destroyed and that Stone had helped to rebuild after 1945. Here he found close friends as well as a recognition of and gratitude for what he had done that the French had never really given him. Not surprisingly, Berlin made him an honorary citizen in 1983. Years earlier, Bonn had already given him the *Bundesverdienstkreuz*. On the occasion of his retirement in 1988, he signed the "Golden Book" of the

Shepard Stone, as director of the Aspen Institute, Berlin, 1980s. (Courtesy of Margaret Macdonald)

city of Berlin. His devotion to the German-American relationship and to the idea that contacts between elites are crucial to any attempt at creating a better understanding between nations also explains why he continued to involve himself in academic exchanges and became instrumental in establishing the McCloy Fellowship program at Harvard University.[147]

He died on 4 May 1990, when his car crashed on a New England mountain road, after he had suffered a heart attack at the wheel. At the time he was on his way to Dartmouth College, his alma mater, to attend a conference on the American impact on West Germany during the late 1940s and early 1950s.[148]

Transatlantic Cultural Relations in the "American Century"

THE STORY OF Shepard Stone's education and professional activities that represents the thread running through this book was designed to provide a window to a range of major problems relating to the European-American relationship during the Cold War period. This chapter offers a summary of our findings and some ideas for future debate.

The first of these problems emerged more indirectly, though clearly enough, and would require further systematic analysis—namely, the operation of transatlantic networks that had grown up the interwar period and were rebuilt after World War II. There has been some writing about a postwar Atlantic elite, though mainly from a political and less from a sociological perspective. But even then, whether the members of this elite were "wise men" or something else, the literature on this subject has focused primarily on a few individuals at the top of the governmental decision-making pyramid.[1] We still have little systematic knowledge about the next layer of these networks—of bankers, manufacturers, civil servants, academics, and intellectuals who have played a crucial role in the fostering of postwar relations between Western Europe and the United States—and what kind of affinities as well as difficulties and misunderstandings arose as they met, talked, and acted together.

The affinities are easier to grasp. They were rooted in personal and even family ties, historical memory, and cultural experience. But the difficulties and misunderstandings should not be played down. Industry and commerce represent cases in point. Although there had been a good deal of international contact and exchange of ideas before and after World War I, each European business system had its own peculiar national culture; its own ways of management within a particular mental and legal structure; its own traditions of labor relations and ethnocentric perceptions of self and of their commercial partners and competitors elsewhere. These and other factors were liable to create tangible differences between, say, the French, Dutch, or British, on the one hand, and the Americans, on the other.

In the case of Germany—still one of the major industrial powers of the postwar world, even after the destruction brought on by the war, and a key strategic player in the Cold War against the Soviet bloc—the difficulties arising from divergent traditions were exacerbated by persistent memories among its neighbors of the death and misery that the Germans had inflicted upon them between 1939 and 1945. Indeed, for perfectly understandable reasons many European and American businessmen as well as others did not want to deal with their West German counterparts and members of a generation that had supported the Nazi dictatorship. Others were prepared to renew old ties. Even if the question of "What did you do during the war?" at first stood between them, the Germans, after a brief period of nonfraternization, were not excluded from the reconstitution of elite networks.

Shepard Stone was one of these "reconstitutionists." He had studied in Berlin in the early 1930s before Hitler's seizure of power. He had been back in Germany as a newspaper journalist thereafter, until he became an officer with the First Army advancing into Hitler's disintegrating Reich in 1944–45. He resumed work at the *New York Times* in 1946 and finally returned to the newly founded Federal Republic for a second longer spell in 1949 to become the director of the Office of Public Affairs (OPA) at the U.S. High Commission (HICOG). The previous chapters have given no more than a survey of the many people he met there and in other parts of Europe professionally and socially. But we have seen how he went about it and how he opened the doors of his house in Falkenstein near Frankfurt and later in Mehlem just south of Bonn to hundreds of guests, Americans and Germans, from all walks of life. He quite consciously wanted the Germans, with their very different traditions of hospitality and sociability, to enjoy the informality that he offered. More than that, he hoped they would emulate it.

Now, it is doubtful that Stone turned his German guests into "good mixers" and cocktail-sipping "Americans." This may have been his hope, but when it came to transatlantic contacts of this kind, whether among businessmen, journalists, officials, or academics, it seems safer to assume that over time there occurred a blending of indigenous traditions and customs with those that were imported by Stone and others from across the Atlantic. No less important, while there were those who were open to integrating these imports into their cultural behavior, others retained their "German formality," either because they did not want to change or were incapable of adaptation. Still, the least Stone achieved with his busy networking as OPA director was that, following the dislocations of the war, a growing number of people who may have known each other by name only actually met. What may appear to be a trivial point thus acquires a larger significance in terms of how Atlantic networks were reconstituted after the war.

If we talk of the interaction of people, we also speak about institutions in which these individuals worked and met. The previous chapters have given ample evidence that the organizational frameworks within which the previously mentioned individuals and groups operated are of considerable significance for an understanding of this period. Dartmouth helped Stone not only to network; it also represented an institutional and normative framework, and so did the *New York Times* with its time-honored traditions and standards of journalism. The same is true of HICOG and the Ford Foundation. At Ford, Stone enjoyed the added advantage that he had not only personal charisma and ideas to offer but also money. People came to him. He did not have to seek them out. Promoting the intersection of "his" circles on both sides of the Atlantic and ultimately around the globe was one of the roles that he believed the Ford Foundation with its millions was particularly suited to undertake. Even though a good deal of research has been done on both HICOG and Ford, it is hoped that this book has thrown new light on their development. Some parts of the story that has been told here were concerned with interdepartmental conflict and rivalries, and Stone also developed considerable skill in the handling of these.

Finally, we have dealt with the history of the CCF, an organization with which Stone was closely connected and whose successor, the International Association for Cultural Freedom, he ultimately headed. Our assessment of this very unique organization has led us into arenas of the postwar history that require further exploration. The first peculiarity of the CCF was that, although it had no endowment or physical assets of its own, it ran a multimillion dollar global enterprise. It had representatives and select membership circles operating in most of Western Europe, the United States, and an array of Asian, African, and Latin American nations. It supported a dozen or more intellectual and scholarly journals in major languages of the world, and it organized large and expensive international conferences on central themes of contemporary concern.

This conglomerate, run by Michael Josselson and his staff out of Paris, had originally been born out of the confrontation with the Soviet bloc and Stalinism. In this sense it was and remained a staunchly anticommunist venture wedded to the totalitarianism paradigm that, in line with the Friedrich-Brzezinski notion that Stalinism and Hitlerism were "basically alike," also propelled its antifascism from an explicitly liberal Western position. It is this opposition to communism, fellow traveling, and rightist radicalism that enabled the CCF to attract some of the best-known intellectuals in North America, Western Europe, and the Third World. These intellectuals lent their pens and oratorial skills to the pursuit of the great postwar conflict between East and West, which was not only about military and economic power, but also about the power of ideas and culture. In addition to stimulating analyses of the confrontation between two power-political and industrial systems, the Cold War has recently also begun to be examined from a cultural perspective, and it also formed a central theme of this book. However, it has been our argument that the Cold War against the East had essentially been won in intellectual terms by the mid-1950s. The people involved in this struggle on the Western side knew this, and yet the CCF and Stone's support of it with Ford Foundation millions continued for more than another decade. Why?

The reasons behind this had little (and certainly less and less) to do with East-West relations and a lot with the European-American relationship. As we have seen, there was another cold culture war being waged. Its issues emerged after 1945 and were related to the desire of America's elites to project an image of the United States not just as the military-political and economic-technological leader of the West, but also as its cultural hegemon. The claim to cultural leadership was to no small degree also a response to a cultural superiority complex that had been strong among Europe's intellectual and educated elites during the interwar years and that, after a brief period of humility, had resurfaced after 1945. When American cultural products arrived in Europe for the first time during the 1920s in quantities that could no longer be ignored, many Europeans rejected them as trashy, vulgar, cheap, mechanical, and primitive. By comparison, European culture was supposedly sophisticated, time-honored, refined, profound, mature and—in contrast to the technological optimism of the Americans—conscious of the dark sides of modernity.

The negative perceptions of American culture were as strong on the European left as they were on the right, though on the right they were mixed with a more comprehensive fear of what the United States represented as a cultural system and a democratic society. For the traditional elites and increasingly also for the conservative *Bildungsbürgertum*, American culture was not for the educated few but one for the "uneducated masses," the *Halbgebildete*. No less significantly, its emergence was linked by European intellectuals, businessmen, and educated people to the rise of mass production and mass consumption as espoused by Taylorism and Fordism, which in turn were deemed to be inseparably connected with mass participation in politics. Adhering to an antidemocratic elitism that they had nourished in the wake of the great revolutionary upheavals of 1789 and 1848, Europe's upper and middle classes became even more deeply fearful of the "common man." If he, as he seemed to be doing in Fordist America, was not only buying mass-produced industrial goods of low quality, but, through the ballot box, also defining the course of national politics and, through the availability of popular culture, even cultural tastes, the end of Western civilization was, in their view, clearly at hand.

Representatives of the European left did not share these conservative, antidemocratic anxieties. They had themselves visions of a new sophisticated culture of the proletarian masses after their liberation from capitalist exploitation, but rejected American mass culture as a modern, secular opium for the gullible. Rationalized production of consumer goods was fine in principle, but only in a society that had abolished capitalism and the profit-motive that drove the Fordist engine of consumerism. This ambivalence helps to explain why so many European intellectuals refused to distance themselves from the Bolshevik experiment, even when its unacceptable human costs became increasingly clear, or why they continued to look for "third way" democratic-socialist solutions that avoided the inhumanities of Stalinism as well as those of Americanism, as they saw it. The fact that fascism with its crimes had been born from the crisis of capitalism and that the Red Army decisively contributed to Hitler's defeat merely added to the tremendous confusion of the mind that Europe's intellectual elites experienced in the 1930s and 1940s. Silone's career is but one case in point. In short, European anti-Americanism was rooted in an older cultural superiority complex that not even the experience of World War II with its barbarisms was able to destroy, either because its implications were simply ignored or because it was presumed to have given the Europeans a glimpse into a civilizational abyss that the "naive" Americans had missed.

Across the Atlantic, intellectuals and educated, well-traveled people like Stone were aware of these European attitudes. They had witnessed them as students in Europe before the war and encountered them again after 1945. Understandably, they wished to project an image of the United States as a nation whose cultural achievements were at least equal to those of Europe and which in fact had become the new center of the avantgarde once domiciled in Paris, Berlin, Vienna, Rome, or London. But they also saw value in American mass culture, its diversity and vibrancy, as

Daniel Bell and others had analyzed it. The CCF became one of the prime vehicles for the transmission of this more comprehensive vision of modern culture. But its leaders and their financial backers faced an uphill struggle. What made their job so difficult in the 1950s was that, just as the culture war against the Soviet Union was being won, forms of American mass culture reappeared in Europe that confirmed European intellectuals and educated people in their views. There were the familar 1920s shapes of Hollywood films and jazz; worse, they were now complemented by the new embodiments of an allegedly vulgar and gender-bending primitivism: Elvis Presley, Bill Haley, and other rock stars.

Nor did it help that the products of a commercialized popular culture were enthusiastically received by a generation of often working-class youths whose riotous behavior merely revived conservative fears of the "masses." Was the rioting and rampaging at rock concerts not typical of the masses's irrationalism and volatility, which Hitler had turned in the direction of violent mass politics during the 1930s? And where would it turn if it became politicized once again? To many older Europeans it was a disturbing scenario.

The reappearance of American popular culture in postwar Europe and the debates it unleashed among politicians, churchmen, and intellectuals have been the subject of a number of very illuminating studies.[2] What has been left out of the analysis of this picture are first of all the heated discussions that Hollywood and Elvis, "Midcult" and "Masscult," generated at the same time in the United States. Indeed, we have also only just begun to see the Atlantic context in which this second cold culture war of the CCF and other American organizations, both public and private, was fought in Europe. It was nothing less than a struggle to combat the cultural anti-Americanism of Western Europe's educated elites, right and left. Millions of dollars were spent in this struggle and it may well be that no other hegemonic power in history has ever invested as much as the United States did after World War II in changing foreigners' perceptions of it as a civilization.

Acting as the spearhead in this struggle, Josselson and his team, having shunted hard-line anticommunists such as Hook in the ACCF into the sidelines, won the support of a significant number of highly regarded European academics, intellectuals, businessmen, and politicians. The motives for their support were not uniform. Some still saw their alliance with the Americans as the most effective means of combatting communism in Eastern and Western Europe. Others regarded it as a way of creating a community that bridged the Atlantic and promoted a culture common to the two continents. Defeating their anti-American opponents was the powerful bond that brought American intellectuals, such as Bell and Schlesinger, together with their European interlocutors inside and outside the CCF, among them Berlin, Silone, and Aron. And yet, however close the relationship in the face of a common enemy and however strong the basic ideological consensus and sense of purpose, the Atlantic still remained a trench whose depth was never openly explored during the 1950s, perhaps for fear of what might be discovered. The chasm became visible only during the crisis years of the 1960s and 1970s, which were, after all, years of great economic and political as well as cultural-ideological conflict.

The best starting point to understand this particular European-American difference is to return to the wider definition of culture to which the members of the ACCF had moved after their defeat of the hard-line anti-communists in their midst. It was a definition that broadened traditional European conceptions of high culture to include, apart from the arts and humanities, the sciences and indeed all elitist creative activity and institutions. At the same time, while not directly promoting or funding American "mass culture," they denied the dangers that the Europeans had traditionally seen in it. Instead they celebrated it. American society was interpreted not as Dwight Macdonald and David Riesman had seen it, but as one that allowed people freely to develop their identity and to express themselves in innumerable nonconformist ways. It was not a cultural desert.

At the same time, Bell's book that had compressed this vision of mass culture into one volume contained another argument that is fundamental to our analysis. While, as we have seen, Bell represented the previously mentioned optimistic view of American society and its culture, his study also provides something like an echo sound with which to fathom the Atlantic deep-sea trench that, thinly covered by Atlanticist appeals to a common heritage, ran between the American and the European members of the CCF, whereby the British offshore islanders, with exceptions often embodied by immigrants from the European Continent, tended to veer more toward the American side.

In its deepest crevices, this trench reached into divergent philosophical traditions and concerned the viability of an "Anglo-Saxon," Deweyian pragmatism and the question of the manageability and rationality of modern industrial societies. Bell, Galbraith, and other American intellectuals shared a managerial optimism that Europeans, still wedded to French and German existentialist thought, had difficulty in accepting. Their utopia stressed the tensions between cultural modernity and the process of capitalist modernization. As we saw, Isaiah Berlin, for example, though familiar with the Oxford school of analytical philosophy, remained ambivalent at heart; for however much he had imbibed, since his arrival from Russia, a pragmatic liberalism and come to reject the irrationalism of the 1930s and the "counterenlightenment," as he called it, his writings retain a pessimism about modernity and an uneasiness about the dark potential of the human soul that is more reminiscent of a Continental-European intellectual tradition. Or take Michael Polanyi, the refugee from Nazism, who was deeply skeptical of science's claims to objectivity and rejected a superficial rationalism.

It is even more tangible in Aron, who in the 1930s had deeply immersed himself in Rickert and Weber, Husserl and Heidegger; the contemplation of American culture and society did not fill him with enthusiasm and a belief in the good potential of modern man, however pro-American he may have been by virtue of sober political calculation in a world threatened by Soviet communism. Unlike some of his American colleagues, he knew that nothing was "more misguided than the attempt to lay claim to Max Weber with a form of empirical social science" that did not "reflect upon the unscientific premises of its own approach and is unconscious— or insufficiently aware—of the lines between its own hypotheses and methods and their roots in a contemporary social situation."[3] Above all, in Aron's view, the optimistic Americans just had no idea of the depths to which humanity could sink and what acts of inhumanity man was capable of perpetrating. For him as well as for Sperber and other Jewish intellectuals the evil of the Holocaust added a special poignancy. This man-made horror, which they had barely escaped, always hovered in the background, even if it took them some time to deal with it not in the abstractly structural terms of the totalitarianism paradigm but as a human tragedy that was most probably inaccessible to the kind of rational analysis that American social scientists assumed all public phenomena to be amenable to.

It might even be argued that in this respect conservative and leftist intellectuals in Europe found themselves strangely in the same boat. Their cultural pessimism and their sense that there were problems that were simply not manageable united them against the "Anglo-Saxons" who in turn tended to have little patience for a "Continental-European" *Sehnsucht nach Schicksal und Tiefe*[4] and whose utopia was not transcendental but oriented toward the solution of human problems in this world. As Hook, the Dewey student, wrote to Josselson in 1964, "in Europe they have the theater of the absurd and in existentialism a philsophy of the absurd."[5] Meanwhile Bertrand Russell continued to mock Hegel's Absolute Idea as "pure thought thinking about pure thought." Returning the disdain, French, Italian, and German intellectuals flatly dismissed as shallow Deweyian pragmatism or British analytical philosophy as espoused by Ayer, the influential Wykeham Professor of Logic at Oxford. And then these intellectuals would reproduce, in the same breath, the older arguments about America. When they visited the United States after the war they merely found their prejudices confirmed. Even as the well-known German political theorist Arnold Bergstraesser saw an Atlantic convergence, he could only cast this happy development in terms of "Western natural law and German *Humanitätsidee* today turning their common face toward each other rather than their antagonistic sides," as they had done in the past. As a result, he added, "their common roots in the Occidental tradition become more clearly visible in historical as well as philosophical perspective."[6]

If we consider the persistence of these traditions, it is no coincidence that Konstantin Jelenski and Pierre Emmanuel would be the two people in the CCF and its successor, the IACF, who, in the 1960s, began openly to talk about the European-American difference in an attempt to redefine the direction of the CCF away from those "Anglo-Saxon" conceptions of politics and culture that had prevailed as long as Josselson was in charge and the money to support his well-oiled "Atlantic" enterprise came from America. Stone, as president of the IACF and a man who was in tune with the CCF's Bellian ethos, had sustained it for many years with Ford Foundation money, and then hoped to perpetuate it, until he was bluntly confronted with those two divergent understandings of culture. But he, too, was too strongly committed to the American way of seeing the world to be able to offer a solution to the inner intellectual crisis of the IACF.

The roots of the crisis that destroyed the association therefore lay very deep. They must be sought in the fact that by the late 1960s the revolt against pragmatism and the "end of ideology" had set in on a broader front on both sides of the Atlantic, promoted by Bell's leftist critics and the rise of a younger generation who believed the managerial-technocratic reformism of the CCF to be itself ideological. They took the liberal-capitalist system and culture that Bell had extolled to task and pointed to the gap between reality and ideology, arguing that the job still to be done required a much more radical approach. Some even called for revolution.

The CCF intellectuals perceived this challenge as a revival of a totalitarianism they had seen in their younger days and accordingly vigorously opposed it. They tried to apply what they thought were the lessons of the

1930s and rallied to the defense of the values they had upheld since the war. In the end they won; the political and economic aims of the New Left were rolled back, and by the late 1970s the student movement had run its course. Capitalism had not been transformed and parliamentary government had survived even the onslaught of the Red Army Faction.

But whatever the ideological differences, from the start there was also an angle to this conflict that was cultural in a broader "American" sense and that was much less acute than the political confrontation of the generations. Only in retrospect can we see its significance more clearly. At least it now appears that the student rebellion in the United States and in Western Europe was more than anything else a movement for a more democratic and individualistic culture. The young revolted against the many social norms and conventions in postwar European and American society that regulated and constrained the freedom of choice and personal expression. The norms that defined gender relations may provide an illustration of this, as we contemplate the changes that have occurred—as well as the work still to be done.

In the same way, attitudes toward mass production, mass consumption, and mass culture have also shifted, partly as a result of generational change. True, there are still some European intellectuals who are vitriolically critical of American popular culture; but the balance seems to have tilted in the opposite direction. As the anthropologist Kaspar Maase put it not too long ago: "Among the upper echelons of business, politics, science, and technology, among the academically trained professions, the right to enjoy the bliss of ordinary culture is claimed extensively. Popular art and entertainment have become the culture of all."[7] Similarly, Richard Peterson has argued that in this respect we have all become "omnivores."[8]

If the Atlantic trench relating to elite attitudes toward modern culture is therefore no longer as deep as it was in the 1950s, the same rapprochement seems to have occurred with regard to philosophical positions. The recent devastating attacks, from within Britain, on Ayer not only as a "hollow man," but also on him as a philosopher who never had "an original idea in his life" and "also never a good" one, reflect a crisis that "Anglo-Saxon" thought has experienced: "His dogmatic empiricism, his conventionalism about logical truth, his emotivism in ethics, his sense-datum theory of perception, his rejection of causal necessity, his 'bundle theory' of objects and persons—none of this seems . . . remotely on the right track." It was because Ayer found positivism so appealing that he had "an excuse not to have to think about hard philosophical questions."[9] Indeed, this failure is exactly what Continental-European intellectuals found so objectionable about "Anglo-Saxon" attempts to grapple with the crisis and its consequences that the twentieth century had seen in its first half and that is still with us the beginning of the twenty-first.

This implies that before we push the European-American rapprochement too far, it is as well to remember that differences in attitude and basic outlook on the human existence continue. They may be difficult to pinpoint exactly, but they may best be gauged from the spirit in which our epoch is viewed. It is certainly striking how Americans seem to approach contemporary problems, however taxing, with a striking optimism, a sense that they can ultimately be solved. In Continental Europe by contrast a cultural pessimism that so deeply affected earlier generations of intellectuals and educated people is much more widespread than in the United States. It was reinforced in the 1990s by the crisis in the Balkans where all the old ghosts of the European past seemed to be rearing their ugly heads again. The same sense of pessimism pervades European debates on Third World overpopulation and poverty, on the destruction of the environment, and on our capacity for violence and cruelty.

But even those in Europe who, like their American counterparts, refuse to lapse into existentialist despair sense that the test of their optimism will ultimately lie in the sphere of political economy, whose evolution is now more than ever in the hands of the practitioners and power brokers than in those of the intellectuals. And in this respect, new differences of view have opened up concerning the viability and promise of the American and European models of organizing a global economy in the midst of the Third Technological Revolution. The telling irony here is that old American Keynesians like Galbraith have considerably more sympathy with the European model than with that of their own country. For the moment, the latter model appears to have gained the upper hand. But, as the Europeans like to point out, its social and cultural costs are tremendous— provided, of course, we subscribe to a broad American definition of culture that Stone and other "Cold War liberals" once stood for and that included, as matter of right, such immaterial goods as education, health, social mobility, and the pursuit of greater equality for all. It was the wider availability of these goods that enabled men (and later also women) of lower-class origin to live fuller and more rewarding lives; to go to the opera or to listen to a symphony, as Stone, the young man from the New England provinces, had done for the first time in Berlin in 1929.

Finally, before we get too carried away by the idea of the intrinsic power of America as a societal model for Europe, let us not forget that it was and still is backed up by the enormous economic clout that, in a period of extended boom, America's media trusts and large corporations possess around the world. Certainly, the generous funding of film and media marketing that, for example, Hollywood throws into the scales are difficult to match. Consequently, the strategy of the Europeans has been to stop resisting and instead to join the Americans because you cannot beat them. At the same time it has become more difficult, at least in economic affairs, to pinpoint what is American and what is not. On closer inspection, the Atlantic is once more a two-lane highway. If the Americanization of Europe continues, we can also see a (re-)Europeanization of the United States.[10]

Shepard Stone moved right in the middle of these European-American affinities and differences. He tried to bridge and to mediate them in practical ways. He used the funds at his disposal to influence attitudes and mentalities. He has rightly been called an "impresario," a "doctor catalyticus,"[11] the man who tried to integrate different traditions during the Cold War. He was not powerful or wealthy enough to move things decisively on his own. But he had the ear of powerful and wealthy people and belonged to a category of advisors whose influence often turns out to have been greater than was visible at the time. Above all, his life and career neatly reflected some of the major developments and struggles of the age and thus hold insights into the developments of the twentieth century that go far beyond the unique and the individual that his life also represented.

List of West German Newspapers
Subsidized by HICOG

Newspapers	Subsidy (in deutschmarks)
1. *Stuttgarter Nachrichten*	400,000
2. *Darmstädter Echo*	300,000
3. *Fuldaer Volkszeitung*	300,000
4. *Westfalen-Zeitung*, Bielefeld	250,000
5. *Giessener Freie Presse*	160,000
6. *Main-Echo*, Aschaffenburg	250,000
7. *Kölnische Rundschau*	200,000
8. *Nordwest-Zeitung*, Oldenburg	200,000
9. *Wittlicher Tageblatt*, Wittlich	50,000
10. *Die Rheinpfalz*, Ludwigshafen	400,000
11. *Das Volk*, Freiburg	150,000
12. *Hessische Nachrichten*, Kassel	400,000
13. *Trierischer Volksfreund*	250,000
14. *Rheinische Post*, Düsseldorf	150,000
15. *Schwäbisches Tageblatt*, Tübingen	400,000
16. *Braunschweiger Zeitung*	150,000
17. *Solinger Tageblatt*	110,000
18. *Flensburger Tageblatt*	300,000
19. *Der Volkswille*, Schweinfurt	150,000
20. *Der Neue Tag*, Weiden	90,000
21. *Süddeutsche Zeitung*, München	500,000
22. *Morgenpost*, Hamburg	150,000
23. *Kölner Stadtanzeiger*	180,000
24. *Neue Württembergische Zeitung*, Göppingen	125,000
25. *Mittelbayerische Zeitung*, Regensburg	300,000
26. *Schwäbische Post*, Aalen	100,000
27. *Nordwestdeutsche Rundschau*, Wilhelmshaven	100,000
28. *Der Allgäuer*, Kempten	230,000
29. *Die Freiheit*, Mainz	100,000

Newspapers	Subsidy (in deutschmarks)
30. *Rheinischer Merkur*, Koblenz	180,000
31. *Generalanzeiger für Bonn und Umgebung*	135,000
32. *Hannoversche Presse*	480,000
33. *Hamburger Freie Presse*	250,000
34. *Frankfurter Rundschau*	1,600,000
35. *Lübecker Nachrichten*	250,000
36. *Westdeutsche Rundschau*, Wuppertal	100,000
37. *Norddeutsche Volkszeitung*, Bremen-Vegesack	40,000
38. *Aachener Volkszeitung*	50,000
39. *Fränkische Landeszeitung*, Ansbach	80,000
40. *Pforzheimer Zeitung*	100,000
41. *Bayerische Rundschau*, Kulmbach	60,000
42. *Nordsee-Zeitung*, Bremerhaven	120,000
43. *Ruhr-Nachrichten*, Dortmund	140,000
44. *Rheinische Zeitung*, Köln	200,000

Source: DCSS, Binder: Personal Files 1978/9, HICOG Current Informational Report, 7 November 1951.

American Foundations Ranked by Assets, 1960

Foundations	Assets in 1960 (1937) (in millions of dollars)
1. Ford Foundation	3,316
2. Rockefeller Foundation	648 (184)
3. Duke Endowment	432
4. Hartford Foundation	414
5. Carnegie Corporation	261 (164)
6. Kellogg Foundation	215 (47)
7. Sloan Foundation	176
8. Lilly Endowment	151
9. Commonwealth Fund	119 (52)
10. Danforth Foundation	110
11. Kresge Foundation	95 (50)
12. Carnegie Institution	89 (37)
13. James Foundation	84
14. Avalon Foundation	74
15. Kettering Foundation	69
16. Fleischmann Foundation	67
17. Hayden Foundation	67
18. Mellon Foundation	59
19. Mayo Foundation	59
20. Rockefeller Brothers Fund	53
21. China Medical Board	52
22. Welch Foundation	51
23. Reynolds Foundation	50
24. Guggenheim Foundation	45 (7)
25. Kress Foundation	45

Source: Adapted from DCSS, Box 8, Loose Materials, Ford Foundation, "Ten-Year Summary, 1951–1960," June 1960.

International Association for Cultural Freedom, Table of Organization

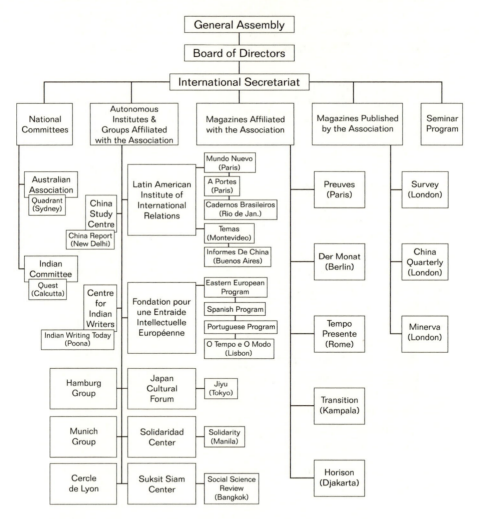

Source: DCSS, Box 10, F. 18, IACF Table of Organization, n.d.

▪▪▪ *Notes* ▪▪▪

Shepard Stone kept his voluminous papers partly in his apartment in Cambridge, Mass., and partly on his farm in Vermont. All materials are now deposited with the Special Collections department of Dartmouth College Library. To put some order into the material, I compiled a provisional inventory and either numbered or lettered the boxes. Other materials were kept in several filing cabinets and are cited by the label on the drawer. Once the Dartmouth Library has cataloged the papers, the file numbering will obviously be more systematic. For the time being, the citation method adopted in the notes is designed to help interested readers to locate a particular file or document. To save space, the Stone Papers will be cited as DCSS. "Dr" stands for Drawer, "F." for Folder.

Other archives consulted include the Ford Foundation Archives, New York (FPA) and the Archive of the Aspen Institute Berlin (AAIB).

INTRODUCTION

1. DCSS, Dr "Old Files," F.: Stone's Correspondence from Europe 28.6.– 15.9.1958, Stone to Nielsen and Slater, 26 July 1959.

2. Ibid., Dr "Countries," F.: W. Nielsen Memos from Europe 1959, Nielsen to Stone, 19 July 1959.

3. Loth 1988.

4. If used in the strict Gramscian sense, the "cultural" in "cultural hegemony" seems redundant. In contemporary parlance and particularly in international relations, however, hegemony is frequently used to describe asymmetrical power relations that are not just cultural. In order to avoid misunderstandings the concept is used here to highlight the cultural focus of this book.

5. See, e.g., Ermarth 1993; Pommerin 1986.

6. See, e.g., Gaddis 1982; Garthoff 1991.

7. Erhard 1957.

8. See, e.g., Rosenberg 1982. Fuller discussion of the literature in Schmidt 1999.

9. See, e.g., Kroes et al. 1993; Fehrenbach and Poiger 2000.

10. Kaelble 1982.

11. See, e.g., Curti 1963; Gemelli 1998.

12. See, e.g., Merle 1987.

13. See, e.g., Wiesen 1998.

14. See Grémion 1995; Coleman 1989; Hochgeschwender 1998; Saunders 2000.

15. See the preface to these notes.

16. Pells 1997.

17. See, e.g., A. Sywottek, "The Americanization of Everyday Life?" in Ermarth 1993, pp. 132–52.

CHAPTER 1

FROM NASHUA AND BERLIN TO PEARL HARBOR

1. Most of the following information about Stone's youth in Nashua stems from manuscript fragments, apparently produced with the aim of publishing his memoirs. They are now at Dartmouth in Box I, F.: Memoirs. Because the fragments do not appear in chronological order, it is difficult to provide a more precise reference. Further information was given by Charlotte Stone and her daughter Margaret MacDonald. See also DCSS, Dr "Germany McCloy Stone," F.: Personal, Stone to Earl [?], 23 March 1953.

2. DCSS, Dr "Hicog I," F.: Letters 1944–45, Lillian Cohen to Stone, 19 February 1945.

3. Ibid., Dr "Speeches," Stone's Speech at Nashua High School, 18 October 1962.

4. Ibid., Box I, F.: Memoirs; ibid., Dr "Hicog IV," F.: 112.4—S. Stone, Lillian Dowd to Stone, 15 March 1952. Dowd was one of Stone's teachers at Nashua High. She now called him "my favorite pupil."

5. Ibid., Box I, F.: Memoirs.

6. Ibid., Box G, F.: Misc. Materials 1951–52, Menu of SS "America," July 1952, with sentence in McCloy's handwriting.

7. Hacker 1997, pp. 231–32.

8. DCSS, Dr "Hicog II," F.: Memoirs, Stone to Tom Sargent, 11 March 1954.

9. Ibid., F.: Correspondence, Stone to Tappe, 2 October 1951. See also ibid., Obituary by Howard Dunham. Stone's essays ibid., Box F, F.: 2 Essays; ibid., Box B, F.: Major Stone 201.

10. Ibid., Box I, F.: Memoirs.

11. Ibid., Box 11, Binder 1: Correspondence 1982–83, Manuscript of Stone's Speech on the Occasion of His Becoming an Honorary Citizen of Berlin, 24 March 1983.

12. Ibid., Box I, F.: Memoirs. In an interview, published in *Lufthansa's Germany*, April 1985, p. 24, he remembered that he bought and read *Mein Kampf*, adding that he never underestimated Hitler.

13. DCSS, Box I, F.: Memoirs. On these attitudes, see more generally: Berghahn 1982; Kaplan 1998.

14. DCSS, Dr "Study," F.: Misc. Correspondence 1975, Bacher to Stone, 27 February 1975.

15. On Read: ibid., Box I, F.: Memoirs; on Teller et al.: *Die Zeit*, 8 April 1988. See also Haxthausen and Suhr 1990; Isherwood 1995.

16. DCSS, Box I, F.: Memoirs, for this and the subsequent quotations.

17. Interview with Charlotte Stone, Cambridge, Mass., 12 January 1994.

302

18. DCSS, Box G, F.: Correspondence with His Wife 1944–45, Stone to his wife, 26 April 1945; F.: Today's Problems in Europe, Charlotte Stone to her husband, 13 May 1945.

19. Ibid., Box I, F.: Memoirs, n.d.

20. DCSS, Box A, F.: Review, Heuss to Stone, 5 February 1946; Box 2, F. 1, Stone to Herzfeld, 22 January 1958, on his attending lectures of the famous historian Friedrich Meinecke. More generally: Döring 1975. On his experiences with Nazi students, see, e.g., his "Hitler und Deutschland," written for *Der Spiegel* in March 1989 in DCSS, Box 12, F. 23.

21. Copy in DCSS, Box E, F.: Stone's Berlin Ph.D. thesis. See the documents in ibid., Box A, F.: Correspondence and Manuscripts 1928–1938, with Oncken's statement of 1 November 1932, Hoetzsch's letter to Stone of 27 December 1932, and the certificate, signed by Fritz Hartung as dean of the philosophical faculty. After 1945 he liked to call himself an "Oncken-Schüler," which certainly enhanced his reputation in Germany, whereas back home in the United States a history Ph.D. from Berlin University no doubt helped him in academic circles.

22. See 16.

23. DCSS, Box B, F.: Misc. Correspondence 1933, Hopkins to Lippmann, 4 March 1933.

24. See pp. 163ff.

25. See pp. 201ff. See also DCSS, Dr "Hicog I," F.: Letters 1944–45, Molony (BBC Bristol) to Stone, 29 July 1944, telling him that she would be taking a vacation in Cambridge in August and adding: "A pity you can't come, too, and I would show you how far an English university transcends a German one."

26. DCSS, Box I, F.: Draft Memoirs III 1933–49.

27. Ibid., Box B, Hopkins to Gannon, 4 March 1933. For the letter to Lippmann, see note 23.

28. Ibid., Box I, F.: Misc. 1933– , Stone to his parents, 9 April 1933. See also his other letters to his family from March and April 1933, ibid., including one to his sister Lillian of 20 March, written on stationery of the Dartmouth Club, New York.

29. Ibid., Box B, F.: Misc. Correspondence 1933, Hopkins to Stone, 20 March 1933.

30. Ibid., Hopkins's Secretary to Wertheimer, 22 August 1933.

31. Ibid., Nashua Telegraph, 7 February 1933. Ibid. also for the material on his other activities.

32. Ibid., Box I, F.: Misc. 1933–, Stone to "Everyone" [i.e., his family], n.d. [March 1933].

33. Ibid., Stone to his parents, n.d. [April? 1933]. See also R. Brownstein, "The *New York Times* on Nazism, 1933–1939," *Midstream* 26 (1980): 14–19.

34. DCSS, Dr "World War II," F.: 1930s Articles, *Current History*, June 1933, pp. 272–78; July 1933, pp. 399–405.

35. Ibid., Box B, F.: Major Stone 201, Interview Manuscript, 11 August 1933.

36. Ibid., Dr "World War II," F.: 1930s Articles, "Democracy Still Lives, Says Masaryk," *New York Times Magazine*, 12 November 1933.

37. DCSS., Box B, F.: Major Stone 201, Interview Manuscript, 31 August 1933.

38. Ibid., Markel to Stone, 5 September 1933.

39. Ibid., Dr "Hicog I," F.: Statement 1955, "Sworn Statement" by Stone, 28 November 1955.

40. See the materials in ibid., Dr "World War II," F.: 1930s Articles.

41. Ibid., Box A, F.: Correspondence and Manuscripts 1928–38, Murrow to Stone, 17 September 1936.

42. Ibid., Clipping of article, n.d.

43. Ibid., Box B, F.: Misc. Correspondence 1933, Murrow to Stone, 6 October 1937.

44. Ibid., Box A, F.: Correspondence and Manuscripts 1928–38, Murrow to Stone, 17 September 1937.

45. Ibid., Box B, F.: Major Stone 201, Polish Consul General to Buell, 21 June 1933.

46. As note 34, for this and the subsequent quotations.

47. DCSS, *Boston Herald*?, 29 October 1933.

48. See Hildebrand 1969, pp. 441–91.

49. *New York Times Magazine*, 3 December 1933.

50. *New York Times* (Sunday edition), 28 January 1934, for this and subsequent quotations. In general, see, e.g., Broszat 1987, pp. 129–49.

51. DCSS, Dr "World War II," F.: 1930s Articles, *Dartmouthian*, 28 February 1934.

52. Ibid., Box B, F.: Misc. Correspondence 1933, Murrow to Stone, 6 October 1937.

53. Ibid., Box A, F.: Correspondence and Manuscripts 1928–38, Manuscript of *CBS Talk*, 30 January 1938.

54. *Commentator*, April 1938, pp. 3–7.

55. Ibid., July 1938, pp. 65–68, for this and subsequent quotations.

56. Stone 1938, for this and subsequent quotations.

57. DCSS, Dr "World War II," F.: 1945–46, Royalty Statement, 11 January 1946.

58. Stone and Baldwin 1938.

59. See the documents in DCSS, Box F, F.: Misc. Personal Correspondence 1938–40.

60. See the materials in ibid., Dr "World War II," F.: 1942.

61. FFA, Heald Office Files, Folder 010499, Stone's speech, 13 October 1965.

62. As notes 33 and 48.

63. *Commentator*, February 1939, pp. 48–51.

64. On the detriorating situation of Jews in Germany in the 1930s, see note 13.

65. The following account is based on the documents in DCSS, Dr "Hicog I," F.: Capt. Stone.

66. On the refugee community in New York, Lowenstein 1989.

CHAPTER 2
DEFEATING AND REBUILDING GERMANY

1. DCSS, Dr "World War II," F.: Letters, Stone's "Diary," entry for 7 December 1941.

2. Ibid., Box I, F.: Correspondence and Memoir Fragments, Fragment "Joining the Army."

3. Ibid., Dr "World War II," F.: Letters, Stone to Baldwin, n.d.

4. Ibid., Markel to Stone, 20 February 1942.

5. Ibid., Stone to Adjutant General, 19 February 1942.

6. As note 2.

7. DCSS, Dr "World War II," F.: Letters, Baldwin's reply at bottom of Stone to Baldwin, n.d.

8. Ibid., F.: Early 1940s, Cantril to Looker, 16 December 1942. On Cantril, a Dartmouth graduate, then working at Princeton University, and on this issue more generally, see M. Hönicke, " 'Know Your Enemy,' " in Fiebig-von Hase and Lehmkuhl 1997, pp. 231–78.

9. As note 2.

10. DCSS., Dr "World War II," F.: Early 1940s, Stone to Beneš, 13 May 1943.

11. Ibid., Box B, F.: C. Stone Letters 1943–44, Charlotte Stone to her husband, 12 December 1943, 17 February 1944, and again 6 March 1944. See also ibid., Box G, F.: Today's Problems in Europe, Charlotte to her husband, 26 December 1944: "I spent Christmas with the parents at Liberty [N.Y.] and we decorated the tree together . . . and I think that the parents were really quite thrilled." On the persistence of such customs among refugees, see Berghahn 1982.

12. Ibid., Box E, F.: Capt. Stone (general), Col. B. A. Dickson to Awards and Decorations Board, 7 May 1945.

13. Ibid., Binder: Personal Files 1980–81, Stone's Draft Manuscript, 15 June 1981. On the situation of the U.S. Army in Britain, see Reynolds 1995.

14. As note 12. See also the letters in DCSS., Box G, F.: Correspondence with His Wife 1944–45.

15. See, e.g., Jaud 1997.

16. DCSS, Box G, F.: Today's Problems in Europe, Charlotte Stone to her husband, 30 November 1944, quoting from Denny's report. On the general situation in the Aachen region, see Henke 1995, pp. 252ff.

17. DCSS, Box G, F.: Correspondence with His Wife 1944–45, Stone to his wife, 1 March 1945.

18. Ibid., Box 12, Loose Correspondence (G-2 file), May to Paine, 19 July 1988.

19. Ibid., Dr "Hicog I," F.: Letters 1944–45, Crossman to Stone, 23 November 1944. Walter Hasenclever was sent to Europe to interrogate POWs and others. See note 49. On the *Edelweisspiraten*, see, e.g., Peukert 1980. See also Robin 1995.

20. DCSS, Box G, F.: Correspondence with His Wife 1944–45, Stone to his wife, 26 April 1945; ibid., F.: Today's Problems in Europe, Charlotte Stone to her husband, 13 May 1945. On this romantic trip, see p. 8.

21. DCSS, Box G, F.: Correspondence with His Wife 1944–45, Stone to his wife, 20 April 1944; ibid., Dr "World War II," F.: Marburg, Report by J. P. Best (PW Combat Team, U.S. First Army) to Stone, 21 April 1945.

22. As note 12.

23. See p. 278. According to Silberberg, he, in his position as intelligence officer of the 47th Infantry Regiment, had heard from the deputy mayor of Pansfelde that in 1943 a large contingent of trucks had, under the cover of darkness, unloaded tons of documents at a remote stately home, Schloss Degenershausen. When Silberberg went to investigate, the owner, Baroness von Bodenhausen, told him not only about the Foreign Office files but also about another archive deposited with Countess von der Asseburg at Schloss Meisdorf, a few miles away. The countess also owned the nearby Burg Falkenstein, where Silberberg discovered hundreds of wooden boxes with books, paintings, and other art objects that had also come from Berlin. Receiving a copy of Silberberg's letter to Dönhoff in turn jogged Stone's memory. He now recalled that Colonel Dickson, the G-2 of the First Army, on getting Silberberg's report, sent Stone to Schloss Degenershausen to investigate further. He found that the baroness was related to the Earl of Douglas and had a letter from P. G. Woodhouse, confirming that she was an anti-Nazi. Recognizing, "as an Oncken student," the importance of the find, Stone, fearing "that German paratroopers might try to destroy the castle," urged Dickson to take the archive to a safe place. According to Stone, it took "a hundred or more 2 1/2-ton trucks to evacuate the documents to Marburg." However, he was unable to inspect the art treasures "because my outfit was ordered to proceed East." Compiled from *Hessische Nachrichten*, 12 February 1948; DCSS, Box 11, Binder 2, Silberberg to Dönhoff, 12 April 1983; Stone to Dönhoff, 25 April 1983; Stone to Silberberg, 25 April 1983.

24. Ibid., Dr "World War II," F.: 1945–46, Report by Stone for the Bulletin of the First Army's G-2 Section, 18 February 1946; Report by J. B. Stanley, 6871 DISCC, APO 758, n.d.

25. See pp. 66. See also J.C.E. Gienow-Hecht, "Friends, Foes, or Reeducators?" in Fiebig-von Hase and Lehmkuhl 1997, pp. 281–300. See also Gienow-Hecht 1999.

26. As note 2.

27. See DCSS, Box E, F.: Stone—Personal, Clay to Sulzberger (*New York Times*), 2 January 1948; Stone to Sulzberger, 3 February 1948. See also Smyser 1999, pp. 53–87.

28. Ibid., Box 10, Loose Materials, Stone to Hurwitz, 13 September 1967. See also Bausch 1992.

29. DCSS, Box E, F.: Stone—201—Press, Stevens to Stone, 20 November 1945; ibid., Box C, F.: Correspondence 1945–46, Heuss to Stone, 20 November 1945.

30. Ibid., Dr "World War II," F.: 1945–46, Report by J. B. Stanley, 6871 DISCC, APO 758, n.d. See also Bermann-Fischer 1967.

31. DCSS, Box G, F.: Correspondence with His Wife 1945–46, Stone to his wife, 27 October 1945. See also ibid., Box A, F.: Review, Sternberger to Stone, 15 May 1946.

32. Ibid., Dr "Study," F.: 1967–74, Allemagne (diverse), Stone to Jan Reifenberg, 3 March 1970, writing on Jan's brother's death. See also ibid., Box A, F.: Review, J. H. Boxer to Stone, 12 May 1946.

33. Interview with Marion Countess Dönhoff, Hamburg, 17 December 1994. See also chapter 9, note 72.

34. DCSS, Binder: Personal Files 1978–79, S. Stone, "Betrachtungen eines amerikanischen Zeitungsfachmanns über die deutsche Presse," 20–21 October 1945, for this and subsequent quotations. See also Hurwitz 1972 and note 25.

35. See, e.g., Hale 1964.

36. DCSS, Dr "World War II," F.: Marburg, Arndt to *Marburger Presse*, 28 October 1945. Arndt later became a prominent SPD politician and the party's legal expert. See also note 8.

37. DCSS, Box G, F.: Correspondence with His Wife 1945–46, Stone to Markel, 12 September 1945.

38. See p. 29.

39. Laqueur 1989.

40. DCSS, Dr "World War II," F.: 1942, Stone to Strong, 3rd, n.d. [November 1940?].

41. Ibid., Dr "Hicog I," F.: Letters 1944–45, Nissen to Stone, 15 October 1944.

42. Ibid., Fehling to Stone, 3 November 1944; Fehling to Stone, 20 December 1944.

43. Ibid., Box B, F.: Personal Correspondence 1945, Abramavicius to Stone, 11 July 1945. See more generally Arad 1980.

44. DCSS, Dr "Hicog I," F.: Letters 1944–45, Read to Stone, 19 February 1945.

45. Ibid., Dr "Hicog II," F.: Correspondence Stone (German), 21 April 1952. On the Morgenthau debate in general, see, e.g., Blum 1972.

46. As note 2 and Shirer 1960.

47. DCSS, Box D, F.: Stone—201—Files II, Stone's Diary (fragment), entry for 7 May 1945.

48. Ibid., Dr "Hicog I," F.: Letters 1944–45, Markel to Stone, 18 December 1944.

49. Ibid., Markel to Stone, 22 March 1945.

50. Ibid., Dr "World War II," F.: Letters, W. Hasenclever, "Psychological Reaction of the German People after the Defeat" (manuscript), n.d. On the youth movement, see Laqueur 1962. See also Borsdorf and Niethammer 1976.

51. DCSS, Box D, F.: Private Correspondence 1943–45, Hasenclever to Charlotte Stone, 6 May 1945; Hasenclever to Charlotte Stone, 31 August 1945.

52. On this conflict, see, e.g., Gimbel 1968; Kaes 1995; Gienow-Hecht 1999.

53. DCSS, Box B, Personal Correspondence 1945, Charlotte Stone to her husband, 20 October 1945. This letter indicates that, however sexually emancipated she may have been as a young woman in Berlin, she did not transgress the traditional framework of middle-class gender relations that existed in the United States and became reinforced in the postwar period. Meanwhile, in England and later, other women found her husband's personal charm quite difficult to resist. However, this is not a modern "American-style" biography, but a "window" to crucial aspects of Cold War history.

54. Ibid., Charlotte Stone to her husband, 23 October 1945; ibid., Box G, F.: Correspondence with His Wife 1945–46, Stone to his wife, 8 October 1945. See also ibid., Stone to his wife, 10 October 1945, with criticisms of President Harry Truman.

55. Ibid., Box G, Stone to his wife, 3 August 1945. But Stone and Dulles kept in touch. On 16 April 1946, Dulles wrote to Stone (ibid., Box A, F.: Review) to get his advice on a manuscript he was writing about the German resistance to Hitler and to talk about other matters. Their cooperation continued throughout the 1950s after Stone joined the Ford Foundation. See also Grose 1994, Thomas 1995, and my comments on pp. 220.

56. DCSS, Box G, F.: Correspondence with His Wife 1945–46, Stone to his wife, 7 September 1945.

57. On Clay and his policies, see Smith 1990, book 3.

58. DCSS, Box G, F.: Correspondence with His Wife 1945–46, Stone to his wife, 18 October 1945.

59. Ibid., Stone to his wife, 20 November 1945.

60. Ibid., Stone to his wife, 6 December 1945.

61. Ibid., F.: Shepard Stone Personal 1946, Cantril to Stone, 28 August 1943.

62. Ibid., Dr "Hicog I," F.: Letters 1944–45, Markel(?) to Stone, 9 August 1944.

63. Ibid., Baldwin to Stone, 13 September 1944.

64. See p. 140. DCSS, Box B, F.: Personal Correspondence 1945, Charlotte Stone to her husband, 4 May 1945.

65. Ibid., Sulzberger to Adjutant General, 1 June 1945.

66. Ibid., Markel to Stone, 30 August 1945; ibid., Box G, F.: Correspondence with His Wife 1945–46, Stone to his wife, 30 August 1945.

67. Ibid., Box F, F.: General German Folder 1945–48, Stone to Markel, 12 September 1945. Apparently he also tried Ed Murrow again at CBS. Ibid., Box G, F.: Shepard Stone Personal 1946, W. S. Paley (CBS) to Stone, 18 February 1946.

68. Ibid., Dr "World War II," F.: Marburg, Markel to Separation Board (War Dept.), 5 November 1945.

69. Ibid., Box G, F.: Correspondence with His Wife 1945–46, Stone to his wife, 22 November 1945; Stone to his wife, 12 December 1945; Stone to his wife, 16 November 1945.

70. Ibid., Hirschfeld to Stone, 11 April 1946.

71. Ibid., Box D, F.: *New York Times* 1947, Stevens to Stone, 30 April 1947. On the background to this shift see notes 25 and 28. In the meantime there had also been the rise of a hard-line anticommunism, soon to turn into McCarthyism. See pp. 63ff.

72. DCSS, Dr "World War II," F.: Personal Letters 1945–, Sternberger to Stone, 20 December 1948.

73. Ibid., Box E, F.: Times Hall Speech, Stone's manuscript of his speech, n.d., for this and subsequent quotations. See also Gienow-Hecht 1999.

74. DCSS, Dr "World War II," F.: 1945–46, Stone to Hilldring, 26 February 1946.

75. Ibid., Box A, F.: Review, Stone to Secretary of War, 15 April 1946.

76. Ibid., Box E, F.: Shepard Stone Personal, Clay to Sulzberger, 2 January 1948; Stone to Sulzberger, 3 February 1948.

77. Ibid., Box E, F.: Shepard Stone Personal, McClure to Stone, 3 December 1948. Bödeker 1993. See also my note 25.

78. DCSS, Box E, F.: Shepard Stone Personal, Stone to McClure, 29 December 1948.

79. Ibid., Box G, F.: Shepard Stone Personal 1946, Stone to Ebbinghaus, 5 June 1946.

80. Ibid., Dr "Hicog I," F.: CFR 1948, Stone's notes for his lecture on 8 March 1948.

81. On reeducation and reorientation, see, e.g., Tent 1988. On the Marshall Plan, see, e.g., Maier and Hoffmann 1984.

CHAPTER 3
PUBLIC OPINION AND HIGH POLITICS IN SEMISOVEREIGN WEST GERMANY

1. On McCloy see, e.g., Bird 1992; Schwartz 1991.

2. DCSS, Box I, F.: Speeches 1980–, Stone's speech at McCloy's ninetieth birthday party on 3 April 1985, n.d.

3. See "Ein Wort über Shepard Stone," *Die Neue Zeitung*, 5 November 1949.

4. Bird 1992, pp. 35–56.

5. See, e.g., Stone recalling (DCSS, Box 12, F. 1, Stone's Speech [probably on the occasion of a memorial service for John Dickey, friend and former president of Dartmouth on 13 June 1989]) that "Jack McCloy, who was my mentor and friend, often recalled his undergraduate days at Amherst when those 'Green Gorillas' [i.e., the Dartmouth football team] would defeat Amherst."

6. The letter was addressed to Tom Sargent, the son of his friend Phil and a student at the Exeter Academy, preparing for a college career. Stone added about McCloy (ibid., Dr "Hicog II," F.: Memoirs, Stone to Sargent, 11 March 1954): that the Harvard Law School gave him "a deep understanding of the importance of law and justice in a democratic society."

7. Ibid., Box 4, F. 1: Correspondence 1949–50, Nicholson to Stone, 24 September 1949.

8. Ibid., F.: Personal 1948–49, Diebold to Stone, 13 October 1949.

9. Ibid., F. 1: Correspondence 1949–50, Stone to Dickey, 28 October 1949.

10. Ibid., Stone to McClure, 15 February 1950; Stone to Neuberger, 20 February 1950.

11. Ibid., Box I, F.: Misc. 1933–, Stone to his family in Nashua, 15 July 1950. He proudly gave them details of the office and his activities.

12. Ibid., Box 4, F. 1: Correspondence 1949–50, Schwartz to Stone, 17 May 1950. Hopkins had been President Roosevelt's right-hand man.

13. Ibid., Schwartz to Stone, 29 June 1950.

14. Ibid., Box 12, F. 13, Stone to Dana Adams Schmidt, 17 February 1950.

15. See pp. 59ff. See also Bödecker 1993 and the literature cited in chapter 2, note 34.

16. DCSS, Box K, F. P, Stone to Praeger, 7 July 1966.

17. Ibid., Box 5, F. 12: Correspondence 1952, A.V. Boerner's memo of a conversation with the McCarthyite American journalist Westbrook Pegler, 2 February 1950. See also pp. 74ff.

18. See ibid., Dr "Hicog II," F.: Expenses—Representation; ibid., F.: Expenses—Household, Stone to Wolfe, 25 August 1950.

19. Ibid., Box I, F.: Misc. 1933–, Stone to his family in Nashua, 31 May 1950; ibid., Stone to his family in Nashua, 15 July 1950. Among his visitors were Hans-Bernd Gisevius, "the former Gestapo fellow who, at the risk of life, had worked throughout the war with Allen Dulles." Later that day, Otto Veit, who had meanwhile become president of the Hessian Reserve Bank, came to see him. There followed a quick trip to Berlin where he lunched with Ernst Reuter, "the remarkable Oberbuergermeister," and General Maxwell Taylor, the U.S. military commander. Back in Frankfurt, he talked to Drew Middleton and Robert Bowie, the HICOG general counsel. On 22 March Sternberger and his wife joined the Stones for dinner with four other guests. At the table there was much talk "about the internal situation in Western Germany, the slow progress of democratization, the necessity of helping the good and positive forces against the more traditional chaps in power." Next day Stone met with Wes Gallagher, the head of the local Associated Press office, and Eugen Kogon. On Saturday, 25 March, he "worked all day at [the] office, had visits from 2 university rectors, 3 politicians, some of our editors, two people seeking money to help refugess." In the evening he had "a group of Marburg University students for dinner . . . to tell us what is happening among students"—not all of which was encouraging. He went to Bad

Nauheim and had dinner at the house of his old friend Jimmy Read, soon to be under him as chief of the Education and Cultural Relations Division, where they were joined by four members of the Bavarian Ministry of Culture to discuss difficult issues of education and Catholic politics in that *Land*.

20. See K. Bird, "Deutschlands Prokonsul 1949," in Lorenz and Machill 1999, pp. 134–35f.

21. As note 11, for this and subsequent quotations.

22. See, e.g., Gillingham 1991; Berghahn 1986, pp. 132ff.

23. See pp. 145ff.

24. In fact, they were beheaded with an ax.

25. See pp. 57f. See also I. Aicher-Scholl, "Offen für neues Denken—Offen für Experimente," in Aicher-Scholl et al. 1988, pp. 13–16; R. Spitz, "Die Wurzeln der Hochschule für Gestaltung Ulm (HfG)," in Knoll 1995, pp. 137–42.

26. Hundhammer was largely responsible for blocking school reform in Bavaria promoted by the Americans after 1945. He was very conservative indeed. See, e.g., Müller 1995.

27. DCSS, box 5, F. 9, Stone to his family in Nashua, 15 July 1950.

28. As note 25.

29. See also DCSS, Dr "Personal Correspondence R–Z," F.: Fragebogen, Review by Stone of Ernst von Salomon's *Der Fragebogen* in the *New York Times Book Review*, 2 January 1955, with a sharp attack on this book.

30. Ibid., box 5, F. 12: Correspondence 1952, Stone to Sulzberger, 27 March 1952.

31. Ibid., Dr "Hicog III," F.: Hicog Budget 1953, Highlight Statement, pp. 75ff., for this and subsequent quotations.

32. On the MSA, see also pp. 60 and 220 ff. See also Hixson 1997.

33. On *Amerika-Häuser*, see also the chapter "America Houses in Germany," in Hicog, ed., *Tenth Quarterly Report on Germany, 1 January–31 March 1952* (DCSS, Dr "World War II," F.: Public Affairs). See also Hein-Kremer 1996; on exchanges, see Schmidt 1999.

34. DCSS, box 5, F. 12, Correspondence 1952, Stone to Taylor, 21 January 1952. On the CFR, see also Wala 1994.

35. Gimbel 1976, and the literature cited in chapter 2, note 81.

36. DCSS, Dr "Hicog IV," F.: Correspondence Stone (New York–U.S.), Stone to Vernon, 21 August 1950.

37. Ibid., Dr "Speeches," F.: SS NYTimes—WQXR Hall Speech, 1952, Stone's notes, n.d.

38. Ibid., Box 12, F. 13: Correspondence 1949–50, Stone to Dozier (*Time-Life*), 15 February 1950: If Dozier read McCloy's speeches in the United States or Stuttgart, "you will have a pretty good idea what I am thinking." See also Fischer and Fischer 1994.

39. See p. 65.

40. DCSS, Box 11, Binder 3, Correspondence 1984–85, McCloy to Truman, 10 September 1950.

41. Ibid., Box 12, F. *13*, Correspondence 1949–50, Schwartz to Stone, 5 October 1950; Dr. "HICOG IV" F.: History, Schwartz to Stone, 9 November 1950.

42. Ibid., F.: Correspondence Stone (New York–U.S.), Stone to Nicholson, 6 November 1950.

43. As note 20.

44. DCSS, Dr "Hicog IV," F.: Correspondence Stone (New York–U.S.), Stone to Byroade, 21 February 1951.

45. Ibid., Stone to Sulzberger, 5 February 1951.

46. Ibid., Dr "Hicog III," F.: Hicog Budget 1953, OPA accounts and budget, n.d.

47. Ibid., Dr "World War II," F.: Public Affairs, E. J. Cramer, "Die Neue Zeitung" in A.V. Boerner, ed., *Semi-Annual Evalutation Report on the Public Affairs Program in Germany*, 1 December 1951–31 May 1952, n.d. On *Neue Zeitung*, see also my chapter 2, note 25.

48. DCSS, Binder: Personal File 1977, Stone to Eva Wallenberg, 17 April 1977. See also ibid., Dr "Old Files," F.: Stone Europe March–May 1958, Stone to McCloy, 4 February 1958, in which he mentioned that, with the Berlin and Frankfurt editions, the paper's circulation was 1.75 million before the 1948 Currency Reform, declining to 200,000 to 250,000 per day thereafter.

49. Ibid., Box F, F.: Letters 1949–53, McCloy to Wallenberg, 28 June 1949.

50. As note 31.

51. Ibid., Dr "World War II," OPA report "Facts about the West German Press" [1952].

52. Ibid., Box 6, F. 3, Kaghan's Memo on "Editorial Bias," 19 January 1951.

53. See pp. 33f.

54. DCSS, Binder: Personal File 1978–79, Kaghan Report on GARIOA Press Fund, 7 November 1951. Subsequent quotations in text are from the Kaghan Report.

55. Ibid., Box I, F.: Misc. 1933–, Stone to his family in Nashua, 31 May 1951.

56. As note 54, also for this and subsequent quotations.

57. See pp. 220ff.

58. Apparent reference to the *Reptilienfond* that Bismarck had established to influence the press after the founding of the German Empire.

59. See the list in appendix I.

60. DCSS, Dr "World War II," F.: Frankfurter Rundschau, Memorandum concerning the "Extension of Credit and Acquisition of Participation (at nominal value of shares) in the Frankfurter Rundschau," n.d.

61. Ibid., Kellermann to Stone, 10 April 1953; Gerold to Stone, 23 March 1953. Kellermann was by then public affairs advisor in the Bureau of German Affairs at the State Department. See also his general account: Kellermann 1978.

62. DCSS, Dr "Hicog II," F.: Correspondence Stone (German), Rudert and Gerold to Stone, 31 March 1952; Stone to Rudert and Gerold, 4 April 1952.

63. *Echo der Woche* had been established with covert HICOG money by the Schopen-Verlag after long negotiations with members of Stone's staff. Schopen had then hired Hans Habe, who was a refugee from Nazism with an American passport, as the paper's editor. Stone had had earlier dealings with Habe when the latter had been responsible for *Die Neue Zeitung*, but they did not get on too well. While HICOG was not involved in the selection of the editors, the money issue drew the Americans in so deeply that they wanted to get out, not least because Stone thought the selection of Habe as editor in chief had been a mistake. When he met Habe "in February or March 1952," he told him that HICOG had no desire "to assume the role of a policy-issuing or policy-controlling agency," but "that, as an American citizen, he [Habe] ought to know by himself what kind of line to take." Two months later HICOG decided "to stop the publishing adventure [!] altogether." If the experience with Habe had taught Stone a lesson about the vagaries of covert funding of newspapers by HICOG, there was still the danger of a leak after the whole project had been buried. Stone's hope had been that Habe would keep quiet. After all, "he had sworn at that time that he would treat the whole deal with the publisher Schopen as a highly secret matter." But Habe did not abide by this agreement. Ibid., Dr "World War II," F.: Hans Habe, N.N. to Stone, 22 November 1954. See also the other documents in this folder and the various books Habe published. See also Gienow-Hecht 1999 on Habe's work in connection with *Die Neue Zeitung*.

64. As note 54.

65. DCSS, Dr "Hicog IV," F.: Correspondence Stone (New York–U.S.A.), Stone to Perry, 27 December 1951.

66. Ibid., Box 5, F. 12, Correspondence 1952, Stone to Lewis, 2 April 1952.

67. Ibid., Stone to Kellermann, 30 June 1952. In a further letter of 16 July, Stone thanked Kellermann for an excellent working relationship and the support the latter had given him from his office in the State Department.

68. Ibid., Box 5, F.: 12, Correspondence 1952, Warburg to Stone, 1 May 1952.

69. He wrote: "Dear Shep: You know it is impossible for me to write an ordinary letter of commendation on your leaving—you are going out with me. But ever since the day you took me for lunch (a very good lunch, by the way, at Sardi's) I have been inspired by your imagination in regard to Germany. If there is anything that we have been able to accomplish here in catching the minds of the German people, it has been due mostly to your imagination and contacts. Everybody knows this and I want you to know that I know it. Your loyalty and devotion to me in my personal interests have been most warming and these have been very fine things to have, but your real contribution has been your imagination and your enthusiasm which have always picked me up when I began to lag a bit. I owe so much to you that I cannot add up the total." Ibid., Box L, F.: Hicog 1952–53, McCloy to Stone (copy), 19 July 1952. See also the transcript of Stone's interviews

with McCloy in Box 3, F. 4, Interview on 14 February 1984: "You and Bob Bowie had a lot of influence on me."

70. Ibid., Dr "Hicog IV," F.: W. Degler, Clipping from *Erie Daily Times* (1952). See also Pegler's other articles, ibid. More generally, see also, e.g., Caute 1978.

71. DCSS, Dr "Old Chrons.," F.: Stone Personal, Dulles's Circular No. 889, 19 February 1953.

72. Ibid., Conant to Secretary of State, 2 March 1953.

73. Ibid., Dr "Hicog II," F.: Memoirs, Stone to Cohn, 5 March 1953.

74. Ibid., Box 5, F. 1, McCloy to Eisenhower, 26 May 1953. See also ibid., Stone to McCloy, 25 May 1953, discussing "a few matters [for McCloy's meeting] with the President that are causing you and many thoughtful people deep concern."

75. *Boston Herald*, 16 June 1953, p. 14.

76. *New York Times*, 26 June 1953, p. 2; DCSS, Box 5, F. 1, Stone to McCloy, 29 May 1953.

77. DCSS, Dr "Hicog II," F.: Senator McCarthy, Stone to Boerner, 31 March 1954.

78. As late as November 1955, he felt obliged to submit a sworn statement to the County of New York in which he refuted a number of allegations that had been reported to him, namely, that he had been "a member of a Communist unit at The New York Times," that he had been "associated, in a subversive way, with Cedric Belfrage, a British subject who was deported from the United States in the summer of 1955," that "pro-Communist books were prevalent in the America Houses operated by Hicog," and a number of other charges. If these charges, which included suspicions against his wife, had been a minor matter, he would not have seen the need to submit thirty-nine pages of refutations and details about his career. Clearly, McCarthyism was a vicious movement. Ibid., Dr "Hicog I," F.: Stone's Statement, "Sworn Statement" by Stone, 28 November 1955.

79. Ibid., Box 6, F. 5, Stone to Sulzberger, 24 September 1951; Sulzberger to Stone, 10 October 1951.

CHAPTER 4

MASS SOCIETY AND THE THREAT OF TOTALITARIANISM

1. The Stone Papers contain quite a large collection of these surveys on a variety of topics. There is no space to evaluate this material here, which should be complemented by the results of emergent West German public opinion polling institutes, most notable the one at Allensbach established by the Noelle-Neumanns. For a digest, see Merritt and Merritt 1980. Overall, the tradition must be seen in the context of the influence that the social sciences enjoyed in American scholarship and politics in these years, a theme that runs through subsequent chapters and also affected the grant-giving priorities of the large foundations. It also

persuaded Stone to try to measure the success of the Ford Foundation's cultural efforts in Europe. See my discussion on p. xi.

2. See also pp. 145ff.

3. See pp. 74ff and 126ff.

4. See, e.g., Sheehan 1989.

5. On "1848" in different European countries, see, e.g., Dowe et al. 2001.

6. See, e.g., T. S. Hamerow, "The Origins of Mass Politics in Germany," in Geiss and Wendt 1973, pp. 105–20.

7. See, e.g., Jones and Retallack 1992.

8. Tocqueville 1945. This is the Henry Reeve Text as revised by Francis Bowen and then further corrected and edited by Philips Bradley. It is significant that many of the fathers of the American Constitution initially conceived of the new political order in terms of classical republicanism based on the principle of representation by elites. The "democratic-populist" and egalitarian element that was also enshrined in the document began to assert itself more strongly in the age of Jackson. See also Jardin 1988.

9. Tocqueville 1945, 2:48–61, for this and subsequent quotations.

10. Pells 1997, p. 97. See also, e.g., D. Strauss 1978.

11. See, e.g., Herman 1997.

12. Le Bon 1899; Barrows 1981.

13. Le Bon [1899] 1910, pp. 13ff., for this and subsequent quotations.

14. Barrows 1981.

15. See, e.g., Wehler 1985.

16. Quoted in Tannenbaum 1976, p. 349.

17. Quoted ibid., p. 348.

18. Tirpitz to Admiral von Stosch, 31 December 1897, in Tirpitz 1921, p. 32.

19. Quoted in Wehler 1995, p. 832.

20. Quoted in Feldman 1966, p. 136.

21. See, e.g., Barclay and Glaser-Schmidt 1997.

22. Quoted in Pommerin 1986, p. 207. See also note 10.

23. See, e.g., Kugler 1987; Fridenson 1972; Bronner 1989.

24. Strasser 1989. To be sure, this modernity was not shared by all upper-class Americans either who observed the "masses" with a good deal of fear and suspicion. See, e.g., Henry Lee Higginson's dictum while fund raising for Harvard: "Educate and save ourselves and our families and our money from the mobs." Quoted in R. Lenman, "From 'Brown Sauce' to 'Plain Air,' " in Forster-Hahn 1996, p. 55.

25. Quoted in Kugler 1987, pp. 315–16.

26. See, e.g., Saunders 1996.

27. See, e.g., Costigliola 1984.

28. See Maase 1997; Gassert 1997, with a good coverage of discourses in the Weimar Republic.

29. Ortega y Gasset [1932] 1969, for this and subsequent quotations.

30. Quoted in E. Nolte, "Die 'herrschenden Klassen' und der Faschismus in Italien," in Schieder 1976, p. 192.

31. On the Cold War, see, e.g., Gaddis 1987.

32. Orwell 1938, 1945.

33. Friedrich and Brzezinski 1956.

34. Arendt 1951. For the totalitarianism debate more broadly, see Gleason 1995.

35. See, e.g. Schapiro 1972.

36. Berghahn 1986, p. 239.

37. H. Arendt, "The Threat of Conformism," in Kohn 1994, pp. 426–27.

38. See, e.g., Muller 1987. See also Canetti 1960.

39. See Judt 1992. See also Kuisel 1993.

40. See p. 128. See also Reynolds 1988.

41. DCSS, Box L, F.: CCF June 1960 Conference, I. Kristol, "High, Low, and Modern" (June 1960).

42. See, e.g., Bender 1987.

43. See, e.g., Krohn 1987. Horkheimer and Adorno's *Dialektik der Aufklärung* first appeared in New York in 1944 under the copyright of the Social Studies Association. The first European version was published in 1947 by Quinto in Amsterdam and republished in Frankfurt in 1981. This essay was a sharp indictment of the culture industry and a scathing verdict on the consumers of mass entertainment. Following the lead by Brooks and others, debates on the meaning and future of American culture had continued among East Coast intellectuals in the 1920s, partly in response to criticisms that they knew their counterparts in Europe were making. But it took the outbreak of the economic depression and the appearance of refugees from fascism to give it greater depth.

44. On Weber's positions, see Mommsen 1984.

45. Wreszin 1994, p. 28.

46. Quoted in ibid., p. 325.

47. Ibid., p. XVII.

48. Ibid., 37.

49. Quoted in ibid., p. 39.

50. Quoted in ibid., p. 40.

51. Ibid., p. 41.

52. Quoted in ibid., p. 82.

53. Ibid., p. 45.

54. Ibid., p. 239.

55. Ibid., p. 140.

56. Pells 1984, pp. 174ff.

57. D. Macdonald, "A Theory of Mass Culture," *Diogenes*, Summer 1953, pp. 1–17, for this and subsequent quotations.

58. Wreszin 1994, p. 293.

59. Ibid., p. 324.

60. Quoted in ibid., p. 292.

61. Ibid., pp. 254–55.

62. See pp. 96ff. See also Fasman 1997, p. 4, referring to their marked elitism.

63. Wreszin 1994, p. 346. See also Fasman 1997, p. 101, quoting Macdonald's critique of the Hollywood spectacle *Ben Hur*: "Bloody in every way—bloody, bloody, and bloody boring."

64. Wreszin 1994, p. 113.

65. Ibid., p. 362.

66. Ibid., p. 353.

67. Bell 1960. See also Waxman 1968.

68. Wreszin 1994, p. 325. See also my discussion on pp. 108f.

69. See, e.g., May 1989; Gans [1974] 1999.

70. Riesman, Glazer, and Denney 1950. See also Whyte 1956; Packard 1957.

71. Bell 1960, for this and subsequent quotations.

72. See also Pells 1997, p. 104, citing the British writer Stephen Spender who, in a 1948 article in the *New York Times Magazine*, had argued that the task in the "battle for the mind of Europe" was to help the Europeans "understand the best in American civilization." Spender became deeply involved in this battle as coeditor of *Encounter* until the journal became embroiled in the scandal over covert CIA funding in 1966 and he withdrew in protest. See pp. 85ff. *Encounter*, like other intellectual journals such as *Der Monat*, *Preuves*, and *Tempo Presente* supported by the Congress for Cultural Freedom (CCF) (see pp. 140ff.), over the years carried many articles portraying American "civilization" in a positive light. On the Ford Foundation's involvement in the campaign, see my discussion on pp. 214ff.

CHAPTER 5
WESTERN INTELLECTUALS AND THE COLD CULTURE WARS OF THE
CONGRESS FOR CULTURAL FREEDOM (CCF)

1. DCSS, Box L, F.: CCF June 1960 Conference, E. Shils, "The Quality of Life in Modern Society" (June 1960), for this and subsequent quotations.

2. B. Rosenberg, "Mass Culture Revisited," in Rosenberg and White 1971, p. 7.

3. E. Shils, "Mass Society and Its Culture," *Daedalus*, Spring 1960, pp. 288–314. The article appeared in a special issue on mass culture and mass media. It is significant that this debate reached its peak at the same time that larger debates about the future viability and dynamism of American capitalism, technocratic government, and politics swept John F. Kennedy and his "youthful" team into power. See also my discussion on pp. 229. The Ford Foundation also became involved in this debate and effort at revitalization; see pp. 239.

4. Rosenberg and White 1971, p. 9.

5. DCSS, Box L, F.: CCF June 1960 Conference, I. Kristol, "High, Low, and Modern" (June 1960), for this and subsequent quotations.

6. See, e.g., Corbin-Schuffels 1996. Among his various books, see Sperber 1982.

7. DCSS, Box L, F.: CCF June 1960 Conference, M. Sperber, "Repudiated Past—Disinherited Present" (June 1960), for this and subsequent quotations.

8. The original reads "back" not "bank." Sperber's fundamental pessimism fits neatly into a debate between the "Continental-European" and "Anglo-Saxon" intellectuals that rent the IACF asunder and that is examined in greater detail on pp. 267ff.

9. DCSS, Box L, F.: CCF June 1960 Conference, R. Hoggart, "The Quality of Cultural Life in Mass Society" (June 1960), for this and subsequent quotations.

10. Coleman 1989; Grémion 1995. Hochgeschwender 1998 focuses on the German CCF, but also contains a sophisticated analysis of the association as a whole. See also Lasch 1969; Saunders 2000.

11. Caute 1973. See also Koestler and Crossman 1950.

12. Orwell 1938, 1945, 1949.

13. See, e.g., Gilbert 1972. See also my chapter 4, note 42.

14. See, e.g., Ryan 1995; Phelps 1997.

15. Quoted in Coleman 1989, p. 161.

16. Neumann 1942.

17. Borkenau 1940.

18. Other influential analysts of the dictatorships that had emerged in Europe were the German Jewish refugees Fraenkel [1941] 1969 and Neumann 1942.

19. Sperber 1982, pp. 52ff.; H. Gruber, "Willi Münzenberg's German Propaganda Empire," *Journal of Modern History* 38 (1966): 278–97; Lottman 1991, pp. 23, 56, 103.

20. Lottman 1991, p. 2.

21. See, e.g., Judt 1992.

22. Ibid., p. 47.

23. Henke and Woller 1991, esp. pp. 192ff.

24. Judt 1992, p. 151.

25. Wilkinson 1981, pp. 27ff.; Ardagh 1970.

26. Quoted in Judt 1992, p. 122. See also Marthy 1991.

27. Ardagh 1970, p. 547.

28. See Todd 1997; Judt 1998, pp. 87ff.; Wilkinson 1981, pp. 80ff.

29. Judt 1992, p. 114.

30. Laqueur 1970, p. 302; Karnow 1996.

31. Quoted in Gleason 1995, p. 60.

32. See, e.g., Reynolds 1988.

33. See, e.g., Barker 1984; Watt 1984. See also pp. 185f for my comments on the implications of the Suez Crisis.

34. Roberts 1996.

35. See, e.g., Kogan 1983.

36. D. Forgass, "The Italian Communist Party and Culture," in Baranski and Lumley 1990, p. 100.

37. Coleman 1989, pp. 142ff.

38. As note 36, p. 98.

39. Wilkinson 1981, pp. 246ff.

40. See also Marelli 1989.

41. See, e.g., Broszat 1987.

42. See, e.g., Naimark 1995.

43. See note 10.

44. See, e.g., Hermand 1989.

45. See p. 80.

46. See F. Meyer-Gosau, "Die Ingenieure der menschlichen Seele," *Text und Kritik* (October 1990), pp. 1–9.

47. Coleman 1989, p. 4. See also Saunders 2000, pp. 17ff.

48. See, e.g., Loth 1988.

49. See, e.g., Koestler 1941. Also see note 12.

50. Ignatieff 1998, p. 228. See also my discussion on pp. 94f.

51. See pp. 94f; also Anderson 1998; Judt 1998, pp. 137ff.

52. Lottman 1991, p. 15.

53. See pp. 94f.

54. Coleman 1989, p. 7. See also Saunders 2000, pp. 66ff.

55. See pp. 189ff.

56. Coleman 1989, p. 15.

57. Ibid., pp. 46ff.; Grémion 1995, p. 22.

58. See, e.g., Grémion 1995, pp. 26ff. See also Saunders 2000, pp. 73ff.

59. People whose names are listed in brackets were unable to come to Berlin.

60. See W. von Eckardt, "Congress for Cultural Freedom," *Hicog Information Bulletin*, September 1950, pp. 18–23.

61. Coleman 1989, p. 37. See also Pells 1984, pp. 340ff.

62. See, e.g., Schrecker 1998. See also my discussion on pp. 74.

63. See pp. 221ff.

64. As Frank Sutton learned from Josselson many years later, Koestler had been "eased out." See FFA, Report 002784, Sutton to Bundy, 21 September 1967.

65. See chapter 6, and chapter 8, pp. 214ff., where the question of the success or failure of this particular approach is being raised. Josselson may be seen to have acted as a bridge between the "Anglo-Saxon" and the Continental European communities of intellectuals and academics. But it also seems that fundamental philosophical differences concerning the role of intellectuals and the nature of cultural activity continued under the surface, covered up largely by the fact that the CCF intellectuals found themselves in the same boat in their fight against their opponents on the right and left and that the funds came from the United States, whether private or public. These larger questions will be taken up in chapter 10. See also Saunders 2000, pp. 201ff.

66. See p. 77.

67. Born in 1903 and a cousin of the author of *Lolita*, Nabokov grew up in St. Petersburg and made a name for himself as a composer of pieces that he wrote for the Ballets Russes de Monte Carlo and for Diaghilev. In 1946–48 he worked in OMGUS's Information Control Division, helping with the revival of musical life in occupied Germany. In 1959 Oskar Fritz Schuh directed the world premiere of his opera *Rasputin* in Cologne. See his memoirs (1973). For his activities in the CCF and as a cultural organizer in Berlin in the 1960s, see my discussion on pp. 234f. See also Saunders 2000, pp. 10, 12f.

68. See Grémion 1995, p. 102. See also Saunders 2000, pp. 115ff.

69. Coleman 1989, p. 56. See also my discussion on pp. 92ff.

70. Kuisel 1993, p. 28.

71. Coleman 1989, p. 56.

72. Ibid.

73. Grémion 1995, p. 141.

74. Coleman 1989, p. 140.

75. Grémion 1995, p. 137.

76. Ibid., pp. 107ff. See also my comments on p. 138, and the literature listed there.

77. Coleman 1995, pp. 104ff. On the Fairfield Foundation, see also my comments on p. 222. See also Saunders 2000, pp. 127, 136ff., 219ff.

78. Grémion 1995, pp. 125ff.

79. Ibid., pp. 153ff.

80. See pp. 222ff..

81. See pp. 103ff.

82. See p. 255.

83. See also pp. 217ff. on the extension of the network to Third World countries and pp. 197f. on the later fate of all these journals. See also Saunders 2000, pp. 215ff.

84. P. Grémion, "Preuves dans le Paris de Guerre Froide" (unpublished manuscript, 1984). See also on pp. 140f my discussion of tensions concerning the orientation of the journal, which in turn related to the conflicts between "Continental European" and "Anglo-Saxon" intellectuals within the CCF/IACF.

85. Coleman 1989, pp. 53–54., 83ff. See also my discussion on pp. 119f and Saunders 2000, p. 101.

86. Grémion 1995, pp. 145ff.

87. Quoted in Coleman 1989, p. 91.

88. Ibid., pp. 83ff.

89. Nenning 1998.

90. Coleman 1989, p. 91.

91. See p. 216. See also Saunders 2000, pp. 27ff.

92. P. Coleman 1989, pp. 93–94.

93. DCSS, Dr "World War II," F.: Stone Washington, Buttles to Lasky, 9 July 1952; Lasky to Buttles, 18 July 1952.

CHAPTER 6
INTERNATIONALIZING THE FORD FOUNDATION

1. Ford Foundation, Financial Statement, 31 December 1951 (n.p., 1952). See also McCarthy 1987; F. X. Sutton, "The Ford Foundation and Europe: Ambitions and Ambivalences," in Gemelli 1998, pp. 21–66.

2. FFA, Box 9, Report of the Trustees, 27 September 1950, p. 4.

3. See the literature cited in chapter 2, note 81.

4. See Appendix II.

5. DCSS, Box 8, Loose Materials, Ford Foundation, "Ten-Year Summary, 1951–1960," June 1960.

6. See p. 143

7. Ford Foundation, Financial Statement, 31 December 1951, n.p. [1952].

8. See Tent 1988.

9. Ford Foundation, *Annual Report for 1951*, 31 December 1951, p. 5.

10. See Bissell 1996. Sutton in Gremelli 1998, p. 23, emphasizes Hoffman's "universalistic approach to international affairs" and "that he was not an eager Cold Warrior, ready to focus on Europe as a critical arena in the struggle against Communism." See also my discussion on pp. 74ff.

11. DCSS, Dr "Old Chrons.," F.: Milton Katz, Katz to Stone, 8 July 1952.

12. Ibid., Dr "Personal Files," F.: Conditions of Peace, "Creating the Conditions of Peace," 3 March 1952, also for the following.

13. Just as he was missed by others at OPA. See ibid., Dr "World War II," F.: Hicog Current, Kimbler to Stone, 30 July 1952.

14. Ibid., Ferry to Stone, 24 June 1952.

15. Ibid., Dr "Old Chrons.," F.: Milton Katz, Katz to Stone, 8 July 1952.

16. Ibid., Dr "Personal Files," F.: Conditions of Peace, Quinn to Stone, 11 August 1952, with the draft attached. The final version that the trustees apparently considered in July 1952 was much briefer, especially in explaining the background to and the objectives of the project. It seems that Katz sent the draft in order to give Stone a fuller picture.

17. Ibid., Binder: Personal Files 1982, Hoffman to Eisenhower, 21 August 1952.

18. DCSS, Box 4, Loose Materials, Stone's Diary, entry for 2 September 1952.

19. See, e.g., Immerman 1990. See also my chapter 7, note 28, and pp. 216ff.

20. DCSS, Box 4, Loose Materials, Stone's Diary, entry for 10 September 1952.

21. Ibid., Box 4, F. 9, W. Park Armstrong Jr. to U.S. Secretary of State, 6 October 1952. This was a briefing document for a meeting between Acheson and McCloy.

22. Ibid., Loose Materials, Stone's Diary, entry for 22 September 1952. Stone added that Clark "was interested in my report that what this country needs is a statement of our principles and philosophy in 125 pages."

23. Ibid., Dr "Correspondence R–Z," F.: Brookings Seminar, Stone's Report to Katz on the Seminar, 15 September 1952.

24. Ibid., Box L, F.: Hicog 1952–53, Stone to Whitman, 14 October 1952.

25. Ibid., Dr "Old Chrons.," F.: Milton Katz, Stone to Hoffman and Katz, 12 November 1952.

26. Stone wrote that they had talked to: "*Washington*—Acheson, Nitze, Bruce, Jessup and other members of the State Department. Sir Oliver Franks [British ambassador]; the Indian ambassador; Leo Pasvolsky; CIA, Pentagon, Public Affairs officials; Clarence Pickett; many Point IV people. *New York*—Representatives at the U.N.—Sir Richard Casey, Selwyn Lloyd, Gladwyn Jebb, David Owen; Indian, Burmese and Pakistan[i] representatives; Lester Pearson. At Columbia—Phil Mosely, Robinson, Bergson, Grayson Kirk, Fox, Franz Neumann, Schuyler Williams. Also Grenville Clark, Chuck Spofford, Hugh Moore; Carnegie, Rockefeller and New York Times people. At Princeton—Ed Earle, Robert Oppenheimer, Jacob Viner, Harold Sprout and others. *Chicago*—Hans Morgenthau, Laird Bell, Jim Douglas and other Political Science people from the University."

27. Ibid., Dr "Personal Files," F.: National Interest, Stone to Katz, 25 November 1952. Toward the end of their collaboration on the project McCloy once remarked that Stone acted as a "sort of 'clearing house' " for him. Ibid., Box 5, F. 1, McCloy to Riemschneider, 13 December 1954.

28. DCSS, Dr "Personal Files," F.: History—Conditions of Peace, McCloy to Hoffman and Katz, 18 December 1952.

29. Ibid. Other ideas contained in the report related to a strengthening of the United Nations and improvements of procedures by which Washington and private groups participated in world affairs at both national and local elite level.

30. Ibid., Dr "Old Chrons.," F.: Milton Katz, Katz to McCloy, 23 December 1952.

31. Ibid., Box L, F.: Hicog 1952–53, Stone to Parker, 27 January 1953.

32. No names were suggested for the other consultants: a German, a Frenchman, an "East European or Russian exile," and an Indian.

33. DCSS, Dr "Personal Files," F.: National Interest, McCloy and Stone to Hoffman and Katz, 18 January 1953.

34. Ibid., F.: Conditions of Peace, Quigley to Stone, 21 January 1953.

35. Ibid., Stone to Quigley, 23 January 1953.

36. Ibid., F.: Personal Correspondence R–Z, May (Ford Foundation) to Katz, 8 July 1953, referring to the meeting on 23 February.

37. Ibid.

38. Ibid., N.N. [McCloy?] to George F. Kennan (State Department), 1 May 1953.

39. Ibid., CFR "Study Group on United States—Soviet Relations" meeting, 6 May 1953. The following group members attended: McCloy (chair), Henry L. Roberts (research secretary), John Blumgart (rapporteur), Frank Altschul (investment banker), Robert Amory (CIA), Robert Bowie (State Department), McGeorge Bundy (Harvard), Merle Fainsod (Harvard), George S. Franklin Jr. (CFR), Howard Johnson (Ford Foundation), Devereux C. Josephs (business executive), J. Rob-

ert Oppenheimer (Institute for Advanced Study, Princeton), Dean Rusk (president, Rockefeller Foundation), Shepard Stone, Henry M. Wriston (president, Brown University). Absent: Hamilton Fish Armstrong (*Foreign Affairs*), Allen W. Dulles (CIA), William T. R. Fox (Columbia), Philip Mosely (Columbia), Charles Spofford (lawyer), Jacob Viner (Princeton).

40. Ibid., N.N. [McCloy?] to Kennan, 1 May 1953. See also Kennan 1972.

41. See p. 162.

42. DCSS, Dr "Old Chrons.," F.: Milton Katz, Stone to Katz, 28 July 1953.

43. Ibid., Box 8, Loose Materials, Ten-Year Summary of Ford Foundation Giving 1951–60 (presented at the meeting of board of trustees in June 1960), n.d.

44. See pp. 178ff.

45. DCSS, Box 9, Loose Materials, "A Review of Progress of the Ford Foundation, January 1951–October 1952," n.d., p. 7.

46. As note 43.

47. See pp. 94ff.

48. See pp. 67ff.

49. FFA, Gaither Papers, Box 1, F. 3, Speier to Gaither, 5 May 1951.

50. DCSS, Dr "Old Chrons.," F.: European Program Paper, Katz to Hoffman et al., 20 March 1952, for this and subsequent quotations.

51. See pp. 172ff.

52. The CED was founded during World War II to provide ideas on the postwar reconstruction of the world economy and had influential businessmen, academics, and policy planners. See, e.g., Collins 1983.

53. The list of names is indicative of the kind of transatlantic networks that Stone would later work with as head of the foundation's international affairs program. See pp. 178ff. See also Leonard 1999.

54. On Maritain, see Schall 1998. On the Friedrich brothers, see Berghahn and Friedrich 1993. Hallstein, then a law professor at Frankfurt University, was to become *Staatssekretär* under Chancellor Konrad Adenauer and later president of the European Commission in Brussels.

55. See the documents in DCSS, Box 5, F. 1.

56. Ibid., Box 12, F. 21, Horkheimer to Stone, 22 June 1953. See also chapter 3, note 30. The Frankfurt Institute was at first supported by HICOG and later by the Ford Foundation. See DCSS, Box 4, F.: Frankfurt 1953, Horkheimer to Stone, 17 September 1953. On Stone's later disappointment during the years of student radicalism, see my p. 273.

57. Ibid., Box 4, F. 26, Aicher-Scholl to Stone, 13 October 1953. See also pp. 57f. for my discussion Stone's first contacts with her while he was still with HICOG.

58. See also p. 57.

59. DCSS, Box 4, F. 26, Aicher-Scholl to Stone, 23 October 1953. The book did appear in English as I. Scholl, *The White Rose* (Middletown, Conn., 1983).

60. DCSS, Box 9, Gaither to Officers and Division Heads, 26 March 1953.

61. Ibid., President's Report to the Trustees [May 1953].

62. Ibid., "A General View of Area One" [May 1953].

63. Ibid., President's Report to the Trustees [June 1953].

64. FFA, Gaither Office Files, Box 1, F. 3, Gaither's memo of his conference with Stone, 8 July 1953.

65. DCSS, Dr "World War II," F.: Reuter, Stone to Reuter, 12 August 1953.

66. Ibid., Box 4, F. 13, Hassolt's Report, 14 September 1953, for this and subsequent quotations.

67. It is interesting that he should refer to this concept, which was coined by Harold Lasswell in World War II to describe the dictatorships of the period.

68. DCSS, Dr "Overseas Trips," F.: Europe (general correspondence) 19.5.–14.6.1953, Wyzanski to Gaither, 8 September 1953, for this and subsequent quotations. See also Saunders 2000, p. 140.

69. See pp. 172ff.

70. DCSS, Dr "Personal Files," F.: Conditions of Peace, Memo by Stone [?] on Conditions of Peace Project, 15 September 1953.

71. Ibid., Box 4, F. 13, Stone to McCloy, 14 September 1953.

72. Ibid., Stone's Notes Relating to the Trip, October 1953.

73. Ibid. See also p. 247 and Saunders 2000, pp. 64–65.

74. DCSS, Box 4, F. 13, Stone's Notes Relating to the Trip, October 1953, for this and subsequent quotations; also see ibid., Dr "Personal Correspondence," F.: Perspectives, Excerpt from Letter by Bondy to Stone [?] (Copy), 27 October 1953.

75. The last sentence is an interesting reflection of the ubiquity of totalitarianism theory. See pp. 92. Stone's summary of his conversation with Bondy is further evidence of why, on his return and later, he pressed for the establishment of a European program to promote positive images of America in Western Europe. See pp. 164.

76. DCSS, Box 4, F. 13, Stone's Notes Relating to the Trip, October 1953. See also ibid., Box F, F.: Letters 1949–53, Stone to Hasenclever, 18 November 1953. See pp. 28.

77. See also DCSS, Dr "Hicog II," F.: Die Neue Zeitung, Wallenberg to Stone, n.d.

78. Ibid., Dr "Old Chrons.," F.: European Program Paper (first drafts), Katz to Carroll, Brown, McPeak, and Price, 16 November 1953. For Katz's "Notes," see p. 156.

79. On Katz's opposition and that of other foundation officials, see also Sutton in Gremelli 1998, pp. 28–29f.

80. DCSS, Dr "Old Chrons.," F.: Old Appointment Book Sheets, Stone's appointment record for 3 November 1953, with his marginal notes about his lunchtime conversation with Laughlin.

81. Ibid., with Stone's marginal notes about his meeting with Price on 3 November at 2.30 P.M.

82. Ibid., F.: Area I (Organization), Stone to Price, 3 December 1953, for this and subsequent quotations.

83. Presumably a reference to the changes in Soviet policy after Stalin's death. See Smyser 1999, pp. 138ff.

84. DCSS., Memo by Stone (? or Johnson), 11 January 1954.

85. Ibid., Dr "Old Chrons.," F.: Area I (Organization), Stone to Price, 14 January 1954, for this and subsequent quotations.

86. Ibid., Box 9, Stone to Price, 21 April 1954.

87. Ibid., Dr "Old Chrons.," F.: Conditions of Peace 1956, Price to International Programs Staff, 28 June 1954.

88. Ibid., Johnson to McCloy, 26 August 1954.

89. Ibid., Dr "Correspondence R–Z," F.: CFR (Conditions of Peace), and ibid., F.: CFR US/USSR Study Group, with other materials relating to the transfer and discussions on Henry Roberts's manuscript. The book was published in 1956. See also DCSS, Dr "Correspondence R–Z," F.: US/USSR General, Moseley to Stone, 23 December 1955.

90. DCSS, Dr "Overseas Trips," F.: European Trip (Report), Stone's "Notes on European Trip–June 15–July 28, 1954" n.d., for this and subsequent quotations.

91. See pp. 157.

92. See pp. 153ff.

93. Compare this passage with what Stone learned from François Bondy. See p. 164.

94. See, e.g., DCSS, Dr "Correspondence R–Z," F.: Intercultural, "Estimated Budget Figures for Intercultural's Program" (1953). 95. Ibid., Starch to Howard, 7 August 1954.

96. Ibid., Dr "Overseas Trips," F.: Europe (general correspondence) 19.5.–14.6.1953, Wyzanski to Gaither, 8 September 1953. Ibid., Dr "Personal Correspondence R–Z," F.: Intercultural, Stone to Laughlin, 19 December 1953. See also note 74 above.

97. Ibid., Dr "Correspondence R–Z," F.: Intercultural, Laughlin to Wyzanski, 2 February 1954, but dictated on 26 January.

98. Ibid., Laughlin to Price, 23 February 1954, but dictated on 20 February. See also chapter 4, note 57.

99. See p. 162.

100. DCSS, Dr "Correspondence R–Z, F.: Intercultural, Laughlin to Price, 21 March 1954.

101. Ibid., Laughlin to Stone, 27 March 954.

102. Ibid., Laughlin to Price, 17 May 1954.

103. See N. Prevots 1998. See also Matthews 1976.

104. DCSS, Dr "Correspondence R–Z," F.: Intercultural, Burkhardt to Price, 6 April 1954.

105. See, e.g., Guibault 1983; Frascina 1985, with a number of relevant contributions; Haddow 1997. See also DCSS, Dr "Old Files," F.: Stone Correspondence from Europe June–September 1958, Stone to Nielsen and Gordon, 21 August 1958, in which he reports on a proposal to bring the American Opera Company to Europe. See also pp. 176f.

106. DCSS, Dr "Correspondence A–Z," F.: Intercultural, Stone to Gaither, 18 November 1954.

107. Ibid., Laughlin to Gaither, 22 December 1954.

108. Ibid., Dr "Overseas Trips," F.: European Trip (Report) 15.6.–28.7. 1954, Stone's "Notes on European Trip," 1 August 1954, p.10. See also ibid., Dr "Germany, McCloy, Stone," F.: Ford Foundation 1953–54, Stone to McCloy, 19 May 1954.

109. See pp. 215ff.

110. See pp. 85ff.

111. Published in *Réalités*, September 1953.

112. As note 77.

113. Ibid., F.: Mrs. McCloy, Stone to Ellen McCloy, 4 May 1954.

CHAPTER 7
PHILANTHROPY AND DIPLOMACY

1. Interview with F. X. Sutton, New York, 22 February 1996.

2. DCSS, Dr "Correspondence R–Z," F.: Intercultural, Laughlin to Garside, 16 August 1954.

3. Ibid., Laughlin to Price, 18 August 1954.

4. Ibid., Dr "Old Chrons.," F.: European Program, Nielsen's Memo "Gaither Conversation," n.d., for this and subsequent quotations.

5. See also pp. 133ff, Tismaneanu 1988, and *Contemporary European History*, no. 3 (1997), with a special issue on "Intellectual Life and the First Crisis of State Socialism in East Central Europe, 1953–1956."

6. Ibid., Dr "Overseas Trip," F.: European Trip (Report) 15.6.–28.7.1954, Katz to Stone, 16 September 1954.

7. Ibid., Dr "Personal Files," F.: European Program Paper (1954), Stone's "Docket Item. European Program," 5 October 1954. Ibid., also several other draft documents relating to a European program in preparation of the trustees meeting in October 1954.

8. Ibid., Dr "Countries," F.: IA—European Program (Evaluation), N.N. to Price, 14 December 1954.

9. Ibid., Box 9, Loose Materials, Stone to Price, 17 December 1954.

10. FFA, Gaither Office Files, Box 1, F. 3, Brown to Program Committee, 25 January 1955.

11. DCSS, Dr "Overseas Trips," F.: Europe (General Corr.) 1955, Stone to Kohn, 18 March 1955.

12. Ibid., Dr "Personal Files," F.: European Program Paper (1954), Draft on IA activities with corrections in Stone's hand, n.d. [1955?].

13. Ibid., Box 9, Loose Materials, Stone to Price, 29 July 1955.

14. FFA, Gaither Office Files, Box 1, F. 3, Nielsen to Gaither, 3 August 1955. Because it was in this period that Dwight Macdonald prepared his study on the foundation in which he criticized it for its dullness, it may well be that he caught the prevailing mood, if perhaps too scathingly, while he was doing his research. See Macdonald 1956. See also the correspondence between Macdonald and Chiaromonte parts of which Michael Wreszin kindly allowed me to see.

15. DCSS, Dr "Old Chrons," F.: Conditions of Peace 1956, Gaither to Foundation Officers and Staff, 24 April 1956.

16. Prior to that he had been president of the Armour Institute of Technology in Chicago for three years and president of the University of Illinois for twelve years. He had a long-standing interest in education in the United States but little international experience. He was not the board's first choice. Later Joseph Slater gave this account of Heald's appointment which is at the same time a classic reflection of how these matters were handled by the East Coast elites in those years: "He was picked on a weekend when they were tired of looking at other candidates, and someone said, how about this fellow Henry Heald down at NYU. And somebody said, well, I don't know him. Why don't you make a couple of calls? It was that kind of recruiting. And they said, he's a very decent intelligent man. Well, that sounds good. But what wasn't looked into was this question of scope, international scene and other things." By the 1960s tensions increased between the board and the president because of the latter's conservatism and caution in questions of international affairs and civil rights support. Ibid., Box 11, Envelope 1, Interview McCloy-Slater, 12 October 1984, pp. 19–20.

17. Ibid., Envelope 2, "Some Dates in FF History for Mr. McCloy," 27 August 1984.

18. F. X. Sutton, "The Ford Foundation and Europe: Ambitions and Ambivalences," in Gemelli 1998, p. 37.

19. Officers and trustees had been worried for some time that ever since 1947 the foundation's endowment consisted very largely of Ford Motor Company stock. In 1955, "the Foundation held 88 per cent of its equity in the Company," reduced to 68 per cent after Ford had gone public in 1956. Thanks to the boom of the previous years, this stock was worth over $6 billion, but what if there were a slump and Ford's values dropped sharply? The way forward seemed to be to diversify in hopes that this would make the endowment more secure and income from it hence more stable and predictable. Accordingly, the foundation disposed of close to 21 million of its 46.3 million shares and used the gains slowly to move, over the next five years, into U.S. government and government agency bonds and notes (48.6 percent), bonds and notes in other American corporations (23.5 percent), fixed and special deposits in American banks (6.0 percent), common and preferred stocks of other American corporations (10.1 percent), bonds and notes

in foreign corporations and governments (5.4 percent), with the rest going into a number of other foreign ventures. By 1962, the foundation's "net worth" (assets, less liabilities and reserves) was $2.2 billion, which included "$1.3 billion (at book value) of Ford Motor Company stock." See DCSS, Dr "Countries," F.: Amsterdam Meeting, "Finances of the Ford Foundation," issued by the Foundation's Office of Reports, 14 September 1962.

20. Ibid., Dr "Overseas Trips," F.: Europe (general correspondence) 19.5.–14.6.1956, Stone to Price, 4 June 1956.

21. Ibid., Dr "Old Chrons.," F.: Program for Europe 1956, Stone's "Program for Europe," 13 September 1956, for this and subsequent quotations.

22. See pp. 103ff and 130ff.

23. DCSS, Dr "Countries," F.: European Program Paper (1956), Price to Heald, 1 October 1956.

24. Quoted in Sutton in Gemelli 1998, p. 39.

25. DCSS, Dr "Personal Correspondence R–Z," F.: Soviet Union 1956–57, Extract from Draft Minutes of the Trustees Meeting of 7 December 1956, 29 December 1956 (for approval by 27 December).

26. Quoted in Sutton in Gemelli 1998, p. 39.

27. FFA, Oral History Project, Interview with Stone, 12 December 1972, Session I, p. 11.

28. On U.S. foreign policy in this period, see, e.g., Divine 1981. See also my discussion on p. 145ff.

29. See, e.g., Garthoff 1985. Subsequently the incoming Kennedy administration drew on McCloy and Stone as advisors on détente.

30. DCSS, Dr "Countries," F.: Amsterdam Meeting, "Finances of the Ford Foundation," issued by the Foundation's Office of Reports, 14 September 1962.

31. Sutton in Gemelli 1998, p. 39.

32. DCSS, Dr "Countries," F.: Stone Europe January–March 1957, Price to Stone, 17 January 1957.

33. Ibid., F.: IA—European Program, Stone to Price, 10 January 1957.

34. Ibid., F.: Stone Europe January–March 1957, Price to Stone, 17 January 1957.

35. Ibid., Price to Stone, 1 February 1957.

36. Ibid., Stone to Price, 21 March 1957.

37. Ibid., Box 9, Loose Materials, IA Report for the Executive Meeting, 25 September 1958.

38. FFA, Heald Office Files, Box 12, F. 150, Herter to Heald, 5 August 1958.

39. DCSS, Box 9, Loose Materials, IA Report for the Executive Meeting, 25 September 1958.

40. Ibid., Binder 1.1.73–31.7.73, Stone to David Rockefeller, 5 March 1973. Over the next couple of years some 160 Polish scholars were selected by the foundation.

41. Ibid.

42. Ibid., Dr "Old Files," F.: IA Policy Directives, Price to Heald, 25 September 1957, for this and subsequent quotations.

43. See pp. 220ff.

44. DCSS, Dr "Countries," F.: Stone—Europe/30 September–30 November 1957, Stone to Price and Nielsen, 18 October 1957; ibid., Box 2, Folder 3, Stone to Flanders, 24 March 1958.

45. Ibid., Box 9, Loose Materials, IA Submission on "Polish Program" to Board of Trustees Meeting on 13 December 1957, n.d.

46. Ibid., Box 2, F. 1, Stone to Chalasinski, 27 January 1958.

47. Ibid., Stone to van Rijckevorsel, 30 January 1958. Stone asked Rijckevorsel, the Dutch consul general in New York, to help secure the issue of a visa for Kolakowski's wife so that she could join her husband in the Netherlands and come to the United States with him. Stone added that Kolakowski "has already made a large contribution in the direction of freedom in Poland." See also ibid., Stone to Josselson, 15 January 1956. Later Kolakowski came permanently to Britain and became well known for his writings on Marxism. See, e.g., Kolakowski 1968 and 1978.

48. DCSS, Box 2, F. 3, IA "Recommended Action for Board Meeting" on Poland and Eastern Europe, 11 March 1958.

49. Ibid. See also ibid., F. 6, Nielsen to Stone, 23 September 1958, concerning the press release for an impending exploratory visit to Yugoslavia by Nielsen, Robert Goheen (Princeton), and Harlan Cleveland (Syracuse University).

50. Ibid., F. 2, Stone to Nielsen, 13 February 1958.

51. Ibid., F. 5, Stone to Nielsen, 26 June 1958.

52. Ibid., Dr "Old Files," F.: Stone's Correspondence from Europe June–September 1958, Stone to Nielsen, 27 July 1958. See also ibid., Stone to Nielsen, 23 July 1958; ibid., Box 2, F. 2, Stone to Central File, 6 March 1958.

53. Ibid., Dr "Countries," F.: Stone—Europe 28.6.–8.9.1958, Nielsen to Stone, 4 September 1958.

54. Ibid., Dr "Old Files," F.: Stone—Europe 28.6.–8.9.1958, Stone to Nielsen, 30 June 1958. See also the other materials relating to Yugoslavia in this folder. On Deakin, who had been invited to attend the celebrations of the anniversary of a major battle by Tito's forces against the Wehrmacht, see also pp. 201ff.

55. DCSS, Box 2, F. 5, Stone's list of contacts compiled for Adlai Stevenson's visit to Poland, 17 June 1958.

56. Ibid., F. 8, Stone to Central Files, 19 November 1958.

57. Ibid., Stone to Heald and Price, 21 November 1958.

58. Ibid., F. 10, Stone to Nielsen et al., 1 February 1959.

59. He was transferred to Vienna, where he represented Poland at the International Atomic Energy Authority. He returned to Warsaw in 1965 to continue work in the Polish Atomic Energy Ministry until 1968, when he fell victim to the anti-

Semitic purges in the Polish CP and lived in retirement until his death in 1992. It was during the 1960s that he and Stone became friends and that the latter helped Leszczynski's daughters to take up their college studies in Britain. See E. Claussen to the author, 10 June 1999.

60. DCSS, Box 4, F. 14, Stone's "Diary" of the trip, April–May 1959, pp. 22ff. The trip was apparently also designed to familiarize Heald with European problems. Stone wheeled out all his contacts for the president, including Brandt, Heinrich von Brentano (then West German foreign minister), Axel von dem Bussche (involved in the July 1944 plot), Heuss, Monnet, Couve de Murville (French foreign minister), Harold Macmillan (British prime minister), Franks (now Lloyds Bank), Alan Bullock, Sir Isaiah Berlin, Sir Hans Krebs, Hugh Gaitskell, Harold Wilson. Other prominent European intellectuals and politicians appeared at various luncheons and dinners. In Berlin Stone asked his contacts to arrange a meeting with students, adding: "I shall never forget the meeting we had many years ago at Mr. McCloy's house with the young students when Henry Ford, Paul Hoffman and others visited Berlin. That meeting, as much as anything else, led to the Ford Foundation grant" to the Free University. Ibid., Dr "Overseas Trips," F.: European Trip 7.4.–13.5.1959, Stone to Hartwich, 23 March 1959. Heald cannot have been but impressed by all this, though it did not necessarily make him more favorably disposed toward Stone's tireless quest to expand the IA program. See my comments on pp. 182f.

61. DCSS, Box 2, F. 14, Stone to Krassowska, 30 September 1959.

62. Ibid., F. 19, Stone to Records Center, 7 December 1959, recording a luncheon he had had with the Polish ambassador to the United Nations.

63. See also ibid., F. 11, Stone to Records Center, 12 March 1959, concerning reports from Polish scholars in West Germany, where, following the Hungarian example in 1956–57, the German Academic Exchange Service (DAAD) had been recruited to handle the program: "These quotes [from the reports] are interesting because they show how the Poles are impressed with economic developments in Germany [and] recognize that the difference in the social and economic systems may be responsible. Without criticizing their own regimes, these quotes indicate that their studies in Germany are having a good effect."

64. Thus plans with regard to Rumania moved very slowly and it took until 1962 for exploratory trips to that country to look promising. See ibid., F. 20, Stone to Deakin, 31 December 1959; ibid., F. 38, Stone to Deakin, 22 January 1962.

65. See ibid., Box 9, Loose Materials, IA "Recommended Action" for Executive Meeting on Exchanges with the USSR, 10 December 1959.

66. Ninkovich 1994, p. 192.

67. See, e.g., Neu 1975.

68. FFA, Heald Office Files, Box 6, F. 76, Everton's Memo "Foundation-Supported Activities Related to Japan," 7 March 1961.

69. DCSS, Box 2, F. 43, Passin to Stone, 13 June 1962. See also ibid., Box L, F.: Japan, Passin's "Report on Passin-Stone Trip to Japan," March 1962.

70. Ibid., Box L, F.: Africa, Heaps to Stone and Ward, 30 January 1962, referring to a "Meeting with State Department on Algerian Situation."

71. On IPI's activities, see, e.g., ibid., Dr "Countries," F.: Stone Memos and Notes on Asia Trip 1960, IPI Report. Monthly Bulletin of the International Press Institute, April 1960. From 1951 onward, the IPI had been receiving various grants from the Ford Foundation for exchanges of journalists and a strengthening of a "free press," mainly in the Third World. See, e.g., ibid., Box 9, Loose Materials, IA "Recommended Action" for the Executive Committee Meeting, 13 July 1956; ibid., box 2, F. 2, Stone to Rykens, 25 February 1958; ibid., F. 42, Stone's Secretary to Rose, 15 May 1962, thanking him for the IPI's ten-year report.

72. Ibid., Box 2, F. 21, Stone to Nielsen (with copy to Gordon and Slater, but "no other distribution"), 4 February 1960. On the CCF's activities, see my discussions on pp. 139ff.

73. DCSS, Box 2, F. 22, Stone to Josselson, 9 March 1960.

74. Ibid., Box L, F.: Misc. 1960– , Nielsen to Stone, 3 August 1960.

75. It was first mooted by him in 1953–4.

76. DCSS, Box 10, F. 7, Kohnstamm to Stone, 8 March 1960.

77. Beitz was highly regarded in Poland because of his attempts during World War II to protect Jews from the Holocaust when he was a young manager in Carpathia. But he also developed a fierce loyalty toward Alfried Krupp whom the Allies had tried at Nuremberg and imprisoned as a war criminal. Beitz became one of the early architects of an opening up to the East and of West German *Ostpolitik*. See the interesting note by Stone to himself on 19 February 1962 (ibid., Dr "Personal Files—Stone Foundations," F.: McCloy [odds and ends]) after a luncheon with Beitz and McCloy. Having discussed possible successors to the aging chancellor Adenauer, Beitz remarked that the "German Government should be pushed by USA to take action in respect of Poland. . . . [The] Germans know [that the] Oder-Neisse [line] is not going to be changed. Should recognize it. Hallstein-Carsten group opposes [this]. Politically possible to recognize [line] if SPD and CDU made [a] joint statement—and SPD is prepared to." Beitz also thought that "Germany should widen trade with Poland which fears [the] Common Market; this [is the] biggest factor to [*sic*] keeping Poland's eyes [directed] toward the West." See also pp. 64f.

78. DCSS, Dr "Personal Files," F.: McCloy (odds and ends), Stone's "Confidential Memorandum," 19 February 1962.

79. Ibid. As Beitz put a somewhat delicate point to his guests, "the Krupp family is dying out. The young 24-year-old [Arndt] Krupp is a 'pansy' and has already been disinherited with a substantial allowance. He spends his time mainly with young friends of his same persuasion and is likely to leave Germany and go back to Mexico." He added "that SPD and CDU officials [had] joined in the plan for a Krupp Foundation. Only Adenauer [was] opposed—because the Krupp Company

was the biggest donor to CDU campaigns, and as a Foundation would not be able to contribute."

80. See *Der Spiegel*, 10 October 1954, pp. 37–38.

81. See Schulze 1995.

82. A history of the Volkswagen Foundation is being prepared at Hamburg University. In part because of its semipublic ownership, its legal structure differs from the American private foundation model and its tax status.

83. DCSS, Dr "Old Files," F.: Asian Trip March–May 1959, Stone to Berg, 10 March 1960. Only "food production" appeared in English.

84. At the meeting Berg asked him to send him information on the foundation's work in India. He would then look into a German contribution. Ibid., Dr "Countries," F.: Stone's European Trip, Stone's Notes of the Meeting (10 February 1960). See also ibid., Box L, F.: Berlin, Stone to Gustav Stein, 25 May 1960. Stein was the BDI's secretary-general and Stone was curious to know whether the meeting at the Oppenheim residence had yielded any results: "Am I correct that a sum of money has been put in the hands of former President Heuss for educational purposes. I hope so. I want very much to talk to my old friend, Professor Heuss, but before I do, it would be helpful to have an answer to this question."

85. Thus Slater to Stone, 24 May 1960 in ibid., Dr "Speeches," F.: Talk on India, for this and subsequent quotations.

86. Ibid., Box 8, Loose Materials, Stone's Notes from Trustees Meeting, 24 June 1960.

87. See, e.g., ibid., Box L, F.: Japan, Passin's "Report on Passin-Stone Trip to Japan," March 1962. During this trip Stone apparently encouraged the establishment of Japanese foundations. Passin concluded: "The situation is ripe for a massive program of cooperation." But progress was slow and in 1967 the Japanese were still studying the operations of American foundations. Stone also tried to get European foundation leaders together for joint discussions of problems and of fresh initiatives and gave lectures to encourage the Europeans to give and to change their tax laws.

88. Ibid., Box 8, Loose Materials, Stone's Notes from Trustees Meeting, 24 June 1960.

89. (New York, 1962). See also p. 192 and Nicholls 2000.

90. DCSS, Box 9, Loose Materials, IA "Recommended Action" for Executive Committee Meeting, 19 March 1959. See also ibid., Box 2, F.11, Stone to Deakin (telegram), 19 March 1959, informing the warden that the grant had been approved. On Deakin's help with IA's Yugoslav program, see my comments on p. 192.

91. Some of these men were in turn linked to the CCF.

92. DCSS, Box 9, Loose Materials, IA "Recommended Action" for Executive Committee Meeting, 19 March 1959.

93. The first contacts appear to have gone back to the summer of 1956 and must be seen in the larger context of the growing coordination of policy delibera-

tions between State Department/CIA and the Foundation. See pp. 220ff. On 5 July 1956, Stone reported to Nielsen (ibid., Dr "Personal Correspondence R–Z," F.: Soviet Union 1956–57) that "our friend in Washington hopes that . . . our little group will take up the problem of our relations with Peiping [sic]; in other words, has the time come for an initiative on our part in respect of China? He feels that the relations between Moscow and Peiping are causing Moscow considerable concern." Mao Zedong's decision of 1958 to embark upon the "Great Leap Forward" added to the American need for information about and scholarly analysis of China. As we now also know, Mao's campaign resulted in a catastrophic famine in which as many as 30 million people are estimated to have died. See Becker 1997. When on 21 October 1958, Stone told Allen Dulles of his plans with Deakin, the latter was delighted, expressed his admiration for Deakin, and hoped that the foundation would support St. Antony's. DCSS, Dr "Old Chrons.," F.: China, Stone to Central file, 24 October 1958. Stone now asked Deakin "to bring up to date the submissions he had made to us earlier this year for China and East European Studies at St. Antony's." Ibid., Stone to Central File, 27 October 1958. He also wrote to Dulles, extolling the scholarly expertise of the Far Eastern experts at Oxford. Ibid., Stone to Dulles, 31 October 1958. In his reply, the CIA boss pointed out that, although the State Department knew "of my interest in gathering information on China and the importance I attach to it," the "decision really" lay with the diplomats. Ibid., Dulles to Stone, 9 November 1958. In December, Stone therefore had discussions with Deputy Under Secretary of State Robert Murphy on "the China Studies problem," informing him that the Foundation was ready to give money to St. Antony's College for this purpose. Ibid., Stone to Record Center, n.d. The trouble was that Assistant Secretary Walter Robertson had taken the view "that one could not always rely upon certain European scholars." Stone protested "that the grantees we had in mind, such as William Deakin, were reliable" and "that we would not attempt to influence any grantee as to whom [sic] would be sent to China." Fortunately Robertson changed his mind, and a few weeks later Stone got the " 'green light to go ahead with that idea.' " Ibid., Stone to Nielsen and Price, 23 January 1959.

94. Quoted in Krige 1999, p. 340.

95. Ibid.

96. See Stone's later remembrance (DCSS, Box I, F.: Memoirs, draft fragment on Bohr, n.d.) that he met Bohr, "when he had turned most of his attention to world peace through control of nuclear weapons." See also the materials in ibid., Dr "Overseas Trips," F.: Niels Bohr.

97. Quoted in Krige 1999, p. 353. See also DCSS, Box 9, Loose Materials, Program Docket for the Meeting of the Trustees, 8–10 December 1955. In this connection mention should also be made of the Joint US-Soviet Study Group and the Pugwash Conferences on Science and World Affairs, founded in 1957. The Harvard biochemist Paul Doty was a leading member of this organization that

was supposed to act as an icebreaker in the Soviet-American nuclear relationship. Doty played a prominent role in the CCF and IACF. See pp. 263f.

98. DCSS, Box 2, F. 2, Stone to Nielsen, 13 February 1958. The Ford Motor Company provided a car for the two days that Bohr spent in Washington. See also ibid., F. 3, Stone to Senator Flanders, 24 March 1958.

99. On these developments, see, e.g., Divine 1981.

100. DCSS, Box 2, F. 2, Stone to Nielsen, 13 February 1958.

101. Ibid., Box 9, Loose Materials, IA "Recommended Action" for Trustees Meeting, 20–21 June 1958.

102. FFA, Heald Office Files, Box 6, F. 70, Heald to McCloy, 14 April 1959. Outside Berlin, Stone's old acquaintance Dolf Sternberger got $150,000 for the Political Science Institute at Heidelberg. A proposal by the more conservative Arnold Bergstraesser for his institute at Freiburg was turned down. DCSS, Box 2, F. 11, Stone to Sternberger, 19 March 1959.

103. DCSS, Dr "Old Files," F.: Stone Correspondence from Europe June–September 1958, Stone to Price and Nielsen, 2 August 1958.

104. Ibid., Box 2, F. 12, Stone to Records Center, 6 April 1959.

105. See Lazarsfeld to Stone, 29 June 1959, in C. Fleck, "Autochthone Provinzialisierung. Universität und Wissenschaft nach dem Ende der nationalsozialistischen Herrschaft in Österreich," in *Österreichische Zeitschrift für Geschichtswissenschaften*, no. 1 (1996), p. 92: "As to the Austrian situation at large, I find it as depressing as before. No brains, no initiative, no colleagiality. Someone should make a study to find out how a country can be intellectually so dead and at the same time have such wonderful musical festivals. There is also, on the conservative side and in large parts of the University a real Anti-Americanism." See also more generally, Wagnleitner 1994.

106. DCSS, Dr "Old Chrons.," F.: European Trip with Heald 1964, IA "Recommended Action" for the Trustees [?] Meeting, 27 April 1961. The grant was to be for $1 million over the first five years of the institute.

107. Ibid., Box 2, F. 10, Stone to Nielsen, 23 January 1959; ibid., F. 1, Stone to Bullock, 3 January 1958; Stone to Veale, 7 January 1958. The foundation later made a grant. Ibid., F. 31, Stone to Bullock, 23 June 1961. See also Bullock [1953] 1964 and "Academic Action Man," *Oxford Today*, no. 1 (1995), pp. 7–9. See also my discussion on pp. 257ff.

108. DCSS, Box 9, Loose Materials, IA "Recommended Action" for Trustees Meeting, 25 September 1959.

109. Quoted in Sutton in Gemelli 1998, p. 37.

110. Ibid.

111. Ignatieff 1998, for this and subsequent quotations.

112. See also pp. 94f.

113. See Ignatieff 1995, pp. 189ff.

114. DCSS, Box 2, F. 10, Stone to Nielsen, 23. January 1959, proudly reporting after a visit to the IISS that it had been a "very good investment." See also ibid., F. 25, Stone to Nielsen and Slater, 26 July 1960.

115. Ibid., Box 9, Loose Materials, IA "Recommended Action" for Trustees Meeting, 11 December 1959. See also ibid., Box 2, F. 1, Stone to Heller, 27 January 1958.

116. See Gemelli 1998.

117. DCSS, Dr "Old Files," F.: Nielsen Memos 1961, Nielsen to Stone, 26 March 1961.

118. Judt 1998, p. 163.

119. See pp. 240f.

120. DCSS, Dr "Old Files," F.: Nielsen Memos 1961, Nielsen to Stone, 26 March 1961.

121. See, e.g., Berghahn 1986. See also my chapter 4.

122. See G. Gemelli, "From Imitation to Competitive Cooperation," in Gemelli 1998, pp. 167–304. See also DCSS, Dr "Overseas Trips," F.: Europe—General Correspondence 1955, Stone to Price, 17 March 1955: "Each year twenty promising workers should be sent to the Harvard Business School and maybe two or three other institutions in this country to study our industrial and business practices and philosophy so that they can go back to Germany with new concepts and with a hope of achieving leading roles in German industry and business." See also Berghahn 1986, pp. 230ff.

123. See Berghahn 1986, p. 254. Later the program was expanded to Asia. See DCSS, Box 8, Loose Materials, IA "Recommended Action" for Trustees Meeting, 20 November 1963, with a request to approve $320,000 "to the Asian Productivity Organization (Tokyo) over a two-year period to assist in the development of international training courses for small-scale business management in Asia."

124. See Kuisel 1981.

125. See Gemelli 1998, p. 177.

126. See also M. Fichter, "Hicog and the Unions in West Germany," in Diefendorf et al. 1993, pp. 257–81.

127. See Berghahn 1986, pp. 248f.

128. See p. 68.

129. See Berghahn 1986, pp. 40ff.

130. See, e.g., Lehmbruch 1979.

131. DCSS, Box 2, F. 26, Stone to Tabatoni, 25 January 1961.

132. Ibid., Box 1, Loose Materials, IA "Recommended Action" for Trustees Meeting, 30 September 1965. Tabatoni apparently hooked up with Gaston Berger with whom he went to the United States to study the Harvard Business School model.

133. See pp. 105ff.

134. See p. xi.

135. DCSS., Dr "Old Files," F.: Stone Correspondence from Europe 28.6.–15.9. 1958, Stone to Nielsen and Slater, 26 July 1958.

136. *Tagesspiegel*, 6 October 1959, p. 4.

137. See p. 182.

138. See also pp. 201ff.

139. See DCSS, Box 9, Loose Materials, IA "Recommended Action" for Executive Committee Meeting, 27 September 1956, with a request to approve $30,000 "to the Carnegie Endowment for International Peace to assist in financing the Bilderberg Conference to be held in the United States in February 1957. See also the interesting reports on this conference in *Die Welt*, 25 November 1957 ("Weite Horizonte für die europäische Kultur") and *Frankfurter Allgemeine Zeitung*, 26 November 1957 ("Kultur der Europäer")—headings that must have dismayed Stone, who was present at the meeting, but reflect problems of cultural perception that are examined further in chapter 9.

140. See DCSS, Box 2, F. 25, Stone to Nielsen, 22 July 1960; ibid., F. 14, Stone to Monnet, 21 July 1959. See also ibid., F. 41, Stone to Record Center, 16 April 1962, relating to plans for an Atlantic Institute. There also developed a "deep interest" in the establishment of a European University in which Monnet and Hallstein were involved and of which Kohnstamm was to be the first president. Ibid., F. 3, Stone to Hallstein, 12 March 1958. A European University Institute was eventually founded, based just outside Florence.

CHAPTER 8
THE CIA, THE FORD FOUNDATION, AND THE DEMISE OF THE CCF EMPIRE

1. See McCarthy 1987; Nielsen 1972, esp. pp. 379ff.

2. See pp. 55ff.

3. See pp. 74ff.

4. DCSS, Box 4, F. 18, Lasky's Memo, August 1953, also for the following. See also Lasky's very positive account which he prepared for ibid., Dr "World War II," F.: Public Affairs, A. V. Boerner, ed., *Semi-Annual Evaluation Report on the Public Affairs Program in Germany* 1.12.51–31.5.1952, pp. 165–66f.

5. *Der Spiegel*, 15 October 1954, p. 37.

6. DCSS, Dr "Correspondence R–Z," F.: Intercultural, Lasky to Stone, 13 April 1954.

7. Ibid., Laughlin to Lasky, 12 April 1954.

8. Ibid., Box 9, Loose Materials, Stone to Price, 21 April 1954.

9. FFA, Box 9, Board of Trustees Meeting, Docket Excerpt May 1954, pp. 46–47 (IA "Recommended Action" for grant to Ernst Reuter Foundation for *Der Monat*).

10. DCSS, Loose Materials, Stone's Memo "Der Monat–Past History," 17 May 1954.

11. Ibid., Dr "Germany McCloy Stone," F.: Ford Foundation 1953–54, Stone to McCloy, 19 May 1954.

12. Ibid., Box 9, Loose Materials, IA "Recommended Action" for Executive Committee Meeting, 27 September 1956.

13. Ibid., Box 2, F. 8, Stone to Bergio, 6 November 1958.

14. Ibid., Box 2, F. 9, Stone to Meyer, 22 December 1958. See also ibid., F. 10, Stone to Lasky, 7 January 1959, and Saunders 2000, pp. 234ff., 341–42f.

15. AAIB, General Correspondence, Lasky's " 'Encounter.' A Brief History," May 1975. See also DCSS, Dr "Old Chrons.," F.: European Trip May–June 1961, Stone to Nielsen, 18 May 1961, reporting, after a lunch with Lasky, that *Encounter* was doing well. The journal had increased its circulation to around 24,000, of which 5,000 went to Africa and Asia.

16. See pp. 255f.

17. DCSS, Dr "Study," F.: 1967–74 Allemagne (divers), Allemann to Stone, 1 August 1970. Allemann had been a radical leftist in the 1930s but later broke with Marxism and became an influential journalist. In the meantime, Walter Hasenclever had also become a full member of the journal's editorial team. DCSS, Box 2, F. 14, Stone to Josselson, 17 July 1959, as Stone was glad to have learned.

18. DCSS, Box K, F.: "H," Harpprecht to Josselson, 27 April 1966. Later Harpprecht became editor of *Der Monat* for a while, before working as a speech writer for Willy Brandt. As the titles of his books demonstrate, he was an untiring interpreter of America to the Germans and a confirmed Atlanticist. See his *Das fremde Land Amerika* (1982), *Amerikaner: Freunde, Fremde, ferne Nachbarn* (1984), and *Die geistigen Grundlagen der atlantischen Gemeinschaft* (1985).

19. DCSS, Dr "Old Chrons.," F.: Congress, Josselson to Stone, 2 May 1966.

20. Ibid., Box K, F.: "H," Harpprecht to Stone, 8 June 1966.

21. See pp. 255f.

22. See pp. 140ff. See also Saunders 2000, pp. 245ff.

23. DCSS, Dr "Old Chrons.," F.: Milton Katz, Stone to Katz, 2 December 1952.

24. Ibid., Dr "Personal Correspondence R–Z," F.: Soviet Union 1956–57, Stone to Files, 17 July 1956.

25. Ibid., Dr "Old Chrons.," F.: Reimbursements 1953, Stone's Travel and Expense Report, 8 June 1953.

26. FFA, Gaither Office Files, Box 1, F. 1, Howard's Notes on Conference, 3 April 1951.

27. Ibid., Gladieux to Gaither, 23 April 1951, paraphrasing Gaither's letter of 18 April.

28. Ibid., Howard to Gaither, 25 April 1951.

29. Ibid., Gaither to Gladieux, 27 April 1951.

30. Ibid., Gaither to Johnson, 1 May 1951.

31. Ibid., F. 3, Speier to Gaither, 5 May 1951. On Speier, see p. 156.

32. Coleman 1989 and Grémion 1995; L. Bushkoff, "Counter-Intelligentsia," *Bostonia*, January–February 1990, pp. 41–45.

33. Born in Latvia on 3 March 1908, Josselson went to high school in Germany and later lived in Paris. He spoke several languages fluently. See also Center for European Studies, Harvard University, A. Collins's Folder on Plans for a Seminar on the CCF, Collins's Notes, 21 December (1986). See also my discussion on p. 133.

34. DCSS, Box L, F.: Ford Foundation/CCF 1966–67, Josselson's Report, n.d. [1967], with corrections in Josselson's hand, for this and subsequent quotations.

35. As note 33.

36. DCSS, Dr "Old Chrons.," F.: CCF, Josselson to Stone, 16 September 1964. The Fairfield Foundation could also be relied upon.

37. Ibid., Box L, F.: Hicog 1952–53, Nabokov to Stone, 17 November 1953.

38. See p. 221.

39. Ibid., Box 4, F. 3, Stone to McCloy, 25 February 1954.

40. DCSS, Dr "Correspondence R–Z," F.: Intercultural, Price to Laughlin, 6 May 1954. Ibid., Box 9, Loose Materials, Stone[?] to Price, 14 April 1954, with attachments under this heading.

41. Ibid., Box 9, Loose Materials, IA "Recommended Action" for Trustees Meeting, appended to a memo titled "Next Dockets," June 1956.

42. Ibid., Box 10, F. 21, Memo "CCF and IACF Receipts from Ford Foundation 1956–1969," n.n., n.d. [1970?].

43. See also ibid., Dr "Personal Files," F.: Organizations—Undisclosed Funds CCF, IA "Recommended Action" (Draft) for Trustees Meeting, [1962?], with a review of past CCF activities and its plans to go global.

44. See p. xi.

45. See p. 223.

46. See p. 221. Nor was Stone particularly enthusiastic. As he wrote to Katz on 2 December 1952 (DCSS, Dr "Old Chrons.," F.: Milton Katz): "I share the feeling that a great deal needs to be done to develop greater understanding among the intellectuals of Western Europe and the United States. I think, however, we should hesitate to have connections with the covert business."

47. DCSS, Dr "Personal Correspondence R–Z," Stone to Meyer, 6 September 1956. See also ibid., Dr "Old Chrons.," F.: Old Appointment Book Sheets, Appointment Record for 10 September 1954, listing a meeting with "Cord Meyer." See also Meyer 1980.

48. Ibid., Nielsen to Stone, 13 September 1956, for this and subsequent quotations.

49. See p. xi.

50. See p. 190.

51. See DCSS, Box 9, F. 15, Stone to Nielsen and Gordon, 14 April 1959: "Mr. Josselson and Mr. Nabokov put on an excellent dinner. . . . The conversation was good, the food was excellent and I think everybody was impressed with the fact

that the Congress calls together men from various parts of the world, men of action and men of thought." Stephen Graubard (interview, Boston, 16 May 1997) called them all "high rollers."

52. DCSS, Box 9, Loose Materials, IA "Recommended Action" for Trustees Meeting, 27–28 September 1957.

53. Ibid., CCF "Program in International Actitivies" (Budget) for Executive Committee Meeting, 15 November 1957.

54. Ibid., Box 2, F. 14, Stone to Josselson, 15 July 1959. When Heuss stepped down from the presidency, Stone wrote to remind him that as a young American student he had attended Heuss's lectures at the Berlin Hochschule für Politik and that they had smoked "peace pipes" when they met in Heidelberg after 1945. See also p. 34.

55. DCSS, Dr "Countries," F.: Stone—Europe 30.9.–8.11.1959, Stones Notes "October 21—Papers—1959—CCF, n.d. [1959]. Once again we hear echoes in Stone's and the CCF's work of the themes that have been analyzed in chapter 4.

56. Ibid., Box 9, Loose Materials, IA "Recommended Action" for Trustees Meeting, 11 December 1959. See also ibid., Dr "Old Chrons.," F.: Congress, Kimbler to Stone, 8 June 1962.

57. Ibid., Dr "Personal Files," F.: Organizations—Undisclosed Funds, Excerpt, n.d. It is not quite clear what happened on the side of the CIA at this time. All we know so far is that Josselson had a row with Meyer in October 1960. See Saunders 2000, p. 342.

58. Ibid., F.: Atlantic Partnership, "Evaluation (1951–61) and Statement of Current Objectives and Policies," December 1961.

59. Ibid., Dr "Personal Files," F.: Atlantic Partnership, IA "Program Submission Concerning Future Program Activities" (prepared for the Ford Foundation's "Special Committee"), Spring 1962.

60. Quoted in ibid., IA Submission "Strengthening the Comprehensive Development of the Atlantic Partnership," March 1963.

61. See p. 232.

62. DCSS, Dr "Personal Files," F.: Atlantic Partnership, IA Submission "Strengthening the Comprehensive Development of the Atlantic Partnership," March 1963. See also FFA, Slater Files, Report 010918, Summary Discussion Paper: Proposal in Support of an Atlantic Partnership, 5 December 1962, which argued that "the Atlantic area, which contains a large part of the world's physical and human resources, may be facing a period of high-level stagnation." To counter this, a system for higher growth rates and the better utilization and distribution of resources are needed, which in turn would "require a new national and international bridge to be built between the public and the private sectors. East-West trade and other avenues should also be explored within this context." See pp. 229f.

63. DCSS, Dr "Personal Files," F.: Atlantic Partnership, IA Submission "Strengthening the Comprehensive Development of the Atlantic Partnership,"

March 1963. This appropriation was to be made "in the expectation that (a) European, Canadian, and other American institutions would provide an additional $60 million to the activities, institutions, and ideas contemplated in the Foundation-supported program, and (b) the leaders and experts referred to in paragraph 4 above would agree to serve on the Foundation's Atlantic Advisory Council which would be established under either of . . . two organizational alternatives."

64. The leaders and experts envisaged for the Atlantic Advisory Council included familiar figures: Monnet, Max Kohnstamm, Kurt Birrenbach, Lester Pearson, and Lord Franks.

65. For a highly illuminating digest of IA strategic thinking in the context of the evolving European-American relationship in the early 1960s, see ibid., Nielsen to Stone and Slater (draft), 4 September 1963. See also the voluminous correspondence about the American-European relationship in ibid., F.: Atlantic Alliance.

66. DCSS, Dr "Personal Files," F.: Organizations—Undisclosed Funds, IA "Recommended Action" for the Trustees [?] Meeting (draft), n.d. [1962?], for this and subsequent quotations. See also chapter 7, note 5 and pp. 103ff. This is why the student rebellion of the late 1960s caused all the more consternation and puzzlement.

67. See pp. 216ff.

68. DCSS, Dr "Personal Files," F.: Organizations—Undisclosed Funds, Stone's Memo, 6 February 1962.

69. Ibid., Dr "Old Chrons.," F.: Congress, Unsigned Compilation of Appreciations Sent to the CCF on Its Tenth Anniversary and at Other Times, n.d. The document was sent, together with other materials, by Josselson to Stone on 23 May 1962.

70. Ibid., Stone to Josselson ("private and confidential [not for FF files]"), 18 April 1962.

71. Ibid., Josselson to Stone, 23 May 1962.

72. See pp. 265ff.

73. Ibid., F.: Congress II, Shils's "Further Thoughts on the Congress in the '60's," March 1962.

74. DCSS, Dr "Personal Files," F.: Organizations—Undisclosed Funds, Stone to McCloy ("copy 1 of 4"), 12 June 1962. Earlier drafts (ibid.) were also numbered 1–4.

75. Ibid., Dr "Old Chrons.," F.: Congress, Josselson to Stone, 15 July [1962].

76. Ibid., Box L, F.: CCF 1966–67, Stone to Josselson, 22 September 1962, for this and subsequent quotations.

77. Ibid., Dr "Personal Files," F.: Organizations—Undisclosed Funds, "Memo on Conversations, January 23 and January 26, between J. E. Slater and Nicholas Nabokov," 30 January 1962. The memo was apparently produced by Slater for the special committee. On Slater, see also pp. 276ff.

78. DCSS, Dr "Old Files," F.: Berlin (general), Brandt to Josselson (draft), n.d. [1962]. See also ibid., Dr "Correspondence R–Z," F.: Berlin, Josselson to Brandt, 24 November 1962.

79. Ibid., Dr "Correspondence R–Z," F.: Berlin 1963, Nabokov to Stone, 11 December 1962. See also Saunders 2000, pp. 351ff.

80. See, e.g., *Tagesspiegel*, 9 January 1963; *Neue Zürcher Zeitung*, 9 January 1963; *Süddeutsche Zeitung*, 9 January 1963, with references to the strategic motives behind this initiative, i.e., to keep West Berlin as a cultural center linked to the "West" after the East German regime and the Soviets had built the Berlin Wall in 1961. See also *Die Zeit*, 2 October 1964. For the considerations behind the founding of the Berlin Aspen Institute in the 1970s, see pp. 276ff. Another Academy was established in postunification Berlin in the 1990s.

81. See DCSS, Dr "Personal Correspondence R–Z," F.: Berlin 1963, "Probable Schedule for 'Artists in Residence' for 1963–64, which included the writer Ingeborg Bachmann (Austria), the sculptor Mario Carvo (Brazil), the composer Luciano Berio (Italy), and the writer W. H. Auden (U.K./U.S.).

82. *New York Times*, 17 May 1964.

83. See p. 168ff. Soon there was also criticism of the whole enterprise. At the Ford Foundation the selection of the first set of artists caused apparent displeasure. See Dr "Personal Correspondence R–Z," F.: Berlin 1963, Nabokov to Stone (copy of a handwritten letter), 8 April 1963. See also *Die Zeit*, 2 October 1964, reporting that many of the invitees were dissatisfied with the program.

84. As note 33.

85. DCSS, Dr "Old Chrons.," F.: Congress 1966, Stone to Josselson, 10 June 1964.

86. See p. 218.

87. Ibid., F.: Congress II, CCF Memorandum "The International Council for Cultural Cooperation," n.d., with a covering note by Josselson, expressing this hope.

88. As note 33, also for the following.

89. See also ibid., Dr "Old Chrons.," F.: CCF 1966, IA "Recommended Action" for Trustees Meeting, n.d. [1966], requesting "approval of a grant of $1,500,000 and appropriation of $5,500,000 over a six-year period" and referring to a "discussion paper" that "outlined the problems of the Congress, particularly its financing, and the steps taken and now completed to separate the CCF from its previous government connection."

90. See pp. 238f.

91. DCSS, Box 11, Envelope 1, Transcripts of Interview with McCloy, 16 August 1984, p. 13.

On Heald, see also p. 182.

92. FFA, Heald Office Files, Box 6, F. 71, "Notes on IA Paper," n.d. For the IA paper itself, see p. 229.

93. DCSS, Box 8, Loose Materials, IA "Recommended Actions" for Trustees Meeting, 12–13 December 1963.

94. Ibid., Minutes of the Trustees Meeting, 24–25 September 1964.

95. Ibid., Box 1, Loose Materials, McDaniel to Officers and Directors, 26 October 1965.

96. Ibid., Box 2, F. 41, Stone to Heald, 16 April 1962. This was in connection with Brandt's and Nabokov's cultural initiative. See pp. 234ff.

97. DCSS, Box 11, Envelope 1, Transcripts of Interview with McCloy, August 15, 1984.

98. See also p. 237, relating to the foundation's spending spree. Now it became clear that this could not be sustained. On Bundy and his brother William, see Bird 1998.

99. DCSS, Dr "Personal Files," F.: Atlantic Partnership, IA's "Planning Budget Request for Fiscal 1966–1967–1968," June 1965.

100. FFA, Bell Papers, Box 12, F. 179, Bundy to Stratton, 23 September 1966.

101. DCSS, Dr "Old Chrons.," F.: Congress 1966, Josselson to Stone, 28 May [1966].

102. FFA, Bell Papers, Box 12, F. 179, Bundy to Stratton, 23 September 1966.

103. See also DCSS, Box L, F.: IACF 1972, Aron to Bundy, 21 September 1966, and ibid., Dr "Old Chrons.," F.: Congress 1966, Kimbler to Ashley, 1 November 1966.

104. Ibid., Dr "Old Chrons.," F.: Congress 1966, IA "Recommended Action" for Trustees Meeting (October 1966). The trustees approved the grant but also "elected to hold action on the appropriation of $5.5 million in abeyance without prejudice." Ibid., McDaniel to Stone, 18 October 1966. Joseph McDaniel then added a footnote: "Mr. Bell is making it clear to Mr. Bundy that we do honor the commitments as stated in p. 5," where the payment dates were listed. See also the announcement in *New York Times*, 2 November 1966.

105. See Coleman 1989, p. 275.

106. DCSS, Binder: Personal File 1983, Stone to Sperber, 18 October 1983.

107. See also pp. 267ff.

108. See p. 227.

109. See, e.g., Patterson 1997. See also p. 103.

110. See p. 207.

111. See pp. 207f. On the renewed technocracy debate in West Germany, see, e.g., Berghahn 1986, pp. 300ff.

112. See, e.g., Williams 1959.

113. Mills 1956. The growing depth of the ideological divide is reflected in what people wrote about each other. Thus Mills had some quite scathing things to say about Bell. It is probably fair to add that in terms of these personal animosities and the remarks they traded with each other the East Coast intellectuals were a match to European intellectuals at different ends of the ideological spectrum. See also Laskin 2000, Podhoretz 1999.

114. (New York, 1962).

115. See, e.g., Katz 1992.

116. *New York Times*, 1 September 1964.

117. Ibid., 4 September 1964.

118. *Nation*, 14 September 1964, p.102.

119. *New York Times*, 19 September 1964.

120. FFA, Heald Office Files, Box 12, F. 152, Heald to Officers and Directors, 4 May 1965.

121. See pp. 189ff.

122. *New York Times*, 26 April 1966.

123. Ibid., 27 April 1966.

124. See, e.g., DCSS, Dr "Old Chrons.," F.: Congress 1966, Graubard to Hunt, 26 May 1966. Stephen Graubard was the editor of *Daedalus*, the journal of the American Academy of Arts and Sciences; Hunt was Josselson's deputy and, like Josselson's, his salary in Paris was paid by the CIA.

125. *New York Times*, 9 May 1966.

126. Ibid., 10 May 1966. Spender stepped down from the *Encounter* editorial board in 1965, to be replaced by Frank Kermode, but he had agreed for his name to appear as contributing editor on the journal's letterhead. Interesting also what Josselson learned about attitudes held by prominent CCF supporters behind the scenes. As he wrote to Stone (DCSS, Dr "Old Chrons.," F.: Congress 1966, Josselson to Stone, 28 May 1966), Spender had called him "in despair from Northwestern University the other day. Dear old Michael Polanyi is going around saying that his life work has been ruined, and even that cynic Irving Kristol who at first pooh-poohed the whole business talked very strangely to me and to Mel on the phone the other day." Fortunately, he added, Nabokov and de Rougemont were "behaving first rate and are causing us no trouble with signing the kind of letter we want them to sign." Finally, "the hardest blows will probably still come when the Isaac Deutschers, Connor Cruise O'Briens, Bertrand Russells will want to take their revenge for our having been right about the Soviet Union and about Stalin in particular." Josselson ended his letter by complaining bitterly about what he thought was the *New York Times*'s irresponsible journalism.

127. *New York Times*, 16 May 1966.

128. DCSS, Dr "Old Chrons.," F.: Congress 1966, Daniel to Lasky, 29 May 1966.

129. Ibid., de Rougemont and Nabokov to the Editor, 27 May 1966; *Nation*, 16 May 1966, pp. 571–78.

130. *Christian Science Monitor*, 16 February 1967.

131. Ibid., 17 February 1967.

132. Washington Post, 21 February 1967. On Lippmann, see also Riccio 1995.

133. *Washington Post* 23 February 1967.

134. Ibid., 28 February 1967.

135. *Ramparts*, March 1967, pp. 29–38. The then radical editor of the journal subsequently took a long ideological journey toward the right. See David Horowitz 1997 and Saunders 2000, pp. 381ff.

136. *New York Review of Books*, April 20, 1967, pp. 16–21.

137. *Christian Science Monitor*, 9 May 1967; *Saturday Evening Post*, 20 May 1967. See also Coleman 1989, p. 238; Bushkoff (note 32), with Braden's reasons for going public. In 1948, Stone wrote the following recommendation for the Dartmouth graduate Braden, then secretary of the Museum of Modern Art, to the CFR's Sub-Committee on Younger Members (DCSS, Dr "Hicog I," F.: CFR 1948): "He early desired to be a publisher, and with that in mind took a job as a printer before he finished school. He soon realized that this was not the way to his goal, however, and in spite of not having finished school persuaded the Director of Admissions of Dartmouth to admit him. He was the outstanding man of his class and became editor of the Dartmouth daily paper. As soon as the war broke out, he believed that this country should do its part, and he himself joined the British Army. . . . He later transferred to the American Army, became a paratrooper, and worked behind the enemy lines. His great interest is international relations." In November 1949 Braden figured as executive secretary of the American Committee on United Europe, of which William Donovan was chairman and Allen Dulles vice-chairman. See DCSS, Box 4, F. 1, Braden to Stone, 16 November 1949. If he had not yet joined the CIA, this position must have been the gateway.

138. DCSS, Dr "A–E Bennington," F.: Johnson/Bondy Project, Staples to Industrial Societies File, 27 February 1967.

139. See the materials in ibid., Box L, F.: Congress 1966–67.

140. As note 33. On Hunt's biography, see Coleman 1989, p. 135.

141. *New York Times*, 8 May 1967. Chiaromonte had no qualms, which got him into an argument with Dwight Macdonald. See Macdonald to Chiaromonte, 10 October 1967. I thank Michael Wreszin for making this letter available to me.

142. DCSS, Box L, F.: Congress 1966–67, Hunt to Josselson, 28 July 1967.

143. Ibid., Box L, F.: Congress 1966–67, Stone's Handwritten Notes of a Trip to Paris, 17 September 1967.

144. FFA, Bell Papers, Box 35, F. 802, Cuninggim to DF [Danforth Foundation?] Trustees, 16 April 1967. See also *Washington Post*, 28 February 1967, and Saunders 2000, pp. 405f.

145. FFA, Bell Papers, Box 35, F. 502, Bell to Bundy 17 April 1967.

146. Quoted in ibid., Cunninggim to DF Trustees, 16 April 1967.

147. DCSS, Dr "A–E Bennington," F.: Johnson/Bondy Project, Stone to Bundy, 17 April 1967.

148. Ibid., footnote by Bundy.

149. Ibid., Binder: Personal File 1974–75, Excerpt from Draft Memoirs by Galbraith [?], n.d. The excerpt continues: "I got hold of the controller of the Congress, whom I had met skiing, and questioned him about where the money came from. He confirmed my suspicions because he did not know. A controller, I

thought, should have a pretty clear idea where his money comes from." The author added that he was not too indignant about his suspicions but decided not to attend any more CCF congresses. Later when the scandal broke he "thought it best not to be too outspoken in my outrage and helped arrange for its [the CCF's] removal to the Ford Foundation." Finally, "a year later [i.e., ca. 1961] in India I encountered a number of similar activities, though all rather more foolish. Supported by the president and Robert Kennedy, I abolished them all." This indicates that the author may have been Galbraith who became U.S. ambassador to India at this time.

150. *Wall Street Journal*, 24 February 1967.

151. See pp. 247f.

152. FFA, Report 002784, Sutton to Bundy and Bell, 21 September 1967.

153. See p. 236.

154. DCSS, Box L, F.: Congress 1966–67, Stone's Notes, 17 September 1967.

155. On Masani and the Indian situation, see Coleman 1989, pp. 199ff., and the correspondence with Masani and others in DCSS, Box L, F.: Congress 1966–67. See also Masani 1977.

156. As note 152.

157. DCSS, Box L, F.: Congress 1966–67, Stone to Bell and Sutton, 21 September 1967. See also ibid., Stone's handwritten notes, dated 20 September 1967, about a meeting with Bell and Sutton on that day.

158. Ibid., Stone to Bell and Sutton, 21 September 1967.

159. Ibid., Josselson to Sutton, 20 September 1967.

CHAPTER 9
COPING WITH THE NEW CULTURE WARS OF THE 1960S AND BEYOND

1. DCSS, Binder: Other Correspondence—Personal and Confidential, Hoffman to Stone, 23 March [1968]. Hoffman was managing director of the UN Special Fund at this time.

2. Ibid., Stone to Hoffman (draft), n.d.

3. Ibid., F.: Pink Copies 4.10.67–28.2.68, Stone to Dickey, 16 October 1967.

4. Ibid., F.: Pink Copies 1.3.68–30.9.68, Stone to Lesczcynski, 24 June 1968.

5. See pp. 132ff.

6. DCSS, Box L, F.: Congress 1966–67, Stone's Notes, 15 May 1967.

7. See p. 237.

8. FFA, Report 009040, Bell to Bundy, 14 October 1966 ("Revised after discussion with Mr. Bundy and approved by him").

9. DCSS, Dr "Personal Correspondence R–Z," F.: Reorganization, Stone and Slater to Bell, 17 October 1966.

10. FFA, Report 009040, Bell and Ward to Bundy, 17 October 1966.

11. Ibid., Bell to Bundy, 19 October 1966.

12. As note 3. He also mentioned to Dickey that there had been suggestions in Washington for him "to take on an East European Embassy. I discouraged the idea because the job did not seem to have enough muscle."

13. DCSS, Box L, F.: Congress 1966–67, Stone's Notes 15 May 1967.

14. According to Stone (ibid.), Bundy said that if Stone took over the CCF, the organization " 'would be stimulated.' He was friendly and cordial [and] thought I would do a positive job for the Congress." When Bundy mentioned Stone's closeness to McCloy, Stone replied that he "was proud to be a McCloy man, but [that] I had also been the man to go into Eastern Europe" and that Bundy was himself a "McCloy man."

15. See p. 256.

16. Born on 3 May 1916 in the Lower Pyrenées, Emmanuel had studied mathematics and philosophy before becoming a secondary school teacher. During World War II he fought in the French resistance and after 1944 first acted as coeditor of the weekly *Les Etoiles*. Subsequently he was head of the British and later the North American service of the French Broadcasting Corporation until 1959, at which point he joined the CCF as literary director and deputy secretary-general. The author of several volumes of poetry, his achievements were recognized when the *Académie française* made him a member. Josselson once called him "one of the finest and most respected French intellectuals today . . . whom we consider as the best acquisition we have made in recent years (after all, he comes from the Catholic fellow-traveling left)." DCSS, Dr "Old Chrons.," F.: Congress 1966–67, Josselson to Stone, 28 May 1966.

17. Ibid., Box L, F.: Congress 1966–67, Stone to Emmanuel, 31 August 1967.

18. Ibid., Emmanuel to Stone, 26 September 1967, for this and subsequent quotations.

19. See Appendix III.

20. See, e.g., DCSS, Box 6, F.: IACF, IACF Memorandum "Congress for Cultural Freedom, 1950–1967," n.d.

21. Ibid., F.: Pink Copies 1.4.1967–29.2.1968, Stone to Dressner, 13 October 1967.

22. The board members were Waldemar Besson, François Bourricaud, Alan Bullock, Daniel Cosio Villegas, John K. Galbraith, Alexander Kwapong, Pedro Lain Entralgo, Luis Lindley Cintra, Shri Krishna Mulgaokar, Edward Shils, Ignazio Silone, Soedjatmoko, Manès Sperber. Ex officio: Masani, Stone, Emmanuel.

23. Ibid., Box L, F.: Basic Documents, IACF Budget for 1968, n.d.

24. FFA, Bell Papers, Box 12, F. 179, Sutton to Bell, 20 September 1967. Sutton ended with a calculation that had apparently also been a factor in the promises given to Stone and that will figure again (see p. 261): "S[hepard]S[tone] will be 60 next March 31. A grant running through calendar 1972 would not quite carry to his 65th birthday."

25. After IPC, Open Court Publishing supported the journal until this company also withdrew. Although there were still some thirty thousand subscribers,

by the spring of 1975 Lasky no longer had enough money to pay for the next issue. AAIB, General Correspondence 1975–, Lasky's Confidential Memorandum, May 1975. For further details, see, e.g., the correspondence in DCSS, Binder 1.8.1971–31.3.1972; ibid., Box L, F.: IACF 1972. But Lasky was enough of a financial wizard to continue independently and attract subsidies, at least for the time being.

26. After the initial IACF subsidy to the journal also had to be cut, Gerd Bucerius, the Hamburg publisher, covered the continuing deficits. But it was quite a financial millstone around his neck, and he was apparently also unhappy with Harpprecht as editor. Stone tried to enlist help from old friends, among them Willy Brandt, Hermann Abs, and Karl Gerold. Other publishers expressed an interest, but did not pursue the matter. In 1972, after Bucerius had finally dropped out, some intellectuals and academics in Berlin thought of creating *Der Neue Monat*, and during 1973 Wolf Jobst Siedler's publishing house put forward its own plans. The story finally came to an end in 1975, when the IACF gave up its title to the *Gesellschaft für Internationale Publizistik* and, with Bucerius apparently contemplating a new journal close to the concerns of the IACF, Stone was informed that "we might very well be interested in the possibility of some fraternal association if he [Bucerius] were agreeable." DCSS, Box 7, Binder 3, Goldstein to Stone, 26 May 1975.

27. DCSS, Binder: Pink Copies 4.10.67–29.2.68, Stone to Neogy, 15 January 1968. *Transitions* had been founded, with CCF help, in Uganda in 1961. It was revived by Henry Louis Gates Jr., and other African American intellectuals in 1995.

28. Ibid., Binder: Pink Copies 3.1.68–30.9.1968, Stone to Cosio Villegas, 16 May 1968.

29. See ibid., various letters in the "Pink Copies" files, 1967ff. On *Quest*, see also Ayyub 1966.

30. Ibid., Binder: Pink Copies 4.10.1967–29.2.1968, Stone to Philips, 12 December 1967; Stone to MacFarquhar, 17 November 1967.

31. See the correspondence in ibid., Box 7, Binder 3. For the subsequent difficulties with Walter Laqueur, the other editor, see ibid., Binder: Pink Copies 4.10.67–29.1.68, Stone to Laqueur, 17 November 1967, and Stone to Laqueur, 10 January 1968. On *Survey* more generally, see Coleman 1989, pp. 99ff.

32. See, e.g., DCSS, Binder: Pink Copies 1.10.68–30.4.69, Stone to Vial, 30 December 1968.

33. See, e.g., ibid., Binder: Pink Copies 1.3.68–30.9.68, Stone to Adorno, 19 June 1968.

34. Ibid., Binder: Pink Copies 1.10.68–30.4.69, Stone to Bryant (Harvard librarian), 9 April 1969. The CCF archive is now at the University of Chicago.

35 See, e.g., ibid., Stone to Vittachi, 24 March 1969.

36. FFA, Bell Papers, Box 12, F. 179, Bell to Sutton, 23 August 1968.

37. DCSS, Binder: Pink Copies 1.3.68–30.9.68, Stone to Sutton, 18 September 1968, repeating and elaborating on the financial plan.

38. Ibid., Box 6, F.: IACF Magazines, Minutes of the IACF Board Meeting on 5–6 December 1968, 28 February 1969.

39. See pp. 269ff.

40. DCSS, Box 10, F. 21, IACF Budget, 10 October 1969.

41. Ibid., IACF "Breakdown of Income and Expenditure 1968 and 1969, Showing Economic Measures Taken in Each Year" (January 1970).

42. Ibid., Box L, F.: Heaps Report, Stone to Swearer, 3 March 1969. The Stone Papers contain numerous other letters of correspondence with other European and Japanese foundations.

43. Ibid., Binder: Pink Copies 1.1.71–31.7.71, Stone to Bullock, 1 July 1971, reporting on a Rockefeller grant of $10,000 over three years which he thought was psychologically important.

44. Ibid., Box L, F.: Private Letters, McLean to Dressner, 17 March 1970.

45. Ibid., Kimbler to Stone, 8 April 1970. Not for the first nor for the last time did Moselle Kimbler, Stone's former assistant at HICOG and later at the Ford Foundation, prove to be helpful in resolving the matter inside the foundation. Moreover, she was "damned mad" at the way this matter had been handled and warned Stone to "keep it in mind." Taking the cue, Stone tried to create counterweights. Thus he rented his farm in Vermont to his "good friend" Tom Lenagh, "the Treasurer of the Ford Foundation." Ibid., F.: Pink Copies 1.8.70–31.12.70, Stone to Galbraith, 16 December 1970. See also ibid., Dr "Study," F.: 1969 Ford Foundation, Swearer to Stone, 18 November 1968, thanking him for the offer of a key to Stone's apartment in Paris.

46. Ibid., F.: IACF 172, Sutton to IR-5, 23 March 1970. Doty was an influential Harvard chemist, a member of the President's Science Advisory Council and close to Henry Kissinger. See also p. 263.

47. Ibid., Box L, F.: Private Letters, Kimbler to Stone, 31 March 1970.

48. Ibid., F.: Heaps Report, Heaps to Bell and Sutton, 3 December 1970.

49. Ibid., F.: Private Letters, Kimbler to Stone, 11 December 1970. Probably Stephen Bechtel who, born on 24 September 1900, built up one of the largest construction and civil engineering firms in the world.

50. Ibid., Kimbler to Stone, 15 December 1970.

51. Ibid., F.: IACF Finances, Bell to Bullock, 6 January 1971.

52. Ibid., F.: Heaps Report, Dressner to Bechtel (draft), January 1971.

53. Ibid., F.: Private Letters, Stone to Hubbard, 29 September 1971.

54. Ibid., Heaps to Stone, 17 December 1970.

55. Ibid., Binder 1.1.71–31.7.71, Stone to Schlumberger, 11 February 1971.

56. Ibid., Stone to Goekjian, 15 June 1971.

57. Ibid., Stone to Shils, 12 February 1971.

58. Ibid., Dr "Study," F.: Allemagne (divers), Jahr to Sommer, 22 February 1971; ibid., Binder 1.1.71–31.7.71, Stone to Shah (Bombay), 7 May 1971.

59. Ibid., Dr "Study," F.: McCloy 1970–73, Stone to McCloy, 6 July 1971.

60. Ibid., Box L, F.: IACF Finances, Stone to Bullock, 22 September 1971.

61. Ibid., Sutton to Stone, 23 September 1971.

62. Ibid., Box 7, Binder 3, IACF Report to the Ford Foundation for 1974, March 1975. Once again Heaps proved "very helpful" in putting the grant through. Ibid., F.: Pink Copies 1.4.72–31.12.72, Stone to Slater, 24 November 1972.

63. See note 24.

64. FFA, Bell Papers, Box 12, F. 179, Heaps to Goodwin, 7 February 1973.

65. FFA, Bell Papers, Box 12, F. 179, Bader to Goodwin, 28 February 1973.

66. DCSS, Box L, F.: Bullock, Bullock to Stone, 15 March 1973.

67. FFA, Bell Papers, Box 12, F. 179, Bell to Bullock, 6 April 1973.

68. Ibid., Heaps to Bell, 4 May 1973.

69. DCSS, Box L, F.: IACF 1974, Stone to Bullock, 25 May 1973. The candidate was apparently Christoph Bertram who certainly qualified as a member of the younger generation. Born in 1937, he had joined the London IISS in 1967 and served as its director from 1974 to 1982. That year he moved to Hamburg to become a senior editor of *Die Zeit* until he was appointed to the directorship of the Stiftung für Wissenschaft und Politik, an influential think tank. On 8 August 1973, Bertram politely informed Stone (ibid., F.: Misc. Correspondence) that he did not wish to pursue the matter. Staying at the IISS in 1973 was clearly a better career choice for him.

70. FFA, Bell Papers, Box 12, F. 179, Sutton to Bell, 8 June 1973, for this and subsequent quotations.

71. As a young student in Berlin, Richard Loewenthal was expelled from the German Communist Party for deviationism in the early 1930s. He eventually had to flee Germany from Nazism and worked as a journalist in London after 1945 until he was appointed to a professorship at the Free University. The rise of leftist student radicalism in the 1960s so alarmed him that he was among the founders of the Bund Freiheit der Wissenschaft, an association of university teachers to combat the perceived totalitarian tendencies among the younger generation. He remained an influential voice in matters of political strategy on the right wing of the SPD. See also his book (1946).

72. Marion Countess Dönhoff, whom Stone knew since the 1940s, had meanwhile become one of the most influential journalists in the Federal Republic. Hailing from an East Prussian noble family, some of whose members had been involved in the July 1944 plot against Hitler, she frequently wrote in Bucerius's *Die Zeit* in a liberal Atlanticist vein. See Sommer 1994. Richard von Weizsäcker, son of Ernst (a high-ranking diplomat in the Nazi Foreign Ministry who was tried at Nuremberg) and brother of Carl Friedrich (the philosopher and physicist involved, with Werner Heisenberg, in nuclear research during the Third Reich), was an up-and-coming CDU politician, soon to become mayor of Berlin and later president of the Federal Republic.

73. As note 70.

74. DCSS, Box L, F.: IACF 1974, Minutes of the IACF Board Meeting, 1–3 July 1973.

75. Born on 1 July 1932 into a miner's family from West Virginia, Joseph Duffy studied theology at Andover Newton Theological School in Massachusetts and worked as a pastor from 1957 to 1960 before gaining a teaching position in urban studies at Hartford Seminary in Connecticut. He later obtained a doctorate there and developed political ambitions, running at one point as a Democratic candidate for the U.S. Senate. He also acted as chairman of the Connecticut branch of the Americans for Democratic Action (ADA). Happily married with two natural children and a foster child, and having established his credentials as a liberal, his candidacy for the position of director general seemed virtually sealed. When the IACF board of directors met in Paris on 19–20 January 1974, Duffy, as "Director General Designate," commented on a paper he had written proposing to move the headquarters to London. But when, after a successful first day, the board reconvened at noon on 20 January, Emmanuel, as the new president and successor to Stone, announced that earlier that day "irreconcilable differences had emerged" between Duffy and the board and "that owing to a personal situation Dr. Duffy would not fill the post of Director General." The IACF was back to square one. Stone continued as president, Emmanuel as director general. The search for a replacement for Duffy was reopened. But relations in the IACF executive, which the financial crisis had done nothing to improve, were even more strained than before. Ibid., Minutes of the IACF Board Meeting, 19–20 January 1974. The story behind this was that Duffy suddenly proposed to bring in his lover as codirector on full pay. Stone and other key people tried to dissuade him from this plan, but when Duffy insisted that he had no enthusiasm for the job unless the woman was at his side, he was told that the deal was off. For details see ibid., Stone to Lindley Cintra, 29 January 1974. After this flap, Watson was obviously a much more solid choice. Born on 10 August 1914, he went to Rugby School and King's College, Cambridge, finishing in 1936 with a first-class honors degree in history. After a brief spell as a journalist, he joined the British diplomatic service, rising to the position of undersecretary of state for foreign affairs until he retired in 1968, but carrying on as a consultant.

76. Ibid., Box 7, Binder 3, Watson to Stone, 23 June 1975.

77. Ibid., Binder: Personal File 1976, Heaps to Watson, 2 September 1976. An application to the Volkswagen Foundation was turned down.

78. Ibid., Binder: Personal File 1977, Watson to Stone, 25 May 1977.

79. Ibid., Memorandum "Administrative Position of IACF," 11 May 1977.

80. The Fondation pour une entraide intellectuelle européenne had been founded in the 1960s and was now chosen to continue the IACF's regional activities. As Watson put it (note 78): "With Pierre Emmanuel, Marion Dönhoff, Kot Jelenski and myself on the Board and Kot and me actively directing its work, the continuity of [the] IACF tradition is assured." *Survey* and *Minerva* also achieved independence and tried to survive by obtaining foundation grants directly.

81. As note 79.

82. DCSS, Binder: Personal File 1978–79, Watson to Stone, 17 January 1978, appending the Resolutions and the Minutes of the IACF board, with the legal details.

83. See FFA, Bell Papers, Box 35, F. 802–4, CIA Orphans.

84. See Saunders 2000, pp. 399ff.

85. See, e.g., chapter 8, note 1.

86. See pp. 242ff.

87. Thus the title of Peter Coleman's 1989 book on the CCF.

88. DCSS, Box I, F.: Correspondence 1970s, Bieber to Bader, 25 August 1971.

89. P. Novick 1988, pp. 415–16.

90. DCSS, Box 6, F.: What Is the IACF? "The Crisis of Rationality," n.d., for this and subsequent quotations.

91. See pp. 82ff.

92. See pp. 106ff.

93. Bell 1973.

94. Servan-Schreiber 1968.

95. DCSS, Dr "Study," F.: Inter-Office Correspondence, Jelenski's "Notes Concerning the Future of the IACF," 14 November 1973, for this and subsequent quotations.

96. See pp. 255ff.

97. See p. 263.

98. DCSS, Box 6, F.: IACF- Directors, Emmanuel's "Remarques personelles sur le nom et sur l'activité de l'Association," 9 May 1968.

99. Quoted in ibid., F.: What Is the IACF? "The Crisis of Rationality," n.d.

100. Ibid., Dr "Study," F.: Inter-Office Correspondence, Emmanuel's Statement, n.d., for this and subsequent quotations.

101. Stone had read the Statement beforehand and had made a few stylistic corrections.

102. See also his criticisms of Vietnam in his "Remarques personelles" (note 98). See also p. 275.

103. Ibid., Box 6, F.: IACF Directors, Minutes of the IACF Board Meeting, 9–10 January 1970, p. 4. On Bullock's notion of European culture, see his "E Pluribus Unum. Cultural Unity vs. Cultural Pluralism. The Outlook for a Renewal of European Culture in the 21st Century," in I. Aicher-Scholl et al. 1998, pp. 81–97. It is interesting that *Preuves* had also been moved in a more "Anglo-Saxon" direction.

104. DCSS, Drawer "Study," F.: 1968–69, Jelenski to Stone, 8 March 1968.

105. Among them: Brandt, Egon Bahr, Axel Springer, and Günter Grass.

106. Ibid., F.: Pink Copies 1.8.70–31.12.70, Stone to Aron, 2 December 1970.

107. Ibid., Binder: Personal File 1974–75, Stone to Hasenclever, 30 May 1975.

108. Ibid., Binder: Pink Copies 1.5.–30.11.1969, Stone to Chinai, 3 July 1969. See also Stone's letter to Robert McNamara, then president of the International Bank for Reconstruction and Development, ibid. Pink Copies 1.3.68–30.9.1960.

109. Ibid., F.: Pink Copies 1.8.70–31.12.70, Stone to Spender, 2 December 1970

110. Ibid., F.: Other Correspondence Pers/Confid., Lasky (telegram) to Shils, 30 October 1967.

111. Ibid., F.: Pink Copies, 1.1.–31.7.1973, Stone to Jacobs, 26 February 1973.

112. Ibid., F.: Pink Copies 1.5.–30.9.1969, Stone to Gordon, 5 November 1969.

113. Ibid., F.: Pink Copies 1.5.–30.11.1969, Stone to Silone, 22 May 1969.

114. Ibid., Dr "Study," F.: Springer 1968–73, Springer to Hillenbrand, 5 February 1973; Springer to Stone, 21 August 1969; Stone to Springer, 15 September 1969.

115. See note 25.

116. Quoted in ibid., Binder: April–May 1970, Michaelis to Stone, 11 May 1970, for this and subsequent quotations.

117. On the stresses that the 1960s imposed on other American intellectuals and their friendships, see Laskin 2000; Podhoretz 1999.

118. DCSS, Binder: April–May 1970, Michaelis to Stone, 15 April 1970.

119. Ibid., Box 7, Binder 3, Minutes of the Meeting of the IACF Board of Directors, 26–27 October 1974, p. 2.

120. Just as the CCF helped Polish and Hungarian intellectuals after 1956, the IACF established a fund in aid of Czechoslovak intellectuals after the suppression of the Prague Spring in 1968. In 1973 Stone made $500 available from this fund for the purchase of some seventy copies of Daniel Bell's new book, *The Coming of Postindustrial Society*, to be sent to intellectuals in the Soviet Union and Eastern Europe. DCSS, F.: Pink Copies, 1.1.–31.7.73, Stone to Bell, 3 May 1973. The association also raised its voice against the dismissal of Angela Davis from her position at the University of California. Ibid., F.: Pink Copies 1.5.–30.11.1969, IACF to Board of Regents, 16 October 1969. See also ibid., Box 6, F.: Angela Davis.

121. Ibid., Box 6, F.: IACF Directors, Minutes of the Meeting of the IACF Board of Directors, 9–10 January 1970, p. 3.

122. Ibid., Dr "Study," F.: Inter-Office Correspondence, Jelenski's "Notes Concerning the Future of the IACF," 14 November 1973.

123. See pp. 270ff.

124. Interview with C. Bertram, Hamburg, 18 December 1994.

125. *New York Times Magazine*, 1 January 1995, pp. 21–22.

126. DCSS, Dr "Personal Correspondence R–Z," F.: Aspen, Stone to Enrich, 23 February 1966.

127. Born on 17 August 1922 in Salt Lake City and with a B.A. from Berkeley, Slater, like Stone, had been posted in Germany after the war, but subsequently joined the diplomatic service where he was deputy assistant secretary of state for education and cultural affairs from 1957 to 1960. In 1960–61 he was president of the Anderson Foundation, then joined Stone's IA program and after Stone's

departure briefly carried on as a program officer for international relations until 1967.

128. AAIB, General Correspondence, Schaetzel to Slater, 5 August 1969.

129. DCSS, Dr "Study," Folder: 1969–72 Slater, Schaetzel to Slater, 15 July 1970.

130. DCSS, Dr "Study," F.: Slater 1969–70, Slater to Stone (28 December 1971).

131. Ibid., Box I, F.: Draft Memoirs "Aspen Berlin," n.d.

132. Ibid., Binder: Personal File 1974–75, Stone to Schuetz, 18 July 1973.

133. Ibid.

134. Ibid., Box I, F.: Aspen Berlin II, Slater to Schuetz, 23 August 1973.

135. Ibid., Schuetz to Slater, 14 September 1973.

136. Hellmuth Becker first met Stone as a representative of boarding schools in connection with the question of support for such establishments as the *Odenwaldschule* to serve as models of postwar school reform. He was also involved in the creation of the Scholl Foundation and the Hochschule für Gestaltung. See pp. 57ff. Becker continued his work in educational reform and became director of the Max-Planck-Institut für Bildungsforschung in West Berlin.

137. DCSS, Box I, F.: Aspen Berlin II, Stone to Slater, 10 September 1973.

138. Ibid., Stone's Notes of a Telephone Call from Herz, 12 September 1973.

139. Ibid., Stone's Notes, 28 September 1973, and other documents in this folder. See also Interview with D. Stobbe, Berlin, 13 August 1996, with interesting details about the visit and its West German domestic politics context.

140. Ibid., F.: Misc. 1933–, Slater to Stone, 5 November 1973.

141 Ibid., Stone to Slater, 22 November 1973.

142. AAIB, General Correspondence, Stone to Slater, 26 March 1974.

143. Ibid., Stone to Slater, 27 May 1974.

144. Ibid., Stone to Anderson, 25 July 1974.

145. Ibid., Bullock to Slater, 12 June 1974.

146. Ibid., List of "Aspen Institute Berlin Conferences," 1974–84, n.d.

147. See Lorenz and Machtill 1999, with several detailed articles on this and other programs.

148. See Ermarth 1993, pp. 203–10, with an article by Stone, published in 1987 but included here because Stone's death prevented him from making a contribution to the conference.

CHAPTER 10
TRANSATLANTIC CULTURAL RELATIONS IN THE "AMERICAN CENTURY"

1. Schulzinger 1984.
2. See, e.g., Kuisel 1993; Fehrenbach and Poiger 2000; Kroes 1996.
3. Mommsen 1984, p. 428.
4. Eickhoff and Korotin 1997.

5. Quoted in Saunders 2000, p. 361.

6. Bergstraesser 1961, p. 247. See also Eisermann 1999, pp. 97, 103ff. and my discussion on p. 88.

7. Maase 1997, pp. 274–75. See also Gans [1974] 1999.

8. Quoted in Gans [1974] 1999, p. 9.

9. C. McGinn, "The Hollow Man's Story: A. J. Ayer and the Philosophy of 'One Damn Thing after Another,' " *Times Literary Supplement*, 25 June 1999, pp. 3–4. See also Rogers 1999.

10. It seems that Stone had something like this in mind when he spoke before the Inter-American Press Association at San Diego on 13 October 1965 (DCSS, Dr "Speeches," F.: Inter-American Press Association): "The arts are no longer confined to the stage or to the museum. They are in our homes, schools, and colleges. Millions of Americans are interested in the arts. What is offered to them in our press is discouraging. For the most part our newspaper criticism—book, drama, film, music, art, and architecture—is not worth the space it gets. It ought to be spiked. The arts and criticism of the arts require knowledge, taste, and appreciation." But, of course, Stone could not end without remarking on what he had been working so hard to change while at the Ford Foundation: "And ignorance abroad of this country's artistic, cultural, and intellectual creativity would be lessened if our newspapers recognized their obligation and above all their opportunities in this area."

11. See p. 276 and DCSS, Box 11, Bound Volume: "Shepard Stone. Briefe zum 75. Geburtstag, 31.3.1983," Deutsch to Stone, 8 March 1983.

••• *Bibliography* •••

Aicher-Scholl, I. et al. 1988. *Ein Buch der Freunde. Shepard Stone zum Achtzig-sten*. Berlin.

Anderson, B. C. 1998. *Raymond Aron*. Lanham, Md.

Arad, Y. 1980. *Ghetto in Flames*. Jerusalem.

Ardagh, J. 1970. *The New France*. Harmondsworth.

Arendt, H. 1951. *The Origins of Totalitarianism*. New York.

Ayyub, A. S. 1966. *Ten Years of Quest*. Bombay.

Baranski, Z. G., and R. Lumley, eds. 1990. *Culture and Conflict in Postwar Italy*. New York.

Barclay, D., and E. Glaser-Schmidt, eds. 1997. *Transatlantic Images and Percep-tions*. New York

Barker, E. 1984. *Britain between the Superpowers*. London.

Barrows, S. 1981. *Distorting Mirrors*. New Haven, Conn.

Bausch, U. M. 1992. *Die Informationspolitik der US-amerikanischen Informa-tion Control Division in Württemberg-Baden von 1945 bis 1949*. Stuttgart.

Becker, J. 1997. *Hungry Ghosts*. New York.

Bell, D. 1960. *The End of Ideology*. Glencoe, Ill.

———. 1973. *The Coming of Postindustrial Society*. New York.

Bender, T. 1987. *New York Intellect*. New York.

Berghahn, M. 1982. *Continental Britons*. Oxford.

Berghahn, V. R. 1986. *The Americanisation of West German Industry, 1945–1973*. New York.

Berghahn, V. R., and P. J. Friedrich. 1993. *Otto A. Friedrich*. Frankfurt.

Bergstraesser, A. 1961. *Politik in Wissenschaft und Bildung*. Freiburg.

Bermann-Fischer, G. 1967. *Bedroht—Bewahrt. Der Weg eines Verlegers*. Frankfurt.

Bird, K. 1992. *The Chairman*. New York.

———. 1998. *The Color of Truth*. New York.

Bissell, R. M., Jr. 1996. *Reflections of a Cold Warrior*. New Haven, Conn.

Blum, J. M. 1972. *Roosevelt and Morgenthau*. Boston.

Bödeker, H. 1993. *Amerikanische Zeitschriften in deutscher Sprache, 1945–1952*. Frankfurt.

Borkenau, F. 1940. *The Totalitarian Enemy*. London.

Borsdorf, U., and L. Niethammer, eds., 1976. *Zwischen Befreiung und Besatzung*. Wuppertal.

Brantlinger, P. 1983. *Bread and Circuses*. Ithaca, N.Y.

Bronner, S. 1989. *Consuming Visions*. New York.

Broszat, M. 1987. *Hitler and the Collapse of the Weimar Republic*. Leamington Spa.

355

Bullock, A, [1953] 1964. *Hitler: A Study in Tyranny*. New York.

Burnham, J. 1941. *The Managerial Revolution*. New York.

Canetti, E. 1960. *Masse und Macht*. Munich.

Caute, D. 1973. *The Fellow-Travellers*. New York.

———. 1978. *The Great Fear*. New York.

Coleman, P. 1989. *The Liberal Conspiracy*. New York.

Collins, R. M. 1983. *The Business Response to Keynes, 1929–1964*. New York.

Corbin-Schuffels, A.-M. 1996. *Manès Sperber*, Berne.

Costigliola, F. 1984. *Awkward Dominion*. Ithaca, N.Y.

Curti, M. 1963. *American Philanthropy Abroad*. New Brunswick, N.J.

Diefendorf, J. M., et al., eds. 1993. *American Policy and the Reconstruction of Germany, 1945–1955. New York*.

Divine, R. A. 1981. *Eisenhower and the Cold War*. Oxford.

Döring, H. 1975. *Der Weimarer Kreis*. Meisenheim.

Dowe, D., et al., eds. 2001. *Europa in 1848*. New York.

Eickhoff, V., and I. Korotin, eds. 1997. *Sehnsucht nach Schicksal und Tiefe*. Vienna.

Eisermann, D. 1999. *Aussenpolitik und Strategiediskussion*. Munich.

Erhard, L. 1957. *Wohlstand für alle*. Düsseldorf.

Ermarth, H. 1993. *America and the Shaping of German Society, 1945–1955*. Providence, R.I.

Fasman, J. 1997. *Learning above the Page*. Senior thesis, Brown University.

Fehrenbach, H. and U. Poiger, eds. 2000. *Transactions, Transgressions, Transformations*. New York.

Feldman, G. D. 1966. *Army, Industry, and Labor*, Princeton, N.J.

Fiebig-von Hase, R. and U. Lehmkuhl, eds. 1997. *Enemy Images in American History*. Oxford.

Fischer, E. J., and H. D. Fischer, eds. 1994. *John J. McCloy*. New York.

Forster-Hahn, F., ed. 1996. *Imagining Modern German Culture, 1889–1910*. Washington, D.C.

Fraenkel, E. [1941] 1969. *The Dual State*. New York.

Frascina, F., ed. 1985. *Pollock and After*. New York.

Fridenson, P. 1972. *Histoire des usines Renault*. Paris.

Friedrich, C. J., and Z. Brzezinski. 1956. *Totalitarian Dictatorship and Autocracy*. New York.

Fukuyama, F. 1999. *The Great Disruption*. New York.

Gaddis, J. L. 1982. *Strategies of Containment*. New York.

———. 1987. *The Long Peace*. Oxford.

Galbraith, J. K. 1999. *Name-Dropping*. Boston.

Gans, H. J. [1974] 1999. *Popular Culture and High Culture*. New York.

Garthoff, R. L. 1985. *Detente and Confrontation*. Washington, D.C.

———. 1991. *Assessing the Adversary*. Washington, D.C.

Gassert, P. 1997. *Amerika im Dritten Reich*. Stuttgart.

Geiss I., and B.-J. Wendt, eds. 1973. *Deutschland in der Weltpolitik des 19. und 20. Jahrhunderts.* Düsseldorf.

Gemelli, G. 1985. *Fernand Braudel.* Paris.

———. 1998. ed., *The Ford Foundation and Europe.* Brussels.

Gienow-Hecht, J.C.E. 1999. *Transmission Impossible.* Baton Rouge, La.

Gilbert, J. 1972. *Writers and Partisans,* New York.

Gillingham, J. 1991. *Coal, Steel, and the Rebirth of Europe, 1945–1955.* New York.

Gimbel, J. 1968. *The American Occupation of Germany.* Stanford, Calif.

———. 1976. *The Origins of the Marshall Plan.* Stanford, Calif.

Gleason, A. 1995. *Totalitarianism.* New York.

Grémion, P. 1995. *Intelligence de l'anticommunisme.* Paris.

Grose, P. 1994. *Gentleman Spy.* Boston.

Guibault, S. 1983. *How New York Stole the Idea of Modern Art.* Chicago.

Hacker, A. 1997. *Money: Who Has How Much and Why.* New York.

Haddow, R. H. 1997. *Pavilions of Plenty.* Washington, D.C.

Hale, O. 1964. *Captive Press in the Third Reich.* Princeton, N.J.

Haxthausen C. W., and H. Suhr, eds. 1990. *Berlin: Culture and Metropolis.* Manchester.

Hein-Kremer, M. 1996. *Die amerikanische Kulturoffensive.* Cologne.

Henke, K.-D. 1995. *Die amerikanische Besetzung Deutschlands.* Munich.

Henke, K.-D., and H. Woller, eds. 1991. *Politische Säuberungen in Europa.* Munich.

Herman, A. 1997. *The Idea of Decline in Western History.* New York.

Hermand, J. 1989. *Kultur im Wiederaufbau.* Munich.

Heuss, Th. 1966. *Aufzeichnungen, 1945–1947.* Tübingen.

Hildebrand, K. 1969. *Vom Reich zum Weltreich.* Munich.

Hixson, W. L. 1997. *Parting the Curtain.* New York.

Hochgeschwender, M. 1998. *Freiheit in der Offensive?* Munich.

Hollander, P. 1992. *Anti-Americanism: Critiques at Home and Abroad.* New York.

Horowitz, D. 1997. *Radical Son.* New York.

Hurwitz, H. 1972. *Die Stunde Null der deutschen Presse.* Cologne.

Ignatieff, M. 1998. *Isaiah Berlin.* New York.

Immerman, R. H., ed. 1990. *John Foster Dulles and the Diplomacy of the Cold War.* Princeton, N.J.

Isherwood, C. 1945. *Goodbye to Berlin.* London.

Jardin, A. 1988. *Tocqueville: A Biography.* New York.

Jaud, R. J. 1997. *Der Landkreis Aachen in der NS-Zeit.* Frankfurt.

Jones, L. E., and J. Retallack, eds. 1992. *Elections, Mass Politics and Social Change in Modern Germany.* New York.

Judt, T. 1992. *Past Imperfect.* Berkeley, Calif.

———. 1998. *The Burden of Responsibility.* Chicago.

Kaelble, H. 1987. *Auf dem Wege zu einer europäischen Gesellschaft*. Munich.

Kaes, A. 1995. "What to Do with Germany." *German Politics and Society* 13: 130–41.

Kaplan, M. 1998. *Between Dignity and Despair*. New York.

Karnow, S. 1996. *Paris in the Fifties*. New York.

Katz, B. 1982. *Herbert Marcuse and the Art of Liberation*. London.

Kellermann, H. J. 1978. *Cultural Relations as an Instrument of US Foreign Policy*. Washington, D.C.

Kennan, G. F. 1972. *Memoirs, 1950–1963*. New York.

Knoll, J. H., ed. 1995. *Internationales Jahrbuch für Erwachsenenbildung*. Cologne.

Koestler, A. 1941. *Darkness at Noon*. New York.

Koestler, A., and R. S. Crossman, eds. 1950. *The God That Failed*. New York.

Kogan, N. 1983. *A Political History of Italy*. New York.

Kohn, J. ed. 1994. *Essays in Understanding*. New York.

Kolakowski, L. 1968. *Alienation of Reason*. Garden City, N.J., 1968.

———. 1978. *Main Currents of Marxism and Beyond*. Oxford.

Kramer, H. 1999. *The Twilight of Intellectuals*. Chicago 1999.

Krige, J. 1999. "The Ford Foundation, European Physics and the Cold War." *Historical Studies in the Physical and Biological Sciences*, 29: 333–61.

Kroes, R. 1996. *If You've Seen One You've Seen the Mall*. Urbana, Ill.

Kroes, R. et al., eds. 1993. *Cultural Transmissions and Receptions*. Amsterdam.

Krohn, C.-D. 1987. *Wissenschaft im Exil*. Frankfurt.

Kugler, A. 1987. "Von der Werkstatt zum Fliessband." *Geschichte und Gesellschaft* 13: 304–39.

Kuisel, R. 1981. *Capitalism and the State in Modern France*. Cambridge.

———. 1993. *Seducing the French*. Berkeley, Calif.

Laqueur, W. 1962. *Young Germany*. London.

———. 1970. *Europe since Hitler*. Harmondsworth.

———. 1989. *The Terrible Secret*. London.

Lasch, C. 1969. *The Agony of the American Left*. New York.

Laskin, D. 2000. *Partisans*. New York.

Le Bon, G. 1899. *La psychologie des foules*. Paris. Translated as *The Crowd* (London, 1910).

Lehmbruch, G., ed. 1979. *Trends towards Corporatist Intermediation*. London.

Leonard, D., ed. 1999. *Crosland and New Labour*. Basingstoke.

Lorenz, S., and M. Machtill, eds. 1999. *Transatlantik*. Opladen.

Loth, W. 1988. *The Division of the World*. New York.

Lottman, H. R. 1991. *The Left Bank*. San Francisco.

Lowenstein, S. 1989. *Frankfort on the Hudson*. Detroit.

Maase, K. 1997. *Grenzenloses Vergnügen*. Frankfurt.

McCarthy, K. D. 1987. "From Cold War to Cultural Deveopment." *Daedalus* (Winter): 93–117.

Macdonald, D. 1956. *The Ford Foundation.* New York.

Maier, C. S., and S. Hoffmann, eds. 1984. *The Marshall Plan: A Retrospective.* Boulder, Colo.

Marelli, S. 1989. *Silone: Intellectuale de la Libertá.* Rimini.

Marthy, J.-P. 1991. *Extreme Occident.* Chicago.

Masani, M. 1977. *Bliss Was It in That Dawn.* Delhi.

Matthews, J. 1976. "Art and Politics in Cold War America." *American Historical Review* (October): 762–87.

May, L., ed. 1989. *Recasting America.* Chicago.

Merle, M. 1987. *The Sociology of International Relations.* New York.

Merritt, A. L., and R. L. Merritt. 1980. *Public Opinion in Semisovereign Germany.* Urbana, Ill.

Meyer, C. 1980. *Facing Reality.* New York.

Mills, C. W. 1956. *The Power Elite.* New York.

Mommsen, W. J. 1984. *Max Weber and German Politics, 1890–1920.* Chicago.

Muller, J. Z. 1987. *The Other God That Failed.* Princeton, N.J.

Müller, W. 1995. *Schulpolitik in Bayern im Spannungsfeld von Kultusbürokratie und Besatzungsmacht, 1945–1949.* Munich.

Nabokov, N. 1973. *Bagazh.* New York.

Naimark, N. 1995. *The Russians in Germany.* Cambridge, Mass.

Nenning, G., ed. 1998. *"Forum."* Vienna.

Neu, C. S. 1975. *Troubled Encounter.* New York.

Neumann, F. 1942. *Behemoth.* New York.

Neumann, S. 1942. *The Permanent Revolution.* New York.

Nicholls, C. 2000. *The History of St. Antony's College, Oxford, 1950–2000.* London.

Nielsen, W. A. 1972. *The Big Foundations.* New York.

Ninkovich, F. 1994. *Modernity and Power.* Chicago.

Novick, P. 1988. *That Noble Dream.* New York.

Ortega y Gasset, J. [1932] 1969. *The Revolt of the Masses.* London.

Orwell, G. 1938. *Homage to Catalonia.* London.

——. 1945. *Animal Farm.* London.

——. 1949. *1984.* London.

Packard, V. 1957. *The Hidden Persuaders.* New York.

Patterson, J. 1997. *Grand Expectations.* New York.

Pells, R. 1984. *The Liberal Mind in a Conservative Age.* New York.

——. 1997. *Not Like Us.* New York.

Peukert, D. K. 1980. *Edelweisspiraten.* Cologne.

Phelps, C. 1997. *Young Sidney Hook.* Ithaca, N.Y.

Podhoretz, N. 1999. *Ex-Friends.* New York.

Pommerin, R., ed. 1986. *Der Kaiser und Amerika.* Cologne-Vienna.

——. 1994. *The American Impact on Postwar Germany.* Oxford.

Prevots, N. 1998. *Dance for Export.* Hanover.

Reynolds, D. 1988. *An Ocean Apart*. London.

———. 1995. *Rich Relations: The American Occupation of Britain*. New York.

Riccio, B. D. 1995. *Walter Lippmann—Odyssee of a Liberal*. New Brunswick, N.J.

Riesman, D., N. Glazer, and R. Denny. 1950. *The Lonely Crowd*. New Haven, Conn.

Roberts, E. A. 1996. The Anglo-Marxists. New York.

Roberts, H. L. 1956. *Russia and America*. New York.

Robin, R. 1995. *Barbed Wire College*. Princeton, N.J.

Rogers, B. 1999. *A. J. Ayer: A Life*. London.

Rosenberg B., and J. M. White, eds. 1971. *Mass Culture Revisited*. New York.

Rosenberg, E. 1982. *Spreading the American Dream*. New York.

Ryan, A. 1995. *John Dewey and the High Tide of American Liberalism*. New York.

Saunders, F. S. 2000. *The Cultural Cold War*. New York.

Saunders, T. 1996. *Hollywood in Berlin*. Berkeley, Calif.

Schall, J. V. 1998. *Jacques Maritain*. Lanham, Md.

Schapiro, L. 1972. *Totalitarianism*. New York.

Schieder, W., ed. 1976. *Faschismus als soziale Bewegung*. Hamburg.

Schmidt, O. 1999. "Protecting the Civil Empire: American Exchange of Person Programs and the Formation of Democratic Elites for Germany, 1945–1960." Ph.D. dissertation, Harvard University.

Schrecker, E. 1998. *Many Are the Crimes*. New York.

Schulze, W. 1995. *Der Stifterverband für die deutsche Wissenschaft, 1920–1995*. Berlin.

Schulzinger, R. D. 1984. *The Wise Men in Foreign Affairs*. New York.

Schwartz, T. A. 1991. *America's Germany*. Cambridge, Mass.

Sering P. [R. Loewenthal] 1946. *Jenseits des Kapitalismus*. Nuremberg.

Servan-Schreiber, J.-J. 1968. *The American Challenge*. New York.

Sheehan, J. 1989. *German History, 1770–1866*. Oxford.

Shirer, W. 1960. *The Rise and Fall of the Third Reich*. London.

Smith, J. E. 1990. *Lucius D. Clay*. New York.

Smyser, W. R. 1999. *From Yalta to Berlin*. New York.

Sommer, Th., ed. 1994. *Was heisst liberal?* Hamburg.

Sperber, M. 1982. *Bis man mir Scherben auf die Augen legt*. Munich.

Stone, S. 1938. *Shadow over Europe*. New York.

Stone, S., and H. Baldwin, eds. 1938. *We Saw It Happen*. New York.

Strasser, S. 1989. *Satisfaction Guaranteed*. New York.

Strauss, D. 1978. *Menace in the West*. Westport, Conn.

Tannenbaum, E. R. 1976. *1900*. Garden City, N.J.

Tent, J. F. 1983. *Mission on the Rhine*, Chicago.

———. 1988. *The Free University*. Bloomington, Ind.

Thomas, E. 1995. *The Very Best Men*. New York.

Tirpitz, A. von. 1921. *Erinnerungen*. Leipzig.

Tismaneanu, V. 1988. *The Crisis of Ideology in Eastern Europe*. New York.

Tocqueville, A. de. 1945. *Democracy in America.*, 2 vols. New York.

Todd, O. 1997. *Albert Camus*. New York.

Wagnleitner, R. 1994. *Coca-Colonization and Cold War*. Chapel Hill, N.C.

Wala, M. 1994. *The Council on Foreign Relations and American Foreign Policy in the Cold War*. Oxford.

Watt, D. C. 1984. *Succeeding John Bull*. Cambridge.

Waxman, C. I. 1968. *The End of Ideology Debate*. New York.

Wehler, H.-U. 1985. *The German Empire, 1871–1918*. Leamington Spa.

———. 1995. *Wehler, Deutsche Gesellschaftsgeschichte*. Vol. 2: *1849–1914*. Munich.

Whyte, W. H. 1956. *The Organization Man*. New York.

Wiesen, J. 1998. "Reconstruction and Recollection." Ph.D. dissertation, Brown University.

Wilkinson, J. D. 1981. *The Intellectual Resistance in Europe*. Cambridge, Mass.

Williams, W. A. 1959. *The Tragedy of American Diplomacy*. New York.

Wreszin, M. 1994. *A Rebel in Defense of Tradition*. New York.

... *Index* ...